Primary Care Psychology

Primary Care Psychology

Edited by
Robert G. Frank
Susan H. McDaniel
James H. Bray
Margaret Heldring

American Psychological Association • *Washington, DC*

Published by
American Psychological Association
750 First Street, NE
Washington, DC 20002
www.apa.org

To order
APA Order Department
P.O. Box 92984
Washington, DC 20090-2984
Tel: (800) 374-2721; Direct: (202) 336-5510
Fax: (202) 336-5502; TDD/TTY: (202) 336-6123
Online: www.apa.org/books/
E-mail: order@apa.org

In the U.K., Europe, Africa, and the Middle East, copies may be ordered from
American Psychological Association
3 Henrietta Street
Covent Garden, London
WC2E 8LU England

Typeset in Goudy by Stephen McDougal, Mechanicsville, MD

Printer: United Book Press, Inc., Baltimore, MD
Cover Designer: Naylor Design, Washington, DC
Technical/Production Editor: Rosemary Moulton

The opinions and statements published are the responsibility of the authors, and such opinions and statements do not necessarily represent the policies of the American Psychological Association.

Library of Congress Cataloging-in-Publication Data

Primary care psychology / [edited by] Robert G. Frank . . . [et al.].
    p. cm.
    ISBN 1-59147-054-4
    1. Medicine and psychology. 2. Primary care (Medicine) I. Frank, Robert G., 1952–

R726.5.P75 2003
610'.1'9—dc21   2003007761

British Library Cataloguing-in-Publication Data
A CIP record is available from the British Library.

Printed in the United States of America
First Edition

CONTENTS

CONTRIBUTORS

Howard Beckman, MD, Rochester Individual Practice Association, Family Medicine, University of Rochester School of Medicine and Dentistry, Rochester, NY

Cynthia D. Belar, PhD, Education Directorate, American Psychological Association, Washington, DC

Maureen M. Black, PhD, Department of Pediatrics, University of Maryland School of Medicine, Baltimore

James H. Bray, PhD, Department of Family and Community Medicine, Baylor College of Medicine, Houston, TX

Cathy Buch, MD, Obstetrics and Gynecology, University of Pennsylvania School of Medicine, Philadelphia

Helen L. Coons, PhD, Women's Mental Health Associates, Philadelphia, PA

Patrick H. DeLeon, PhD, Administrative Assistant to Senator Daniel Inouye, United States Senate, Washington, DC

W. David Driscoll, PsyD, independent practice, Rochester, NY

Irene Easling, PhD, Department of Family and Community Medicine, Baylor College of Medicine, Houston, TX

Michael F. Enright, PhD, independent practice, Jackson Hole, WY

Janet E. Farmer, PhD, Department of Health Psychology, University of Missouri—Columbia

Robert G. Frank, PhD, College of Health Professions, Florida Center for Medicaid Issues, University of Florida, Gainesville

Richard Frankel, PhD, Richard L. Roudebush Veterans Affairs Medical Center, Indianapolis, IN

Esther L. Freeman, PhD, independent practice, Virginia Beach, VA

Elsie Go Lu, PhD, Department of Human Resources, IDEA Inc., Brea, CA

Erik J. Groessl, PhD, Department of Family and Preventive Medicine, University of California, San Diego

Kristopher J. Hagglund, PhD, College of Health Professions, University of Missouri—Columbia

William E. Haley, PhD, Department of Gerontology, University of South Florida, Tampa

David S. Hargrove, PhD, Department of Psychology, University of Mississippi, Oxford

Margaret Heldring, PhD, America's HealthTogether, Washington, DC

Jeri Hepworth, PhD, Department of Family Medicine, University of Connecticut School of Medicine, Hartford

Eileen M. Hoffman, MD, independent practice, Internal Medicine, New York, NY

Suzanne B. Johnson, PhD, College of Medicine, Florida State University, Tallahassee

Robert M. Kaplan, PhD, Department of Family and Preventive Medicine, University of California, San Diego

Eugene P. McCabe, PsyD, independent practice, Rochester, NY

Susan H. McDaniel, PhD, Department of Psychiatry and Family Medicine, University of Rochester School of Medicine and Dentistry, Rochester, NY

Diana Morgenstern, MD, MedCases, Inc., Philadelphia, PA

Laura Nabors, PhD, Department of Psychology, University of Cincinnati, Cincinnati, OH

Thomas L. Patterson, PhD, Department of Psychiatry, University of California, San Diego

Randy Phelps, PhD, Practice Directorate, American Psychological Association, Washington, DC

Geoffrey M. Reed, PhD, Professional Development, American Psychological Association, Washington, DC

Nina P. Rossomando, PhD, independent practice, Waterford, CT

Nancy B. Ruddy, PhD, Hunterdon Family Practice Residency, Flemington, NJ

Joseph E. Scherger, MD, MPH, College of Medicine, Florida State University, Tallahassee

Carolyn S. Schroeder, PhD, Department of Human Development and Family Life, University of Kansas, Lawrence

Brian D. Smedley, PhD, Institute of Medicine, Washington, DC

Meg I. Striepe, PhD, Center for Research on Women, Wellesley College, Wellesley, MA

Jack G. Wiggins, PhD, independent practice, Fountain Hills, AZ

Paul G. Wilson, PhD, Air Force Substance Abuse Research and Program Development, Bolling Air Force Base, Washington, DC

FOREWORD

JOSEPH E. SCHERGER

Someday, the U.S. health care system will get it. Integrating psychologists into primary care makes the system more effective, allows for early recognition and intervention in the pervasive psychosocial nature of health and illness, and will save a ton of money by avoiding needless tests and treatments. The parallel realm of mental health services has not been trained to integrate into primary health care. This groundbreaking text will help jumpstart this long-overdue and ripe process.

Primary care psychology is a collaborative effort of pioneering psychologists who have spent their careers as teachers, researchers, and providers in primary care settings. They more than see the potential of this integration; they are passionate about making it happen. They have dissected, analyzed, and created models for effective primary care psychology. Psychologists are not just mental health providers but health providers. Psychosocial care is not done optimally when separated from the biopsychosocial context. If only the administrators in today's health care systems knew that!

As a primary care physician, I am deeply appreciative of the respect and understanding the chapter authors have for the role of the primary care provider. There is no competition described here, no power play to wrestle part of health care away from physicians or nurses. The spirit of collaboration exudes from these pages. The authors know and describe well the synergy that results from bringing psychologists into the primary health care team.

By lucky circumstances, I have spent my career working in collaboration with psychologists. Trained as a family physician in the 1970s, I experienced the birth of family medicine and its training model of having one or more psychologists as full-time faculty. Entering a small town National Health Service Corps practice in 1978, psychologist Margie Hackett opened up next door to my practice. For 14 years, we collaborated with many patients, and that set me up for the academic collaborations I have enjoyed since. Psychologists working with primary care physicians and nurses is how health care in a community should be delivered.

The authors of the chapters in *Primary Care Psychology* do a great job of avoiding the Cartesian split of one professional for the mind and another for the body. They appreciate and promote the role of primary care physicians providing much, if not most, of primary mental health care. In addition to common depression, anxiety disorders, and stress-related illnesses, other problems such as chest pain, headaches, back pain, and obesity (the list is very long) are often primarily psychosocial. Sometimes the brief visit elucidates for the patient the psychosocial nature of the problem, and that is all that is needed. Information can be effective therapy. Other times, the management of the psychosocial problem needs intensive work, and the psychologist on site may provide what a primary care physician does not have the time or expertise to do. A double-helix integration occurs when the psychologist tunes in on physical problems and enlists the help of the primary care provider.

I am also excited by how the changes in technology can facilitate relationship-centered care, linking the work of primary care psychologists with physicians and the rest of the health care team. It is already clear that health care of the 21st century will be vastly different than the healthcare of the 20th century. Electronic mail and the Internet have opened up a new world of connectivity and collaboration. Psychologists have made important contributions to medical informatics. Asynchronous communication available 24/7 allows the patient and providers to express themselves anytime and anywhere, freeing the care process from time-limited visits and forming a truly continuous dialogue. Patients may be more articulate about their problems at home, in a bathrobe. Providers may attach patient information documents to their responses. Electronic mail and the Internet do not replace face-to-face visits. Physicians still need to see and touch their patients, and vice versa. However, their offices are bottlenecks of episodic care which by themselves do a poor job of healing and meeting our patients' needs. The main advances of quality care for the 21st century are the best use of information technology and collaborative teams that provide systematic care with a highly empowered patient and family.

Primary Care Psychology is a turn-of-the-century book. I hope that there will be many editions of this work that will play a key role in finally bringing collaborative health care to a ready, willing, and deserving population. Enough research has been done to bring collaborative health care mainstream. Let's get on with it.

PREFACE

When someone asks "Who is your doctor?" people answer with the name of their primary care provider. Primary care is the foundation of all health care. One clinician is responsible for, or coordinates, comprehensive, first-stop health care using specialists to handle specific aspects of care. Primary care provides continuous care that emphasizes the importance of the relationship between the clinician and the patient.[1]

To achieve this continuous, coordinated care, primary care clinicians must develop effective interpersonal relationships with their patients. They must address the emotional and psychological aspects of illness, including depression, anxiety, response to trauma and change, and family stress. Addressing these interpersonal and emotional issues as they affect health is a big agenda for one provider. The importance of the interpersonal relationship in primary care, as well as recognition of the importance of psychological functioning to health outcomes, has created remarkable opportunities for psychologists. This book examines the role of psychologists in various primary care settings and capacities. Primary care is more than just a team.

Over the last 20 years, an increasing number of psychologists have found opportunities in primary care settings. The magnitude of the opportunities for psychologists, combined with the value of psychology's contributions, has spawned the specialty of primary care psychology. Primary care psychology is the specialty of psychology devoted to practice, teaching, and research on the delivery of continuous, comprehensive, coordinated health care that occurs as the first point of professional contact to maintain health and treat illness.

---

[1]Donaldson, M., Yordy, K., & Vanselow, N. (Eds.). (1994). The new definition and an explanation of terms. In *Defining primary care: An interim report* (Part 3, pp. 15–33). Washington, DC: National Academy Press.

The development of primary care psychology has been supported within the profession of psychology. In 1995, the Committee for the Advancement of Professional Psychology (CAPP) of the American Psychological Association (APA) appointed an eight-member task force to review the opportunities and obstacles for psychologists in primary care. The task force included the four of us, as well as psychologists Jack Wiggins, William Haley, and Suzanne Bennett Johnson; Elsie Go Lu served as the CAPP liaison to the task force. Randy Phelps and Geoffrey Reed of the APA Practice Directorate staffed the task force, which worked for two years to develop a set of recommendations regarding primary care psychology. In 1996, the task force issued its final recommendations to CAPP. In its work, the task force found there has been significant progress in the development of primary care psychology, yet the specialty lacked a coherent framework. The task force provided a range of recommendations to aid theoretical and practical development of the area.

As part of its work, the Primary Care Task Force sponsored a series of well-received presentations at the Annual Convention of the American Psychological Association. The strong demand for information on primary care psychology led the members of the task force to recognize the need for a groundbreaking textbook on primary care psychology. Thus began the work on this book, which was designed to provide a comprehensive overview of primary care psychology as it exists at this point in time.

We were all drawn to primary care psychology long before it became an identified area within psychology. Common to each of our journeys was an interest in the integration of psychology and health and practical concerns about ways to best achieve effective, integrated health care. Susan H. McDaniel started teaching in the University of Rochester Family Medicine Department in 1982. Collaborating with medical colleagues, she developed a curriculum to teach primary care physicians how to detect psychological problems in their patients and when to refer patients to a psychologist. The program was very successful, but she still had difficulty getting mental health professionals to collaborate on family medicine cases. In 1986, somewhat in desperation, she started the Family Medicine Behavioral Health Service (BHS) to see if more collaboration would occur when physicians, nurses, and psychologists worked side by side. From the beginning, it worked like a charm. By 2002, the BHS included six part-time faculty and three primary care family psychology post-doctoral fellows working in the BHS with physicians, residents, fellows, and nurse practitioners. The clinic has become a laboratory for experimentation and innovation in collaborative care.

James H. Bray came to primary care psychology through his work on relationships between family processes and health. After joining the Department of Family Medicine at Baylor University's College of Medicine in 1987, he focused his teaching and research on the role of psychologists in primary care. His work at Baylor has expanded to include adolescent substance abuse and the effects of family stress on adjustment and health of adults and children. Bray made collaboration with primary care practitioners a major initiative as a member of the APA Rural Health Task Force and as the 1995 president of the APA Division 43 (Family Psychology).

Margaret Heldring's interest in primary care psychology began before she became a psychologist when she was working as a counselor for Planned Parenthood. She became intrigued by the relationship between mental and physical health. Her love for hearing the stories of people's lives led her to become a psychologist. She became the coordinator of behavioral sciences for a family practice residency in Seattle, Washington. After years of teaching and practicing in primary care at the University of Washington and in Seattle, she moved into public policy and politics, where she has looked for opportunities to promote primary care psychology. Her work in public policy includes serving as health advisor to Sen. Bill Bradley (D–NJ) during his 2000 Presidential campaign.

Robert Frank's interest in the area of primary care psychology grew from his work in rehabilitation. Working as part of a health care team providing comprehensive services to people with chronic conditions, it became clear that a stronger integration of services and links to traditional primary care were needed. At the same time, the impact of public policy on the health outcomes of these individuals became more apparent. This led him to pursue roles in federal and state health policy with special interests in the development of comprehensive, affordable health care systems.

The volume is divided into three parts. The first part asks "What Is Primary Care Psychology?" The four chapters in it define primary care psychology and examine unique aspects of clinical care for psychologists working in primary care. In chapter 1, we examine the concept of primary care and the role of psychologists in primary care settings. In the second chapter, Phelps and Reed review changes in health care delivery systems and how the changes will affect psychology. In chapter 3, Frankel and Beckman discuss the critical elements of the physician–patient relationship. In chapter 4, the last chapter in Part I, McDaniel, Hargrove, Belar, Schroeder, and Freeman review the essential curriculum for education in primary care psychology.

Part II, entitled "The Practice of Primary Care Psychology," includes five chapters that focus on practical issues psychologists encounter in the broad array of settings comprising primary care. In chapter 5, Haley and his colleagues on the CAPP Primary Care Task Force provide practical tips for practice in primary care psychology settings. This chapter is designed to help psychologists understand the essential ingredients of primary care practice. Chapter 6, authored by McDaniel and Hepworth, introduces the concept of collaborative family health care. This chapter describes the role of psychologists as part of the collaborative family health care team in primary care settings and examines issues of power and dependency that must be confronted. Primary care is characterized by the presence of an effective, interpersonal relationship between the provider and patient. In chapter 7, Driscoll and McCabe provide practical advice from their successful independent practice on how to succeed as a private primary care psychologist. In chapter 8, Ruddy and Schroeder address difficult issues that can arise as primary care psychologists collaborate with primary care physicians. In chapter 9, Wilson describes an innovative program implemented by the Air Force to integrate primary care and behavioral health services.

Chapters 10 through 14 examine areas of practice and application of primary care psychology. Pediatrics comprises one of the largest sectors of primary care. In chapter 10, Black and Nabors review issues confronting collaboration between psychologists and pediatricians in primary care settings. Coons, Morgenstern, Hoffman, Striepe, and Buch provide in chapter 11 a similar overview and suggestions for the development of effective collaborations for psychologists wanting to work in obstetrics–gynecology. In chapter 12, Haley reviews challenges and opportunities for psychologists working in geropsychology. Bray, Enright, and Easling examine in chapter 13 opportunities for psychologists in rural settings. In chapter 14, Frank, Hagglund, and Farmer suggest that coordinated, integrated health care can be provided through several approaches. They suggest a "Cardinal Symptoms model" that is focused on dominant health complaints that can be effective in addressing chronic care demands.

The chapters in Part IV address the interface between primary care health care delivery systems and health policy. These chapters are designed to provide readers with an understanding of policy and reimbursement issues that are likely to affect primary care in the future. In chapter 15, Heldring discusses current as well as historical trends in health policy and implications for primary care psychology. In chapter 16, Kaplan, Patterson, and Groessl consider how resources are allocated in health care. They describe the use of quality of life as an outcome measure and apply it in primary care settings. In the last chapter, DeLeon, Rossomando, and Smedley consider primary care psychology as part of the discipline of professional psychology that holds great promise.

We have attempted to present primary care psychology in its broadest conceptualization. The Primary Care Task Force recognized that primary care psychology could be applied to a broader array of settings, beginning with family medicine, internal medicine, and pediatrics. Given that the field is young, we chose to seek the outer parameters; we included areas such as obstetrics and gynecology (which many advocate as a primary care specialty) and areas of chronic care that have less claim to current definitions of primary care.

Despite its rapid growth and the interest created among psychologists, physicians, nurse practitioners, and other health professionals, primary care psychology is plagued by some of the same labeling problems encountered in other disciplines and fields of psychology. Use of the phrases *mental health services, mental health services integrated into health settings, behavioral health services*, and *psychological services* is inconsistent across settings. In this volume, the authors have used the term that best fits their view of primary care psychology. As recognition of the basis of psychology as a health profession grows, we assume there will be a migration toward calling these services *psychological services*. As the evolution continues, however, we have opted to focus this discussion on the substance of primary care psychology rather than the labels.

From the start, this volume has enjoyed the support of a number of groups and individuals. The Practice Directorate of the APA, directed by Russ Newman, supported the Primary Care Task Force. Randy Phelps and Geoffrey Reed provided remarkable knowledge and helped keep the group focused. Anthony Chu of the APA Practice Directorate provided support to the task force. During the development of the text, Joyce Hudson at the University of Florida kept us organized and provided cheerful support at each step of the process. Specific long-term collaborations with primary care physicians have informed this work, especially those of Thomas Campbell, MD, with Susan H. McDaniel; John Rogers, MD, and Bob Rakel, MD, with James H. Bray; Coleen Kivalahan, MD, with Robert G. Frank; and, for Margaret Heldring, the residents of Seattle's Swedish Hospital Medical Center Family Practice Residency from 1983 to 1990, especially those who went on to form the Uptown Family Practice.

We hope this book will stimulate more work to define primary care psychology. The field is young and holds great promise. Each of us was drawn to the area of primary care psychology because of a common interest in the creation of truly integrated health care addressing psychological and physical health. Primary care psychology may be the best way to achieve this ideal.

I

WHAT IS PRIMARY CARE PSYCHOLOGY?

1

EDUCATION, PRACTICE, AND RESEARCH OPPORTUNITIES FOR PSYCHOLOGISTS IN PRIMARY CARE

JAMES H. BRAY, ROBERT G. FRANK, SUSAN H. McDANIEL, AND MARGARET HELDRING

The emphasis on primary care in the health care system provides psychologists with expanded opportunities and roles in the delivery of behavioral health services. These opportunities require additional knowledge of primary care and different skills in caring for primary care patients that reflect the evolution of psychology from being a *mental health* profession to a full partner in the *health* professions. Psychologists have a long history of collaboration with physicians and other health care providers; however, this has primarily been in the mental health arena. There is generally a paucity of pre- and postdoctoral training to help psychologists work in primary care medicine. In this chapter we review the definition of *primary care*, the role of psychologists in primary care settings, and issues to consider in collaborating successfully with primary care clinicians.

James H. Bray's work on this chapter was partially supported by Grant RO1 AA08864 from the National Institute on Alcoholism and Alcohol Abuse and Grant 5 D45 HP5018 from the Health Resources and Services Administration.

WHAT IS PRIMARY CARE, AND WHO PROVIDES IT?

The Institute of Medicine defines *primary care* as "the provision of integrated, accessible health care services by clinicians who are accountable for addressing a large majority of personal health care needs, developing a sustained partnership with patients, and practicing in the context of family and community" (Donaldson, Yordy, & Vanselow, 1994, p. 15).

Primary care practitioners (PCPs) are usually the points of entry for patients into the health care system. Practitioners provide continuous and comprehensive medical care for patients over a period of time, both in sickness and in health, and coordinate all the health care needs of their patients. Furthermore, practitioners assume *continuing responsibility* for individual patient follow-up and community health problems (American Academy of Family Physicians, 1994; Rakel, 2002). PCPs believe that providing this kind of care requires that they get to know their patients and families over time and develop a long-term relationship with them. Specific aspects of primary care include the following.

1. It is *first-contact care*, serving as a point of entry for patients and their families into the health care system. Patients often present undifferentiated problems or symptoms that are vague and include multiple symptoms that may involve various bodily systems (e.g., "I don't feel well," or "My stomach hurts all the time"). PCPs diagnose, rule out, and treat a broad spectrum of illness that ranges from severe or life-threatening disease to minor, self-limiting problems (Crabtree, Miller, & Stange, 2001; Kroenke & Mangelsdorff, 1989; Miller, McDaniel, Crabtree, & Stange, 2001). This often leads to a focus on biomedical problems and disease.

    First-contact care is generally viewed as being associated with decreases in mortality and morbidity (Rakel, 2002). The efficacy of quick access to prenatal care, immunization, early treatments to prevent rheumatic fever, and detection of anemia and asthma have been described well (e.g., Starfield, 1992). Individuals cared for by PCPs have fewer hospital days, and this care is believed to decrease inappropriate use of specialty and emergency care services (Hurley, Freund, & Taylor, 1989; Moore, 1979).

2. It is *continuous care*, by virtue of the fact that a PCP cares for patients and families over a period of time, both in sickness and in health. This type of care includes prevention services and routine checkups, in addition to treatment for illnesses (Crabtree et al., 2001; Rakel, 2002). There is an emphasis in primary care on enhancing health through prevention and

health promotion rather than focusing solely on treatment of disease. In the field of psychology there is not yet the "well-person" checkup to prevent behavioral health problems, although this has been proposed in several arenas (e.g., pediatrics and marital and family functioning; Bray & Rogers, 1995).

Patients who receive comprehensive, continuing health care have fewer hospitalizations, fewer operations, and make fewer trips to their doctor than those who do not have a regular, accessible PCP (Rakel, 2002). Children who receive health care from an identifiable, regular source are more likely to receive preventive health care, such as immunizations; are twice as likely to keep follow-up appointments; and are less likely to use an emergency room "unnecessarily." These children are more likely to take prescribed antibiotics and receive treatment for childhood behavioral problems (Becker, Drachman, & Kirscht, 1974).

3. It is *comprehensive care*, in that it relies on all the major disciplines, including medical specialists (e.g., cardiologists), allied health professionals (e.g., physical therapy, dietetics), and mental and behavioral health professionals. Primary care systems yield higher consumer satisfaction, and comprehensiveness appears to be one of the critical factors in achieving that satisfaction. The Institute of Medicine (2001) noted that comprehensive primary care facilities employ health care practitioners who: (a) are willing to handle, without referral, the majority of problems arising in a health care practice; (b) are willing to admit to, and follow patients in, the hospital; (c) are willing to admit to, and follow patients in, nursing homes or convalescent sites; (d) are willing to provide home visits; (e) routinely engage in preventive health activities, such as immunization, detection of hypertension, and control risk factors for coronary artery disease; (f) assess lifestyle factors that may contribute to morbidity or mortality, such as diet, exercise, injury prevention, family planning, and adolescent behavior; and (g) support community health programs. Referral rates are inversely correlated to the comprehensiveness of a primary care practice. For example, Forrest et al. (1999) noted in a large study of pediatricians that approximately 2% of patients were referred for consultation or joint management with specialists. Although most referrals were to surgical subspecialists (52.3%), over 8% were to mental health practitioners (Forrest et al., 1999).

4. It serves a *coordinative function* for all the health care needs of the patient. This is the role of the coach or quarterback by

which the PCP manages and directs all of the medical and other care. In the last 10 years, the emphasis on the PCP as the manager of access to other health care services and providers has been fundamental to most managed-care plans.

The Council on Graduate Medical Education (1992) outlined four critical content areas within primary care services: (a) health promotion and disease prevention, (b) assessment and evaluation of common symptoms and physical signs, (c) management of acute and chronic medical conditions, and (d) identification of appropriate referral of other needed health services. Primary care differs from specialty care in the breadth of disorders addressed (Council on Graduate Medical Education, 1992; Rakel, 2002). For PCPs, 25 diagnoses account for 50% of all office visits (Schappert, 1999). Included among these diagnoses are conditions frequently treated by psychologists, such as depression, anxiety, obesity, and low-back pain. The breadth of diagnoses seen in primary care contrasts sharply to that of subspecialties. For example, within specialties such as dermatology and psychiatry, only 5 diagnoses account for more than 50% of the office visits (Marsland, Wood, & Mayo, 1976).

5. It assumes *continuing responsibility* for individual patient follow-up and community health problems. The goal of the PCP is to maintain an ongoing relationship to the individual patient and his or her family and community across the life span, from birth to death. It is argued that by knowing a patient and his or her family, the PCP is able to render better and more economical care (Rakel, 2002). This perspective fits with some views of the role of psychologists as providing intermittent care across the life cycle (Bray, 1996).

6. It is a highly *personalized type of care* (American Academy of Family Physicians, 1994). PCPs get to know their patients and families over time and develop a long-term relationship with them. This means getting to know the whole person, not just his or her biomedical functioning, a goal that is sometimes difficult to achieve in this age of rapidly changing health care systems.

A more common determination of a PCP is whether the clinician takes care of undifferentiated symptoms and routine health problems, such as checking patients' blood pressure and caring for common illnesses, such as colds, infections, hypertension, or depression (Bray, 1996; Rakel, 2002). Three medical specialties are the core providers of primary care: (a) family physicians, (b) general internal medicine physicians, and (c) general pediatricians.

Other specialties that are sometimes included are obstetricians–gynecologists and family nurse practitioners.

In most managed health care systems, PCPs are the "gatekeepers" for entry into the medical system. This means that a person with a health or mental health problem must first see his or her PCP before he or she can see another provider, such as a psychologist or cardiologist. If the PCP feels it is within his or her scope of practice to treat the problem, then he or she will provide the treatment and not provide a referral to a specialist. For example, the initial Agency for Healthcare Research and Quality (AHRQ; formerly the Agency for Health Care Policy and Research, 1999) guidelines for treatment of depression indicate that a PCP should try a trial of antidepressant medication before referring the patient for psychotherapy.

This type of managed-care system can place added burdens on PCPs, who must provide health care services to all patients and are part of a triangle between patients and specialists. Patients sometimes resent having to see their PCP just to get a referral and may be upset if they are not approved to see the specialist. By being a part of the primary health care team, psychologists can work collaboratively with PCPs and avoid being part of the PCP–patient–specialist triangle.

PRIMARY CARE PSYCHOLOGY

Where do psychologists fit within primary care? Are psychologists PCPs? According to Rakel (1995), one of the originators of the family physician movement, "Primary care, to be done well, requires extensive training specifically tailored to problems frequently seen in primary care. These include the early detection, diagnosis, and treatment of *depression* [italics added], . . . and the care of those with chronic and terminal illnesses" (p. 7). These are clearly areas where psychologists can provide services. Furthermore, deGruy (1996) argued that there is a parallel primary care mental health system that does not necessarily require PCPs for referral. In these cases, patients can directly seek behavioral health services without going through their PCPs.

Although psychologists are not trained to take blood pressure or treat the common cold, they are trained to treat the most common behavioral health problems, such as depression and anxiety, and to provide behavioral interventions to prevent or intervene with major health problems (Bray, 1996; Million, Green, & Meagher, 1982). For example, prevention of cardiovascular disease or cancer through lifestyle modification, weight management, smoking cessation, or stress management are areas in which psychologists have developed effective interventions. In addition, many of the chronic diseases, such as diabetes, hypertension, or chronic back pain, can be helped or treated effectively through behavioral interventions (Holland & Rowland, 1989; Routh, 1988; Stager & Fordyce, 1982). Adherence to medical regimens is critical to effective health outcomes. In many chronic health conditions, adherence issues, such as following a diet, smoking cessation, taking medications appropriately, or performing exercise, are integral to good outcomes. Psychological factors mediate these compliance behaviors. Psychologists have much to offer in the development and management of compliance programs. Thus, psychologists are able to provide primary care behavioral health services and to diagnose or manage a number of health problems seen in primary care settings.

Primary care psychology is the provision of health and mental health services that includes the prevention of disease and the promotion of healthy behaviors in individuals, families, and communities. The communities most relevant for primary care include those of the patient and health care providers. Primary care psychologists are experts in: (a) assessment and evaluation of common psychosocial symptoms, signs, and problems that are seen in primary care patients; (b) psychosocial management of acute and chronic health and illness conditions with which primary care patients often present; (c) collaboration with other PCPs and primary care teams; and (d) identifying appropriate experts for referral and collaboration. Primary care psychologists have a basic understanding of the common biomedical conditions seen within primary care, the medical and pharmacological treatments of those conditions, and how they interact and affect the psychosocial functioning of patients and their families and communities. In this case, *family* is broadly defined as the patient's network of committed relationships (Pequegnat & Bray, 1997). In addition, primary care psychologists are generalist providers who are trained to evaluate, treat, and refer patients from birth through death across the life span (Bray, 1996).

In July 1995, the American Psychological Association Committee for the Advancement of Professional Practice convened a Primary Care Task Force to examine the role of psychologists in primary medical care (Primary Care Task Force, 1996). A core assumption of the task force was that psychology is a health profession, not just a mental health profession (Bray, 1996; Haley et al., 1998). The task force believes that psychologists and psychological services are essential to the primary health care team whose purpose is to deliver cost-effective and clinically effective comprehensive care.

The task force discussed several models of psychology in primary care. One concept that gained support was that psychologists should contribute to comprehensive health care. This type of care is provided over time, is coordinated with other members of the health care team, and uses specialists and subspecialists as needed. Comprehensive care makes use of community resources and recognizes the role of systems, such as families and contextual factors, in health and illness. Primary comprehensive health care teams emphasize prevention, education, consultation, evaluation, and treatment. Furthermore, this care rests on a growing fund of knowledge and the science that underlies collaboration and the biopsychosocial or systemic model (Bray, 1996; Haley et al., 1998).

The Primary Care Task Force identified three major characteristics of psychologists providing primary care psychology. First, many psychologists work directly in a primary care setting. This could be a clinic, a group practice, or with an individual medical practitioner. This could also include both clinical and educational services, such as teaching in a family medicine or pediatric residency.

Second, primary care psychologists are capable of working with all patients seen in the setting. This means that they can work with the broad range of psychosocial problems found in primary care settings. In addition, such psychologists may serve as consultants to the other PCPs, such as family physicians or nurse practitioners, regarding patient care issues, doctor–patient issues, or system issues. Furthermore, primary care psychologists are able to provide interventions for behavioral and interpersonal components of medical problems, such as facilitating compliance with medical regimens, lifestyle changes, reducing complications due to surgery, and dealing with individual and family dysfunction related to the stress of coping with illness.

Third, primary care psychologists contribute to patients' total health care, both in sickness and in health. Psychologists in primary care are not limited solely to the assessment and treatment of mental disorders. In essence, this model of psychology requires that the psychologist provider be a *generalist* and be able to treat the full range of psychological and behavioral problems, from birth to death, with individuals and families, that present in these settings.

The Committee for the Advancement of Professional Practice Primary Care Task Force also recognized that psychologists provide "psychological primary care" in diverse settings that focus on individuals with chronic health conditions. The skills and knowledge needed to provide these services have significant overlap with the skills required to practice psychology in a primary care setting (Primary Care Task Force, 1996, p. 2). Making psychological services available in chronic medical or tertiary care settings makes clinical and financial sense.

The recognition of psychological disorders presenting as general medical illnesses and the provision of psychological services can lead to a decline in general medical services, a phenomenon commonly referred to as a *cost offset effect* (Olfson, Sing, & Slesinger, 1999). In addition, alcohol and drug abuse may have substantial morbidity costs associated with advanced states of the condition (Sherin & Kaiser, 2002). Psychological treatment may prevent unnecessary medical care and reduce future demands on medical resources or substitute for mental health services provided by PCPs.

It is interesting that cost offsets are less likely to be observed in psychiatric illnesses, such as schizophrenia, bipolar disorder, or other severe forms of mental illness (England, 1999). Individuals with these diagnoses are not likely to use excessive medical services. Indeed, individuals with severe mental illness are more likely to be underserved. At the other end of the spectrum, cost offsets are unlikely to occur among individuals who are socioeconomically disadvantaged. In this group, provision of psychological and mental health treatment may lead to an appropriate increase in medical services, where previously unmet needs are recognized. Olfson et al. (1999) noted the correlation between poor psychological functioning and physical health. These authors found that in one health maintenance organization review of primary care patients with depression or anxiety, annual costs were twice as high for patients with these disorders. The increases were noted across pharmacy, laboratory, general medical care, and specialty care. Similar observations have been made among older primary care patients (see chap. 12, this volume). Psychological treatment has been shown to have the greatest cost offset among three patient groups: (a) distressed elderly inpatients; (b) primary care outpatients with multiple, unexplained somatic complaints; and (c) nonelderly adults with alcoholism. Mental health interventions have been found to be associated with an average 10% reduction in inpatient medical care costs for medically ill inpatients (Mumford et al., 1984).

MENTAL, BEHAVIORAL, AND INTERPERSONAL HEALTH PROBLEMS IN PRIMARY CARE

PCPs are usually the first health care professionals to encounter mental health problems. As deGruy (1996) stated in his report on behalf of the Committee on the Future of Primary Care for the Institute of Medicine, "a major portion of mental health care is rendered in the primary care setting, *and always will be* [italics added]" (p. 285). Prevalence studies of psychiatric disorders in primary care have yielded a wide range of estimates, with estimates of diagnosable psychiatric disorders in primary care ranging from 16% to 43% (Barrett et al., 1988). Nonpsychiatric physicians write over 50% of the prescriptions for psychotropic medications in the United States and provide the vast majority of diagnosis and treatment of mental health problems (deGruy, 1996). It is estimated that between 10% and 20% of the population consults a primary care clinician during the course of a year because of a mental health concern (Hankin & Oktay, 1979; Schulberg & Burns, 1988). In many cases, patients in managed-care systems are more likely to seek treatment from their PCP than from a mental health specialist (Sturm, Camp, & Wells, 2001).

Despite the high prevalence of certain mental disorders in primary care settings (Katon & Sullivan, 1990), PCPs often overlook these types of problems and focus on the diagnosis and treatment of physical health symptoms (deGruy, 1996; Eisenberg, 1992; Higgins, 1994). Estimated rates of failure by PCPs to detect psychiatric disorders range from one half to two thirds (deGruy,

1996), with women more likely to be properly diagnosed with depression than men (Bertakis et al., 2001). Considerably higher rates of nonrecognition were found when stringent diagnostic criteria were used and when patients presented with physical rather than psychological complaints (Bridges & Goldberg, 1985; Kirmayer et al., 1993). Recent studies indicate that PCPs are likely to recognize depressed patients but do not provide adequate follow-up to ensure proper treatment (Carney et al., 1999; Simon & Von Korff, 1995).

Obesity is a current national U.S. concern. Groups such as the American Association of Diabetes and the Office of the Surgeon General have targeted this epidemic problem, especially among youth. Opportunities for prevention of diabetes through lifestyle and health education will grow as PCPs focus on this major health problem. Psychologists are well suited to offer health education programs, family counseling, and interventions to enhance compliance with prevention and treatment (Brownell, 1998; Foreyt & Goodrick, 1994)

Inadequate interviewing skills and experience in the management of psychosocial problems and mental disorders are two factors related to the nonrecognition of such problems (Ormel & Tiemens, 1995). Insufficient knowledge of diagnostic criteria is another factor (deGruy, 1996). In a study that used standardized patients, few of the 47 participating PCPs knew or used the *Diagnostic and Statistical Manual of Mental Disorders* (*DSM–IV*; American Psychiatric Association, 1994) diagnostic criteria for depression (Badger, deGruy, et al., 1994). Instead, most PCPs use more general *International Classification of Diseases* (*ICD–10*, World Health Organization, 1994) diagnoses for common disorders such as depression.

Lack of time to interview patients is another barrier to accurate diagnosis (Philbrick et al., 1996). Lipkin (1996) found that generalist physicians spend an average of 12 minutes with a patient, which makes it more difficult to conduct extensive psychiatric interviews and assessments. Physicians sometimes fail to recognize mental disorders in patients presenting with physical symptoms, especially nonspecific symptoms, such as fatigue, sleep problems, and multiple pains.

Primary care patients contribute to the lack of accurate diagnosis by consistently underreporting personal distress to physicians. In a study of primary care in rural counties of California, Good and her colleagues (1987) found that only 20% to 30% of patients with emotional distress, family problems, behavioral problems, or some combination of these, reported them to their PCPs.

The expense of not diagnosing and treating these types of problems can be staggering (Simon et al., 2001). For example, the costs associated with depression have been estimated as high as $43.7 billion/year (Greenberg, Stiglin, Finkelstein, & Berndt, 1993). In addition, anxiety and depression result in higher medical utilization rates and costs (Simon, Ormel, VonKorff,

& Barlow, 1995; Simon et al., 2001). (See chap. 9, this volume, for further information about this.)

Thus, there is a critical need for the appropriate diagnosis and treatment of common types of mental, behavioral, and interpersonal health problems seen in primary care settings. However, it is important that psychologists understand that most treatments of mental health problems occur in the medical system and are provided by nonpsychiatric physicians (Campbell et al., 1992; deGruy, 1996). It is estimated that between 40% and 60% of primary care medical visits are due to psychosocial problems and not to diagnosable physiological disease. Furthermore, Kroenke and Mangelsdorff (1989) found that, of patients from an internal medicine clinic, only 16% had clear organic causes of their problems, and 10% had clear psychological problems, but nearly 80% of patients had significant psychological distress. Primary care is also a context in which serious interpersonal problems emerge (Snugg & Inui, 1992). Kerker, Horwitz, Leventhal, Plichta, and Leaf (2000) reported that 4.2% of mothers in primary care report child abuse. In primary care, the lifetime prevalence of partner violence is about 40% (Hamberger, Saunders, & Hovey, 1992; Saunders, Hamberger, & Hovey, 1993). Saunders et al. (1993) found that women with a history of violent relationships visit their PCPs more frequently than women who have not been abused.

As the renowned family physician Tom Campbell and his colleagues (Campbell et al., 1992) stated:

> The vast majority of patients with mental health disorders are treated solely in the medical sector by non-psychiatrists, most of who[m] have inadequate training to deal with these problems. Many well-trained physicians want to develop good working relationships with psychologists and other mental health professionals to whom they can confidently refer their patients with serious emotional and relational problems. (p. 196)

These facts point to the need for psychological services in primary care settings.

LACK OF PSYCHOLOGIST PARTICIPATION IN PRIMARY CARE

Does all this mean that a psychologist should see the majority of patients with psychosocial problems in primary care? Probably not. For example, if someone develops a cold due to being susceptible to a virus because of increased stress, then he or she would probably benefit most from a proper medical diagnosis and treatment. Recurrent stress and viral infections may, however, be a good reason to refer a patient for psychological treatment. Many patients do not need or want to see a psychologist and prefer to be treated by their PCP (Orleans, George, Houpt, & Brodie, 1985; Von Korff & Myers, 1987). They have an ongoing relationship with the provider and do not want to be referred out to any other professional. This occurs with other types of referrals, such as to medical specialists, as well (Olfson, 1991). Appropriate and skillful referral is a key issue if the PCP feels the patient really needs to see a psychologist.

In addition, many of the psychosocial problems seen by PCPs are in the very early stages of development, that is, before a formal psychiatric diagnosis is warranted. For example, a patients might see his or her PCP because of fatigue related to situational sleep problems and stress that has not yet developed into a diagnosable mental health problem. The PCP provides basic empathy, advice, support, or symptom relief with medications that prevent the progression of the problem.

These problems are often due to psychological reactions to difficult social situations, such as poverty, lack of adequate resources, and so on, which are not typically handled by psychologists. Social workers are often involved in these types of problems, although systems and community-oriented psychologists can certainly provide important help. Psychologists are unfortunately often isolated from the primary care medical system. Thus, the professionals best trained to assess and treat psychosocial problems may not be available to medical professionals and the patients who need these services. The change from psychologists as mental health professionals to health care professionals will require special training on how to work closely with PCPs.

EDUCATIONAL NEEDS AND OPPORTUNITIES IN PRIMARY CARE

As we discussed earlier, psychologists are not regularly trained to work with PCPs and often do not have access to the general health care system. Most clinical or counseling psychology training programs do not provide training in basic biomedicine, access to primary care training sites, or expertise in primary care behavioral health and family problems (McDaniel, Hepworth, & Doherty, 1992; Primary Care Task Force, 1996). Furthermore, there are few opportunities at internship sites for training in primary care settings. A few exceptions are opportunities in pediatric settings or health psychology rotations; however, even in these sites there is often an emphasis on providing mental health interventions or specialized behavioral health interventions rather than being integrated into the primary care health system. Furthermore, there are only a few postdoctoral training opportunities and continuing education programs for learning about primary care.

Effective collaboration between behavioral health practitioners and physicians requires recognition of: (a) differences in conceptual orientations and training (biomedical vs. psychosocial), (b) different languages based on training (medical jargon vs. psychological jargon), (c) divergent practice styles (time differences, confidentiality issues), (d) difficulties in accessibility to various providers (problems with referral and managed-care issues), and (e) noncongruent expectations for assessment and treatment (Bray & Rogers, 1995, 1997; McDaniel et al., 1992). Training and experience in these areas are essential.

A model primary care curriculum has recently been developed and is described in chapter 4 of this volume. In brief, this curriculum describes the core knowledge, skills, and training for graduates in primary care psychology, which include biological components of health and disease; cognitive components; affective components; sociocultural components; behavior and developmental aspects; health policy and health care systems; common primary care problems; clinical assessment of common conditions; chemical interventions; interprofessional collaboration; and ethical, legal, and professional issues in primary care.

Another educational opportunity for psychologists is to provide education and training for medical students, resident physicians, and those in continuing postgraduate medical education. Most primary care residency programs require training in behavioral science, which includes information on psychology and mental health topics. It is important in providing educational activities for physicians to remember that they are most interested in case-based practical discussions with an emphasis on how to use the information to treat their patients. They are usually not interested in academic reviews of the literature or theoretical discussions. A guiding rule of thumb is the answer the question "How will this lecture help the physician better treat his or her next patient?"

Some programs, such as family medicine, pediatrics, physical medicine and rehabilitation require behavioral science faculty who provide formal educational activities, for example, lectures, seminars, case consultation, or precepting (Bray, 1996; Bray & McDaniel, 1998). *Precepting* involves reviewing cases and seeing patients in a medical clinic. A variety of methods are used, including case discussions, videotape reviews of cases, live observation via one-way mirrors or video, or collaborative patient care. Each of these provides psychologists with opportunities to teach physicians about behavioral, mental health, and systemic issues and how psychologists can be part of the treatment process. Many programs or clinics employ part-time faculty. These may be paid or voluntary positions. The advantage for psychologists is to gain patient referrals and access to medical providers for consultations.

PRACTICE NEEDS AND OPPORTUNITIES IN PRIMARY CARE

With the increase in managed health care and integrated health care systems, PCPs are under added pressure to diagnose and treat a broad spectrum of biomedical and psychosocial problems. Thus, they benefit from greater access to behavioral health practitioners (Coleman, Patrick, Eagle, &

Hermalin, 1979; MacDonald, Baloun, & McKenna, 1995). Collaborative practice between psychologists and physicians is one method to meet the multiple needs of primary care patients (Bray & Rogers, 1995, 1997; McDaniel et al., 1992). Collaborative treatment models are addressed in detail in chapters 5 through 9 of this volume. Collaborative practice will be enhanced by recent approval of new billing CPT codes that facilitate the provision of psychological services for medical conditions. These new CPT codes allow psychologists to bill for treatment of patients with medical, nonmental health diagnoses (e.g., hypertension or diabetes).

RESEARCH NEEDS AND OPPORTUNITIES IN PRIMARY CARE

Psychologists have much to offer primary care in the research domain. Most physicians, and especially PCPs, are not trained in formal research methods and have limited interest in conducting formal research. Although physicians have more training in biomedical sciences than do most psychologists, they often have limited knowledge about statistics or psychological research methods. Their research training is usually in epidemiology research methods, which use a different language and description for research than those used in psychology training. However, the vast majority of physicians recognize the importance of research and science for medical practice and are thus interested in clinically oriented research. In addition, with the new emphasis on evidence-based medicine and managed care there is increasing pressure to use the results of clinical trials and outcome studies to inform medical practice and to conduct patient satisfaction surveys (Miller et al., 2001). All of these factors create excellent opportunities for psychologists to conduct research and evaluations in primary care settings. (See chap. 9 for an example of research on collaborative care.)

There are some important differences between psychological and medical approaches to consider in conducting research in primary care settings. First, most physicians are interested in research to provide better patient care; they want practical answers to pressing patient care problems. In contrast, psychologists are often interested in more basic processes or theory. Second, given the demanding nature of medical practice, research needs to be able to be integrated into and not disrupt patient care. These differences reflect the divergent values and training between physicians and psychologists.

Primary care presents unique problems for research that is sensitive to comorbidities and subthreshold syndromes (deGruy, 1996). *Subthreshold syndromes* are observed when patients present with symptoms that create distress and discomfort but do not meet the requirements for a formal diagnosis. The identification and treatment of psychological mental disorders in primary care is critical. Problems such as depression and anxiety often present differently for patients in primary care settings, and their relationships to other medical problems, such as diabetes and hypertension, is complex. Sub-threshold syndromes, such as mixed anxiety–depression, do not meet *DSM* criteria but are prevalent and related to other health problems. There is also a need to examine high comorbidity syndromes, such as posttraumatic stress disorder; somatizing syndromes; and other medical complaints, such as chronic pain or disease. These problems are often frustrating for PCPs to treat.

Psychologists can develop and study innovative models of service delivery in primary care settings. Many clinical delivery systems are developing integrated medical–behavioral health services in primary care settings (see chaps. 2, 9, and 14, this volume, and McKay & Frank, in press). These models often rely on proprietary data and are not addressed in the scientific literature; as a consequence, there is little available research on mental health "carve-ins" or "carve-outs." This might include observational studies of the innumerable natural experiments now underway in the health care system. A recent series of articles by Crabtree and colleagues (Crabtree et al., 2001; Miller et al., 2001) that observed primary care practices from the ground up exemplifies this type of research. Furthermore, it is important to conduct tests of the effectiveness and cost-effectiveness of different collaborative and consultative modes between mental health professionals and primary care clinicians.

Psychologists can also provide assistance in the development of patient satisfaction surveys and evaluations to demonstrate and evaluate medical and psychological health care. Managed-care companies are now requiring that medical groups provide evidence of patient satisfaction to renew contracts. These are just a few examples of the much-needed research in primary care. As more emphasis is placed on primary care treatment, traditional funding agencies, such as the National Institute of Mental Health or the National Institute on Alcoholism and Alcohol Abuse, are emphasizing research in primary care.

CONCLUSIONS

With the move from specialized medical care to primary medical care and the increase in integrated, managed health care services, it is essential that psychologists expand their practices into the general health care arena. Psychologists can provide important diagnostic and intervention services that enhance treatment options to patients in primary care settings. In addition, psychologists can provide valuable systems consultation to primary health care teams and providers, educational training, and much-needed research expertise.

Psychologists need to gain additional training and experience in working in primary care settings to be effective clinicians, educators, and researchers in these arenas. This type of training needs to be offered in both graduate psychology programs and in continuing education programs to familiarize psychologists with primary health care and psychological interventions for primary care patients. Finally, psychologists will need to shift their focus from an exclusively psychosocial orientation to a biopsychosocial orientation to fully integrate themselves into the general health care system. The movement from mental health to health care provider is an exciting opportunity to expand the roles and areas of practice for psychologists.

REFERENCES

Agency for Healthcare Research and Quality. (1999). *Treatment of depression—Newer pharmacotherapies*. Evidence Report/Technology Assessment: Number 7. AHCRP Publication No. 99-E014, Rockville, MD. www.ahrq.gov/clinic/epsums/deprsumm.htm

American Academy of Family Physicians (AAFP). (1994). Directors' newsletter, AAFP revises primary care definition and exhibit. *AAFP Reporter*, *1*, 1.

American Psychiatric Association (1994). *Diagnostic and statistical manual of mental disorders (4th ed.)*. Washington, DC: Author.

Badger, L. W., deGruy, F. V., Hartman, J., Plant, M. A., Leeper, J., Ficken, R., et al. (1994). Psychosocial interest, medical interviews, and the recognition of depression. *Archives of Family Medicine*, *3*, 899–907.

Barrett, J. E., Barrett, J. A., Oxman, T. E., & Gerber, P. D. (1988). The prevalence of psychiatric disorders in a primary care practice. *Archives of General Psychiatry*, *45*, 1100–1106.

Becker, M. H., Drachman, D. H., & Kirscht, J. P. (1974). Continuity of the pediatrician: New support for an old shibboleth. *Medical Care*, *84*, 599–605.

Bray, J. H. (1996). Psychologists as primary care practitioners. In R. J. Resnick & R. H. Rozensky (Eds.), *To your health: Psychology across the lifespan* (pp. 89–100). Washington, DC: American Psychological Association.

Bray, J. H., & McDaniel, S. H. (1998). Behavioral health practice in primary care settings. In L. VandeCreek, S. Knapp, & T. L. Jackson (Eds.), *Innovations in clinical practice: A source book.* (Vol. 16, pp. 313–323). Sarasota, FL: Professional Resource Press.

Bray, J. H., & Rogers, J. C. (1995). Linking psychologists and family physicians for collaborative practice. *Professional Psychology: Research and Practice*, *26*, 132–138.

Bray, J. H. & Rogers, J. C. (1997). The linkages project: Training behavioral health professionals for collaborative practice with primary care physicians. *Families, Systems, and Health*, *15*, 55–63.

Bridges, K. W., & Goldberg, D. P. (1985). Somatic presentations of DSM–III psychiatric disorders in primary care. *Journal of Psychosomatic Research*, *29*, 563–569.

Brownell, K. D. (1998). Diet, exercise, and behavioral intervention: The nonpharmacological approach. *European Journal of Clinical Investigation*, *28*, 19–21.

Campbell, T. L., McDaniel, S. H., & Seaburn, D. (1992). Family systems medicine: New opportunities for psychologists. In T. J. Akamatsu, M. A. Parris-Stephens, S. E. Hobfoll, & J. H. Crowther (Eds.), *Family health psychology* (pp. 193–215). Washington DC: Hemisphere.

Carney, P. A., Dietrich, A. J., Eliassen S., Owen, M., & Badger, L. W. (1999). Recognizing and managing depression in primary care: A standardized patient study. *Journal of Family Practice, 48*, 965–972.

Coleman, J. V., Patrick, D. L., Eagle, J., & Hermalin, J. A. (1979). Collaboration, consultation, and referral in an integrated health–mental health program at an HMO. *Social Work in Health Care, 5*, 83–96.

Council on Graduate Medical Education. (1992). *Improving access to health care through workforce reform: Directions for the 21st century: Executive Summary*. Washington, DC: U.S. Department of Health and Human Services.

Crabtree, B. F., Miller, W. L., & Stange, K. C. (2001). Understanding practice from the ground up. *Journal of Family Practice, 50*, 881–887.

deGruy, F. (1996). Mental health care in the primary care setting. In M. S. Donaldson, K. D. Yordy, K N. Lohr, & N. A. Vanselow (Eds.), *Primary care: American's health in a new era* (pp. 285–311). Washington, DC: National Academy Press.

Donaldson, M., Yordy, K., & Vanselow, N. (Eds.). (1994). *Defining primary care: An interim report. Committee on the Future of Primary Care, Division of Health Care Services, Institute of Medicine* (Part 3, pp. 15–33), Washington, DC: National Academy Press.

Eisenberg, L. (1992). Treating depression and anxiety in primary care: Closing the gap between knowledge and practice. *New England Journal of Medicine, 326*, 1080–1084.

England, M. J. (1999). Capturing mental health cost offsets. *Health Affairs, 18*, 91–93.

Foreyt, J. P., & Goodrick, G. K. (1994). *Living without dieting*. New York: Warner Books.

Forrest, C. B., Glade, G. B., Baker, A. E., Bocian, A. B., Kang, M., & Starfield, B. (1999). The pediatric primary–specialty care interface: How pediatricians refer children and adolescents to specialty care. *Archives of Pediatric and Adolescent Medicine, 153*, 705–714.

Good, M. J. D., Good, B. J., & Cleary, P. D. (1987). Do patient attitudes influence physician recognition of psychosocial problems in primary care? *Journal of Family Practice, 25*, 53–59.

Greenberg, P. E., Stiglin, L. E., Finkelstein, S. N., & Berndt, E. R. (1993). The economic burden of depression in 1990. *Journal of Clinical Psychiatry, 54*, 405–418.

Haley, W. E., McDaniel, S. H., Bray, J. H., Frank, R. G., Heldring, M., Johnson, S. B., et al. (1998). Psychological practice in primary care settings: Practical tips for clinicians. *Professional Psychology: Research and Practice, 29*, 237–244.

Hamberger, L. K., Saunders, D. G., & Hovey, M. (1992). Prevalence of domestic violence in community practice andrate of physician inquiry. *Family Medicine, 24*, 283–287.

Hankin, J. R., & Oktay, J. S. (1979). *Mental disorder and primary care: An analytical view of the literature*. In National Institute of Mental Health, Series D, No. 5. DHEW publication No. (ADM) 78-661. Government Printing Office.

Higgins, E. S. (1994). A review of unrecognized mental illness in primary care. *Archives of Family Medicine, 3,* 908–917.

Holland, J. C., & Rowland, J. H. (Eds.). (1989). *Handbook of psychoonocology: Psychological care of the patient with cancer*. New York: Oxford University Press.

Hurley, R. E., Freund, D. A., & Taylor, D. E. (1989). Emergency room use and primary care case management: Evidence from four Medicaid demonstration projects. *American Journal of Public Health, 79,* 843–846.

Institute of Medicine. (2001). *Crossing the quality chasm: A new health system for the 21st century*. Washington, DC: The National Academies Press.

Katon, W., & Sullivan, M. D. (1990). Depression and chronic medical illness. *Journal of Clinical Psychiatry, 51,* 3–11.

Kerker, B. D., Horwitz, S. M., Leventhal, J. M., Plichta, S., & Leaf, P. J. (2000). Identification of violence in the home: Pediatric and parental reports. *Archives of Pediatrics and Adolescent Medicine, 154,* 457–462.

Kirmayer, L. J., Robbins, J. M., Dworkind, M., & Yaffe, M. J. (1993). Somatization and the recognition of depression and anxiety in primary care . *American Journal of Psychiatry, 150,* 734–741.

Kroenke, K., & Mangelsdorff, D. (1989). Common symptoms in ambulatory care: Incidence, evaluation, therapy, and outcome. *American Journal of Medicine, 86,* 262–266.

Lipkin, M. (1996). Patient education and counseling in the context of modern patient–physician–family communication. *Patient Education & Counseling, 27,* 5–11.

MacDonald, A. S., Baloun, E. T., & McKenna, Q. L. (1995). Emerging models of integrated health systems. *GFP Notes, 8,* 1–5.

Marsland, D.W., Wood, M., & Mayo, F., (1976.) A databank for patient care, curriculum, and research in family practice: 526,196 Patient Problems. In J. P. Geyman (Ed.), *Content of family practice: A statewide study in Virginia with its clinical, educational and research implications*. New York: Appleton–Century Crofts.

McDaniel, S. H., Hepworth, J., & Doherty, W. J. (1992). *Medical family therapy*. New York: Basic Books.

McKay, N., & Frank, R. G. (in press). Payment for clinical services: From fundamentals to practice considerations. In R. G. Frank, J. Wallander, & A. Baum (Eds.), *Handbook of clinical health psychology: Models and perspectives in health psychology*. Washington, DC: American Psychological Association.

Miller, W. L., McDaniel, R. R., Crabtree, B. F., & Stange, K. C. (2001). Practice jazz: Understanding variation in family practice using complexity science. *Journal of Family Practice, 50,* 872–878.

Million, T., Green, C., & Meagher, R. (Eds.) (1982). *Handbook of clinical health psychology*. New York: Plenum.

Moore, S. (1979). Cost containment through risk sharing by primary care physicians. *New England Journal of Medicine, 300*, 1359–1362.

Mumford, E., Schlesinger, H. J., Glass, G. V., Patrick, C., Cuerdon, T. (1984). A new look at evidence about reduced cost of medical utilization following mental health treatment. *American Journal of Psychiatry, 141*, 1145–1158.

Olfson, M. (1991). Primary care patients who refuse specialized mental health services. *Archives of Internal Medicine, 151*, 129–132.

Olfson, M., Sing, M., & Slesinger, H., J. (1999). Mental health/medical cost care offsets: Opportunities for managed care. *Health Affairs, 18*, 79–93.

Orleans, C., George, L., Houpt, J., & Brodie, H. (1985). How primary care physicians treat psychiatric disorders: A national survey of family practitioners. *American Journal of Psychiatry, 142*, 52–57.

Ormel, J., & Tiemens, B. (1995). Recognition and treatment of mental illness in primary care. *General Hospital Psychiatry, 17*, 160–164.

Pequegnat, W., & Bray, J. H. (1997). Families and HIV/AIDS: Introduction to the special series. *Journal of Family Psychology, 11*, 3–10.

Philbrick, J. T., Connelly, J. E., & Wofford, A. B. (1996). The prevalence of mental disorders in rural office practice. *Journal of General Internal Medicine, 11*, 9–15.

Primary Care Task Force. (1996). *Final report to the Committee for the Advancement of Professional Psychology*, American Psychological Association, Washington, DC.

Rakel, R. E. (2002). The family physician. In R. E. Rakel (Ed.), *Textbook of family practice 6th Edition* (pp. 3–18). Philadelphia: W. B. Saunders.

Routh, D. K. (Ed.). (1988). *Handbook of pediatric psychology*. New York: Guilford Press.

Saunders, D. G., Hamberger, K., & Hovey, M. (1993). Indicators of woman abuse based on chart review at a family practice center. *Archives of Family Medicine, 2*, 537–543.

Schappert, M. (1999). 1997 *Summary: National ambulatory medical care survey* (Advance Data Vital Health Statistics, No. 305). Washington, DC: U.S. Government Printing Office.

Schulberg, H. C., & Burns, B. (1988). Mental disorders in primary care: Epidemiologic, diagnostic, and treatment research directions. *General Hospital Psychiatry, 10*, 79–87.

Sherin, K., & Kaiser, G. (2002). Alcohol abuse. In R. E. Rakel (Ed.), *Textbook of family practice* (6th ed., pp. 1513–1522). Philadelphia: W. B. Saunders.

Simon, G. E., & Von Korff, M. (1995). Recognition, management, and outcomes of depression in primary care. *Archives of Family Medicine, 4*, 99–105.

Simon, G. E., Barber, C., Birnbaum, H. G., Frank, R. G., Greenberg, P. E., Rose, R. M., et al. (2001). Depression and work productivity: The comparative costs of treatment versus nontreatment. *Journal of Occupational and Environmental Medicine, 43*, 2–9.

Simon, G. E., Ormel, J., VonKorff, M., & Barlow, W. (1995). Health care costs associated with depressive and anxiety disorders in primary care. *American Journal of Psychiatry, 152*, 352–357.

Snugg, N. K., & Inui, T. (1992). Primary care physicians' response to domestic violence: Opening Pandora's box. *Journal of the American Medical Association, 267,* 3157–3193.

Stager, J., & Fordyce, W. (1982). Behavioral health care in the management of chronic pain. In T. Million, C. Green, & R. Meagher (Eds.), *Handbook of clinical health psychology* (pp. 467–498). New York: Plenum.

Starfield, B. (1992). *Primary care: Concept, evaluation and policy.* New York: Oxford University Press.

Sturm, M. R., Camp, P., & Wells, K. B. (2001). Effects of cost–containment strategies within managed care on continuity of the relationship between patients with depression and their primary care providers. *Medical Care, 39,* 1075 1085.

Von Korff, M., & Myers, L. (1987). The primary care physician and psychiatric services. *General Hospital Psychiatry, 9,* 235–240.

World Health Organization (1994). *International statistical classification of diseases and related health problems—10th revision.* Geneva, Switzerland: Author.

2

THE INTEGRATION AND CONSOLIDATION OF HEALTH CARE: IMPLICATIONS FOR PSYCHOLOGY IN PRIMARY CARE

RANDY PHELPS AND GEOFFREY M. REED

The integration and consolidation of the U.S. health care system has become increasingly apparent to practitioners, consumers, and policymakers, with the delivery model rapidly shifting away from individual and group practices to one dominated by corporate conglomerates. In its current state of evolution, the system can best be characterized as employer focused; market driven; and largely governed by the rules of free enterprise and big business, including a preoccupation with cost and short-term profitability. Also, it is a system in which economic pressures have forced a reexamination of many issues for the field of psychology, including the discipline's emphasis on specialty-based care and a renewed focus on models of primary care. Although these changes may appear recent, they are actually the result of public policy and marketplace developments over at the least the last 50 years. In this chapter we highlight some of the forces that have reshaped health care dur-

We thank Russ Newman, American Psychological Association Executive Director for Professional Practice, for his contributions to the preparation of this chapter.

ing that time and consider the implications of the delivery system's evolution for psychology's involvement in primary care at the outset of the 21st century.

THE TRANSFORMATION OF HEALTH CARE

Public Policy

Government intervention has been an integral dynamic in the evolution of the delivery system. Starr (1982) noted, for example, that a failed attempt to enact national health insurance legislation during the 1940s was an early impetus for the growth of today's employer-based health insurance system. Also, corporate dominance of the current delivery system has its roots in public policy of the 1960s. The enactment during those years of the Medicare and Medicaid programs for elderly and poor individuals made the development of for-profit service delivery increasingly attractive for investors. The infusion of public funds into these programs led to the emergence of increasingly interlocking connections between hospitals and medical schools with corporate entities such as drug companies and medical equipment suppliers.

The corporatization of health care got another boost from federal legislation in the 1970s. Prepaid health plans, or *health maintenance organizations* (HMOs), had actually been on the scene for several decades but did not affect the larger marketplace until after the passage of the federal HMO Act of 1973. That legislation, as well as additional enabling legislation that followed, resulted in even more accelerated growth in market-driven health care.

In 1993, national health reform legislation proposed by then-President Clinton sought to curtail the explosive growth of health care costs and to increase access to care for 37 million uninsured members of the nation. The plan embraced many elements of a market-driven system, including employer-based coverage, cost controls, integrated service delivery, and competitive purchasing. However, the plan also established vast new powers of government regulation, and as a result it failed in large measure because of massive opposition from the business community to increased government involvement. As had occurred in the 1940s, though, the failure of a national plan furthered investment in marketplace and corporate solutions to the problems of health care delivery.

Third-Party Payment

Employer-paid health plans became increasingly prevalent after World War II, introducing employers as a significant third party between providers and patients. By 1960, 69% of the population was enrolled in some form of employer-based health insurance program (VandenBos, 1993). With the advent of Medicare and Medicaid, the government entered the third-party system for an additional segment of the population. By 1995, approximately 224 million of the total U.S. population of 264 million were insured as a result of employer-provided and government health care coverage (Edmunds et al., 1997).

By inserting employers and government between patients and providers, the third-party payment system removes consumers as the primary purchasers of care. As such, governments and businesses wield tremendous power in the marketplace to demand competitive prices from suppliers of health care. As the purchasers of care, they control the nature of competition in the market through the prequalification of plans, the negotiation of premiums, and the definitions of benefits and performance standards (Edmunds et al., 1997).

Corporatization

As noted, the influx in the 1960s of public money into health care set in motion the formation of large-scale corporate enterprises, thus beginning an ongoing shift from nonprofit and government-owned delivery systems to corporate-owned, for-profit systems that has continued into the present. By 1980, the editor of the *New England Journal of Medicine* described the "new medical–industrial complex," referring to the interconnections between health care and the corporate sector, as well as the growing number of profit-driven businesses such as dialysis centers and walk-in clinics selling their services directly to the public (Relman, 1980).

Corporate expansion into health care proceeded at an explosive pace in the decade to follow. The 1980s saw the formation of large hospital-based delivery systems as companies acquired and linked previously independent private and nonprofit hospitals. As a result, the health care industry became more consolidated, with ownership and control increasingly held by fewer regional and national corporations. In 1997, the five largest health care firms controlled 50% of the market, as a result of national consolidations (Feldman, Wholey, & Christianson, 1999).

Industry Consolidation

The current state of industry consolidation had its beginnings in those corporate hospital mergers and acquisitions, although such consolidations reached an all-time high by the end of the 20th century. The merger and acquisition frenzy was by no means unique to health care, although the tremendous boom came later to health care than to other industries. As is apparent from industries such as transportation, banking, and telecommunications, however, mergers and acquisitions are a typical by-product of corporatization. When companies become established in the marketplace and grow, they begin to merge with other companies and take over their competitors.

A prime example is the Hospital Corporation of America (HCA). In 1968, HCA began as a small for-profit system in Nashville, Tennessee, that, through aggressive acquisitions and its eventual merger with Columbia Healthcare, grew into the single largest health care provider in the country. In 1970, HCA controlled 23 for-profit hospitals. By 1997, Columbia/HCA operated more than 200 home care systems and 342 hospitals in 38 states, representing 6.7% of all U.S. hospitals, and it became the largest biller of Medicare in the country, with Medicare reimbursements in 1996 totaling more than one third of its $20 billion revenue.

Within behavioral health care, the 1990s in particular were a time of industry concentration and consolidation (Freeman & Trabin, 1994). A large number of independent companies went by the wayside in a short time through mergers and acquisitions, and the market share of those remaining increased drastically. In 1993, 17 behavioral health care companies accounted for 80 million covered lives (Oss, 1993). By mid-1998, 181 million Americans were covered for behavioral health services, with 142 million of them in a managed behavioral health plan. Over 80%, or 118 million, of these Americans were covered by only six behavioral health companies, and 42% (60 million) were covered by a single company, Magellan Health Services.

Ownership and Control

Through corporate restructuring and diversification, small organizations operating in single markets gave way to conglomerate enterprises and multiple corporations, often organized under holding companies and operating in a wide variety of markets. It was not uncommon for these entities to own both nonprofit and for-profit subsidiaries offering services in the same health care markets.

It is interesting that the ownership of local health care operations by corporate conglomerates was given further impetus by government initiatives of the 1970s and 1980s to prevent fraud and abuse. Those initiatives, the so-called Stark provisions (after their principal advocate, California Rep. Fortney Stark), fueled perceptions that health care providers were routinely abusing the system for profit. Moreover, they heralded a posture by government regulators that persists into the present day: that government policing of health care is necessary to control fraud and abuse in the system.

The Stark provisions included "anti-kickback" statutes and prohibitions against self-referral. Anti-kickback statutes were instituted first at the federal level and later at the state level to prevent fee splitting and payments between provider organizations for patient referrals. Additional legislation was enacted to prevent self-referrals, that is, those in which the patient was referred to a facility for other services that was ostensibly separate but was actually owned by the referring source. A typical example was a situation in which a physician referred a patient to a laboratory or diagnostic facility in which the same physician had an undisclosed full or part ownership. These initiatives hastened consolidation, because separate entities could become part of a single company to overcome self-referral prohibitions. If the physician's services and those of the laboratory were offered by the same corporate entity, then no laws would be broken.

Corporatization has led to the decline of free-standing, locally owned institutions in favor of large, multi-institutional systems controlled not by community-based hospital boards aware of local needs but by regional or national health care corporations. The managers and stockholders of these companies are typically removed from, and therefore may feel little accountability to, consumers at the point of service delivery.

The impact on health care professionals has been profound. As Webb (1996) put it, "The status of practitioners, regardless of discipline, is shifting from being an owner to being an employee" (p. 167). The implication of this shift has been significant for psychology, which as a profession has steadfastly held to the solo and small-group model of service delivery. As small business owners, psychologists have limited opportunity to compete with multi-institutional systems, and the profession's lack of success at gaining widespread access to hospital privileges has meant that few psychologists have the same options as their physician colleagues for moving into more integral roles and ownership positions in these largely hospital-based systems.

Cost Containment and Risk Allocation

The sheer magnitude and growth of health care expenditures, as well as the threat these costs pose to the U.S. economy, has reinforced a preoccupation with cost containment in the present system. One model of cost control has been to introduce *business efficiency* into health care through corporatization and consolidation. By becoming large enough to capitalize on economies of scale and to control provider–supplier costs, corporations can minimize their expenditures. Another model of cost control is the *free market economy* approach, a perspective that emphasizes minimal government intervention in health care to permit the marketplace to deal with cost issues through competition unfettered by regulatory control.

Cost containment in modern health care has relied mostly on *supply side* strategies, such as limiting patient access to care and managing utilization (Newman & Reed, 1996). Whereas traditional indemnity insurance uses patient cost-sharing mechanisms such as deductibles and copayments to limit utilization and reduce costs, the typical managed care reimbursement system, *capitation*, focuses on provider behavior to affect access and limit costs (Edmunds et al., 1997; Grumbach & Bodenheimer, 1995). *Simple capitation* involves paying the provider a fixed price for a specified set of services to a defined group of recipients. As the managed care market has matured, more complex capitation schemes have become increasingly prevalent.

These complex models include *subcapitation arrangements*, which are essentially subcontracts; *specialty-population capitation*, in which providers are paid a single premium for all services to a specific population, such as the frail elderly; and *global case rates*, in which the provider receives a lump sum for a defined episode of care, such as heart bypass surgery or depression treatment (Darves, 1998).

The common element of these capitation models is the shifting of financial risk from the managed care entity to the provider. Risk sharing creates strong incentives to limit patient services, because the provider is at financial risk if the cost of the care delivered exceeds the capitation payment. Hybrid reimbursement systems that combine capitation with additional payments or penalties in the form of bonuses or withheld fees can further enhance the incentive to limit care (Landon, Wilson, & Cleary, 1998).

Utilization management, a more intrusive form of utilization review, is another mechanism for cost reduction through influencing provider behavior. It involves scrutiny of the clinical activities of the provider to determine whether the services are appropriate and necessary, as defined by the managed care company. Utilization management techniques include prospective review, use of treatment protocols and guidelines, and case management for high-cost services or illnesses. The method of cost control is simple and direct: denial of payment for services deemed unnecessary (Grumbach & Bodenheimer, 1995).

Organized Systems of Care

In 1982, Starr reported that corporate expansion in health care was proceeding along the lines of both horizontal and vertical integration. *Horizontal integration* involves the acquisition of multiple institutions of the same type across geographic areas. The dramatic growth of for-profit psychiatric hospital chains during the 1980s is an example, as are the mergers and acquisitions described previously.

In contrast, a *vertically integrated* system is a network of organizations that provides or arranges to provide an integrated and coordinated continuum of services to a defined population (Shortell, Gillies, & Anderson, 1994). Such systems are typically referred to as *organized systems of care*, and they may include primary care providers, specialists, ambulatory care centers, home health care agencies, hospitals, and so on. The goal of these organized systems differs dramatically from those of a single entity such as a hospital. Organized systems typically encompass disease prevention, health promotion, acute illness treatment, rehabilitation, and chronic disease management to improve the health and well-being of a community or population (Shortell, Gillies, Anderson, Erickson, & Mitchell, 1996).

Early forecasts that organized systems of care would eventually dominate health care proved to be incorrect. Indeed, the marketplace shifted in the latter part of the 1990s to vertical dis-integration, with horizontal consolidation becoming the predominant market strategy (Lesser & Ginsburg, 2000). The premise underlying the early prediction was that the best way to control health care value—that is, cost *and* quality—was to control all of the organization, financing, and delivery as closely as possible, in ways that were responsive to regional demographics and economics (Newman & Reed, 1996). This vision of vertically integrated systems that provide a seamless, coordinated continuum of health care across settings, types, and levels of care was consistent with strong demands from the purchaser community for "one-stop shopping."

Despite the fact that most managed care companies typically offer "soup to nuts" plans that appear from the purchaser's perspective to be organized systems of care, the vast majority of these systems have been slow to integrate at a clinical level. Although integrated care holds the promise of better care, in actuality managed care plans have been rewarded in the marketplace for driving down costs through reducing provider reimbursement, restricting health care access, and transferring risk rather than for enhancing quality. It is much easier and more profitable to subcontract for those parts of the system that are difficult and costly to provide and to evade the clinical and fiscal accountability that a vertically integrated system implies. As a result, health plans have increasingly chosen to contract out significant components of their delivery system and to focus primarily on risk allocation in their contracting.

The second factor limiting development of true organized care systems is the tremendous underdevelopment and undercapitalization of health care information systems. Providing seamless services—or even tracking individual patients across a continuum of care—requires a fully integrated, probably electronic, medical record and a seamless flow of information throughout all parts of the system.

The Growth of Managed Care Delivery Systems

Hand in hand—and perhaps synonymous—with the corporatization of health care has been the increasing dominance of managed care in the health care marketplace. Although certain forms of managed care had their roots in the early 1900s, it was the federal HMO Act of 1973 that ushered in the modern era of managed care (see DeLeon, VandenBos, & Bulatao, 1991). That legislation required businesses with more than 25 employees to offer at least one qualified HMO plan in their health benefits package as an alternative to conventional insurance, if such a plan was available in the vicinity and requested inclusion. To qualify, the HMO had to provide beneficiaries not only with basic medical care and hospitalization but also with a wide range of other services, including diagnostic and laboratory services as well as emergency, mental health, alcohol and substance abuse, and home health services.

The HMO movement was predicated on the assumption that traditional fee-for-service indemnity health plans provided an incentive to health care professionals to deliver expensive and unnecessary treatment as well as costly and excessive diagnostic services. In contrast, prepaid comprehensive plans were thought to reverse this incentive by rewarding the maintenance of health and the prevention of illness.

Early data showed that HMOs could reduce overall health care costs by reducing use of inpatient services, the most expensive component of care. In 1978, Congress amended its 1973 HMO legislation to increase federal aid for HMO development after it was found that hospital expenses for federal employees in the Kaiser system were substantially lower than the national average (Edmunds et al., 1997). Those data showed that Kaiser subscribers had only 349 days of hospitalization per 1,000 persons, whereas the national average was 1,149 hospital days per 1,000 (Starr, 1982).

Demonstration by early managed care plans of their ability to contain costs propelled the development of a number of increasingly complex organizational models in the HMO markets of the 1970s and 1980s, such as pure staff or group models, independent practice associations (IPA), and network models (Landon et al., 1998). However, most present-day managed care plans are *mixed model* plans made up of complex, contractually based networks of multiple IPAs and provider groups. Furthermore, most managed care organizations offer purchasers multiple options as "products" from which to choose. These products may include HMO coverage, preferred provider organizations (PPO), point-of-service plans (POS), and plans for Medicare and Medicaid beneficiaries.

Privatization of public programs through government contracts with managed care companies was also an important trend in the 1990s (Reed, Levant, Stout, Murphy, & Phelps, 2001). In 1991, only 2.7 million of the total 28.3 million Medicaid recipients in the United States (<10%) were enrolled in managed care plans, but by 1995 that figure had grown to over 30%, or 11.6 million of 36.2 million recipients (Health Care Financing Administration, 1996). Coverage for Medicare recipients has also been increasingly directed away from fee-for-service plans as federal policymakers have turned to managed care as a means of controlling costs. From 1991 to 1995, the percentage of Medicare recipients enrolled in managed care plans almost doubled to 10%, and by 1995 three out of four beneficiaries had a choice of at least one managed care plan (Health Care Financing Administration, 1995). By 2000, however, managed care companies had begun to withdraw from these markets, citing a lack of profitability.

ERISA

Another federal statute which has had a tremendous, albeit unintended impact on the character of market-driven health care in this country is the Employee Retirement Income Security Act (ERISA), passed in 1974 to prevent misuse of employee pension funds and to encourage employers to provide worker benefits. It established uniform federal standards for employee welfare benefits plans, including health plans. One consequence of this legislation is that if an employer fully or partially self-insures its own health plan, that plan is regulated by the federal ERISA statute rather than by state insurance laws (Fuchs, 1997).

Subsequent to the passage of ERISA, corporations soon found that they could save on health care costs by underwriting their own health plans instead of purchasing coverage from insurance companies. By self-insuring, the employer's plan would be exempt from potentially costly state requirements such as taxes on insurance premiums, specific benefit requirements, and mandated provider laws. Because these plans can ignore state laws requiring mental health coverage or consumer freedom to choose providers, one practical result of ERISA has been to reduce access to some mental health care and to exclude coverage for psychological services by some self-insured plans (Newman & Bricklin, 1991).

Moreover, ERISA pre-empts the growing number of state laws attempting to regulate the managed care industry. Employer-purchased plans may therefore be unresponsive to state mandates to provide patient protections for managed care enrollees. Patients who are injured as a result of a managed care company's negligence through the inappropriate denial of services or provision of substandard care can seek legal redress in almost every state. However, for patients receiving services from a managed care plan purchased by a self-insured company, ERISA removes this option. Thus, ERISA evolved into a shield of immunity protecting managed care organizations from potential liability for negligent or inadequate care.

The impact of the ERISA pre-emption on the U.S. health care system has been enormous, for the single reason that most workers and their families in this country receive their health care through self-insured benefit plans. The Employment Retirement Income Security Act covers over 2.5 million private sector plans that provide health benefits to 125 million Americans ("Pension and Welfare Benefits Administration testimony," 1998).

THE RISE OF PRIMARY CARE

From the postwar period until the late 1980s and early 1990s, health care policy and health insurance coverage emphasized acute care, short-term hospital care, and surgery. Little attention was devoted to serious initiatives to maintain health, and only minimal investments were made in public health strategies to broadly promote healthy communities and individuals (Pew Health Professions Commission, 1995).

During this period, payment systems for providers and health care facilities were based on circumscribed procedures, and reimbursement was higher for inpatient care than for outpatient care. Thus, health care systems had economic incentives to hospitalize patients and to provide expensive inpatient procedures. Conversely, health care providers and health care systems actually had economic disincentives to emphasize prevention, early intervention, and treatment in less restrictive environments (Newman & Reed, 1996). These services were typically not reimbursable, because prevention and early intervention services are not procedure based and are generally provided on an outpatient basis, and the individuals who receive them may not carry a diagnosis.

Driven by this pattern of reimbursement arrangements as well as an explosion in specialized medical knowledge and medical technology, this period was also a time of tremendous specialization among health care professionals. By 1992, only about one third of practicing physicians could be considered generalists, down from half as recently as 1960. Only 13% of medical school graduates in 1992 were choosing to enroll in residencies that would prepare them to practice as primary care physicians. As the Pew Health Professions Commission (1995) put it, "the ideal of specialization came to dominate the patterns of training, the orientation of professionalism, and the ways in which health care services are reimbursed" (p. 8).

These patterns supported a high-technology, episode-based approach to care provided by an array of specialists focusing on individual organ systems (Institute of Medicine, 1994). It is not surprising that health care costs exploded, rising from $27.1 billion in 1960 to $675 billion, or 12.2% of the gross national product, in 1990. In constant dollars, this represented an increase of over 400% (see VandenBos, 1993). At the time of the Clinton health care reform proposal, national health expenditures were absorbing 14% of the GNP, or one-seventh of the total economy (White House Domestic Policy Council, 1993). In 1996, the total cost of national health care actually exceeded $1 trillion for the first time in history (" '96 Health Spending," 1998).

A basic premise of the early HMO movement was that costs could be contained by reducing demand for more expensive specialty-based care. Prewar, populist HMOs emphasized primary care, disease prevention, and health promotion as a means of improving population health, thus reducing the need for specialty care. Although this rhetoric has been retained by modern managed care organizations, the more recent emphasis on primary care has been largely driven by the cost containment interests of managed care organizations, employers, and state governments. This is partly related to the fact that primary care professionals can provide services at lower cost than their specialist counterparts (Starfield, 1997).

More important, however, is that primary care physicians were increasingly expected to assume the role of principal gatekeepers for these systems, limiting the flow of patients to more expensive specialist providers. In that sense, they were involved with the rationing of services. Indeed, in many systems, and certainly under capitated payment arrangements, there are incentives for primary care providers *not* to refer patients to specialists. The role of primary care providers as gatekeepers has increasingly been eroded, however, because of such factors as market responses and public policy changes to support consumer demand for direct access to specialists, as well as the move away from vertically integrated systems in the marketplace.

The way in which primary care physicians have been used in a managed care-dominated marketplace has in many ways has been at odds with the clinical values of their tradition. Until the second half of the 20th century, personal health care was generally provided to patients by physicians with whom they had continuing and trusting relationships, by whom they were well-known, and who viewed their concerns in the context of a biopsychosocial model (Engel, 1977) that included their families and communities. The hope for many contemporary primary care practitioners has been that the renewed emphasis on primary care within modern health care organizations would foster a return to this model.

Instead, the predominance of economic factors has exacerbated what Eisenberg (1995) called the "monetarization" of medicine, in which the interaction between provider and patient is reduced to being perfunctory and formulaic. Similarly, psychologist Barbara Gutek (1995) wrote of the distinction between *relationships* and *encounters*. In contrast to relationships, encounters

> typically consist of a single interaction between a customer and a provider, and they are typically fleeting rather than lengthy. Over time, the customer's successive contacts involve different providers so that provider and customer are strangers to each other. Most important, each of these providers is expected to be functionally equivalent. (pp. 7–8)

Many health professionals have felt that organizational changes in the delivery system and the increasing dominance of managed care systems have accelerated a movement from the therapeutic relationship to health-related service encounters. As though guided by the industrial principles of the assembly line, health care has been increasingly broken down into smaller and smaller discrete units of service offered by generic providers.

Another aspect of this trend has been an increased emphasis on treatment guidelines, part of what has sometimes been referred to as *evidence-based medicine*. The function of a guideline is to identify the most effective treatments for a particular condition, with the intended results that the quality of care offered to the patient will be increased and that variability in the care offered to a patient will be reduced. However, many of the guidelines offered by managed care organizations conflated the goals of cost containment and quality assurance, thereby attempting to control costs through decisions about treatment rather than about benefits (see Stricker et al., 1999, for a detailed discussion). An excessive or rigid reliance on guidelines as a substitute for expert clinical judgment is certainly likely to undermine the treatment relationship. Moreover, complex clinical situations rarely lend themselves to treatments that can be applied in step-by-step cookbook fashion.

The impact of these trends has been particularly strong in primary care. Although generalist primary care providers will continue to occupy a role in the future health care system, whether it is as biopsychosocial healers or cookbook technicians, remains to be seen. In part, this question rests on difficult choices with which we as a society have not yet grappled regarding the type of health care we want, who should have access to it, and how much we are willing to pay.

IMPLICATIONS FOR PSYCHOLOGY IN PRIMARY CARE

Psychologists have experienced tremendous pressures as a result of these sweeping changes in the health care delivery system. Corporate mergers and takeovers, market demands for lower cost providers, managed care's cost controls, and public policy measures that pre-empt earlier gains, such as freedom of choice laws, have all directly affected psychologists. Indeed, these factors have created barriers and declining opportunities that pose threats to the very existence of traditional psychological practice. To ensure the profession's future, psychologists must not only weather these challenges but also continue to evolve and expand as a discipline to overcome them.

In spite of such pressures to change, professional psychology has been slow to diversify beyond its traditions as a specialty discipline of independent mental health practitioners. As an example, a 1995 study by the American Psychological Association (APA) of almost 16,000 practicing psychologists found that 4 out of 5 reported negative effects of managed care on their practices (Phelps, Eisman, & Kohout, 1998). Yet the majority of study participants were continuing to devote three quarters of their time to providing traditional mental health assessment and psychotherapy services in independent practice settings.

Only a small number of these respondents were working outside mental health and in the broader delivery system, with about 13% reporting medical settings as their primary work site. There were some generational differences, however, with recent graduates more likely than previous generations to work in medical settings. About 20% of psychologists licensed in the 1990s were practicing in these settings. Nevertheless, private practice was still the most likely setting for these young psychologists, with 40% of them in independent practice.

Opportunities in Primary Care

Nowhere is the opportunity for professional psychology to expand its roles in the changing health care system greater than in the primary care arena. The justification for more widespread integration of psychological services in primary care settings is obvious, because research has consistently indicated that mental health problems are highly overrepresented, yet poorly detected, in these settings (Danton, Altrocchi, Antonuccio, & Basta, 1994; Katon & Sullivan, 1990; Magill & Garrett, 1988; Regier, Goldberg & Taube, 1978; VandenBos & DeLeon, 1988).

There are far greater contributions that psychologists can bring to primary care beyond mental health evaluation and treatment, however. Medical use can be substantially reduced through the availability of behavioral interventions in the primary care setting (Sobel, 1994). Research has consistently shown that psychological interventions are as clinically effective as, and are dramatically less expensive than, somatic interventions across a wide variety of illnesses and disorders, including cardiovascular disease, diabetes, traumatic brain injury, and somatization (Friedman, Sobel, Myers, Caudill, & Benson, 1995; Groth-Marnat & Elkins, 1996). Also, data regarding the efficacy of psychological interventions for chronic pain are so compelling that the National Institutes of Health has called for wider acceptance and use of behavioral treatments in conjunction with typical medical care (National Institutes of Health, 1995).

Despite strong empirical evidence supporting psychological interventions in health care settings and the considerable clinical, consultation, research, and systems skills that psychologists have to offer, movement of the field into primary care has occurred quite slowly. To be sure, psychologists have been involved as consultants and as members of treatment teams in primary and tertiary health care settings for many years, although in relatively small numbers. To more broadly capitalize on the opportunities and expand its involvement in primary care, however, the profession will have to overcome a number of significant barriers both within the discipline and beyond. What is needed are systematic and concerted efforts by organized psychology to address these obstacles through advocacy and the development of supportive policy; enhancement of training models; and more widespread education of the public, purchasers of care, and policymakers about the value of psychologists' services in these settings. Examples of some of these efforts by the profession are described next.

Advocacy and Policy Development

In late 1994, APA's Committee for the Advancement of Professional Practice commissioned a Primary Care Task Force to advise the association about specific actions to maximize psychology's role as a health care profession generally and as a primary care profession specifically. In its final report, the task force acknowledged that changes in the health care system have challenged traditional models of service delivery but have also created new opportunities for psychologists to become full partners in the health care system. The report asserted that the greatest challenge facing professional psychology today is assuring that it is viewed not solely as a mental health profession but as a full-fledged health care profession, and its authors warned that if "psychology fails to be recognized as such, the problems the profession now faces will only grow with time" (American Psychological Association, Committee for the Advancement of Professional Practice, 1996, p. 4). The report outlined more than 30 specific recommendations for needed advocacy activities, including initiatives involving training and education, financing and reimbursement systems, organized delivery systems, professional advocacy, and research. The task force also published an article describing the culture of primary care medicine and offering practical tips for the adaptation of psychological practice to primary care (Haley et al., 1998).

In 1995, APA's Board of Professional Affairs, which has particular responsibility for the development of internal policy for professional psychology, commissioned a work group to examine policy issues involved in the application of psychological services to people with physical disorders, including psychosocial treatments related to medical conditions and direct psychological treatments of medical disorders. The Work Group on Expanding the Role of Psychology in the Health Care Delivery System made numerous recommendations regarding policy development and collaboration with other groups within APA to support the continued growth of psychology in this arena. In addition, the work group examined ethical, legal, malpractice, and professional issues unique to psychological practice in medical settings. The group also addressed training models, including promoting the use of individualized learning and continuing education for practicing psychologists interested in transitioning into health care settings, and it developed a self-assessment model for evaluating the necessary specialized knowledge and skills.

The Board of Professional Affairs also championed the need for a broader recognition of psychologists as *health service providers*. It developed the following designation, which was approved as APA policy by the Council of Representatives at its February 1996 meeting:

> Psychologists are recognized as Health Service Providers if they are duly trained and experienced in the delivery of preventive, assessment, diagnostic and therapeutic intervention services relative to the psychological and physical health of consumers, based on: 1) having completed scientific and professional training resulting in a doctoral degree in psychology; 2) having completed an internship and supervised experience in health care settings; and 3) having been licensed as psychologists at the independent practice level. (DeLeon, 1996, p. 842)

In a different but related arena, support has been building within the profession to expand psychology's scope of practice to include prescriptive authority. After several years of study by governance groups of the association, APA's Council of Representatives adopted policies supporting the prescriptive authority movement within the field. At its August 1996 meeting, the council approved two documents describing APA's policy positions for training and credentialing of psychologists to prescribe medication: "Recommended Postdoctoral Training in Psychopharmacology Prescription Privileges" and "Model Legislation for Prescriptive Authority" (DeLeon, 1997).

The prescriptive authority movement represents an important opportunity for the future expansion of psychology's role in health care generally and in primary care particularly. As a front-line practitioner equipped with not only psychological assessment and intervention skills but also psychopharmacological treatments, a primary care psychologist would be positioned to offer less medically driven, more biopsychosocially balanced care to patients. A recent review of his practice by one of the prescribing psychologists from the Department of Defense Psychopharmacology Demonstration Project (PDP), Morgan T. Sammons, provides some supportive evidence. Surveying his cases, Sammons found that, despite his option to prescribe, he was more likely to use psychological interventions and less likely to medicate patients than his medical colleagues (Sammons, cited in DeLeon, 1998).

The PDP was a congressionally mandated demonstration program to train military psychologists to prescribe psychotropic medications. It ran from 1991 to 1997. Ten military psychologists completed the program in what became one of the most intensively studied and widely scrutinized experiments in the training of nonphysicians for prescriptive authority. Both the military and the Congress commissioned a number of objective, external evaluations of the program during its existence. A retrospective analysis of those studies concluded that the PDP successfully achieved its primary objective: to demonstrate that licensed psychologists could be trained to provide safe, high-quality pharmacological care (Newman, Phelps, Sammons, Dunivin, & Cullen, 2000).

The PDP has served as a foundation for the profession's efforts to include prescriptive authority in state licensing laws and for the further development of a psychological model for prescribing. At the outset of the 21st century, legislative initiatives for psychologists' prescriptive authority have gained considerable momentum, assisted by financial resources and technical assistance from APA to the state psychological associations. In March 2002, New Mexico became the first state to institute such a law, when Gov. Gary Johnson signed House Bill 170, authorizing properly trained psychologists to prescribe psychotropic medications.

At that time, 31 state psychological associations had prescription privileges task forces working on legislation, and 13 states had introduced prescribing bills over the preceding 10-year period. Several state psychological associations had also instituted training programs consistent with the APA's recommended postdoctoral training guidelines (DeLeon, 1997; Dunivin & Orabona, 1999).

Training

The evolution of the health care system has serious implications for the education, training, and professional development of psychologists. In response to changes in the system, the format of undergraduate medical education and residency programs in psychiatry has been revamped to emphasize a problem-based learning curriculum, team-based learning, and experience in outpatient settings. Psychology's training models, by contrast, have changed little. A 1998 APA survey of training programs found that only 43 doctoral psychology programs provided education and training in clinical health psychology, and only a handful of those emphasized primary care. Among more than 500 internship programs, 36% offered training in psychological interventions for patients with medical disorders, but only 2% offered a major rotation in primary care (American Psychological Association, Education Directorate, 1998).

Generic training in professional psychology is a necessary, but not a sufficient, basis for competent practice in primary health care. To further expand the field's inroads into primary care, training models need to be enhanced to include health promotion and prevention and the biological, cognitive, affective, social, and intrapersonal bases of health and disease. In addition to their general clinical skills, psychologists require the ability to function effectively in multidisciplinary teams; knowledge of the language, ethics, and culture of medical settings; skills in general health assessment; and an understanding of the specialized procedures and technologies appropriate to the populations with which they work.

External Advocacy and Education

A great deal of APA's primary care advocacy has focused on addressing external barriers to psychology's evolution as a comprehensive health care profession. For example, APA has engaged in demonstration projects involving the integration of psychological services with physical health services delivery, in contrast to service delivery, in which behavioral services and their financing are "carved out" or independent from the of rest of the system. Some have argued that the wave of the future in health care will be *carve-ins*, the integration of physical health and mental health services (Kiesler, 2000). Until then, the widespread prevalence in the marketplace of carve-outs makes it extremely difficult for the benefits of integrated systems, such as cost offsets and reduced medical utilization, to be realized. The goal of APA's ongoing initiatives has been to demonstrate to marketplace decision makers and plan purchasers the value of integrated services in terms of both clinical and financial efficacy.

There are also barriers to greater involvement by psychology that are inherent in the diagnostic and procedure coding schemes used by public and private payer systems for reimbursement. Psychologists have been typically prevented from using physical health diagnostic codes and have been restricted to a few reimbursable procedures, the majority of which are limited to psychotherapy services. Consequently, APA has advocated for the American Medical Association to expand its current procedural terminology coding system to more accurately reflect the work psychologists do in health care systems. The American Psychological Association successfully gained six new "health and behavior" assessment and intervention procedure codes in 2002, as well as reimbursement for them by Medicare. In addition, APA has been a key player in the development of the World Health Organization's diagnostic system based on the functional aspects of illnesses and disorders, the International Classification of Functioning, Disability and Health.

The American Psychological Association has also worked to address resistances and stereotypical views about the profession held by policymakers. As an example, the U.S. Public Health Service was unwilling in the early 1990s to include psychology in its primary care prevention initiatives, on the basis of the rationale that psychologists did not give immunization injections. Neither had APA ever been invited to participate in the Public Health Service Primary Care Policy Fellowship, a program to train primary care leaders to better affect health policy at the national, state, and local levels. After a 3-year advocacy campaign by APA, however, every psychologist nominated by APA to the fellowship since 1998 has been accepted into the program.

THE FUTURE OF PSYCHOLOGY IN PRIMARY CARE

Psychology has an important stake in advocating for a model of primary care based on the biopsychosocial model of health. The integration of mental and general health care that this model implies will require a greater degree of collaboration than ever before among psychologists, primary care physicians, and other mental health and primary care clinicians (see Meyer & McLaughlin, 1998). However, such a collaborative model offers potentially great benefit to the consumers and purchasers of health care.

It is obvious that the extent to which this model of primary care can offer opportunities for psychology depends on the field's continued survival and growth. Although the discipline's narrow identity as a mental health specialty was appropriate in earlier stages of psychology's development, rigid adherence to this position ignores the breadth and diversity of the field and its members' training. Psychology is at risk in the context of tremendous and ongoing changes in the health care system if psychologists fail to expand their own conceptualization of the profession.

Thus, organized psychology and individual psychologists must be advocates for quality health care in general, rather than confining themselves narrowly to mental health issues. As a part of this expanded advocacy, the field must work toward broader recognition as a health care profession and widespread acceptance of psychologists as health service providers. Public messages should emphasize the expertise of psychologists in health promotion and disease prevention, as team members in primary care settings, and as providers of interventions for conditions generally considered medical in nature (see Newman & Reed, 1996).

In terms of professional practice, the integration of psychologists into the teams of physicians, nurses, and other professionals used in primary care clinics must be promoted at a policy level, in graduate and postgraduate psychology training, and by individual psychologists in specific work settings. This will require psychologists to adopt a truly biopsychosocial model of health and to conceptualize psychological practice as including a continuum of activities from the traditional psychotherapeutic care of individuals with emotional disturbances to the direct treatment of illness and disease. Psychology professionals must also rethink the field's traditional isolationist position with respect to other health care professionals. Both successful advocacy for patterns of health care that will benefit the American public and the integration of psychology into the larger health care delivery system will require collaboration with other disciplines at all levels. In this regard, the interests and outcomes of psychologists will rise and fall with those of other health care professionals.

REFERENCES

American Psychological Association, Committee for the Advancement of Professional Practice Primary Care Task Force. (1996). *Primary Care Task Force final report.* Washington, DC: Author.

American Psychological Association, Education Directorate. (1998). *Interprofessional health care services in primary care settings: Implications for professional education and training of psychologists.* (Substance Abuse and Mental Health Services Administration/Health Resources and Services Administration Work Order 97M220464).Washington, DC: Author.

Danton, W. G., Altrocchi, J., Antonuccio, D., & Basta, R. (1994). Nondrug treatment of anxiety. *American Family Physician, 10,* 161–166.

Darves, B. (1998). Whatever happened to capitation? *Physician's Practice Digest, 8,* 30–31.

DeLeon, P. H. (1996). Proceedings of the American Psychological Association, Incorporated, for the Year 1995: Minutes of the annual meeting of the Council of Representatives, August 10 and 13, 1995, New York, NY, and February 16–18, 1996, Washington, DC. *American Psychologist, 51,* 805–848.

DeLeon, P. H. (1997). Proceedings of the American Psychological Association, Incorporated, for the Year 1996: Minutes of the annual meeting of the Council of Representatives, August 8 and 11, 1996, Toronto, Ontario, Canada, and February 21–23, 1997, Washington, DC. *American Psychologist, 52,* 813–868.

DeLeon, P. H. (1998). Washington scene: The maturation of the profession continues. *Psychotherapy Bulletin, 33,* 7–12.

DeLeon, P. H., VandenBos, G. R., & Bulatao, E. Q. (1991). Managed mental health care: A history of the federal policy initiative. *Professional Psychology: Research and Practice, 22,* 15–25.

Dunivin, D. L., & Orabona, E. (1999). Department of Defense Psychopharmacology Demonstration Project: Fellows' perspectives on didactic curriculum. *Professional Psychology: Research and Practice, 30,* 510–518.

Edmunds, M., Frank, R., Hogan, M., McCarty, D., Robinson-Beale, R., & Weisner, C. (Eds.). (1997). *Managing managed care: Quality improvement in behavioral health.* Washington, DC: National Academy Press.

Eisenberg, L. (1995). Medicine: Molecular, monetary, or more than both? *Journal of the American Medical Association, 274,* 331–334.

Engel, G. L. (1977). The need for a new medical model: A challenge for biomedicine. *Science, 196,* 129–136.

Feldman, R. D., Wholey, D. R., & Christianson, J. B. (1999). HMO consolidations: How national mergers affect local markets. *Health Affairs, 18,* 96–104.

Freeman, M. A., & Trabin, T. (1994). *Managed behavioral health care: History, models, key issues, and future course.* Washington, DC: Substance Abuse and Mental Health Services Administration, Center for Mental Health Services.

Friedman, R., Sobel, D., Myers, P., Caudill, M., & Benson, H. (1995). Behavioral medicine, clinical health psychology, and cost offset. *Health Psychology, 14,* 509–518.

Fuchs, B. C. (1997, October 8). *Managed health care: Federal and state regulation* (CRS Report for Congress). Washington, DC: Library of Congress, Congressional Research Service.

Groth-Marnat, G., & Elkins, G. (1996). Professional psychologists in general health care settings: A review of the financial efficacy of direct treatment interventions. *Professional Psychology: Research & Practice, 27,* 161–174.

Grumbach, K., & Bodenheimer, T. (1995). Mechanisms for controlling costs. *Journal of the American Medical Association, 273,* 1223–1230.

Gutek, B. A. (1995). *The dynamics of service: Reflections on the changing nature of customer/provider interactions.* San Francisco: Jossey-Bass.

Haley, W. E., McDaniel, S. H., Bray, J. H., Frank, R. G., Heldring, M., Johnson, S. B., et al. (1998). Psychological practice in primary care settings: Practical tips for clinicians. *Professional Psychology: Research and Practice, 29,* 237–244.

Health Care Financing Administration. (1995). *Medicare managed care report: December, 1995.* Baltimore: Author.

Health Care Financing Administration. (1996). *Medicaid managed care enrollment report: Summary statistics.* Baltimore: Author.

Institute of Medicine. (1994). *Defining primary care: An interim report*. Washington, DC: National Academy Press.

Katon, W., & Sullivan, M. D. (1990). Depression and chronic medical illness. *Journal of Clinical Psychiatry, 51*, 3–11.

Kiesler, C. A. (2000). The next wave of change for psychology and mental health services in the health care revolution. *American Psychologist, 55*, 481–487.

Landon, B. E., Wilson, I. B., & Cleary, P. D. (1998). A conceptual model of the effects of health care organizations on the quality of medical care. *Journal of the American Medical Association, 17*, 1377–1382.

Lesser, C. S., & Ginsburg, P. B. (2000). Update on the nation's health care system: 1997–1999. *Health Affairs, 19*, 206–216.

Magill, M. K., & Garrett, R. W. (1988). Behavioral and psychiatric problems. In R. B. Taylor (Ed.), *Family medicine* (3rd ed., pp. 534–562). New York: Springer-Verlag.

Meyer, M. E., & McLaughlin, C. J. (Eds.). (1998). *Between mind, brain, and managed care: The now and future world of academic psychiatry*. Washington, DC: American Psychiatric Press.

National Institutes of Health. (1995, October). *Integration of behavioral and relaxation approaches into the treatment of chronic pain and insomnia* (NIH Technology Assessment Statement). Washington, DC: Author.

Newman, R., & Bricklin, P. M. (1991). Parameters of managed mental health care: Legal, ethical and professional guidelines. *Professional Psychology: Research and Practice, 22*, 26–35.

Newman, R., Phelps, R., Sammons, M. T., Dunivin, D. L., & Cullen, E. A. (2000). Evaluation of the Psychopharmacology Demonstration Project: A retrospective analysis. *Professional Psychology: Research and Practice, 31*, 598–603.

Newman, R., & Reed, G. M. (1996). Psychology as a health care profession: Its evolution and future directions. In R. J. Resnick & R. H. Rozensky (Eds.), *Health psychology through the life span: Practice and research opportunities* (pp. 11–26). Washington, DC: American Psychological Association.

'96 health spending rise smallest in 36 years. (1998, January 12). *Modern Healthcare*, p. 3.

Oss, M. (1993). *Managed behavioral health market share in the United States 1993: An Open Minds publication*. Gettysburg, PA: Behavioral Health Industry News.

Pension and Welfare Benefits Administration: Testimony before the Committee on Labor, Health and Human Services and Education, of the United States Senate, 105th Cong. (1998). (testimony of Olena Berg).

Pew Health Professions Commission. (1995). *Critical challenges: Revitalizing the health professions for the twenty-first century*. San Francisco: University of California, Center for Health Professions.

Phelps, R., Eisman, E. J., & Kohout, J. (1998). Psychological practice and managed care: Results of the CAPP practitioner survey. *Professional Psychology: Research and Practice, 29*, 31–36.

Reed, G. M., Levant, R. F., Stout, C. E., Murphy, M. J., & Phelps, R. (2001). Psychology in the current mental health marketplace. *Professional Psychology: Research and Practice, 32*, 65–70.

Regier, D. A., Goldberg, I. D., & Taube, C. A. (1978). The de facto U.S. mental health services system: A public health perspective. *Archives of General Psychiatry, 35*, 685–693.

Relman, A. S. (1980). The new medical–industrial complex. *New England Journal of Medicine, 303*, 963–970.

Shortell, S. M., Gillies, R. R., & Anderson, D. A. (1994). The new world of managed care: Creating organized delivery systems. *Health Affairs, 13*, 46–64.

Shortell, S. M., Gillies, R. R., Anderson, D. A., Erickson, K. M., & Mitchell, J. B. (1996). *Remaking healthcare in America.* San Francisco: Jossey-Bass.

Sobel, D. S. (1994). Mind matters, money matters: The cost-effectiveness of clinical behavioral medicine. In S. Blumenthal, K. Matthews, & S. Weiss (Eds.), *New research frontiers in behavioral medicine: Proceedings of the national conference.* Washington, DC: National Institutes of Health.

Starfield, B. (1997). The future of primary care in a managed care era. *International Journal of Health Services, 27*, 687–696.

Starr, P. (1982). *The social transformation of American medicine.* New York: Basic Books.

Stricker, G., Abrahamson, D. J., Bologna, N. C., Hollon, S. D., Robinson, E. A., & Reed, G. M. (1999). Treatment guidelines: The good, the bad, and the ugly. *Psychotherapy, 36*, 69–79.

VandenBos, G. R. (1993). U.S. mental health policy: Proactive evolution in the midst of health care reform. *American Psychologist, 48*, 283–290.

VandenBos, G. R., & DeLeon, P. H. (1988). The use of psychotherapy to improve physical health. *Psychotherapy, 25*, 335–343.

Webb, C. E. (1996). The corporatization of health care: Effects on accreditation and integrity. In M. Osterweis, C. J. McLaughlin, H. R. Mannasse Jr., & C. L. Hopper (Eds.), *The U.S. health workforce: Power, politics, and policy* (pp. 167–174). Washington, DC: Association of Academic Health Centers.

White House Domestic Policy Council. (1993). *The President's health security plan: The Clinton blueprint.* New York: Times Books/Random House.

3

THE PHYSICIAN–PATIENT RELATIONSHIP

RICHARD FRANKEL AND HOWARD BECKMAN

To effectively collaborate in a health care setting, it is essential for each person to understand and ultimately respect the unique contribution persons from other disciplines bring to the situation, be it working with patients, their families, or other health care professionals. In this chapter we describe the physician–patient relationship in the context of primary care medical practice. Because access to most medical care in the United States is organized around encounters with primary care physicians as the initial point of entry, we have chosen to direct our comments toward the experience of these primary care practitioners. Understanding the goals of primary care and the standards to which physicians are held is critical to successful collaboration. After describing the elements of primary care, we present a case study from one physician's practice to illustrate the challenges and opportunities involved in a typical medical interview. We then discuss some ways in which physicians and other health professionals can most effectively work together on an interdisciplinary team.

We gratefully acknowledge Jenny Speice and Susan McDaniel for reading and commenting on drafts of this chapter.

Our goal is to explore the similarities and differences between practicing psychologists and physicians as they approach clinical work. As our case is described, please consider your responsibilities in a similar situation and compare them with those of the medical practitioner we describe. By identifying the areas of overlap and, more important, the areas that are left unaddressed by a physician, psychologists can more confidently understand their role in collaborating with physicians and truly create a world of options and opportunities in caring for patients. The heart of an interdisciplinary team is being able to know and understand others' roles and to feel known and understood in one's own role.

UNDERSTANDING WHAT PRIMARY CARE PHYSICIANS DO

Goals of Primary Care

The responsibilities of a primary care practitioner are to offer access to comprehensive medical care, provide continuity of relationship, and integrate information and services provided by other practitioners (Albert & Charney, 1975). The goals of practice include (a) successfully making and managing biological, psychological, and social diagnoses and treatments; (b) providing support to patients of all backgrounds, in all stages of illness and disease; (c) communicating information about diagnosis, evaluation, treatment, prevention, and prognosis; (d) caring for patients with chronic illness; and (e) preventing disability and disease through early detection, education, persuasion, and preventive treatments (Goroll, May, & Mulley, 1987). Given these daunting goals, only a limited number can be addressed at any one office visit, even in the best of circumstances. To complicate things, primary care practitioners have a mean time of about 16 minutes to conduct office consultations with patients, whether they are initiating or providing ongoing care (Levinson, Roter, Mullolly, Dull, & Frankel, 1997). Despite these challenges, most primary care physicians' passion for their work derives from the satisfaction achieved in solving and managing complex problems. This is where the skills of teamwork are essential, as the following case example illustrates.

CASE STUDY: Mrs. Salek and Dr. Brent
Mrs. Mary Salek has been a patient of Dr. Christine Brent for 5 years. Mrs. Salek is 56 years old and is followed in the office for diabetes mellitus, complicated by peripheral neuropathy and renal failure, hypertension, peripheral vascular disease, and chronic bronchitis. For these illnesses, she takes nine medications, which presents an economic burden, because her insurance pays only 80% of the cost. The Saleks have a combined income of $955 per month, and her medicines cost $178 per month. She is angry about the cost. She and her husband live together in a single-family home (1,500 sq. ft.) where she provides child care for her four-

year-old granddaughter. Her daughter often asks her to babysit on weekends. Mrs. Salek loves to go camping. Unfortunately, foot pain associated with her peripheral neuropathy has limited her ability to get about. Anemia further adds to her fatigue. As a result, camping is no longer an option for her.

Mrs. Salek invariably enters the exam room angry. "My feet hurt. My blood sugar is up. My daughter is driving me crazy. Even though it's fall and my favorite time of year, I can't go camping. Life is just not worth living."

Dr. Brent sits back in her chair and sighs. She is overwhelmed by the number, severity, and chronicity of Mrs. Salek's problems. This visit is scheduled for 25 minutes, 10 minutes extra having been added because of the patient's known complexity. She asks, "Why do you think your blood sugar is up?", focusing on the problem she believes is most important. They then spend 10 minutes discussing diet, the stresses in Mrs. Salek's life, and the therapeutic options available to her. She describes terrible pain related to her peripheral neuropathy, a direct result of her diabetes. They then spend an additional 2 minutes discussing the availability of a new medication that some physicians have found helpful for patients with peripheral neuropathy. Mrs. Salek says, "I'll try anything if you think it might help." Dr. Brent takes another 2 minutes to determine whether the new medication will adversely affect any of Mrs. Salek's nine other medications. At the end of the visit, Dr. Brent writes a prescription that adds $67/month to Mrs. Salek's medication costs. With 4 minutes left, Dr. Brent asks, "Is anything else bothering you?", and Mrs. Salek describes four more problems. Dr. Brent concentrates on one of the easier ones and tells her they will have to cover the other problems next time. With 1 minute left, Dr. Brent says, "Mrs. Salek, I know things haven't been going so well for you lately. Do you really feel that life isn't worth living?" "No, I guess not Dr. Brent," Mrs. Salek replies; "thanks for your help today." With this brief exchange, the visit ends.

As a primary care physician, Dr. Brent is often confronted by patients who have more problems than can be handled in the usual allotted time. Perhaps more important, she experiences a constant struggle to determine the relative importance of biological, psychological, and social problems. Most physicians feel a primary responsibility and are trained to evaluate and treat biomedical problems first. From Dr. Brent's perspective, improving control of Mrs. Salek's diabetes seemed most important to address. Indeed, the discussion of her diabetes turned to her disabling peripheral neuropathy, for which a promising new medication was available. At the end of the visit, Dr. Brent felt she had done something of value but also felt frustrated by what was left unattended.

The number of possible issues to be discussed in any one visit often exceeds the time allotted to explore them. In fact, the mean number of concerns patients bring to the typical office visit is three (Kaplan, Gandek,

Greenfield, Rogers, & Ware, 1995; Stewart, Brown, Levenstein, McCracken, & McWhinney, 1986). When chronically ill patients are seen, the number of unvoiced concerns often outnumbers those articulated. For instance, Mrs. Salek described financial difficulties yet, later in the visit, Dr. Brent prescribed another expensive medication, believing it was the best available. In addition, Mrs. Salek's relationship with her daughter, one of her greatest stressors, was not discussed at all. Dr. Brent simply could not cover all these issues. Rather, like many primary care physicians, she used her continuity relationship with Mrs. Salek and her clinical judgment to decide what to cover in the current visit and what to put on her agenda for subsequent visits.

Dr. Brent also knows she is part of a larger community of health professionals available to consult and manage the many problems that are simultaneously in play in the physician–patient relationship. In fact, Mrs. Salek is also being seen by Jason Sloan, PhD, a clinical psychologist suggested by Dr. Brent and who practices near her home. How these medical professionals understand each other's roles in caring for Mrs. Salek is critical to successful team practice. Worried about Mrs. Salek's statement about life not being worth living, Dr. Brent decided to call Dr. Sloan and let him know what Mrs. Salek had said. Dr. Sloan said that he was aware of Mrs. Salek's suicidal ideation and related that Mrs. Salek had been upset recently by some family problems but was not, in his opinion, at risk for harming herself. Dr. Brent said that she was grateful for Dr. Sloan's input, and they both agreed to talk again after Mrs. Salek's next visit to Dr. Brent, 1 month hence.

Integrating the input of multiple consultants is an additional responsibility of primary care physicians. Although each practitioner is responsible for communicating with others involved in a patient's care, it is the primary care physician whom society and the courts hold legally responsible for this task. Although she did not directly address the issue of suicide in detail with Mrs. Salek, Dr. Brent was aware of its potential and sought to coordinate her perspective with another medical professional involved in the patient's care. The task of coordinating clinical, pathologic, radiologic, and laboratory data is an important, time-consuming component of the physician's role, and one that is not generally visible to the patient.

In the next section, we describe the approach many physicians are taught to use in gathering data and responding to patient concerns. We present the model with an eye toward illustrating some of the routine challenges physicians face in the medical interview and how these may differ from the approach psychologists are trained to take.

THE MEDICAL INTERVIEW: CHALLENGES AND OPPORTUNITIES

The average primary care physician in the United States conducts between 120,000 and 160,000 interviews in a practice lifetime, making the interview the most frequent clinical activity in which physicians engage (Lipkin et al., 1995). Scholarship about the medical interview has been ongoing since the 1930s and has gained momentum over the last 20 years; in fact, the MedLine database now lists more than 10,000 articles relating to this topic. Several models of the primary care interview have been proposed recently, and there is growing agreement that the basic tasks include agenda setting, relationship building, and diagnostic news delivery and treatment planning. We now illustrate some of the challenges and opportunities primary care physicians face in the interview by returning to Dr. Brent and Mrs. Salek at the beginning of their next scheduled visit.

Negotiating an Agenda

Dr. Brent had some unfinished issues from the prior visit that she wanted to discuss with Mrs. Salek. Aware that she had only touched on her statement about life not being worth living in the last visit, and armed with the information she had gotten from consulting Dr. Sloan, Dr. Brent was eager to explore in more depth the meaning of Mrs. Salek's statement. In addition, she wanted to find out whether Mrs. Salek had used the new medication for her neuropathy.

After greeting Mrs. Salek, Dr. Brent said, "I was concerned after our last visit that you said with some of your problems that life was not worth living." The two talked for 7 minutes about Mrs. Salek's feelings and frustration about her life, at which point Dr. Brent encouraged her to talk more about this with Dr. Sloan and shifted the discussion to the new medication. Mrs. Salek responded, "I didn't have the money to fill the prescription." They then talked about the family's financial problems. At the end of the visit, as Mrs. Salek prepared to leave, she said, "Oh, by the way; I've got this new sore on my ankle. Is it important?" Dr. Brent was compelled to reopen the visit and spend an additional 8 minutes caring for Mrs. Salek's foot ulcer.

After the visit, Dr. Brent felt frustrated. She thought to herself,

> Why didn't she bring up this issue at the beginning of the visit, so that I could appropriately evaluate and treat it? An ulcer in a diabetic is important, and she knows that as well as I do. Early treatment can prevent consequences as serious as amputation.

The answer to this question appears to be inadequate agenda setting on Dr. Brent's part. In reviewing the opening of routine visits to primary care internists, Beckman and Frankel (1984) found that patients' concerns were not solicited at all in 25% of the consultations, and only 23% of the patients were able to articulate their complete list of problems without being interrupted. In 51 of the 52 visits in which the physician interrupted at the beginning of the visit, patients did not complete their responses. The mean time from soliciting problems to interruption was 18 seconds, and most patients were interrupted after the first stated concern. Fifteen years later, Marvel, Epstein, Flowers, and Beckman (1999) also found that in 25% of return visits, the patient's agenda was not solicited. In this study of experienced family physicians, the mean time to interruption was 23 seconds and occurred most frequently after the patient's first expressed concern. Of note is that patients who were allowed to finish their statement of concerns took a mean of 32 seconds to finish.

Another important aspect of agenda setting is prioritization. In both Beckman and Frankel's (1984) and Marvel et al.'s (1999) studies of agenda setting, the most likely place for interruption to occur was after the patient's first stated concern. The most likely reason for the frequency of interruption at this point is an assumption on the physician's part that the first stated concern voiced by a patient is the most important "presenting concern." Evidence from Beckman and Frankel's study and one by Rost and Frankel (1993) suggest that this approach to agenda setting is flawed.

Beckman and Frankel (1984) abstracted all the concerns voiced by patients in the encounters they studied whether they were interrupted or not. They found that there was no statistical association between the order of concerns (first, second, third, fourth) and their clinical or medical importance. Likewise, Rost and Frankel (1993) studied the concerns of a group of elderly diabetic patients, asking them, prior to their medical visits, to list both the concerns they hoped to address with their physicians and the importance of those concerns from their perspective. Most patients had multiple problems and stated that it was their third concern that was most important from their perspective. Reviews of the taped encounters revealed, however, that 85% of the time they never got beyond their first agenda item and were thus unable to raise their most important concerns for discussion.

It is clear that in the world of patient experiences there is no easy way to predict the scope, importance, and sequence of concerns. The only way to effectively establish an agenda is to ask, prioritize, and negotiate, all of which can be accomplished within a mean additional time of 39 seconds.

Dr. Brent had decided on the agenda before the visit, and as a result there was no solicitation of concerns. In other words, there was no opportunity at the beginning of the visit for Mrs. Salek to mention the ulcer on her ankle. In failing to solicit any interim concerns, Dr. Brent inadvertently limited the beginning of the visit in a way that caused her great frustration at its conclusion.

The tension between physician and patient agendas in the face of limited time is perhaps the hallmark of modern medical care and a problem that will not yield to an either–or solution. Instead, soliciting the complete agenda and then negotiating what is possible to accomplish in the visit's allotted time is the preferred strategy. By using such an agenda, Dr. Brent might have begun the visit by saying, "Mrs. Salek, I want to talk with you about something you said last time, but before I do, are there any things that you were hoping to discuss today?" At that point, Mrs. Salek would likely have identified the ulcer, the neuropathy, and her financial problems, to which Dr. Brent might then have responded,

> I really do want to talk with you about the neuropathy and the comment you made that life was not worth living. How about if we also talk about the ulcer on your ankle and, if time permits, about your finances?

The result is a more focused discussion of mutually agreed-on issues. Additional concerns for which there is insufficient time can be placed on the agenda for the next visit.

Relationship Building

Establishing and maintaining safe, trusting, therapeutic relationships is at the heart of successful clinical practice. Despite the documented benefits of positive relationships on the process and outcomes of care, and the increased risk of dissatisfaction, disenrollment, and medical malpractice where relationships are strained or difficult, there is evidence that primary care physicians do poorly at developing key relationship skills such as empathy (Maguire et al., 1986). One recent study found that physicians responded to empathic opportunities very infrequently (Suchman et al., 1997); the researchers also identified a dominant pattern in which patients' hints or indirect references to emotions were deflected via abrupt shifts in topic. It appears that most physicians' response to affect or the potential for affect is avoidance, leaving patients feeling misunderstood and uncared for. The etiology of physician preferences for facts over feelings has several possible causes, ranging from underrecognition of facial and nonverbal cues of emotion; to differences in professional cultural norms; to medical education itself, which is often harsh and abusive. Whatever the cause, physicians' responses to patients' expression of emotion appears to be suboptimal.

In the interim between visits, Dr. Brent had done some more thinking about her relationship with Mrs. Salek. She decided that, despite her frustrations, she wanted to provide additional emotional and psychological support to help Mrs. Salek cope with the complexity of her problems and the increasing physical limitations they were placing on her. She just wasn't sure how. Because she had agreed to call Dr. Sloan after Mrs. Salek's visit, she decided to start there. Dr. Sloan was quite understanding and helpful in giving Dr. Brent a list of pertinent Web sites and local organizations. Dr. Brent did an Internet search on relationship building and discovered evidence that the skills she was interested in could be taught, learned, and put into practice with both short- and long-term effects (Maguire et al., 1986). One area in which she took special interest was the role of verbal and nonverbal behavior in relationship building (DiMatteo et al., 1986). Dr. Brent's search also turned up a daylong continuing education workshop on improving relationship skills, which she decided to attend. Motivated to try her new skills, she decided to apply what she had learned in her next visit with Mrs. Salek.

After opening the visit, Dr. Brent asked Mrs. Salek how the treatment for her foot ulcer was going. "It's healing well," Mrs. Salek replied, but Dr. Brent noticed a sad expression on her face. She reflected, "You seem sad," and Mrs. Salek began crying. "My mother had an ulcer like this, and they had to amputate her leg. If I become wheelchair bound and can't go camping, I'd rather be dead." Dr. Brent had opened a "window of opportunity" (Branch & Malik, 1993). By observing the discrepancy between her patient's words and nonverbal behavior, Dr. Brent was able to facilitate the expression of Mrs. Salek's emotional distress, improve her own understanding of the context of her concerns, and provide the support she desired. Best of all, the entire exchange had taken a little more than 2 minutes.

Given the chance to share their fears and concerns, patients often become more willing and able to work together with the physician. Recent evidence suggests that patients who are encouraged to speak or write about the emotional distress associated with chronic illness experience significant physiological benefits (Smyth et al., 1999). By facilitating her expression of emotion, Dr. Brent discovered that Mrs. Salek's fear of incapacity was related to the memory of her mother's last year of life, during which she developed an ulcer that was not treated, a fact of which she had been unaware prior to the visit. The ulcer penetrated to the mother's bone, and she developed osteomyelitis (a bone infection), which caused her a great deal of pain and resulted in her becoming wheelchair bound.

Mrs. Salek had no intention of reliving her mother's experience and vowed that she would rather kill herself than live like her mother had. By expanding the social and emotional context of Mrs. Salek's concern, Dr. Brent was better able to respond to Mrs. Salek's underlying fears and address them in a meaningful way. For example, she was able to arrange for Mrs. Salek to review her foot care with a nurse educator and to explore her fears and concerns with Dr. Sloan as well as herself. By the end of the visit, Dr. Brent was feeling refreshed and eager to help Mrs. Salek with a problem she understood and could do something about. Mrs. Salek left the visit thanking Dr. Brent for her caring and concern, remarking that at last she felt as though someone, other than her psychologist, really understood her and her concerns. Dr. Brent had learned an important lesson about the human dimension in primary medical care and the power of the relationship.

DELIVERING DIAGNOSTIC RECOMMENDATIONS AND NEGOTIATING TREATMENT DECISIONS

Dr. Brent left the visit feeling that she had achieved her goal of understanding and supporting Mrs. Salek's concerns about the quality of her life.

Moreover, she felt that for the first time in their 5-year relationship she had gotten to the heart of one of Mrs. Salek's numerous problems and was genuinely happy because she knew that, unlike her mother, Mrs. Salek had an excellent chance of responding to treatment. Dr. Brent was looking forward to her next visit with Mrs. Salek and eager to address another puzzle in her care: recent fluctuations in blood pressure that she suspected might mean that Mrs. Salek wasn't taking her blood pressure medications as prescribed.

After greeting Mrs. Salek at the beginning of their next visit and commenting on how much progress she thought they'd made during their last visit, Dr. Brent suggested that they focus on blood pressure in addition to any concerns Mrs. Salek might have. Mrs. Salek readily agreed and said that she was feeling a lot better about her life and about feeling understood by her doctor. The following dialogue then ensued.

Doctor (D): You know, your blood pressure readings over the last several visits have varied quite a bit, and I'm not sure why. Let me ask you a few questions about it.

Patient (P): Okay.

D: How's it going with your high blood pressure medication? Is it pretty easy to remember to take it?

P: Yeah, I don't have any trouble remembering.

D: I know we changed your medication dose awhile back. Have you noticed any side effects?

P: No, not really. Maybe I go to the bathroom a little more frequently.

D: That's to be expected.

P: I see.

D: Let's see, you're taking hydro chloro-thrazide, HCTZ. Is that right?

P: Yes.

D: Okay, good. Well, keep up the good work, and we'll keep working to stabilize your readings.

Dr. Brent continued with the rest of the visit but still felt puzzled by Mrs. Salek's blood pressure fluctuations. She felt convinced by her discussion with Mrs. Salek that she was taking her medicine. Dr. Brent concluded that she would either have to increase Mrs. Salek's dose of HCTZ, which she was anxious about doing, because of the side effects it might cause her, or to try her on yet another significantly more expensive drug. Dr. Brent felt caught between two undesirable options, neither of which was likely to be of great benefit to Mrs. Salek.

Primary care physicians diagnose and treat a range of medical and psychological conditions. The literature on treatment adherence is remarkable in that it shows that anywhere from 40% to 80% of patients do not follow the recommendations they are given (Dunbar-Jacob & Schlenk, 2001; Sackett & Snow, 1979). More recently, some investigators have also begun to focus on the medical interview itself as a source of miscommunication that can affect rates of adherence. Two recent studies have suggested that the directness, or "information intensity," of discussions about adherence is one determinant of outcomes (Frankel & Beckman, 1989; Steele et al., 1990).

In reviewing Dr. Brent's approach to adherence, several issues are worth mentioning. First, Dr. Brent's question to Mrs. Salek about her medications—"How's it going with your blood pressure medication? Is it pretty easy to remember to take it?"—assumes rather than demonstrates adherence. The question with adherence is not simply remembering to take medication but when it is appropriate or suggested to do so. Mrs. Salek's answer is truthful: She has no difficulty remembering to take her HCTZ. The problem is that her idea of when to take it and Dr. Brent's assumption about when she takes it differ.

Second, Dr. Brent did not really evaluate Ms. Salek's knowledge of her regimen. She reminded her of the name of her medication and the fact that the dosage had changed recently. A more partnershiplike approach, in which she asked Mrs. Salek to name her medications and dosage changes, would place more responsibility for management and adherence with Mrs. Salek. This more explicit approach has been shown to improve adherence (Williams et al., 1998).

Finally, Dr. Brent congratulated Mrs. Salek for a job well done, based on the information she had. As we will see, Mrs. Salek was taking her medication only when she felt symptomatic. Dr. Brent unwittingly reinforced this behavior by saying "Good, keep up the good work." Research in this area suggests that Dr. Brent's approach is typical of 80% to 85% of physicians (Steele et al., 1990).

For purposes of comparison, we return to the same point in the encounter and illustrate how it might have gone differently.

D: Your blood pressure readings over the last several visits have varied quite a bit, and I'm not sure why. Let me ask you a few questions about it.

P: Okay.

D: First, can you name for me your blood pressure medication?

P: I think it's called HCTZ.

D: That's right. Next, can you tell me the dose you're taking?

P: We changed it from 200 mg to 300 mg a little while back.

D: Right. And how many times a day do you take your medication?

P: Well, I'm supposed to take it three times a day.

D: What do you mean by "supposed to"?

P: Well, I really only take my blood pressure medicine when I get headaches. That's how I know my pressure is up. You know, my medications are so expensive I have to conserve where I can.

D: I see. So what you're telling me is that you only take HCTZ when you get headaches, and your headaches are a sign to you that your blood pressure is up.

P: That's right.

D: Mrs. Salek, I'm so glad we had this conversation, because I'm pretty sure I know why your blood pressure readings have been so variable. A lot of people, including yourself, believe that headaches and other signs like them indicate increased blood pressure. The fact is that you can't feel high blood pressure. If you take your medication only at those times you think it's up, you can actually increase your risk of heart problems.

P: I didn't know that.

It is striking how using an indirect versus an information intensive interviewing style affects the direction of the encounter. Mrs. Salek's nonadherence was not a product of willful determination to frustrate her doctor; rather, it was a practical strategy based on her understanding of hypertension and the need to save money. Neither was Dr. Brent's approach born of a desire to be ambiguous; it was instead the consequence of tacit assumptions and a lack of explicit attention to the issue of adherence and the critical importance of assembling an accurate picture of the patient's behavior.

Delivering Bad News

Over the past several visits, Dr. Brent had been buoyed by her improved relationship with Mrs. Salek and its obvious impact on her health and outlook. As a result, it was with shock and sadness that she read the results of a routine blood test that she had ordered because of Mrs. Salek's anemia. The test revealed an abnormally high white count (55,000), mostly composed of lymphocytes: a low platelet count (80,000) and a hematocrit of 28, indicating acute lymphocytic leukemia (ALL).

Dr. Brent felt as though she were in a quandary—how could she tell Mrs. Salek that she had a potentially fatal disease in the face of the progress she had been making with her other medical conditions? More troubling to Dr. Brent was the fact that, despite having been in practice for almost 10 years, her experience in delivering bad news was based entirely on intuition and without benefit of formal training. After a quick consultation with an oncologist colleague, whom she knew dealt with bad news frequently, and a review of the literature, Dr. Brent discovered that she was not alone.

One resource Dr. Brent's literature search turned up was an article by Arthur Nahill (1999) entitled "Apologies to Mr. O: A Doctor Reflects on Delivering the Bad News," in which the author reflected on his experience in this area.

> I begin with a confession long overdue, on admission of guilt. Through-out my 10 year medical career, I have repeatedly engaged in a practice for which I have never been formally trained: The delivery of bad news. Not a single hour of medical school or residency was dedicated to the skills necessary to communicate unwelcome news—news that could ir-revocably alter the trajectory of another's life. (Nahill, 1999, p. 2)

As she investigated further, Dr. Brent discovered that unlike other ar-eas of the medical interview where there was strong research evidence link-ing communication skills with outcomes of care this was not the case for delivering bad news. For example, she found a literature review conducted by Ptacek and Eberhardt (1996) that evaluated more than 400 studies of bad news in the last decade found and only a handful were based on experimental or quasi-experimental methods. The rest were based on opinion and observa-tions of small, nonrepresentative samples.

In the medical education literature, Dr. Brent found an early study by Maguire et al. (1986) that suggested that although medical students who were given video feedback coaching on communication skills retained those skills 5 years into practice, delivering bad news was an exception in which experimental and control students both did poorly. To her relief, a later study by Maguire and colleagues (1996) involving senior oncologists showed sub-stantial changes in communicating bad news according to consensus guide-lines suggested by Girgis and Samson-Fisher (1995).

Taking all of the information she had gathered, Dr. Brent noted some common themes she found throughout the literature relating to the timing of bad news, responding to emotion, and patient comprehension. From the previous workshop she had attended, Dr. Brent had learned that role play with a standardized patient—an actor or actress trained to simulate various patient problems—was an excellent way of learning new skills without the added pressure of it being "real life."

Dr. Brent called the education department of a local medical school and was able to arrange a practice session for delivering bad news. To work on her skills in telling Mrs. Salek the bad news, Dr. Brent practiced with the standardized patient who agreed to play the role of a 56-year-old woman with the same problems as Mrs. Salek. A communication skills instructor with training in how to deliver bad news agreed to provide feedback.

Dr. Brent's first try at delivering the bad news to the standardized pa-tient (SP) follows.

D: You know, I wanted to just tell you that the blood test we did for your anemia has come back positive.

SP: That's good, isn't it?

D: [stammering] Well, actually—no; it's not good. You see, your white count was very high—around 55,000, mostly lymphocytes—and your platelet count was low, around 80,000. Also your hematocrit was 28.

SP: So what does that mean?

D: Well, I've been struggling all week for a way to tell you this, and it's really hard for me, but the fact is that the blood test indicates that you have a type of leukemia called acute lymphocytic leukemia, sometimes called ALL.

SP: [Visibly shaken] Does that mean I have cancer?

D: Yes, I'm afraid it does.

SP: [Tearfully] Oh my god, what am I going to do?

D: There are a number of different treatments available for ALL, depending on how far advanced it is. We can consider a course of chemotherapy and possibly radiation to try to bring the leukemia into remission. I would like you to see an oncologist who can help you understand the various options better. Do you have any questions at this point?

SP: [Head lowered, shakes her head no]

At this point, the instructor stopped the session and began to review the videotape with Dr. Brent. The instructor asked first what Dr. Brent was trying to accomplish in the opening segment of the interview. Dr. Brent stated that she wanted to ease the patient into the bad news. When asked if there was anything else, Dr. Brent replied, "I was very nervous about telling her, and it was hard to control my own anxiety."

The instructor pointed out to Dr. Brent that her attempt to ease the patient into the bad news had actually confused the patient, because she did not know whether a positive test result was good or bad. In addition, a lot of technical terms, which the patient was unlikely to know, were used in describing her condition. Finally, the instructor pointed out that, as well meaning as it was, Dr. Brent's focus on her own difficulty in delivering the news may have prevented her from actually focusing on the patient's needs at that moment, a behavior characteristic of many physicians without training in how to deliver bad news.

The instructor suggested, and Dr. Brent agreed, to make the following changes in the bad news delivery based on the best available evidence for effectiveness in communication. The instructor suggested that first, after attending the patient's comfort, Dr. Brent identify the reason for the visit early on by saying something like, "The reason I've asked you to come in today is to talk about the results of the blood tests I did because you were feeling tired," and to follow that with a succinct statement of the bad news: "I'm afraid I have some bad news to share with you about the results, because they show that you have a type of cancer." At this point, the instructor asked Dr. Brent if she would like to replay the scene trying out the new skills. She did and reported that she felt it had gone much more smoothly. This was confirmed by the standardized patient, who felt less confused about the nature of the news.

There were two other areas of discussion between the instructor and Dr. Brent: one involving Dr. Brent's own struggle to share the information most appropriately and usefully and the second having to do with the aftermath of the delivery. The instructor pointed out to Dr. Brent that her stating how difficult it was for her to deliver the news to the patient put an additional burden on the patient to respond both to the news and to the provider's difficulty in delivering it. It was suggested to Dr. Brent that one way to handle such conflicts is to talk with a colleague or friend about the challenge and to try to make the actual telling of the bad news focused as much as possible on the patient. Dr. Brent acknowledged that it would make things a lot easier in talking with Mrs. Salek if she didn't feel so alone and scared about sharing such bad news. She volunteered that it might be useful to talk with Dr. Sloan (who was also seeing Mrs. Salek) and agreed to talk with him before her next appointment with Mrs. Salek.

Turning to the aftermath of delivering the news, the instructor reflected to Dr. Brent that she very quickly moved from delivering the news to a description of various treatment options. Also, although it was true that this response followed the patient's statement "Oh my god, what am I going to do?" it was also a statement of strong emotion to which Dr. Brent failed to respond. The instructor suggested that an empathic statement such as "I know this is very difficult for you, and I want you to know that I will be here for you," would give the patient an opportunity to respond to the news emotionally, which is an important step in accepting and coping with the diagnosis. Dr. Brent practiced this response with the standardized patient and found that it deepened and strengthened their relationship. At the end of the session, Dr. Brent stated that she felt much more confident and competent in her approach to talking with Mrs. Salek, because she'd had an opportunity to learn and practice the skills she would need rather than leaving it to her intuition. Although she was still uncomfortable about what she would have to do in telling Mrs. Salek the bad news, Dr. Brent felt capable and much less alone in the process.

CONCLUSION

Our first goal in this chapter was to illustrate some of the challenges and opportunities psychologists have in working with primary care physicians. We began by noting that a gap in understanding currently exists among practicing psychologists in knowing what primary care physicians do. Using a longitudinal case study synthesized from several actual cases, we described a typical primary care approach to the interview, along with some of the current thinking from scholars regarding the medical interview about approaches that optimize communication and outcomes of care. In using this approach, we sought to show both the complexity of the responsibility physicians assume in providing care and how their approach to interviewing and problem solving compares with that of psychologists.

In closing, we offer the following observation: In its broadest sense, the question of collaboration between psychologists and primary care physicians is part of a broader social context in which professionals relate. Students of quality processes, understanding the conditions under which goods and services are produced, point out that there are two general paradigms, or worldviews regarding quality that prevail (Suchman, 1998). The first is a paradigm of control in which hierarchy and power are used to control individuals and force them to comply with externally applied norms or expectations. Psychologists and physicians working in such an arrangement are unlikely to succeed in establishing functional partnerships. In contexts as disparate as automobile assembly lines and the cockpits of commercial airlines, it has been shown that hierarchical relationships based on control lead to poorly produced automobiles and airline accidents and incidents.

The contrasting paradigm is based on relationship. In this paradigm, individuals have autonomy to act and are assumed to seek and share responsibility. The paradigm of relationship is based on principles of mutual respect and unconditional positive regard. Mistakes and errors within the relational paradigm are opportunities for all to learn and grow, not occasions for punishment and humiliation. Programs based on the relational paradigm have been used in business and industry, with impressive results.

In medicine, and perhaps psychology, practitioners are at least a generation away from seeing any wholesale shift from control to relationship. We view this as unfortunate for both disciplines and even more unfortunate for our patients, who are exceedingly clear in stating that it is the relationship that is the primary determinant of their satisfaction. Nonetheless, we believe that change is occurring, and the evidence base for the value of relationship-based collaborative care is growing. We invite readers to reflect on how they currently interact with their physician or psychologist colleagues and commit themselves to making these relationships more satisfying and successful through improved collaboration.

REFERENCES

Albert, J. J., & Charney, E. (1975). *The education of physicians for primary care* (DHEW Publication No. 74-31B). Washington, DC: U.S. Government Printing Office.

Beckman, H. B., & Frankel, R. M. (1984). The effect of physician behavior on the collection of data. *Annals of Internal Medicine, 101*, 692–696.

Branch, W. T., & Malik, T. K. (1993). Using "windows of opportunities" in brief interviews to understand patients' concerns. *Journal of the American Medical Association, 269*, 1667–1668.

DiMatteo, M. R., Hays, R. D., & Prince, L. M. (1986). Relationship of physicians' nonverbal communication skill to patient satisfaction, appointment noncompliance, and physician workload. *Health Psychology, 5*, 581–594.

Dunbar-Jacob, J., & Schlenk, E. (2001). Patient adherence to treatment regimen. In A. Baom, T. Reveson, & J. E. Singer (Eds.), *Handbook of health psychology*. Mahwah, NJ: Lawrence Erlbaum.

Frankel, R. M., & Beckman, H. B. (1989). Conversation and compliance with medical recommendations: An application of micro-analysis in medicine. In L. B. Dervin, L. Grossberg, B. O'Keefe, & E. Wartella (Eds.), *Rethinking communication: Volume II. Paradigm exemplars* (pp. 60–74). Beverly Hills, CA: Sage.

Girgis, A., & Sanson-Fisher, R. W. (1995). Breaking bad news: Consensus guidelines for medical practitioners. *Journal of Clinical Oncology, 133*, 2449–2456.

Goroll, A. H., May, L. A., & Mulley, A. G. (1987). *Primary care medicine: Office evaluation and management of the adult patient*. London: Lippincott.

Kaplan, S. H., Gandek, B., Greenfield, S., Rogers, W., & Ware, J. E. (1995). Patient and visit characteristics related to physicians' participatory decision-making style: Results from the Medical Outcomes Study. *Medical Care, 33*, 1176–1187.

Levinson, W., Roter, D. L., Mullolly, J. P., Dull, V. T., & Frankel, R. M. (1997). Physician–patient communication: The relationship with malpractice claims among primary care physicians and surgeons. *Journal of the American Medical Association, 277*, 553–559.

Lipkin, M. J., Frankel, R. M., Beckman, A. B., Chavon, R., & Fine, D. (1995). Performing the interview. In M. J. Lipkin, S. M. Putnam, & A. Lazare (Eds.), *The medical interview* (pp. 65–82). New York: Springer-Verlag.

Maguire, P., Booth, K., Elliott, C., & Hillard, V. (1996). Helping health professionals involved in cancer care acquire key interviewing skills—The impact of workshops. *European Journal of Cancer, 32A*, 1486–1489.

Maguire, P., Fairbairn, S., & Fletcher, C. (1986). Consultation skills of young doctors: I. Benefits of feedback training in interviewing as students persist. *British Medical Journal Clinical Research Edition, 292*, 1573–1576.

Marvel, M. K., Epstein, R. M., Flowers, K., & Beckman, H. B. (1999). Soliciting the patient's agenda: Have we improved? *Journal of the American Medical Association, 281*, 283–287.

Nahill, A. (1999, August 9). Apologies to Mr. O: A doctor reflects on delivering the bad news. *Boston Globe*, p. C2.

Ptacek, J. T., & Eberhardt, T. L. (1996). Breaking bad news: A review of the literature. *Journal of the American Medical Association, 276*, 496–502.

Rost, K., & Frankel, R. M. (1993). The introduction of the older patient's problems in the medical visit. *Journal of Aging and Health, 5*, 387–401.

Sackett, D. L., & Snow, J. C. (1979). The magnitude of compliance and non-compliance. In R. B. Haynes & D. L. Sackett (Eds.), *Compliance in health care* (pp. 11–22). Baltimore: Johns Hopkins University Press.

Smyth, J. M., Stone, A. A., Hoerwitz, A., & Kaell, A. (1999). Effects of writing about stressful experiences on symptom reduction in patients with asthma or rheumatoid arthritis. *Journal of the American Medical Association, 281,* 1304–1309.

Steele, D. J., Jackson, T. C., & Gutmann, M. C. (1990). Have you been taking your pills? The adherence-monitoring sequence in the medical interview. *Journal of Family Practice, 30,* 294–299.

Stewart, M., Brown, J., Levenstein, J., McCracken, E., & McWhinney, I. R. (1986) The patient-centered clinical method: 3. Changes in residents' performance over two months of training. *Family Practice, 3,* 164–167.

Suchman, A. L. (1998). Control and relation: Two foundational values and their consequences. In A. L. Suchman & P. Hinton-Walker (Eds.), *Partnerships in healthcare: Transforming relational process* (pp. 9–18). Rochester, NY: University of Rochester Press.

Suchman, A. L., Markakis, K., Beckman, H. B., & Frankel, R. M. (1997). A model of empathic communication in the medical interview. *Journal of the American Medical Association, 277,* 678–682.

Williams, G. C., Rodin, G. C., Ryan, R. M., Grolnik, W. S., & Deci, E. (1998). Autonomous regulation and long-term medication adherence in adult outpatients. *Health Psychology, 17,* 269–276.

4

RECOMMENDATIONS FOR EDUCATION AND TRAINING IN PRIMARY CARE PSYCHOLOGY

SUSAN H. McDANIEL, DAVID S. HARGROVE, CYNTHIA D. BELAR, CAROLYN S. SCHROEDER, AND ESTHER L. FREEMAN

As the range of contexts of psychological research and practice expands into primary care settings, training opportunities are necessary for psychologists to gain the relevant skills for effective involvement in health care teams. At this point there are few organized, sequential experiences that enable psychologists to learn the information and gain the skills necessary for working in primary care settings. As the psychological knowledge and skills useful for primary care evolve, it is important to organize them and design pedagogical techniques that enhance acquisition. These skills may be learned in diverse settings and under different conditions, and psychological practitioners from a variety of training backgrounds may seek to become involved.

The purpose of this chapter is to propose an organized sequence of knowledge and skills for psychologists who wish to practice and conduct research in primary care settings.[1] These skills may involve operation at the level of

---

The development of this curriculum was funded in 1999 and 2000 by an Interdivisional Grant from the American Psychological Association.
[1]For examples of training programs in primary care, see McDaniel, Belar, Schroeder, Hargrove, and Freeman (2002).

the family or emotional system or individually based prescriptive clinical techniques, such as biofeedback or specific psychotherapeutic interventions. The proposed curriculum is designed for formal training programs, such as predoctoral, internship, or postdoctoral experiences, or for individuals who seek to enhance their competency in the skills required for working in primary care through self-guided or continuing education. First, the need for such training is demonstrated. To respond to this need, the traditional role of psychologists as providers of mental health services is expanded to embrace the larger, more inclusive set of responsibilities of the psychologist as health professional. Second, the specific core knowledge and skills necessary for work in primary care settings are identified, along with specific suggestions for resources and exercises to develop the knowledge and skills. Finally, the different levels of training in primary care are described from the graduate to postgraduate level.

THE NEED FOR TRAINING PSYCHOLOGISTS IN PRIMARY CARE

A psychologist who works in primary care is a general practitioner who has skills in the psychological assessment of and intervention with common health problems of patients and families throughout the life span. Primary care psychologists work collaboratively with other health care professionals to provide continuity of care and to help identify important questions for research using a biopsychosocial model. Thus, the curriculum for education and training of generalist psychologists is distinguished by its breadth and comprehensiveness, its provision of opportunities to work with health care professionals other than those in the mental health field, and its explicit attention to experiences involving continuity of care within a systems perspective. The obligation to evaluate and understand the mechanisms by which systems operate to produce specified outcomes also is inherent in psychologists' role.

Currently, applied psychology training programs in clinical, counseling, and school psychology typically train people for general research and practice, leaving specialization training to postdoctoral and continuing education experiences. Although training may follow different models, the Guidelines and Principles for Accreditation of Programs in Professional Psychology (American Psychological Association, 2000) reflect a core value of broad and general preparation for practice at the entry level. The curriculum proposed in this chapter assumes basic doctoral training in psychology. Within professional psychology, it represents a merging of knowledge, skills, and attitudes fundamental to clinical, counseling, and school psychology with the focus areas of family, clinical child, pediatric, and clinical health psychology that are relevant for primary care psychology. As noted in chapter 1, traditional training programs do not train psychologists for work in primary care settings; a curriculum to guide such training is needed.

LEVELS OF EDUCATION AND TRAINING IN
PRIMARY CARE PSYCHOLOGY

Professional psychologists have historically been trained in Boulder model programs, with an integration of science and practice at the core of their work (Raimy, 1950). The perspective of science (including knowledge of focused, contextually relevant research and useful methodologies for both basic and applied inquiry) grounds the psychologist as a member of the interdisciplinary primary health care team.

Multiple levels of education and training must be addressed as the profession of psychology moves toward the future in primary care. At one level, students can prepare for practice in primary care as part of their initial preparation for careers as professional psychologists; this will require preparatory experiences in both academic and clinical primary care settings. This training optimally begins at the undergraduate level, as students entering the field may have backgrounds not only in psychology but also in biology and sociology. Graduate programs then provide additional coursework and practica. Other students may become primary care psychologists through education and training at the internship and postdoctoral levels. Yet another pathway to competence in primary care can be pursued by psychologists who are already at the level of independent practice and who seek to expand their practices to include primary care work. There are several available means of expanding practice into primary care. For example, in a fellowship model, a psychologist may take an extended leave (for a year or two) from a practice to engage in education and training designed for primary care work.[2]

Another approach to gaining primary care psychology knowledge and skills involves supervised self-study. This approach includes taking relevant graduate-level courses, continuing education courses, or both, as well as receiving supervision in a primary health care setting. Working with an experienced primary care psychologist is critical for this advanced level of training. This curriculum is designed so that it may be adapted by predoctoral psychology training programs, internship settings, postdoctoral programs, and by individuals pursuing self-study and continuing education.

PRIMARY CARE PSYCHOLOGY: CORE KNOWLEDGE AND SKILLS

This curriculum was developed with the assumption that effective training of psychologists for work in primary care settings takes place within a biopsychosocial context (Engel, 1977). This model emphasizes the reciprocal and dynamic influence of biological, psychological, and social forces on

---

[2]We would like to acknowledge the helpful reviews of the curriculum offered by Penny Bruker, Mark Larson, Ellen Poleshuck, Nancy Ruddy, David Seaburn, Sam Sears, and Linda Travis.

etiology, experience of illness, and treatment of disease. Although the interaction among components is integral to the experience of illness, in the context of training the component parts must be identified and clearly articulated.

This curriculum is based on several assumptions.

- Primary care psychologists (like other primary care professionals) are generalists, who play multiple roles on the primary health care team. This is consistent with traditional generalist training for psychologists in clinical, counseling, and school psychology.
- The education and training of psychologists must be developmental, biopsychosocial, and systemic in nature.
- Primary care requires knowledge of prevention and wellness.
- Primary care is collaborative in nature.
- Primary care problems often have a relational dimension, requiring education about patient–family, physician–patient, and other important relationships.
- Primary care psychologists bring to the health care team expertise in behavioral health, developmental psychology, psychopathology, family and systems issues, and research skills.
- Primary care is practiced in many different kinds of settings, including rural and urban sites, ambulatory and inpatient settings, private and government-owned clinics, community-based and academic health centers, independent practices, and health maintenance organizations. Psychologists must understand the context of the practice and the population that it serves (McDaniel, Belar, Schroeder, Hargrove, & Freeman, 2002).

The resources for the development of this curriculum were the following:

- published literature relevant to primary care psychology (e.g., Belar, 1980, 1991a, 1997; Belar & Deardorff, 1995; Bray & McDaniel, 1998; Campbell, McDaniel, & Seaburn, 1992; Diekstra & Jansen, 1988; Drotar, 1995; Elliott & Kaplow, 1997; Hargrove & Keller, 1997; McDaniel & Campbell, 1986, 1997; McDaniel, Campbell, & Seaburn, 1990; McDaniel, Hepworth, & Doherty, 1992; M. C. Roberts et al., 1998; Schroeder, 1997; Strohsahl, 1996; Zilberg & Carmody, 1995);
- relevant American Psychological Association task force reports (e.g., *Interprofessional Health Care Services in Primary Care Settings: Implications for the Education and Training of Psychologists*, American Psychological Association, 1998; *Primary Care*

Task Force Final Report, American Psychological Association, 1996);

- the perspectives of the authors and consulting reviewers;[3]
- data on the most common presenting conditions in ambulatory care (1997 National Ambulatory Medical Care Survey; Woodwell, 1999);
- Data concerning the leading causes of morbidity and mortality that can be prevented or reduced through behavioral interventions (Friedman, Sobel, Myers, Caudill, & Benson, 1995; U.S. Department of Health and Human Services, 1999).

This proposed curriculum is comprehensive, but not exhaustive. Broad educational objectives are followed by specific descriptions of knowledge and skills. To facilitate implementation, each educational objective section is followed by a selection of references to the knowledge base in the literature and then suggestions for experiential training. These exercises are meant to be illustrative, not prescriptive.

The following are the components of a comprehensive primary care psychology curriculum, assuming a strong generalist background in professional psychology.

1. Biological Components of Health and Illness

Objective: to understand the biological components of health, illness, and disease and the interaction between biology and behavior, including:

    a. general knowledge of human anatomy, physiology, and pathophysiology, and

    b. general knowledge of pharmacology, with a special focus on those medications with known effects on behavior.

Resources: Abraido-Lanza (1997); Berkow and Fletcher (1992); Bernard and Krupat (1994); Buelow and Herbert (1995); McDaniel and Campbell (1999); Kiecolt-Glaser and Glaser (1995); Lovallo (1997); McPhee, Lingappa, Ganong, and Lange (1997); Noble, Levinson, Modest, Young, and Greene (1995); *Physicians' Desk Reference* (1998); Reiss and Aman (1998); *Steadman's Medical Dictionary* (1990); Wingard, Brody, Larner, and Schwartz (1991); see also http://www.onhealth.com.

Possible coursework: pathophysiology, neuroscience, genetics, pharmacology.

Exercises:

    1. Identify a primary care physician and arrange for consultation about the biological aspects of the illness of a particular

---

[3]The components and objectives of this curriculum were first reported in McDaniel et al. (2002).

patient. Research and discuss the potential biological and behavioral effects of medications used to treat that illness.

2. Go to a medical library and view a continuing medical education videotape on the illness.

3. Check the Discovery Health TV schedule (http://www.discoveryhealth.com) for upcoming programs related to medical problems and advances.

4. Call a disease-focused organization for information, such as the American Diabetes Association for literature on Type I and Type II diabetes. After you understand rudimentary information regarding these illnesses, meet with a nutritionist to understand the diabetic diet. Also, attend a support group to learn about the real-life problems this disease and its management cause.

5. Shadow a primary care physician or nurse practitioner (or both), seeing patients for half a day. Notice the nature of their work, the number of psychosocial problems that are directly or indirectly presented, and what you might say to be helpful when collaborating.

2. Cognitive Components of Health and Illness

Objective: to understand how learning, memory, perception, and cognition can influence health and health behavior, including

a. knowledge of health belief models of patients and their families and how these beliefs influence identification of health problems, help seeking, and adherence to treatment regimens;

b. knowledge of beliefs and attitudes that mediate help seeking;

c. knowledge of cognitive factors that influence reactions to initial diagnoses and the processing of health information;

d. knowledge of the impact of biologic factors on cognitive functioning.

Resources: Baum, Revenson, and Singer (2001); Bernard and Krupat (1994); Connor and Norman (1995); Kemeny and Gruenewald (2000); Rolland (1994); Wright, Watson, and Bell (1996).

Exercises:

1. Interview an ill person to learn about his or her personal and family beliefs about the illness and his or her beliefs about the cause of illness and its most appropriate treatment. Compare this to the beliefs held by the medical profession regarding this illness.

2. In supervision, describe your own family illness history and how this affects your health beliefs.

3. List 10 medical illnesses that can affect cognitive functioning.
4. Reflect on the last time you made an appointment to see your primary care provider. What were your beliefs about the need for that appointment and what might transpire? How did your expectations match with what occurred during the visit?

3. Affective Components of Health and Illness

Objective: to understand how emotions and motivation can influence health and health behavior, including
   a. knowledge of how affect influences cognition and attitudes that mediate help seeking;
   b. knowledge of affective factors that influence reactions to initial diagnoses and the processing of health information;
   c. knowledge of affective reactions to illness, injury, and disability; and
   d. knowledge of medical problems that can present as affective disorders (e.g., thyroid disorders, steroid reactions, etc.).

Resources: Baum et al. (2001); Lazarus (1999); Pennebaker (1995).

Exercises:
   1. Interview a patient and inquire as to his or her feelings regarding going to a physician, receiving a diagnosis, participating in treatment, and telling friends and family about the illness.
   2. Do an imagery exercise in which you imagine you have just been given the diagnosis of a chronic illness.
   3. Reflect on the last time you made an appointment to see your primary care provider. What emotions did you experience regarding the need for that appointment and what might transpire? How did you feel during the visit?
   4. List five medical problems that might present as depression or anxiety.
   5. Consider how cognitive and affective components might interact in health or illness. Examine a blemish on your body and ascribe to it various meanings as listed below. With each meaning, examine the different feelings that might arise along with the different perceptions.

Ascribed meanings:
   - a scar from a childhood injury during a summer vacation,
   - a scar from childhood physical abuse,
   - a scar from a successfully excised skin cancer,

- a scar from an excised malignant melanoma,
- a scar from self-mutilative behavior during adolescence, and
- a scar from a criminal attack.

4. Behavioral and Developmental Aspects of Health and Illness

Objective: to understand behavioral aspects of health, help-seeking behavior, response to illness and treatment, and prevention, as well as how development and individual differences may interact with cognitive, affective, and behavioral components:
 a. knowledge of behavioral risk factors for problems seen in primary care;
 b. knowledge of relationships among coping styles and health;
 c. knowledge of the relationships among age, developmental context, and health;
 d. knowledge of the impact of psychopathology on response to illness and recovery; and
 e. knowledge of how operant and classical conditioning affect health and health behavior.

Resources: Ammerman and Campo (1998a, 1998b); Arnett (2000); Bernard and Krupat (1994); Carter and McGoldrick (1999); Cassem and Hackett (1997); Kaplan, Sallis, and Patterson (1993); Kiecolt-Glaser and Glaser (1995); McConnaughy, DiClemente, Prochaska, and Velicer (1989); Prochaska, Norcross, and DiClemente (1994); A. R. Roberts (1995); Rolland (1987, 1990); Thompson and Gustafson (1995).

Exercises:
 1. Interview three patients from different stages of the life cycle to understand their experiences of health and illness, including preventive behaviors, help-seeking behaviors, coping with and adaptation to the stress of illness, and compliance with treatment regimens.
 2. Interview the family of a person with a chronic illness to determine the family's perspective of the illness and its effect on the identified patient and on the functioning of the family.
 3. Sit in on a group for the caregivers of patients with Alzheimer's disease to learn about its effects on the family.
 4. Talk to a pediatrician or family physician about the developmental differences involved in examining young children, preteens, and teens, listening for issues of privacy, body image/anxiety, dependency, and so on. Ask how the physician handles issues of inclusion and confidentiality with the child's parents.

5. Arrange to visit a clinic treating children with asthma, diabetes, or nutritional problems. Observe the children and families in the waiting room and talk with the health professional about the nature of the child's problems and what developmental or behavioral factors are promoting or inhibiting treatment.

6. Contact the local chapter of the Tourette Syndrome Association and ask to attend a parent meeting. Arrange to talk with two parents and their children about the problems they experience in coping with the disorder as well as ways they have learned to cope with it and how this has changed over time.

5. Sociocultural Components of Health and Illness

Objective: to understand social and cultural factors in the development of health problems, access to health care, help-seeking behavior, and adherence to treatment and prevention. This includes the following:

    a. knowledge of the impact of interpersonal relationships on health and health behavior and awareness of

        1) partner and family influences;

        2) the impact of health professional(s), patient, and family communication on health; and

        3) the positive and negative effects of the social network and health;

    b. knowledge of relationships among ethnicity, race, culture, and health behavior and disease management;

    c. knowledge of socioeconomic factors in health status and health care, including

        1) knowledge of the relationship between socioeconomic status and health and

        2) knowledge of socioeconomic and sociopolitical factors specific to a local community with respect to practice and resources;

    d. knowledge of relationships between religion and health;

    e. knowledge of issues related to sexual orientation and health;

    f. knowledge of issues related to disability and health;

    g. knowledge of issues related to gender and health;

    h. knowledge of health care consumer groups and their impact of health policy and health care delivery.

Resources: Abraido-Lanza (1997); Batshaw (1997); Bleckman and Brownell (1998); Campbell and Patterson (1995); Candib (1995); Doherty and Campbell (1988); Gallant, Keita, and Royak-Schaler (1997); Garcia-Coll and Meyer (1993); Giachello and Belgrave (1997); House, Landis, and

Umberson (1988); Kaplan et al. (1993); Kazarian and Evans (2001); Mann and Kato (1996); McDaniel and Campbell (1996, 2000); McDaniel et al. (1990); McGoldrick, Giordano, and Pearce (1996); Olkin (1999); Pasco (1983); Richards and Bergin (1999); Rolland (1994); Shewchuck and Elliott (2001); Uchino, Cacioppo, and Kiecolt-Glaser (1996); Zerbe (1999).

Possible coursework: families, systems, and health; medical sociology; medical anthropology.

Exercises:
1. Describe the effect of your ethnicity on your family's health beliefs. Illustrate it with an illness event and the family's approach to its treatment. Share the written description with a colleague from a different ethnic group and compare experiences.
2. List the age, ethnicity, religion, class, and geographic region of five patients. Describe and compare the effect of these social factors on their health beliefs.
3. Spend time in the clinic or emergency room of a hospital that serves poor people to learn the impact of economics on medical care.
4. Interview people from different economic groups regarding their attitudes and comfort level with the health care system.
5. Interview a hospital social worker about the problems of patients with no insurance.
6. Visit a gay community health center, if there is one in your area, to learn its members' perspective on the impact of AIDS and what types of support these patients need. Learn also about your community's resources for these patients.
7. Interview a blind person, a person in a wheelchair, or another otherly abled person to learn about their health care needs.
8. Make rounds with a hospital chaplain.
9. Arrange for an experience in which you are, for a specific period of time—at least half a day—confined to a wheelchair or blindfolded and must function within your usual context.

6. Health Policy and Health Care Systems

Objective: to understand how health policy and health care systems affects health.
    a. awareness of impact of health policy on health and health care, including
        1) knowledge of health care financing,
        2) awareness of behavioral health carve-outs as impediments to integrated primary care,

3) knowledge of the underinsured and uninsured: their health care needs and community strategies to care for them, and

4) knowledge of trends in health policy;

b. knowledge of specific characteristics and sociopolitical features of the health care system, including

1) awareness of health care system design and

2) awareness of the impact of mind–body dualism on the design of health care services;

c. knowledge of specific characteristics and sociopolitical features of primary care, including awareness of

1) the role of primary care in the current health care system and its differences from the mental health system,

2) similarities and differences between primary and specialty care and how referrals and communications between them generally occur, and

3) similarities and differences in various primary care settings (family practice, obstetrics–gynecology, pediatrics, general internal medicine, geriatrics).

Resources: Bower (2000); Campbell et al. (2000); Chiles, Lambert, and Hatch (1999); Cummings (1996); Druss, Rohrbaugh, and Rosenheck (1999); Fisher and Ransom (1997); Frank et al. (2002); Haagland, Kewman, and Ashkanazi (2000); Institute of Medicine (1996); Kaplan (2000); Kiesler (2000); Mauksch and Leahy (1993); Mullen (1998); Pew Health Professions Commission (1995); Pruitt, Klapow, Epping-Jordan, and Dresselhaus (1998); Shortell, Gillies, and Anderson (1994); Strosahl (2000).

Exercises:

1. Investigate and describe the specific Medicaid plan for covering children's health and mental health care in your state.

2. Use local resources to determine the percentage of uninsured people in your county. Interview a physician or clerk in a local emergency department to find out what percentage of people are treated who have no insurance, the nature of their problems, and how these services are covered.

3. Speak to three people over the age of 70 and list the medications they take. Go to the pharmacy and learn what the total costs are per month and what part the patient pays. Find out the average Social Security income of a 70-year-old.

4. Talk to a transplant patient about the cost of his or her care and medications.

7. Common Primary Care Problems

Objective: to acquire knowledge concerning the biological, cognitive, affective, behavioral, and interpersonal aspects of the most common conditions and issues seen in primary care (see Exhibit 4.1), with a specific focus on the following as relevant:

a. etiology,
b. signs and symptoms,
c. illness course,
d. relevant treatments,
e. prognosis,
f. psychophysiological components,
g. methods for primary and secondary prevention, and
h. interpersonal and cultural context.

Resources: Baum, Newman, Weinman, West, and McManus (1997); Baum et al. (2001); Berkow and Fletcher (1992); Bleckman and Brownell (1998); Camic and Knight (1998); Campbell (1997); deGruy (1997); Feinstein and Brewer (1999); Gatchel and Blanchard (1993); McDaniel et al. (1990); Olfson et al. (1997); Sartorius et al. (1993); Schulberg (2001); Schurman, Kramer, and Mitchell (1985); Von Korff and Simon (1996); Weiss (2000).

Exercises:

1. Investigate four common primary care problems; describe their incidence and recommended treatment.
2. Write a case study of one of your patients who has a concurrent physical problem drawn from the list above. Describe the characteristics of the illness with respect to etiology, signs and symptoms, illness course, and so on (i.e., items a–h, listed above).
3. Attend at least two illness support groups (for asthma, breast cancer, fibromyalgia, multiple sclerosis, etc.) to learn what it is like for patients who live with these diseases.
4. Arrange to talk with a pediatrician or nurse practitioner about his or her evaluation and treatment of a common pediatric problem, such as childhood attention-deficit disorder. Prior to the meeting, research the problem and its evaluation and treatment in primary care.

8. Clinical Assessment of Common Primary Care Conditions

Objective: to acquire knowledge and expertise in the assessment of relevant cognitive, affective, behavioral, relational, social, and psychophysiological components for all common conditions seen in primary care, including:

a. knowledge of common medical assessment methods and ability to move through a medical assessment process to case formulation using the biopsychosocial model;
b. the ability to detect subthreshold clinical problems;
c. knowledge of mental health problems, such as anxiety and depression, how they might present differently in primary care

EXHIBIT 4.1
Common Conditions Seen in Primary Care

Abdominal pain
Adjustment disorders
Anxiety disorders
Arthritis
Asthma
Attention-deficit/hyperactivity disorder
Back pain
Birth control
Chest pain
Chronic obstructive pulmonary disease
Depression
Dermatitis
Developmental problems (toileting, sleep, oppositional behavior, social
  relationships, learning, puberty, marriage, aging, death)
Diabetes
Domestic violence
Earache
Family issues (e.g., divorce, blended families)
Fatigue
Grief reactions
Heart disease
Hypertension
Headache
Injury (falls, sprains and strains, motor vehicle accidents, assault)
Insomnia
Nonadherence to medical regimes
Obesity
Pain
Pregnancy
Sedentary lifestyle
Sexual disorders
Sexual trauma (sexual abuse, rape)
Sleep disorders
Somatoform disorders
Stress reactions
Substance use and abuse
Tobacco use
Upper respiratory (sore throat, cough)
Urinary problems (incontinence, infections)

Note. This table is based on Woodoll (1999), Weiss (2000), and Schroeder (1997).

than in specialty mental health clinics, and their association
with certain medical illnesses;

d. expertise in targeted, brief interviewing methods;

e. knowledge of and expertise in the use of empirically supported
psychometrics relevant to common primary care conditions;
and

1) awareness of limitations of traditional measures in primary care settings,

2) knowledge of normative data relevant to primary care, and

3) knowledge of and skills with brief screening instruments;
f. expertise in triage;
g. skills in obtaining information from collateral persons;
h. skills in working under time demand pressures;
i. skills in starting with an undifferentiated clinical population and sorting through various domains of information quickly;
j. skills in targeting the assessment to the referral question in language that is meaningful to the person who made the referral; and
k. the ability to conduct assessments in medical settings, such as an examination room, the emergency department, or a hospital bed.

Resources: Achenbach (1991); Badger et al. (1994); Belar and Deardorff (1995); Camic and Knight (1998); Haley et al. (1998); Heldring (1995); Holden and Schuman (1995); McDaniel et al. (1997); Radnitz, Bockian, and Moran (2000); M. C. Roberts (1995); Rozensky, Sweet, and Tovian (1997); Schroeder and Gordon (2002); Sears, Danda, and Evans (1999); Spielberger, Gorsuch, and Lushene (1970); Spitzer et al. (1995).

Exercises:
1. Write an assessment of the psychological (intrapsychic and interpersonal) factors associated with a patient with a common primary care problem, like headaches. Include your plan for coordinating assessment with the primary care professional.
2. Research a measure, such as the Child Behavior Checklist (Achenbach, 1991) the State–Trait Anxiety Inventory (Spielberger et al., 1970), or the Child Somatization Inventory (Walker & Green, 1989). Investigate the norms to determine how the instrument could be used in a primary care setting.
3. Interview patients and family members in health care settings, such as the emergency room and the county health department.
4. Attend two home visits with a hospice or home health care nurse.
5. Describe the assessment process for a 6-year-old who presents with encopresis due to chronic constipation.

9. Clinical Interventions in Primary Care

Objective: to acquire knowledge and skill in implementing empirically supported and awareness of other clinically supported interventions for the prevention and treatment of the most common conditions in primary care, including:

a. skills in developing a psychological treatment plan to include in collaborative care;

b. skills in individual, couples and family, and group therapy;

c. skills in supportive, cognitive–behavioral, crisis intervention, family systems approaches, psychoeducation, and relapse prevention;

d. skills in case management;

e. skills in negotiating treatment plans that are mutually acceptable to the patient, family, and health care team;

f. skills in increasing motivation for change and adherence;

g. skills in implementing interventions through other providers;

h. knowledge of community resources;

i. skills in designing culturally sensitive interventions for local populations;

j. practical, concrete, problem-solving skills; and

k. a plan regarding when to refer patients who need a more intense level of care (e.g., partial hospitalization, emergency care, full hospitalization).

Resources: American Psychological Association (1995, 1997a); Camic and Knight (1998); Campbell and McDaniel (1997); Campbell and Patterson (1995); Center for the Advancement of Health and The Center for Health Studies, Group Health Cooperative of Puget Sound (1996); Cummings and Cummings (1997); DeGood, Crawford, and Jongsma (1999); Diekstra and Jansen (1988); Eisenberg (1992); Feinstein and Brewer (1999); Frank et al. (2002); Glenn (1984); Goodheart and Lansing (1997); Haley (1996); James and Folen (1999); Koocher and Pollin (1995); McConnaughy et al. (1989); McDaniel, Harkness, and Epstein (2001); McDaniel et al. (1992); Mikesell, Lusterman, and McDaniel (1995); Miller and Cohen (2001); Miranda, Hohmann, Attkisson, and Larson (1994); Nicassio and Smith (1995); Prochaska et al. (1994); Raimy (1950); A. R. Roberts (1995); M. C. Roberts (1995); Robinson (1998); Ruddy and McDaniel (1995); Schroeder, Goolsby, and Stangler (1975); Spirito (1998); Stein (1985); Walker and Greene (1989); Weissman and Klerman (1993); Wynne, McDaniel, and Weber (1986); Zilberg and Carmody (1995).

Exercises:

1. For a patient with a common primary care problem, develop an intervention plan that is collaborative in nature, involving the psychological, physical, and social health of the patient. Also, describe the process by which a collaborative treatment plan is developed among the patient, family, and health care team.

2. Design a cognitive–behavioral treatment plan for a patient with depression who sees you in the primary care setting only once a month.

3. Choose a common pediatric problem and determine whether there are any American Academy of Pediatrics recommended guidelines for the assessment and treatment of the problem. Write a critique, comparing these findings with what is actually done in practice (as reported by pediatricians and nurse practitioners you interview). If appropriate, write a list of recommendations on how more appropriate assessment and treatment could be incorporated into clinical practice.

4. Develop an intervention plan that is collaborative in nature to treat a 6-year-old child with encopresis due to chronic constipation.

5. Outline the steps you would take to intervene with a 12-year-old who is having a panic attack during a physical examination.

6. A physician prescribes a great deal of stimulant medication and asks you to develop a cost-effective way to determine if the medication is indicated and, if so, how to determine the most appropriate dose. Write an outline of how you would proceed in consulting with this physician.

10. Interprofessional Collaboration in Primary Care

Objective: to acquire knowledge and skill in interprofessional primary health care, including:

a. knowledge of other disciplines integrally involved in primary care (including, but not limited to, family practitioners, pediatricians, internists, obstetricians–gynecologists, nurse practitioners, registered nurses, licensed practical nurses, physician assistants, nutritionists, midwives, alternative healers, social workers), with special attention to the following:

1) roles and functions,
2) education and training background,
3) scope-of-practice and boundary issues, and
4) values and priorities;

b. expertise in collaboration with other professions, including the following:

1) ability to discriminate individual differences from discipline differences,
2) skills in coordination of care across the life span,
3) skills in clear communication with other disciplines, and
4) skills in cocreating an integrated treatment plan;

c. expertise in consultation, such as
   1) patient-centered approaches,
   2) consultee-focused strategies, and
   3) brief curbside methods;
d. knowledge of medical specialties frequently consulted by primary care providers, especially skill in referral to and managing consultations with other providers.

Resources: Belar (1995); Belar and Deardorff (1995); Blount (1998); Bray (1996); Doherty, McDaniel, and Baird (1996); Drotar (1995); Druss et al. (1999); Dym and Berman (1996); Frank et al. (2002); Fraser and Greenhalgh (2001); Garner and Orelove (1994); LaBaron and Zeltzer (1985); Lazarus (1999); McConnaughy et al. (1989); McDaniel (1995); McDaniel and Campbell (1996, 1997); McDaniel, Campbell, & Seaburn (1990, 1995); McDaniel and Landau-Stanton (1992); Pace, Chaney, Mullins, and Olson (1995); Rivo and Satcher (1993); Rivo, Saultz, Wartman, and DeWitt (1994); Schroeder (1996); Seaburn, Lorenz, Gunn, Gawinski, and Mauksch (1996); Talen, Graham, and Walbroehl (1994); Wynne et al. (1986); Zeiss and Steffen (1996); see also chapter 8, this volume, and http:// www.urmc.rochester.edu/ smd/psych/family/mft_ms.html and http://www.onhealth.com.

Possible coursework: Take any course in which other health care professionals are enrolled.

Exercises:
1. Shadow experienced primary care psychologists.
2. Observe half-day patient sessions of primary care physicians and nurses.
3. Makes rounds with a primary care physician in the hospital.
4. Attend a nurses' meeting during their change of shifts.
5. Study the Web sites of other health care professions' national organizations.
6. Select a representative primary care case and develop an interdisciplinary treatment plan; for example:

Christine is a 43-year-old single mother of two sons, ages 10 and 14. She has been coming to the clinic for over 6 years and is well known to the team. The team consists of a psychologist, a nurse, a physician, a nutritionist, and a pharmacist. Christine is clinically obese, weighing 180 lbs at 5 ft, 2 in., practices poor nutrition, and does not exercise. She has gained 30 lbs in the last 18 months. She has been resistant to the idea of talking with the psychologist on the team.

Address the following issues:
a. How would you assess this patient? What are her strengths, and what are her problems?

    b.   What treatment plan would you as a psychologist put forward?
    c.   Talk to other professionals and describe the treatment plan of at least two other disciplines.
    d.   Describe an integrated treatment plan.
    e.   Which team members should play a primary role with this patient? Which should play a secondary role?
    f.   What are the potential medical and psychosocial complications in treating this patient?
    g.   Obtain supervision/consultation from a health professional who is not a psychologist.

11. Ethical Issues in Primary Care

Objective: to be able to identify the distinctive ethical issues encountered in primary care practice, including, but not limited to, awareness of
    a.   the multiple consumers of services and identification of potential role conflicts;
    b.   problems encountered in team functioning, for example, diffusion of responsibility;
    c.   the psychologist's scope of practice;
    d.   distinctive issues related to informed consent and confidentiality (negotiating with the patient to share relevant information with the primary care team);
    e.   the potential for dual relationships; and
    f.   management issues when you are involved with multiple family members across the life span.

Resources: Belar and Deardorff (1995); Frank et al. (2002); Gottlieb (1995); McDaniel, Hepworth, and Doherty (1997); Seaburn et al. (1996).

Possible coursework: interdisciplinary course in medical ethics.

Exercises:
    1.   Discuss the ethical issues in the following primary care case:

    Mr. Brown is seeing you for marital therapy. He discloses in an individual interview that he is having unprotected sex with men about once a month. His health professional is unaware of this activity. How should you handle confidentiality in this situation?

    2.   Develop a plan for a mother who reports bruising her child while spanking him.
    3.   Describe the ethical and legal considerations that influence your plan.

12. Legal Issues in Primary Care

Objective: to be able to identify the distinctive legal issues often encountered in primary care practice, including, but not limited to:

a. practice within scope of licensure and
b. possibilities of shared liability.

Resources: Belar and Deardorff (1995).

Possible coursework: legal aspects of health care.

Exercises:
1. Investigate the legal constraints on business practice between psychologists and other health professionals. In your state, is it best to have merged practices, or must collaborative practices be separate corporations?
2. A noncustodial parent demands to see the medical records of his or her child who has had repeated urinary tract infections. Research and discuss the legal issues involved.

13. Professional Issues in Primary Care

Objective: to be aware of and skilled in the special professional issues found in primary care practice, including:
a. differences between on-site and off-site collaborative practice;
b. differences between working with one versus multiple groups of primary care providers;
c. the effect of a psychologist's own personal and family issues with illness, disability, and death and dying;
d. personality issues in collaborative practice;
e. reimbursement issues in managed care, Medicaid, Medicare, and other insurances, including differences in coverage for medical and psychological care;
f. the ability to address decisions regarding amount of nonreimbursed services to provide to referral sources (e.g., curbside consults, triage);
g. knowledge and skill in relevant marketing strategies;
h. consideration of salaried versus fee-for-service models in primary care;
i. commitment to lifelong learning and skills in self-assessment of knowledge and competencies; and
j. the ability to function in different roles (team leader, direct service provider, consultant, case manager).

Resources: American Psychological Association (1997b); Belar (1991a, 1995); Frank et al. (2002); Frank and Ross (1995); Haley et al. (1998); Mann and Kato (1996); McDaniel et al. (1990, 1992); Nathan (1998); Schurman et al. (1985); Strosahl (2000).

Exercises:

1. Construct a strategy for seeking reimbursement in your community for psychoeducational groups and collaborative sessions (i.e., sessions at which there is more than one clinician present).
2. Write a justification to an insurance company for a child to be treated by a psychologist for attention-deficit/hyperactivity disorder.
3. Write a 1-page advocacy statement for inclusion of psychological services in primary care for submission to your state legislature.

REFERENCES

Abraido-Lanza, A. F. (1997). Task group V: Adaptive health behaviors. *Journal of Gender, Culture, and Health, 2,* 143–161.

Achenbach, T. M. (1991). *Manual for the Child Behavior Checklist.* Burlington: Department of Psychiatry, University of Vermont.

American Psychological Association. (1995). *Final report of the Board of Educational Affairs Working Group to develop a Level I Curriculum for Psychopharmacology Education and Training.* Washington, DC: Author.

American Psychological Association (1997a). *Final report of the Board of Educational Affairs Working Group on Psychopharmacology Education and Training: Curriculum for Level 2 training in psychopharmacology.* Washington, DC: Author.

American Psychological Association. (1997b). *Proceedings from the National Working Conference on Supply and Demand: Training employment opportunities in professional psychology.* Washington, DC: Author.

American Psychological Association. (1998). *Interprofessional health care services in primary care settings: Implications for professional education and training of psychologists* (Substance Abuse and Mental Health Services Administration/Health Resources and Services Adminisitration Work Order 97M220464). Washington, DC: Author.

American Psychological Association. (2000). *Guidelines and principles for accreditation of programs in professional psychology.* Washington, DC: Author.

American Psychological Association, Committee for the Advancement of Professional Psychology Primary Care Task Force. (1996). *Primary Care Task Force final report.* Washington, DC: American Psychological Association.

Ammerman, R. T., & Campo, J. V. (Eds.). (1998a). *Handbook of pediatric psychology and psychiatry: Vol. 1. Psychological and psychiatric issues in pediatric settings.* New York: Allyn & Bacon.

Ammerman, R. T., & Campo, J. V. (Eds.). (1998b). *Handbook of pediatric psychology and psychiatry: Vol. 2. Disease, injury, and illness.* New York: Allyn & Bacon.

Arnett, J. J. (2000). Emerging adulthood: A theory of development from the late teens through the twenties. *American Psychologist, 55,* 469–480.

Badger, L. W., deGruy, F., Hartman, J., Plant, M. A., Leeper, J., Anderson, R., et al. (1994). Patient presentation, interview content and the detection of depression by primary care physicians. *Psychosomatic Medicine, 56,* 128–135.

Batshaw, M. L. (Ed.). (1997). *Children with disabilities* (4th ed.). Baltimore: Brooks.

Baum, A., Newman, S., Weinman, J., West, R., & McManus, C. (Eds.). (1997). *Cambridge handbook of psychology, health, and medicine.* New York: Cambridge University Press.

Baum, A., Revenson, T. A., & Singer, J. E. (Eds.). (2001). *Handbook of health psychology.* Mahwah, NJ: Erlbaum.

Belar, C. D. (1980). Training the clinical psychology student in behavioral medicine. *Professional Psychology: Research and Practice, 11,* 620–627.

Belar, C. D. (1991). Issues in training in clinical health psychologists. In M. A. Jansen & J. Weinman (Eds.), *The international development of health psychology* (pp. 91–98). New York: Harwood Academic.

Belar, C. D. (1995). Collaboration in capitated care: Challenges for psychology. *Professional Psychology: Research and Practice, 26,* 139–146.

Belar, C. D. (1997). Clinical health psychology: A specialty for the 21st century. *Health Psychology, 16,* 411–416.

Belar, C. D., & Deardorff, W. W. (1995). *Clinical health psychology in medical settings: A practitioner's guidebook.* Washington, DC: American Psychological Association.

Berkow, R., & Fletcher, A. (Eds.). (1992). *The Merck manual of diagnosis and therapy.* Rahway, NJ: Merck.

Bernard, L. C., & Krupat, E. (1994). *Health psychology: Biopsychosocial factors in health and illness.* Orlando, FL: Harcourt Brace.

Bleckman, E., & Brownell, K. (1998), *Behavioral medicine and women's health: A comprehensive handbook.* New York: Guilford Press.

Blount, A. (1998). *Integrated primary care: The future of medical and mental health collaboration.* New York: Norton.

Bower, P. (2000). Systematic review of the effect of on-site mental health professionals on the clinical behavior of general practitioners. *British Medical Journal, 320,* 614–617.

Bray, J. H. (1996). Psychologists as primary care practitioners. In R. J. Resnick & R. H. Rozensky (Eds.), *Health psychology through the life span: Practice and research opportunities* (pp. 89–99). Washington, DC: American Psychological Association.

Bray, J. H., & McDaniel, S. H. (1998). Behavioral health practice in primary care settings. *Innovations in Clinical Practice: A Source Book, 16,* 313–323.

Buelow, G., & Herbert, S. (1995). *Counselor's resource on psychiatric medications: Issues of treatment and referral.* Pacific Grove, CA: Brooks/Cole.

Camic, P. M., & Knight, S. J. (Eds.). (1998). *Clinical handbook of health psychology.* Kirkland, WA: Hogrefe & Huber.

Campbell, T. L. (1997). Research reports: Domestic violence in primary care. *Families, Systems, and Health, 15,* 345–350.

Campbell, T. L., Franks, P., Fiscela, K., McDaniel, S. H., Zwanzeger, J., Mooney, C., et al. (2000). Do physicians who diagnose more mental health disorders generate lower health care costs? *Journal of Family Practice, 49,* 305–310.

Campbell, T. L., & McDaniel, S. H. (1997, Summer). Branching out: A randomized trial of collaborative family healthcare for distressed high utilizers of medical systems. *American Family Therapy Academy Newsletter,* 7–9.

Campbell, T. L., McDaniel, S. H., & Seaburn, D. B. (1992). Family systems medicine: New opportunities for psychologists. In T. J. Akamatsu, M. A. Stephens, S. E. Hobfoll, & J. H. Crowther (Eds.), *Family health psychology* (pp. 193–215). Washington, DC: Hemisphere.

Campbell, T. L., & Patterson, J. (1995). The effectiveness of family interventions in the treatment of physical illness. *Journal of Martial and Family Therapy, 21,* 545–584.

Candib, L. (1995). *Medicine and the family: A feminist perspective.* New York: Basic Books.

Carter, E., & McGoldrick, M. (1999). *The expanded family life cycle.* New York: Allyn & Bacon.

Cassem, N., & Hackett, T. (Eds.). (1997). *Massachusetts General Hospital handbook of general hospital psychiatry.* St. Louis, MO: Mosby.

Center for the Advancement of Health & The Center for Health Studies, Group Health Cooperative of Puget Sound. (1996). *An indexed bibliography on self-management for people with chronic disease.* Washington, DC: Center for the Advancement of Health.

Chiles, J. A., Lambert, M. J., & Hatch, A. L. (1999). The impact of psychological interventions on medical cost offset: A meta-analytic review. *Clinical Psychology: Science and Practice, 6,* 204–221.

Connor, M., & Norman, P. (Eds.). (1995). *Predicting health behavior: Research and practice with social cognition models.* Washington, DC: Taylor & Francis.

Cummings, N. A. (1996). The new structure of health care and a role for psychology. In R. J. Resnick & R. H. Rozensky (Eds.), *Health psychology through the life span: Practice and research opportunities* (pp. 27–38). Washington, DC: American Psychological Association.

Cummings, N. A., & Cummings, J. L. (Eds.). (1997). *Behavioral health in primary care: A guide for clinical integration.* Madison, CT: International Universities Press.

DeGood, D. E., Crawford, A. L., & Jongsma, A. E. (1999). *The behavioral medicine treatment planner.* New York: Wiley.

deGruy, F. V. (1997). Mental healthcare in the primary care setting: A paradigm problem. *Families, Systems, & Health, 15,* 3–40.

Diekstra, R. F., & Jansen, M. A. (1988). Psychology's role in the new health care systems: The importance of psychological interventions in primary health care. *Psychotherapy, 25*, 344–359.

Doherty, W. J., & Campbell, T. L. (1988). *Families and health.* Beverly Hills, CA: Sage.

Doherty, W., McDaniel, S. H., & Baird, M. (1996). Five levels of primary care/behavioral healthcare collaboration. *Behavioral Health Tomorrow, 5*, 25–27.

Drotar, D. (1995). *Consulting with pediatricians: Psychological perspectives.* New York: Plenum.

Druss, B. G., Rohrbaugh, R. M., & Rosenheck, R. A. (1999). Depressive symptoms and health costs in older medical patients. *American Journal of Psychiatry, 156*, 477–479.

Dym, B., & Berman, S. (1996). The primary health care team: Family physician and family therapist in joint practice. *Family Systems Medicine, 4*, 9–21.

Eisenberg, L. (1992). Treating depression and anxiety in primary care: Closing the gap between knowledge and practice. *New England Journal of Medicine, 326*, 1080–1084.

Elliott, T. R.. & Kaplow, J. C. (1997). Training psychologists for a future in evolving health care delivery systems: Building a better Boulder model. *Journal of Clinical Psychology in Medical Settings, 4*, 255–267.

Engel, G. (1977). The need for a new medical model: A challenge for biomedicine. *Science, 196*, 129–136.

Feinstein, R. E., & Brewer, A. A. (Eds.). (1999). *Primary care psychiatry and behavioral medicine: Brief office treatment and management pathways.* New York: Springer.

Fisher, L., & Ransom, D. C. (1997). Developing a strategy for managing behavioral healthcare within the context of primary care. *Archives of Family Medicine, 6*, 324–333.

Frank, R. G., & Ross, M. (1995). The changing workforce: This role of health psychology. *Health Psychology, 14*, 519–525.

Fraser, S. W., & Greenhalgh, T. (2001). Coping with complexity: Educating for capability. *British Medical Journal, 323*, 799–803.

Friedman, R., Sobel, D., Myers, P., Caudill, M., & Benson, H. (1995). Behavioral medicine, clinical health psychology, and cost offset. *Health Psychology, 14*, 509–518.

Gallant, S. J., Keita, G. P., & Royak-Schaler, R. (Eds.). (1997). *Health care for women: Psychological, social, and behavioral influences.* Washington, DC: American Psychological Association.

Garcia-Coll, C. T., & Meyer, E. C. (1993). The socio-cultural context of infant development. In C. H. Zeanah Jr. (Ed.), *Handbook of infant mental health* (pp. 56–70). New York: Guilford Press.

Garner, H. G., & Orelove, F. P. (Eds.). (1994). *Teamwork in human services: Models and applications across the life span.* Newton, MA: Butterworth–Heinemann.

Gatchel, R. J., & Blanchard, E. B. (1993). *Psychophysiological disorders: Research and clinical applications*. Washington, DC: American Psychological Association.

Giachello, A. L., & Belgrave, F. (1997). Task Group IV: Health care systems and behavior. *Journal of Gender, Culture, and Health, 2*, 163–173.

Glenn, M. (1984). *On diagnosis: A systemic approach*. New York: Brunner/Mazel.

Goodheart, C. D., & Lansing, M. H. (1997). *Treating people with chronic disease: A psychological guide*. Washington, DC: American Psychological Association.

Gottlieb, M. (1995). Ethical dilemmas in change of format and live supervision. In R. H. Mikesell, D. D. Lusterman, & S. H. McDaniel (Eds.), *Integrating family therapy: Handbook of family psychology and systems theory* (pp. 561–569). Washington, DC: American Psychological Association.

Haagland, K. J., Kewman, D. G., & Ashkanazi, G. S. (2000). Medicare and prospective payment systems. In R. G. Frank & T. R. Elliott (Eds.), *Handbook of rehabilitation psychology* (pp. 603–614). Washington, DC: American Psychological Association.

Haley, W. E. (1996). The medical context of psychotherapy with the elderly. In S. Zarit & R. Knight (Eds.), *A guide to psychotherapy and aging: Effective clinical interventions in a life-stage context* (pp. 221–239). Washington, DC: American Psychological Association.

Haley, W. E., McDaniel, S. H., Bray, J. H., Frank, R. G., Heldring, M., Johnson, S. B., et al. (1998). Psychological practice in primary care settings: Practical tips for clinicians. *Professional Psychology: Research and Practice, 29*, 237–244.

Hargrove, D. S., & Keller, P. A. (1997). Collaboration with community mental health centers. In J. Morris (Ed.), *Practicing psychology in rural settings: Hospital privileges and collaborative care* (pp. 67–80). Washington, DC: American Psychological Association.

Heldring, M. (1995). Primary health care for women: What is it and who provides it? *Journal of Clinical Psychology in Medical Settings, 2*, 39–48.

Holden, E. W., & Schuman, W. B. (1995). The detection and management of mental health disorders in pediatric primary care. *Journal of Clinical Psychology in Medical Settings, 2*, 71–87.

House, J., Landis, K., & Umberson, D. (1988, July 29). Social relationships and health. *Science, 241*, 540–545.

Institute of Medicine. (1996). *Primary care: America's health in a new era*. Washington, DC: National Academy Press.

James, L. C., & Folen, R. A. (1999). A paradigm shift in the scope of practice for health psychologists: Training health psychologists to be primary care case managers. *Professional Psychology: Research and Practice, 30*, 352–356.

Kaplan, R. M. (2000). Two pathways to prevention. *American Psychologist, 55*, 382–396.

Kaplan, R. M., Sallis, J. F., & Patterson, T. L. (1993). *Health and human behavior*. New York: McGraw-Hill.

Kazarian, S., & Evans, D. R. (2001). *Handbook of cultural health psychology*. New York: Academic Press.

Kemeny, M. E., & Gruenewald, T. L. (2000). Affect, cognition, the immune system, and health. *Progress in Brain Research, 122*, 291–308.

Kiecolt-Glaser, J. K., & Glaser, R. (1995). Psychoneuroimmunology and health consequences: Data and shared mechanisms. *Psychosomatic Medicine, 57*, 267–274.

Kiesler, C. A. (2000). The next wave of change for psychology and mental health services in the health care revolution. *American Psychologist, 55*, 481–487.

Koocher, G. P., & Pollin, I. (1995). Medical crisis counseling: A new service delivery model. *Journal of Clinical Psychology in Medical Settings, 1*, 291–299.

LaBaron, S., & Zeltzer, L. (1985). Pediatrics and psychology: A collaboration that works. *Journal of Developmental and Behavioral Pediatrics, 6*, 157–161.

Lazarus, R. S. (1999). *Stress and emotion: A new synthesis.* New York: Springer.

Lovallo, W. R. (1997). *Stress and health: Biological and psychological interactions.* Thousand Oaks, CA: Sage.

Mann, T., & Kato, P. M. (Eds.). (1996). *Handbook of diversity issues in health psychology.* New York: Perseus Books.

Mauksch, L. B., & Leahy, D. (1993). Collaboration between primary care medicine and mental health in an HMO. *Family Systems Medicine, 11*, 121–135.

McConnaughy, E. A., DiClemente, C. C., Prochaska, J. O., & Velicer, W. F. (1989). Stages of change in psychotherapy: A follow-up report. *Psychotherapy, 26*, 494–503.

McDaniel, S. H. (1995). Collaboration between psychologists and family physicians: Implementing the biopsychosocial model. *Professional Psychology: Research and Practice, 26*, 117–122.

McDaniel, S. H., Belar, C., Schroeder, C., Hargrove, D. S., & Freeman, C. (2002). A training curriculum for professional psychologists in primary care. *Professional Psychology: Research and Practice, 33*, 65–72.

McDaniel, S. H., & Campbell, T. L. (1986). Physicians and family therapists: The risk of collaboration. *Family Systems Medicine, 4*, 4–8.

McDaniel, S. H., & Campbell, T. L. (1996). Training collaboration. *Families, Systems & Health, 14*, 147–150.

McDaniel, S. H., & Campbell, T. L. (1997). Training health professionals to collaborate. *Families, Systems, & Health, 15*, 353–360.

McDaniel, S. H., & Campbell, T. L. (Eds.). (1999). Genetic testing and families [Special issue]. *Families, Systems, & Health, 17*(1).

McDaniel, S. H., & Campbell, T. L. (Eds.). (2000). Consumers and collaborative care [Special issue]. *Families, Systems, & Health, 18*(2).

McDaniel, S. H., Campbell, T. L., & Seaburn, D. B. (1990). *Family-oriented primary care: A manual for medical providers.* New York: Springer-Verlag.

McDaniel, S. H., Campbell, T. L., & Seaburn, D. B. (1995). Principles for collaboration between health and mental health providers in primary care. *Family Systems Medicine, 13*, 283–298.

McDaniel, S. H., Harkness, J., & Epstein, R. (2001). Differentiation before death: Medical family therapy for a woman with end-stage Crohn's disease and her son. *American Journal of Family Therapy, 29*, 375–396.

McDaniel, S. H., Hepworth, J., & Doherty, W. J. (1992). *Medical family therapy: A biopsychosocial approach to families with health problems*. New York: Basic Books.

McDaniel, S. H., Hepworth, J., & Doherty, W. J. (1997). *The shared experience of illness: Stories of patients, families, and their therapists*. New York: Basic Books.

McDaniel, S. H., & Landau-Stanton, J. (1992). The University of Rochester Family Therapy Training Program. *American Journal of Family Therapy, 20,* 361–365.

McDaniel, S. H., & Speice, J. (2001). What family psychology has to offer women's health: The example of conversion, somatization, infertility treatment and genetic testing. *Professional Psychology: Research and Practice, 32,* 44–51.

McGoldrick, M., Giordano, J., & Pearce, J. (1996). *Ethnicity and family therapy*. New York: Guilford Press.

McPhee, S. J., Lingappa, V. R., Ganong, W. F., & Lange, J. D. (Eds.). (1997). *Pathophysiology of disease: An introduction to clinical medicine* (2nd ed.). New York: McGraw-Hill.

Mikesell, R., Lusterman, D. D., & McDaniel, S. H. (1995). *Integrating family therapy: Handbook for systems, theory, and family psychology*. Washington, DC: American Psychological Association.

Miller, G. E., & Cohen, S. (2001). Psychological interventions and the immune system: A meta-analytic review and critique. *Health Psychology, 20,* 47–63.

Miranda, J., Hohmann, A. A., Attkisson, C. C., & Larson, D. B. (1994). *Mental disorders in primary care*. San Francisco: Jossey-Bass.

Mullen, F. (1998). The Mona Lisa of health policy: Primary care at home and abroad. *Health Affairs, 17,* 118–126.

Nathan, P. E. (1998). Practice guidelines: Not yet ideal. *American Psychologist, 53,* 290–299.

Nicassio, P., & Smith, T. (Eds.). (1995). *Managing chronic illness: A biopsychosocial perspective*. Washington, DC: American Psychological Association.

Noble, J., Levinson, W., Modest, G., Young, M. J., & Greene, H. (1995). *Textbook of primary care medicine*. New York: Mosby.

Olfson, M., Fireman, B., Weissman, M. M., Leon, A. C., Sheehan, D. V., Kathol, R. G., et al. (1997). Mental disorder and disability among patients in a primary group practice. *American Journal of Psychiatry, 154,* 1734–1740.

Olkin, R. (1999). *What psychotherapists should know about disability*. New York: Guilford Press.

Pace, T. M., Chaney, J. M., Mullins, L. L., & Olson, R. A. (1995). Psychological consultation with primary care physicians: Obstacles and opportunities in the medical setting. *Professional Psychology: Research and Practice, 26,* 123–131.

Pasco, G. C. (1983). Patient satisfaction in primary health care: A literature review and analysis. *Evaluation and Program Planning, 6,* 185–210.

Pennebaker, J. W. (Ed.). (1995). *Emotion, disclosure, and health*. Washington, DC: American Psychological Association.

Pew Health Professions Commission. (1995). *Critical challenges: Revitalizing the health professions for the twenty-first century*. San Francisco: University of California Center for the Health Professions.

Physicians' desk reference. (1998). Montvale, NJ: Medical Economics Data Production.

Prochaska, J. O., Norcross, J. C., & DiClemente, C. C. (1994). *Changing for good*. New York: William Morrow.

Pruitt, S. D., Klapow, J. C., Epping-Jordan, J. E., & Dresselhaus, T. (1998). Moving behavioral medicine to the front line: A model for the integration of behavioral and medical services in primary care. *Professional Psychology: Research and Practice, 29*, 230–236.

Radnitz, C. L., Bockian, N., & Moran, A. (2000). Assessment of psychopathology and personality in people with physical disabilities. In R. G. Frank & T. R. Elliott (Eds.), *Handbook of rehabilitation psychology* (pp. 291–310). Washington, DC: American Psychological Association.

Raimy, V. C. (Ed.). (1950). *Training in clinical psychology*. New York: Prentice Hall.

Reiss, S., & Aman, M. G. (1998). *Psychotropic medication and developmental disabilities: The international consensus handbook*. Columbus: Ohio State University.

Richards, P. S., & Bergin, A. E. (1999). *Handbook of psychotherapy and religious diversity*. Washington, DC: American Psychological Association.

Rivo, M. L., & Satcher, D. (1993). Improving access to health care through physician workforce reform: Directions for the 21st century. Third report of the Council on Graduate Medical Education. *Journal of the American Medical Association, 270*, 1074–1078.

Rivo, M. L., Saultz, J. W., Wartman, S. A., & DeWitt, T. G. (1994). Defining the generalist physician's training. *Journal of the American Medical Association, 271*, 1499–1504.

Roberts, A. R. (Ed.). (1995). *Crisis intervention and time-limited cognitive therapy*. Thousand Oaks, CA: Sage.

Roberts, M. C. (Ed.). (1995). *Handbook of pediatric psychology* (2nd ed.). New York: Guilford Press.

Roberts, M. C., Carlson, C. C., Erickson, M. T., Friedman, R. M., LaGreca, A. M., Lemanek, K. L., et al. (1998). A model for training psychologists to provide services for children and adolescents. *Professional Psychology: Research and Practice, 29*, 293–299.

Robinson, P. (1998). Behavioral health services in primary care: A new perspective for treating depression. *Clinical Psychology: Science and Practice, 5*, 77–93.

Rolland, J. S. (1987). Chronic illness and the life cycle: A conceptual framework. *Family Process, 26*, 203–221.

Rolland, J. S. (1990). Anticipatory loss: A family systems developmental framework. *Family Process, 29*, 229–244.

Rolland, J. S. (1994). *Families, illness, and disability*. New York: Basic Books.

Rozensky, R. H., Sweet, J. J., & Tovian, S. M. (1997). *Psychological assessment in medical settings*. New York: Plenum.

Ruddy, N. B., & McDaniel, S. H. (1995). Domestic violence in primary care: The psychologist's role. *Journal of Clinical Psychology in Medical Settings, 2*, 49–69.

Sartorius, N., Ustun, B., Costa e Silva, J.-A., Goldberg, D., Lecrubier, Y., Oremel, J., et al. (1993). An international study of psychological problems in primary care. *Archives of General Psychiatry, 50*, 819.

Schroeder, C. S. (1996). Psychologists and pediatricians in collaborative practice. In R. J. Resnick & R. H. Rozensky (Eds.), *Health psychology through the life span: Practice and research opportunities* (pp. 109–131). Washington, DC: American Psychological Association.

Schroeder, C. S. (1997). Conducting an integrated practice in a pediatric setting. In R. J. Illback, C. Cobb, & H. Joseph (Eds.), *Integrated services for children and families: Opportunities for psychological practice* (pp. 221–255). Washington, DC: American Psychological Association.

Schroeder, C. S., Goolsby, E., & Stangler, S. (1975). Preventive services in a private pediatric practice. *Journal of Clinical Child Psychology, 4*, 32–33.

Schroeder, C. S., & Gordon, B. N. (2002). *Assessment and treatment of childhood problems: A practitioner's guide* (2nd ed.). New York: Guilford Press.

Schulberg, H. C. (2001). Treating depression in primary care practice: Applications of research findings. *Journal of Family Practice, 50*, 535–537.

Schurman, R. A., Kramer, P. D., & Mitchell, J. B. (1985). The hidden mental health network: Treatment of mental illness by nonpsychiatrist physicians. *Archives of General Psychiatry, 42*, 89–94.

Seaburn, D. B., Lorenz, A., Gunn, W., Gawinski, B., & Mauksch, L. (1996). *Models of collaboration*. New York: Basic Books.

Sears, S. F., Danda, C. E., & Evans, G. D. (1999). PRIME-MD and rural primary care: Detecting depression in a low-income rural population. *Professional Psychology: Research and Practice, 30*, 357–360.

Shewchuk, R., & Elliott, T. (2001). Family caregiving in chronic disease and disability. In R. G. Frank & T. R. Elliott (Eds.), *Handbook of rehabilitation psychology* (pp. 553–564). Washington, DC: American Psychological Association.

Shortell, S. M., Gillies, R. R., & Anderson, D. A. (1994). The new world of managed care: Creating organized delivery systems. *Health Affairs, 13*, 46–64.

Spielberger, C. D., Gorsuch, R. L., & Lushene, R. (1970). *The State–Trait Anxiety Inventory manual*. Palo Alto, CA: Consulting Psychologists Press.

Spirito, A. (Ed.). (1999). Empirically supported treatment in pediatric psychology [Special series]. *Journal of Pediatric Psychology, 24*, 87–90.

Spitzer, R. L., Kroenke, K., Linzer, M., Hahn, S. R., Williams, J. B., deGruy, F. V., et al. (1995). Health-related quality of life in primary care patients with mental disorders: Results from the PRIME-MD 1000 study. *Journal of the American Medical Association, 274*, 1511–1517.

Steadman's medical dictionary (25th ed.). (1990). Baltimore: Williams & Wilkins.

Stein, H. F. (1985). *The psychodynamics of medical practice: Unconscious factors in patient care.* Berkeley: University of California Press.

Strosahl, K. (1996). Confessions of a behavior therapist in primary care: The odyssey and the ecstasy. *Cognitive and Behavioral Practice, 3,* 1–28.

Strosahl, K. (2000). The psychologist in primary health care. In A. J. Kent & M. Hersen (Eds.), *A psychologist's proactive guide to managed mental health care* (pp. 87–112). Mahwah, NJ: Erlbaum.

Talen, M. R., Graham, M. C., & Walbroehl, G. (1994). Introducing multiprofessional team concepts and practices into the curriculum: A challenge for health care educators *Family Systems Medicine, 12,* 354–360.

Thompson, R. J., & Gustafson, K. E. (1995). *Adaptation to chronic childhood illness.* Washington, DC: American Psychological Association.

Uchino, B. N., Cacioppo, J. T., & Kiecolt-Glaser, J. K. (1996). The relationship between social support and physiological processes: A review with emphasis on the underlying mechanisms and implications for health. *Psychological Bulletin, 119,* 488–531.

U.S. Department of Health and Human Services. (1999). *Mental health: A Report of the Surgeon General. Executive summary.* Rockville, MD: Author.

Von Korff, M., & Simon, G. (1996). The prevalence and impact of psychological disorders in primary care: HMO research needed to improve care. *HMO Practice, 10,* 150–155.

Walker, L. S., & Greene, J. W. (1989). Children with recurrent abdominal pain and their parents: More somatic complaints, anxiety, and depression than other patient families? *Journal of Pediatric Psychology, 14,* 231–243.

Weiss, B. (2000). *20 common problems in primary care.* New York: McGraw-Hill.

Weissman, M. M., & Klerman, G. (1993). Interpersonal counseling for stress and distress in primary care settings. In G. L. Klerman & W. W. Weismman (Eds.), *New applications of interpersonal psychotherapy* (pp. 295–318). Washington, DC: American Psychiatric Press.

Wingard, L. B., Brody, T. M., Larner, J., & Schwartz, A. (1991). *Human pharmacology: Molecular to clinical.* St. Louis, MO: Mosby Year Book.

Woodwell, D. A. (1999). *The 1997 National Ambulatory Medical Survey: 1997 summary.* Hyattsville, MD: U.S. Department of Health and Human Services, Centers for Disease Control and Prevention, National Center for Health Statistics.

Wright, L., Watson, W., & Bell, J. (1996). *Beliefs: The heart of healing in families and illness.* New York: Basic Books.

Wynne, L., McDaniel, S. H., & Weber, T. (1986). *Systems consultation: A new approach for family therapy.* New York: Guilford Press.

Zeiss, A. M., & Steffen, A. M. (1996). Interdisciplinary health care teams: The basic unit of geriatric care. In L. L. Carstensen, B. A. Edelstein, & L. Dornbrand

(Eds.), *The practical handbook of clinical gerontology* (pp. 423–450). Thousand Oaks, CA: Sage.

Zerbe, K. J. (1999). *Women's mental health in primary care*. Philadelphia: W. B. Saunders.

Zilberg, N. J., & Carmody, T. P. (1995). New directions for the education of clinical psychologists: The primary care setting, the VA's PRIME program, and the in-depth generalist model. *Journal of Clinical Psychology in Medical Settings, 2,* 109–127.

II

THE PRACTICE OF PRIMARY
CARE PSYCHOLOGY

II

5

PSYCHOLOGICAL PRACTICE IN PRIMARY CARE SETTINGS: PRACTICAL TIPS FOR CLINICIANS

WILLIAM E. HALEY, SUSAN H. McDANIEL, JAMES H. BRAY, ROBERT G. FRANK, MARGARET HELDRING, SUZANNE B. JOHNSON, ELSIE GO LU, GEOFFREY M. REED, AND JACK G. WIGGINS

Primary care is now the linchpin of the new health care delivery system. This focus on primary care creates both threats to the conventional independent practice of psychology and new opportunities for collaboration

This chapter was originally published as an article in *Professional Psychology: Research and Practice, 29*, pp. 237–244. Copyright 1998 by the American Psychological Association (APA). Reprinted with permission.

The original article was developed by the Committee for the Advancement of Professional Practice (CAPP) Task Force on Primary Care, APA. The members were William E. Haley, Department of Gerontology, University of South Florida; Susan H. McDaniel, Department of Family Medicine, University of Rochester; James H. Bray, Department of Family Medicine, Baylor College of Medicine; Robert G. Frank, College of Health Professions, University of Florida; Margaret Heldring, Director of Research, National Issues Project; Suzanne Bennett Johnson, Center for Pediatric Psychology and Family Studies, University of Florida; Elsie Go Lu, Fullerton, CA; Geoffrey M. Reed, Practice Directorate, APA; and Jack G. Wiggins, Fountain Hills, AZ.

The original article was completed with support from the APA CAPP as part of the efforts of the Task Force on Primary Care. We greatly appreciate the support of Randy Phelps and Anthony Chuukwu and the comments made by Robert Resnick on a draft of the article.

Correspondence concerning this material should be addressed to William E. Haley, Department of Gerontology, SOC 107, University of South Florida, Tampa, Florida 33620. Electronic mail may be sent to whaley@luna.cas.usf.edu.

and direct participation in the delivery of primary care services. In terms of threat, a psychologist whose solo or small-group practice has focused predominately on private, office-based psychological assessment and psychotherapy faces increasing economic pressures created by market-driven reforms, managed care, and other limits to traditional fee-for-service psychological services (Frank & VandenBos, 1994). Managed care systems increasingly rely on primary care providers (including physicians in family medicine, general internal medicine, pediatrics, and sometimes obstetrics–gynecology) to screen and triage patients with a wide range of medical and psychological problems. These physicians are the gatekeepers for referral to all specialists, including psychologists. In terms of opportunity, psychologists who shift their practices to work closely with these providers as part of an integrated delivery system are most likely to continue to deliver services to a wide variety of patients (Shortell, Gillies, & Anderson, 1994).

Many patients who present in primary care settings have psychological problems that often are not detected or treated appropriately by primary care providers (Higgins, 1994). Some of these patients present with relatively minor physical symptoms (e.g., undifferentiated pain, sleep disturbance) that may be closely related to psychological stressors. Other patients have chronic illnesses that are associated with significant psychological distress and disability. Psychological disorders among primary care patients are associated with increased disability, increased use of health services, and reduced quality of life (e.g., Callahan, Hui, Nienaber, Musick, & Tierney, 1994; Kroenke & Mangelsdorff, 1989; Spitzer et al., 1995). These findings and the demonstrated effectiveness of psychological interventions (e.g., Barlow, 1994) suggest that psychologists are needed to ensure adequate treatment of psychological disorders in primary care.

With this opportunity, however, comes a need for psychologists to adapt their practice style to the unique characteristics of primary care. A number of sources describe in detail the current state of knowledge concerning the interface of psychology, health care, and primary care (e.g., Belar & Deardorff, 1995; Blanchard, 1994; McDaniel, Hepworth, & Doherty, 1992), though little of this information is aimed at practitioners who are skilled in general psychology practice but know little of the culture and expectations of medical group practice. In this article, we present an overview of practical clinical issues faced by practitioners who plan to work in primary care settings. We do not address financial, business, and contractual issues related to primary care; these essential issues have been addressed in the American Psychological Association (APA) Practitioner's Toolbox Series and related APA publications (e.g., APA Practice Directorate, 1996; Yenney & APA Practice Directorate, 1994). With the caveat that ethical practice requires an in-depth understanding of issues related to practice in health care settings, we offer 10 tips for developing successful psychological services in a primary care setting.

PRACTICAL TIPS FOR CLINICIANS

1. *Don't wait for your patients to come to you.*

Conventional practice models that rely on physician referral of patients to a psychologist have a number of serious flaws. First, an extensive literature documents that primary care physicians commonly fail to detect common psychological problems, such as depression and anxiety (Eisenberg, 1992; Higgins, 1994), and that up to 50% of medical patients commonly fail to follow through on mental health referrals (e.g., Callahan, Hendrie, et al., 1994). This failure to follow through is partly due to the inconvenience of making separate medical and psychological appointments but is also because of the stigma associated for many Americans with mental disorders. Furthermore, unless referrals to a psychologist are handled very skillfully by the physician, patients may hear the message that their problems are not real or are "all in their head"—not a mindset conducive to encouraging follow-up for psychological services. Organized delivery systems that have been the most successful in merging psychology and primary care services have located the two programs in the same clinic. Physical proximity has a number of advantages (Bray & Rogers, 1995; McDaniel, Hepworth, & Doherty, 1992). When the behavioral health group is located at the same site as the rest of health care, it is simpler for the primary care provider to personally introduce the patient to the psychologist. During the introduction, the referring physician or advanced practice nurse can address any questions arising about the referral. Location of the behavioral health group on the same site as the primary care group has other advantages. Psychological services are viewed as part of the primary care system, overcoming the stigma often associated with outside referral. In addition, locating behavioral health services within or next to primary care clinics ensures that behavioral health services are visible to those who refer services. All providers are facing increased demands for efficient practice. Referrals requiring inconvenience by the referring individual are less likely to occur. By having behavioral health services adjacent to the primary care service, the primary care provider is frequently reminded of this referral option. Perhaps the most critical variable is accessibility. The most important communications that occur within such relationships may take place in informal consultations between the physician or other provider and the psychologist. If the psychologist is not available, it's almost impossible to build strong relationships with physicians and other health care providers. As one member of a physician–psychologist pair who were attempting to build a collaborative linkage reported, "Across the street is too far" (Bray & Rogers, 1995, p. 136). Although physical proximity helps ensure referrals from primary care providers, more sophisticated interactions are also available. Integrating psychology into primary care can facilitate the referral process. Although there are many considerations involved in determining the best model for structure of a practice, creation of a common entry point for primary care and behavioral health services is generally the most helpful to consumers. Consolidation of services at the point of entry requires integrated information systems. Common information systems ensure patients will not have to provide insurance and demographic information across multiple providers—a feature patients appreciate. Office overhead can be reduced by this approach as well. Another option is for psychologists interested in health care to consider outreach to patients in their homes. Home health care is one of the fastest growing areas in health care; the number of licensed home health agencies grew by 50% between 1990 and 1995 (Prospective Payment Assessment Commission, 1996). To date, psychologists have directed little attention to this sector of care. As this area grows, however, it will be important for psychologists to consider how to adapt their services to this delivery approach. In general, home health care has focused on the delivery of health services to individuals with chronic illnesses. Because health care spending for these individuals constitutes approximately 68% of all health care spending (Frank & VandenBos, 1994), this sector is likely to grow in the future. For example, during the last few years, the use of home-based services has grown dramatically in the treatment of individuals with severe and persistent mental illness. Psychologists providing services to individuals with chronic health needs will need to consider how best to provide their services within the context of a home health care delivery system.

2. *Many of your patients really are sick.*

Most psychologists are taught to ask questions about a new patient's physical health as part of any assessment. It is important to do much more than a cursory review of physical functioning, especially if the patient is referred from or within a primary care setting. This process involves careful interviewing of the patient and family about relevant health events and current functioning, with particular emphasis on the patient's subjective view of his or her illness. It also involves active collaboration with the patient's primary care physician or nurse practitioner. Although careful health assessment is critical, communication among providers is equally important to avoid unnecessary duplication of effort. In fact, one of the most helpful aspects of practicing in a medical setting is the opportunity for the psychologist to get immediate consultation from the physician concerning the likely impact of medical problems on psychological functioning. For example, information from lung function tests or about staging or prognosis of cancer may be essential in planning psychological services for some patients (Haley, 1996). Close collaboration with a physician, particularly when the focus of treatment is on a physical symptom, can also minimize malpractice risks related to accusations of practicing medicine without a license (Belar & Deardorff, 1995). Psychologists may be accustomed to helping patients develop confidence and trust in their feelings. However, psychologists may spend so much time focused on thoughts and emotions that they overlook the importance of physical experience. Physical functioning affects individual and family dynamics and vice versa, much more than is acknowledged in most theories of psychotherapy (McDaniel et al., 1992). Although we psychologists often accuse physicians of somatic fixation (overfocusing on the physical and ignoring the psychosocial), we must guard against psychosocial fixation (overfocusing on the psychological experience and avoiding the somatic; McDaniel, Campbell, & Seaburn, 1990). For example, it is reasonable to assume that with a man who had a heart attack 2 years ago and now presents with marital difficulties, a detailed medical history is likely to be relevant to the assessment of a relationship conflict. Detailed information about the prognosis of a given illness and its likely effects on the patient's daily functioning should be integrated into the psychologist's treatment plan. Beyond the realities of any physical limitations or disabilities, illness or accidents serve as wake-up calls to the human psyche. They are reminders of our mortality and, as such, affect a patient and family's functioning and defensive structure. Some people respond to threatened loss by strengthening their emotional and practical resolve: They order their priorities, increase intimacy with those they care about, and do the most with the time they have left. Others go underground with their psychic response to physical events, presenting with child behavior problems, marital problems, work problems, depression, or anxiety. A thorough assessment may reveal these problems to be directly linked to their own or a loved one's illness, disability, or death (McDaniel et al., 1992). For that reason, psychologists need to obtain a thorough physical history for all patients and their close family members, regardless of presenting complaint.

3. No more Lone Ranger—Join the posse.

Collaboration with other health care providers requires an integrated, biopsychosocial model of patient care (McDaniel et al., 1992). Together with the rest of the health care team, psychologists can provide patients with comprehensive services that avoid artificial distinctions between mental and physical health. Successful collaboration involves the following: developing a collegial relationship with the referring provider, eliciting his or her explanation about the patient's problems, clarifying any questions, and securing his or her support for the psychological treatment. Joint sessions with the physician or nurse can be particularly useful for initial sessions, particularly for patients who are reluctant regarding referral (especially somatizing patients), for patients who experience a dramatic change in functioning, and for patients for whom the psychological and the physical complications are unusually complex. These sessions can take place either at the physician's or the psychologist's office, depending on each professional's schedule and accessibility. The psychologist should be prepared to spend some of the time scheduled for a session traveling back and forth to the physician's office if the patient would benefit. Even a brief, 15-minute session with both mental and physical health care providers together can be a very powerful experience for patients struggling with health problems. Arguably the most important trend in the current health care marketplace is increasing levels of integration. The traditional lines separating hospitals, providers, and insurers have begun to blur. There is increasing consumer demand for so-called one-stop shopping in health care services. Only by integrating various aspects of health care can a seamless, coordinated continuum of health care be provided. Organized delivery systems may encompass primary care providers, specialists, ambulatory care centers, home health care agencies, and so on. These systems may be owned by or associated with insurance products, grow out of established health maintenance organizations, or be based on provider service networks. Signposts of this increasing integration include "downsizing of acute care capacity, consolidation of programs and services, development of cross-institutional clinical service lines [horizontal ellipsis], expansion of the number of primary care physicians, and growth in both primary care and multi-disciplinary group practices" (Shortell, Gillies, & Anderson, 1994, p. 62). All of these changes are clearly characterized by an increased emphasis on primary care. Furthermore, these patterns of service delivery are based largely on multidisciplinary teams. These changes provide important opportunities for us psychologists, but in order to participate, many of us need to make significant changes in the way we practice our profession. In particular, participation in the health care system will require the ability to work closely in more flexible ways with other specialists. Participation within primary care delivery—whether as a specialty consultant or as a full team member—depends on developing strong working alliances with other professionals. However, our training has often not equipped us to become team players, given the solo practitioner competitive models of many academic faculties and clinical practices (Belar, 1995). A number of variables facilitate the development of collaborative interdisciplinary relationships (Tsukuda, 1990). One of the most basic is a working knowledge of other professions' methods of training and their approach to problem conceptualization and inquiry; also important is a respect for their areas of expertise. Psychologists can take practical and incremental steps toward developing team-based patterns of practice. An early step might be to develop group practices of psychologists. Such groups help render the theoretical diversity within our profession an advantage, rather than a liability, and can relieve psychologists of feeling overwhelmed and burdened by the sense of having to know everything. Another step is for groups to establish informal linkages with primary care physicians. These linkages strengthen referral bases, educate us psychologists about the needs for our services that exist on the front lines of health care, and prepare us to participate in integrated health care delivery systems. These linkages can eventually lead to the development of multidisciplinary primary care practices with psychologists as integral members. Assessment and enhancement of provider–patient communication is one of the most important roles for the psychologist serving on a health care delivery team. Patients and families learn about the patient's illness and its management from the health care provider. However, numerous studies have documented patients' poor understanding of their medical condition and its treatment (e.g., Johnson et al., 1982; Page, Verstraete, Robb, & Etzwiler, 1981). In order to be effective, the psychologists must learn about the patient's illness, including what the physician believes the patient and family have been told. The psychologist's discussion with the patient and family about the illness and its management will often uncover numerous discrepancies between the patient's and the medical provider's perceptions. The psychologist should review these discrepancies with the medical members of the team and devise a plan to correct the miscommunication. The psychologist may meet with the patient and the medical provider to ensure a clearer understanding of patient needs and provider expectations. The psychologist may devise both tools that become part of the clinic's standard practice for assessing patient knowledge and improved methods for ensuring accurate understanding of medical provider recommendations at each clinic visit (e.g., easy-to-understand, written, take-home health care information). In other words, the psychologist can serve as a consultant to a health care team about an individual patient, or the psychologist can serve as a consultant to the health care clinic or system in which the health care team operates. Both are important roles.

4. Psychotherapy ain't enough.

Psychologists practicing in clinical settings have traditionally thought of themselves as mental health practitioners, with psychological testing and psychotherapy as their major tools of the trade. This model is now considered a limited and limiting formulary. Political and marketplace variables have shaped a new health care environment over the last several years. The opportunities to apply psychology's fund of knowledge to social and public health problems like violence, drug and alcohol abuse, family dysfunction, and community breakdown are increasingly evident to psychologists and policymakers alike. Cutting-edge programs designed to prevent or address these problems are collaborative and systemic in nature. The key words of the emerging health care system, especially at the primary care level, are integration, prevention, outreach, and community-oriented. In response, psychologists must broaden their roles and contributions to both the private sector and public health care systems. Psychologists must be more visible in the community. If mental health practitioners remain sequestered in private offices while providing traditional services, they risk oblivion. In short, psychotherapy ain't enough. Psychologists in primary health care settings can and do provide a variety of services and play multiple roles (Bray, 1996; Resnick & Rozensky, 1996). These services and roles include clinical and consultation services, education, research, personal and program development, community outreach, policy making, and political advocacy. Capitated reimbursement systems will increasingly provide incentives to primary care practitioners to collaborate with psychologists demonstrating generalist skills and personal and professional flexibility. The range of services psychologists can provide should include the following:

1. Clinical services include assessment and evaluation; individual, family, and group psychotherapy; psychoeducational groups; referral for additional services; crisis intervention; and follow-up care. Settings may vary from the exam room, to the home, to the bedside on an inpatient unit or in a nursing home and may include such topics as dealing with terminal illness and bereavement.
2. Consultation services may be provided to the patient or family (or both) as well as to other health care providers, including physicians, nurse practitioners, and nurses; consultation may occur on a regular schedule or may be an impromptu curbside consult in the exam room. Topics for consultation can range from conventional mental health issues to such areas as evaluation of competency to consent to treatment.
3. Education services may be provided, such as those offered to the entire health care team as well as to the patient, family, and community and continuing medical education on health psychology, behavioral health, psychological disorders, the provider–patient relationship, compliance with the medical regimen, stress management, and interviewing skills.
4. Psychologists can be particularly useful in establishing a research program in a health care setting that could provide necessary data about health care utilization, outcomes, patient satisfaction, prevalence and incidence, and effective treatment and health promotion strategies.
5. Primary health care providers and psychologists must increasingly integrate with their local communities in a manner that supports a continuum of care and reflects cultural sensitivity and competence; psychologists can help develop these partnerships and facilitate this level of collaboration.
6. Psychologists can work with all components of a primary health care team to provide ongoing review, growth, and change to the team and its programs.
7. With a health care market and environment in flux, it is essential for providers at the primary care level to inform public policy and participate in the political process; psychologists can work with their primary care partners to be a credible voice and advocate for a comprehensive model of primary health care at the state and federal levels.
8. Psychologists have opportunities to support the professional development of their primary care partners and colleagues in

the form of Balint Groups (groups that reflect on the doctor–patient relationship), stress management seminars, and other self-care activities. Although other members of the health care team typically take the lead in educating the patient and family about a disease, the psychologist can prove to be an important partner in the design, administration, and evaluation of educational programs. Psychologists are well aware of both the motivational and disruptive role anxiety can have on learning. They understand the importance of shaping behavior and reinforcing successive approximations to new skill acquisition. They appreciate the limits a child's cognitive developmental level will place on what the child learns about an illness and how much responsibility for health care is reasonable to expect from a child and how much should be shared by other family members. Psychologists view the patient in a social context of family, work, and friends and quickly appreciate both the assets and liabilities this social context can present. Once again, the psychologist's role in addressing these issues is valuable and important at both the individual patient level and the health care system level. Psychologists are experts at assessing and facilitating change in human behavior. Behavior is critical to patient care, whether the illness is acute or chronic and whether the intervention is an invasive medical procedure or an instruction to change lifestyle habits. The treatment of acute illness often requires behavioral interventions for some specified period of time (e.g., taking daily medication for an infection; drinking extra fluids for a cold; using crutches for a broken leg). Chronic diseases typically demand complex, lifelong behavioral interventions (e.g., administering daily insulin injections and testing blood glucose for patients with insulin dependent diabetes mellitus; quitting smoking, reducing fat and salt intake, and increasing exercise for patients with heart disease; avoiding triggers and selecting appropriate medications for patients with asthma). Even invasive medical procedures conducted in an outpatient clinic or in a hospital require a number of patient cooperative behaviors (e.g., venipuncture; placement of a catheter or a nasogastric tube; mammogram procedures). The psychologist can serve as the expert who not only assesses patient behavior, but also designs strategies to enhance cooperative or healthy behavior. This expertise can be offered at the individual level or at the broader level of system design. Medical illness is associated with more than physical distress; it often generates considerable emotional distress as well (Kroenke &

Mangelsdorff, 1989). Disease diagnosis and invasive medical procedures are typically associated with considerable anxiety in both the patient and family. Many individuals actually avoid health care (e.g., refuse screening tests; avoid going to the dentist) because of psychological or medically related fears. Others feel guilty, blaming themselves for the onset of the disease. Others may become depressed as they face physical limitations or a shortened life span. Still others become angry at providers' "incompetence" or at a family member's unwillingness to appropriately care for his or her disease. Once again, the psychologist has a special appreciation for the affect generated by physical disease or dysfunction within the patient and within the family unit. The psychologist can (a) assess the type and extent of this affect and how it affects the patient's health care and (b) devise methods to reduce stress and provide more successful coping strategies.

5. *Patients don't know why they are seeing you unless you tell them.*

Most primary care patients with psychosocial problems initially present to their physician with physical symptomatology rather than psychological or behavioral symptoms. Even in cases where patients are aware of psychological problems, such as anxiety, depression, or marital conflict, they frequently want their primary care physician to treat the problem (Bray & Rogers, 1997). Thus, the referring physician and treating psychologist need to consider this context when working together. A patient may also be reluctant to consult with a psychologist because of negative stereotypes of mental health providers, concerns that the physician is covertly indicating that the patient is "crazy," or fears about talking to a new provider. In some cases, physicians may feel frustrated with their treatment of the patient and the patient may misinterpret that frustration, resulting in feelings of rejection or a sense that the physician does not believe that the symptoms are real. Particularly when patients have physical complaints, the physician and psychologist need to avoid the message that the physical symptoms are not real health problems and are just in the patient's head. A useful therapeutic approach is to have the physician indicate that he or she needs help from a specialist but that the physician will still provide other needed medical care (i.e., the physician is not dumping the patient). An alternative is for the physician to indicate that the problem the patient is currently experiencing is beyond the physician's expertise and thus requires specialty care (Bray & Rogers, 1997). The psychologist needs to be aware of this context when accepting referrals from a primary care provider (McDaniel et al., 1992). In addition, it is important for the psychologist to negotiate with the primary care provider how he or she (the psychologist) intends to collaborate and what kind of information the provider expects from the psychologist about the patient (Bray & Rogers, 1997). Most primary care physicians expect some type of communication about their patients from consulting doctors (Rakel, 1995). The amount and frequency of such information varies considerably among providers, although a typical format involves a paragraph or two describing the diagnosis, formulation, and treatment recommendations. However, if no follow-up information is provided, primary care physicians are likely to stop making referrals to these providers. During the first meeting with patients, it is important to clarify their understanding about why their physician referred them to the psychologist. Misconceptions or concerns can be addressed at this time, and reassurance can be offered that the psychologist will be working with their physician to provide optimal treatment for their problems. It is also important to clarify confidentiality issues so that the patient understands and is in agreement with the psychologist and physician sharing information (Bray & Rogers, 1995). A joint meeting with the patient, physician, and psychologist (usually in the physician's office) may be a means to deal with patients who are resistant to referral (Bray & Rogers, 1997; Dym & Berman, 1986). Such meetings have the added benefit of allowing the psychologist to model for the physician the type of rationale for referral that will be well-received by patients in medical settings.

6. *Hurry up.*

There are important differences in practice styles between physicians and psychologists (Bray & Rogers, 1997). In a typical outpatient primary care setting, a physician sees at least one patient every 15 minutes. In a similar manner, when patients visit a primary care physician, they are generally presenting with problems for which they seek immediate and concrete solutions. When seeking a consultation from a psychologist or other provider, "physicians are likely to expect clear statements of observed facts and specific intervention recommendations" (Pace, Chaney, Mullins, & Olson, 1995, p. 125). Most outpatient psychologists, on the other hand, see individual clients for 45 to 50 minutes. For psychologists who use interpersonal, psychodynamic, or family systems orientations, work with an individual may be viewed as an experiential and personal undertaking focused more on methods and processes than concrete solutions (Pace et al., 1995). From these premises, areas of culture clash can be anticipated. One of the most striking has to do with the relationship between work and time. Within medical settings, the pace is far more rapid and results are expected far more quickly. Psychologists are likely to experience the perception of time within these settings to be markedly different from that of more familiar environments. Psychologists may find themselves feeling caught by expectations to produce unreasonable outcomes within insufficient periods of time. There are several basic strategies for managing some of the potential time-related problems that are inherent in physician–psychologist collaborations in primary care settings. Most important is a shift to a problem-focused approach to consultation—at least in one's initial encounters with a patient and early in the development of a relationship with a particular physician. Thus, it is extremely important to focus and clarify the referral question (Belar & Deardorff, 1995). Physicians who are not used to working with psychologists may not be good at this and may make only a general request for consultation or at best write a note such as "Evaluate for possible depression." It may be necessary to talk further with the physician to find out exactly what is expected from the consultation, what specific information is needed, and what working hypotheses are to be confirmed or disconfirmed. It is also important to understand how this information may be relevant for the physician's treatment plan for the patient. Such clarification provides the framework for a focused consultation that can more quickly provide the answers the physician is seeking. This discussion can also reveal any unreasonable expectations on the physician's part, such as getting a lifelong alcohol abuser to stop drinking so that he or she can have a liver transplant the following month. Psychologists may initially be uncomfortable with providing what may seem like a limited and incomplete assessment. However, recommendations for further exploration of additional areas or for expanded psychological treatments can easily be made in the consultation report. In a similar manner, reports need to be completed quickly—if possible on the day the patient was seen. This style may be different for psychologists used to spending hours laboring over assessment reports. It is also vital for the psychologist to be aware of and respect the demands on the physician's time. Thus, the psychologist should try to focus his or her own requests for information and background. The physician is likely to be more willing to invest time in discussing patients at length as it becomes clear that this is useful. For example, McDaniel (1995) described conducting occasional conjoint patient visits with a physician colleague. Such conjoint visits are obviously an intensive use of provider time. Opportunities for such innovative and more intensive forms of work are more likely to become available once a strong working alliance is established. On a similar topic, although many psychologists have been trained to write lengthy and elegant reports, such notes will not be read in medical settings. A standard rule of thumb is that anything longer than a page will not be read. In instances where a longer note is necessary to provide details and documentation, a summary section of about a paragraph will be necessary to summarize the most critical information. In medical settings, case presentations are also typically brief and to the point. The medical team will not be interested in a 15-minute speculative report; rather, the essential findings, along with specific recommendations, are required.

7. Don't give any tests you can't carry in a briefcase.

Psychological assessment can represent one of the unique contributions psychologists make in medical settings (Belar & Deardorff, 1995). Physicians and other professionals in health care settings value objective information on patients' depression, cognition, or daily functioning. In fact, over time, physicians may come to view psychological assessment as equivalent to laboratory tests; they may become comfortable in citing the patient's depression score or score on a cognitive screening test as an indication of severity and improvement over time. In addition to selecting instruments with ideal psychometric features, psychologists should also consider the following variables when selecting assessment instruments for use in medical settings: the acceptability to medical patients, the acceptability to physicians and other health care providers, and the time required for the assessment. Patients in medical settings are likely to be particularly averse to assessments that lack face validity and that strongly emphasize severe psychopathology. Some instruments may also not be appropriate because they are too lengthy, especially if the patient's stamina is poor. In medical settings, patients may be seen with more severe sensory or physical impairments, including deafness, blindness, and paralysis. Some patients may also be too weak or impaired to complete certain tests. In addition, psychologists should be careful that instruments have been appropriately normed and validated on populations seen in primary care settings, such as older adults. Specific suggestions for assessment instruments useful with medical populations have been reviewed elsewhere (Belar & Deardorff, 1995), and adaptations necessary for assessment of older adults with medical problems or sensory impairments are reviewed in several recent sources (Haley, 1996; Kaszniak, 1996). Use of brief screening instruments by primary care providers can also enhance the identification of patients who might benefit from referral to the psychologist (Higgins, 1994).

8. *Stand up for what you know, and ask about what you don't know.*

Psychologists and primary care physicians have important complementary areas of expertise. The psychologist who begins work in a primary care setting must demonstrate his or her psychological expertise to other health care providers. This expertise should include the ability to offer decisive opinions about behavioral issues in patient care; the psychologist should also be an expert on research findings concerning psychological aspects of health. Particularly in clinical training settings, physicians are accustomed to challenging each other and citing recent research related to patient care; psychologists have much to offer in this type of exchange. In many ways, this ability for a well-informed psychologist to communicate as a peer with the physician is one of the unique contributions psychologists, as opposed to social workers and counselors, make to health care settings. Psychologists should communicate their knowledge while avoiding unnecessary jargon—a courtesy that will likely be returned by experts in biomedicine. Psychologists should not allow themselves to be bullied by the occasional overly brusque physician who may not be accustomed to having a PhD, PsyD, or EdD as a colleague. In most cases, collaboration that is based on mutual respect can be developed. The psychologist should also demonstrate a willingness to be trained and educated on topics beyond his or her expertise. Physicians do not generally expect psychologists to understand the complexities of medical conditions and the terminology involved. However, if physicians are convinced that the psychologist has something to offer, they are generally willing to explain. Comfort and familiarity with a new setting and vocabulary comes fairly quickly in the context of such two-way relationships. Although psychologists bring with them generic training in psychological assessment and treatment, they will be most successful in a medical care setting if they can translate their knowledge and expertise into the particular health care setting they are working in. In some cases, this may mean developing an in-depth knowledge about a particular disease or population, whereas in other settings, a broad variety of medical problems are seen across the life cycle. In either case, the psychologist will need to acquire necessary medical information from other members of the health care team and will need to adapt psychological expertise to the special needs and concerns of medically ill or physically compromised patients. It would be a mistake to assume that training and experience in a traditional mental health setting can be immediately and directly translated to the larger medical health care context without appropriate training, supervision, or consultation related to health psychology and medical family psychology. Successful integration into the health care team will require an honest appraisal by the psychologist of the limitations of prior experience and training as well as a willingness to acquire new knowledge and skills and to learn to practice in a context that has different norms than mental health settings. The psychologist who is comfortable admitting ignorance and asking questions will quickly acquire the information needed through conversations, workshops on collaboration, and reading. The psychologist who wishes to appear medically sophisticated and is too embarrassed to ask for translations of medical jargon runs the risk of confusing the patient further and can never be a truly effective member of the health care team.

9. *No specialists allowed—Be prepared for anything and everything.*

Psychologists working in primary care settings need to be generalists (Bray, 1996). Psychologists can expect to see a tremendous variety of medical and psychological problems that have a broad range of impact and frequently do not fit *Diagnostic and Statistical Manual of Mental Disorders* criteria. Although it is common for psychologists who are specialists in health psychology or behavioral medicine to focus on a particular medical disorder, such as the psychological aspects of diabetes or obesity, or a particular aspect of psychological practice, such as biofeedback or clinical neuropsychology (e.g., see Blanchard, 1994), in many primary care settings such specialization is not an advantage. Patients present with a wide variety of medical problems or with multiple medical disorders. Even patients seen in settings that focus on a specific medical problem, such as diabetes or Alzheimer's disease, often have several complex medical and psychosocial problems. Thus, psychologists in primary care settings must remain aware of advances in a variety of areas and be competent to conduct initial screenings for the full range of psychosocial disorders. Physicians in primary care settings will expect the psychologist to be an expert on the full range of psychosocial and mental disorders. Patients with schizophrenia or with bipolar disorder are commonly seen in primary care settings, and these conditions are often managed by the primary care physician. Thus, the psychologist will commonly be asked to provide a consultation relevant to the adequacy of psychological–psychiatric care delivered by another mental health practitioner. In medical settings, patients can present with numerous physical and psychological symptoms that psychologists are unprepared for by academic training or life experiences. The diversity of presenting problems in primary care is often overwhelming. Psychologists lacking experience in primary care settings may be poorly prepared for these encounters; thus, experience and training in medical settings are essential. For example, in medical settings, psychologists will be exposed to medical problems that are commonly discussed or viewed only in the medical office. Patients with amputations, sores, rashes, or coughs will routinely offer these for inspection to the psychologist. Psychologists may also encounter patients who are severely or terminally ill and will have the experience of working with patients who die during the course of treatment. In supervising psychology interns in medical settings, these stressful events are commonly a focus of supervision, and psychologists who are redirecting their practices toward medical populations must expect that the transition may be stressful.

10. Refer out when necessary.

Whether the psychologist works in a primary care setting seeing a variety of patient problems or in a specialty clinic seeing a particular type of patient, the need to refer will rapidly become apparent. Working as a member of a health care team typically demands relatively rapid consultation about a large number of patients. Rarely does the psychologist have the luxury to do comprehensive psychological assessments that demand multiple test procedures and extensive personal interviews. Rather, the psychologist sees the patient, often for less than an hour, and makes a recommendation. Just as the physician may elect to refer the patient for additional diagnostic studies, the psychologist may elect to refer the patient for more extensive psychological evaluation. For example, the psychologist may be concerned about the cognitive capability of the patient and may refer the patient for a full intellectual assessment. Or the psychologist may be concerned that the patient may have a significant thought or affective disorder and may refer the patient for a more complete personality assessment. Most patients will not need this type of extensive evaluation, but the psychologist must be prepared to evaluate relatively quickly and triage those patients that do. In a similar manner, the psychologist member of a health care team does not have the time or the training to provide the appropriate psychological treatment for all patients that come to his or her attention. Once again, the psychologist must be prepared to assess relatively quickly what type of intervention the patient needs and identify an appropriate referral to provide that care. Just as the physician may refer a patient to a specialist for a particular medical procedure, the psychologist may refer the patient to a behavioral specialist with expertise in a particular type of care. For example, the overweight, newly diagnosed patient with diabetes may be referred to a psychologist who specializes in weight reduction programs. The patient with a substance abuse problem may be referred to a specialist in the treatment of drug or alcohol abuse. The family of an asthmatic adolescent who is being nonadherent with medical care as a way of expressing angry independence may be referred to a family therapist. In most cases, the psychologist makes an assessment as to whether the psychosocial problems presented can be rather rapidly addressed within the context of the clinic environment over the course of two or three sessions. These cases may be treated within the confines of the health care clinic, whereas more complex cases, which require either more extensive intervention or specialized intervention outside the training and experience of the psychologist, are typically referred elsewhere. However, the psychologist provides an important link between the psychological specialist to whom the patient is referred and the heath care team. This link occurs at the point of referral when the referring psychologist informs the specialist as to the reasons for the referral. It also occurs later when the patient returns to the health care clinic for routine care and the reasons for the referral are reviewed and any progress is noted. If warranted, additional contact with the specialist to whom the patient was referred may be initiated. At the time of the referral and on subsequent occasions when additional communication with the specialist may occur, issues of patient consent, assent, and confidentiality must be addressed.

FINAL COMMENTS

To survive in a changing health care environment, psychologists must increasingly define themselves as health care providers and be prepared to contribute to patient care in primary care settings. Although many of the assessment and intervention skills that are appropriate in traditional clinical settings can be adapted to the primary care setting, psychologists must proceed with caution when beginning work in health care settings. They must ensure that they practice within the scope of their expertise and competence and should seek out consultation and advanced training in health psychology as appropriate. Psychology has a great deal to offer to primary care; both health care providers and patients welcome psychologists' skills in attending to the full range of medical and psychosocial problems that make good health care more than delivery of medical services. Psychologists who can successfully focus their training in this area or shift their practices to health care settings will find this a very rewarding area of practice.

REFERENCES

American Psychological Association Practice Directorate (with Coopers & Lybrand, L. L. P.). (1996). *Contracting with organized delivery systems: Selecting, evaluating, and negotiating contracts.* Washington, DC: American Psychological Association.

Barlow, D. H. (1994). Psychological interventions in the era of managed competition. *Clinical Psychology: Science and Practice, 1,* 109–122.

Belar, C. D. (1995). Collaboration in capitated care: Challenges for psychology. *Professional Psychology: Research and Practice, 26,* 139–146.

Belar, C. D., & Deardorff, W. W. (1995). *Clinical health psychology in medical settings: A practitioner's guidebook.* Washington, DC: American Psychological Association.

Blanchard, E. B. (1994). Behavioral medicine and health psychology. In A. E. Bergin & S. L. Garfield (Eds.), *Handbook of psychotherapy and behavior change* (4th ed., pp. 701–733). New York: Wiley.

Bray, J. H. (1996). Psychologists as primary care providers. In R. H. Rozensky & R. J. Resnick (Eds.), *To your health: Psychology across the lifespan* (pp. 89–100). Washington, DC: American Psychological Association.

Bray, J. H., & Rogers, J. C. (1995). Linking psychologists and family physicians for collaborative practice. *Professional Psychology: Research and Practice, 26,* 132–138.

Bray, J. H., & Rogers, J. C. (1997). The linkages project: Training behavioral health professionals for collaborative practice with primary care physicians. *Families, Systems, and Health, 15,* 55–63.

Callahan, C. M., Hendrie, H. C., Dittus, R. S., Brater, D. C., Hui, S. L., & Tierney, W. M. (1994). Improving treatment of late-life depression in primary care: A randomized clinical trial. *Journal of the American Geriatrics Society, 42,* 839–846.

Callahan, C. M., Hui, S. L., Nienaber, N. A., Musick, B. S., & Tierney, W. M. (1994). Longitudinal study of depression and health services use among elderly primary care patients. *Journal of the American Geriatrics Society, 42,* 833–838.

Dym, B., & Berman, S. (1986). The primary health care team: Family physician and family therapist in joint practice. *Family Systems Medicine, 4,* 9–21.

Eisenberg, L. (1992). Treating depression and anxiety in primary care: Closing the gap between knowledge and practice. *New England Journal of Medicine, 326,* 1080–1084.

Frank, R. G., & VandenBos, G. R. (1994). Health care reform: The 1993–1994 evolution. *American Psychologist, 94,* 851–854.

Haley, W. E. (1996). The medical context of psychotherapy with the elderly. In S. Zarit & B. Knight (Eds.), *A guide to psychotherapy and aging: Effective clinical interventions in a life-stage context* (pp. 221–239). Washington, DC: American Psychological Association.

Higgins, E. S. (1994). A review of unrecognized mental illness in primary care. *Archives of Family Medicine, 3,* 908–917.

Johnson, S. B., Pollak, R., Silverstein, J., Rosenbloom, A., Spillar, R., McCallum, M., et al. (1982). Cognitive and behavioral knowledge about insulin-dependent diabetes among children and parents. *Pediatrics, 69,* 708–713.

Kaszniak, A. W. (1996). Techniques and instruments for assessment of the elderly. In S. Zarit & B. Knight (Eds.), *A guide to psychotherapy and aging: Effective clinical interventions in a life-stage context* (pp. 163–219). Washington, DC: American Psychological Association.

Kroenke, K., & Mangelsdorff, D. (1989). Common symptoms in ambulatory care: Incidence, evaluation, therapy, and outcome. *The American Journal of Medicine, 86,* 262–266.

McDaniel, S. H. (1995). Collaboration between psychologists and family physicians: Implementing the biopsychosocial model. *Professional Psychology: Research and Practice, 26,* 117–122.

McDaniel, S. H., Campbell, T., & Seaburn, D. (1990). *Family-oriented primary care: A manual for medical providers.* New York: Springer-Verlag.

McDaniel, S. H., Hepworth, J., & Doherty, W. J. (1992). *Medical family therapy: A biopsychosocial approach for families with health problems.* New York: Basic Books.

Pace, T. M., Chaney, J. M., Mullins, L. L., & Olson, R. A. (1995). Psychological consultation with primary care physicians: Obstacles and opportunities in the medical setting. *Professional Psychology: Research and Practice, 26,* 123–131.

Page, P., Verstraete, D., Robb, J., & Etzwiler, D. (1981). Patient recall of self-care recommendations in diabetes. *Diabetes Care, 4,* 96–98.

Prospective Payment Assessment Commission. (1996, March 1). *Report and recommendations to the Congress.* Washington, DC: Author.

Rakel, R. E. (1995). The family physician. In R. E. Rakel (Ed.), *Textbook of family practice* (5th ed., pp. 3–19). Philadelphia: W. B. Saunders.

Resnick, R. J, & Rozensky, R. H. (Eds.). (1996). *Health psychology through the lifespan: Practical and research opportunities.* Washington, DC: American Psychological Association.

Shortell, S. M., Gillies, R. R., & Anderson, D. A. (1994). The new world of managed care: Creating organized delivery systems. *Health Affairs, 13,* 46–64.

Spitzer, R. L., Kroenke, K., Linzer, M., Hahn, S. R., Williams, J. B. W., deGruy, F. V., et al. (1995). Health-related quality of life in primary care patients with mental disorders: Results from the PRIME-MD 1000 Study. *Journal of the American Medical Association, 274,* 1511–1517.

Tsukuda, R. A. (1990). Interdisciplinary collaboration: Teamwork in geriatrics. In C. K. Cassell, D. E. Riesenberg, L. B. Sorenson, & J. R. Walsh (Eds.), *Geriatric medicine* (2nd ed., pp. 668–678). New York: Springer-Verlag.

Yenney, S., & American Psychological Association Practice Directorate. (1994). *Business strategies for a caring profession: A practitioner's guidebook.* Washington, DC: American Psychological Association.

6

FAMILY PSYCHOLOGY IN PRIMARY CARE: MANAGING ISSUES OF POWER AND DEPENDENCY THROUGH COLLABORATION

SUSAN H. McDANIEL AND JERI HEPWORTH

Practicing psychologists, by nature and by training, traditionally work independently to provide a wide variety of assessment, treatment, and consultative services. The opportunity to participate in integrated care delivery, and the evolution of health care delivery and reimbursement, are changing that tradition of independence. With systems theory, family psychology offers a way to conceptualize, operationalize, and evaluate this collaboration with patients, families, and the rest of the health care team. The literature in family health psychology to date focuses on the treatment of health problems such as lifestyle changes, chronic illness, terminal illness, somatization (McDaniel, Hepworth, & Doherty, 1992, 1997), cancer (Friedrich, 1997; Wellisch, 1995), childhood illness (Wood, 1995), and women's health (McDaniel & Speice, 2001).

This chapter is an expansion of a plenary address, "Cooperation and Solidarity: New Strategies for Healthcare Systems," given by Susan H. McDaniel at the Lindauer Psychotherapie Wochen in Lindau, Germany, on April 29, 1999.

Systems theory also illuminates the workings of health care teams (McDaniel, Campbell, & Seaburn, 1990; Seaburn, Lorenz, Gunn, Gawinski, & Mauksch, 1996).[1] In recent times, the complexity of health care and the recognition that multiple people are needed to deliver high-quality services has led to a growing movement named *Collaborative Family Health Care* that began in the United States and has spread through Europe and other continents (Bloch, 1993, 1994; see also http://www.chfcc.org). Collaborative care requires a different approach to the traditional use of power and hierarchy to manage the patient's, family's, and team's roles in the care of illness and disease.

In this chapter we synthesize this emerging field, with an emphasis on the role of the family psychologist. We describe the role of psychologists as part of collaborative family health care in primary care settings, with particular attention to managing issues of power and dependency in the doctor–patient–family relationships. *Families* in this context refers to the significant others involved in a patient's health care, or "any group of people related biologically, emotionally, or legally" (McDaniel et al., 1990). These relationships are characterized by a "network of mutual commitment," part of the definition of *family* recognized by the National Institute of Mental Health (Pequegnat & Bray, 1997). We focus on the importance of families in primary care and health-oriented psychotherapy and conclude with descriptions, difficulties, and examples of interprofessional collaboration from primary care practice.

Collaboration among patients, families, psychologists, and primary care clinicians allows for prevention and the comprehensive treatment of many prevalent primary care problems, whether acute, chronic, psychosomatic, or terminal. It is rare with any chronic or complex problem for one primary care professional to accomplish all that is needed. The addition of a psychologist to a primary care team allows for a host of problems to be addressed successfully and comprehensively.

> For example, Eleanor,[2] a 37-year-old investment banker, made frequent visits to her family physician, Dr. Keller, with questions about rashes and blemishes, abdominal cramps, and lumps in her throat. At each visit her complaints initially seemed appropriate, but later in the interview she asked if the symptoms could signify cancer. Without using unnecessary tests, Dr. Keller was usually able to help Eleanor recognize a pattern of excessive fear and worry. Eleanor was generally reassured, and even joked about her concerns, but still made frequent visits.
>
> After a series of three visits within several weeks, Dr. Keller asked Eleanor to meet with a family psychologist in the office to address her

---

[1]See also articles in the journal *Families, Systems & Health* (http://www.fsh.org).
[2]All case material used in this chapter is factual and drawn from our work in primary care. Names and other identifying information have been changed to protect confidentiality.

concerns and fears. Dr. Keller made it clear that she could not promise that Eleanor would never develop cancer but that they would continue to work together to monitor and screen as necessary. Although initially reluctant, Eleanor was willing to meet with Dr. Keller and therapist for a short visit and elected to return for a series of visits with the psychologist. After a few visits, Eleanor recognized how her sense of responsibility and control in her family and work lives contrasted with her inability to control all aspects of her health. In sessions with her husband, she realized how her sense of responsibility and fear of losing control had increased her attention to her physical symptoms. With increasing vigilance, she had increasing anxiety about relatively minor physical symptoms. As Eleanor and her husband began to share more responsibility for home and children, Eleanor felt less anxiety in general, including less anxiety about her health, and she decreased her office visits.

Collaboration among physicians, psychologists, patients, and families is required for multifaceted cases such as Eleanor and her family. Cases that reflect a complicated mix of psychosocial and medical issues are daily occurrences in primary care practices. When patients and families have few strategies to cope with these problems, and with the psychosocial challenges of dis-ease and disease, they frequently turn for assistance to their primary care professionals. In collaborative practice, primary care physicians can then turn to psychologists. The collaborative family health care approach focuses on relationships in three areas: (a) patients in relation to families and significant others; (b) psychologists in relation to other members of the health care team; and (c) relationships among the patient, the family, and the health care system. Each kind of relationship involves a choice about how to manage hierarchy and power that can result in health or dysfunction.

POWER AND COLLABORATION

The most effective way of using one's power as a psychologist, physician, or other health professional, is to give it away—that is, to recognize the power of the patient and the power of the family as partners with professionals in health care. *Collaboration* means, simply, "working together" (*American Heritage Dictionary*, 1991). It is a distribution of power that recognizes each party's point of view. It is also a functional interdependency among patients, families, and the health care team that counteracts the difficulties that can arise from the traditional, one-up, one-down power hierarchy of most professional–patient relationships.

Power as a Relational Concept

Primary care psychologists frequently deal with the abuses of power in the family that are at the root of many health problems. Freud was correct when at the beginning of his career he claimed that family violence itself (not *fantasies* of family violence) is the cause of so many emotional disorders (Freud, 1893/1962, 1898/1962). Clinicians now know that the prevention and treatment of family violence, specifically sexual and physical abuse, would go a long way toward treating many of our patients' emotional and somatizing problems. Many patients with a history of childhood neglect or abuse somatize (Katon, 1985). They focus on physical experience and do not learn an emotional language to process affect. In this way, they acknowledge pain without speaking directly about the abuse or the intense emotions experienced.

It is not surprising that many of the common primary care problems are relationally based (McDaniel & deGruy, 1996). Many scientific and humanistic advances in the 20th century involved understanding the part in relation to the whole. In the early 1900s, the Russian philosopher Bakhtin (1927/1997) declared the romantic notion of self-wrong; he said we *only* have our relational selves. Harry Stack Sullivan (1953) focused on the importance of interpersonal relationships in the development of mental health problems. It is the disruption of these relationships that often results in prevalent primary care problems, such as domestic violence, depression, and the somatoform disorders. The primary care psychologist helps the health care team understand the patient's individual psychodynamics as well as his or her context and its relation to the presenting complaint.

Power and dependency are relational concepts with great influence on the etiology and the treatment of many primary care disorders. Domination and dependency are two opposing, relational strategies that we humans, whether patients or professionals, use to manage our existential angst. Traditional relationships between health professionals and patients replicate the parent–child hierarchical relationship, in which the professional-as-parent knows and understands all, and the patient-as-child is the passive recipient of the professional's knowledge, advice, and caring. For some groups of patients, this authoritarian approach is effective, perhaps because it is familiar. These patients wish for the professional to be powerful so they can be dependent. However, for many patients and for many professionals, this kind of relationship may encourage resistance.

Definition of Power

The *American Heritage Dictionary* (1991) lists four definitions of *power*, the first being "the ability or capacity to act or perform effectively." It is this first definition that is embraced in collaborative health care. Not until the fourth definition is power defined as "the ability or official capacity to exercise control or authority." It is the delusion of control, often outside awareness, that causes trouble in physicians' roles as clinicians. Unfortunately, it is this fourth definition of power, the one that implies the domination and "power-over," that is associated with medicine by patients and many health professionals as well.

Problems of power and dependency are well known in medicine. Problems related to the doctor–patient hierarchy are especially prominent when there are differences between the physician and patient with regard to class, race, and ethnicity. It is well documented that patients from lower socioeconomic classes get less information, less talk, and less reinforcement from physicians than patients of a higher social class (Candib, 1995). Less information translates into less power for the patient. This search for information and equity in power is reflected in the recent trend in the United States in which many people with resources augment or abandon allopathic medicine for a variety of alternative therapies, preferring a clinician–patient relationship that respects patient autonomy and is more of a partnership. Psychologists on primary care teams may facilitate partnership in place of hierarchy in the doctor–patient relationship. For example, ensuring that patients and family members feel involved in making important decisions regarding treatment reduces the chance of noncompliance with the plan.

What professionals believe about power over others influences the way they structure treatment, the questions they ask, and the outcomes they seek. The truth is that, in an existential sense, people are all fundamentally powerless. As professionals, physicians or psychologists may cover up their fear that they have limited power. Instead, they may wield the power that comes with status as a way to be "helpful" to their patients—or at least that is what they tell themselves. Jungian analyst Adolf Guggenbuhl-Craig (1971) wrote extensively about the Shadow side of the psychotherapist—the destructive part in all of us that may deny our own aggression or ignorance. A patient can become the holder of all illness, all problems, all sins, and the clinician the holder of all health, all knowledge, all truth. When this polarization occurs, the patient is reinforced for continuing to be weak and dependent, and the professional is reinforced for being all-knowing and powerful. In this power-as-domination model both parties are incomplete and symptomatic. With such polarizing responses it can become difficult for patients and clinicians to share their expertise and create mutually agreeable health care plans. Effective care requires conscious attention to ways to minimize extreme positions and devise consensual understanding and collaborative treatment.

Collaboration as Shared Power

For any health professional, the antidote to power as domination is shared power, or caring. *Caring* consists of being present, listening, demonstrating a willingness to help, and an ability to understand (Suchman, 1997). Caring is operationalized through a fully collaborative relationship with the patient. It involves many of the foundational skills of professional psychology: active listening and empathy, in addition to careful diagnosis. Collaboration involves respectful partnership and shared power, power that is distributed among health professionals, patients, and families in the seeking of appropriate diagnoses and mutually acceptable treatment plans. The psychologist on the primary care team both models and consults about these skills.

A collaborative exchange is characterized by a spirit of shared inquiry, people talking *with* rather than *to* each other. Inherent in this approach is the idea that the power of each party is fully recognized: the power of the physician, the psychologist, and the nurse to diagnose and suggest treatment; the power of the patient to make sense of the illness experience, decide and embark on the best course for treatment; and the power of the family or social group to provide a healing environment, or not. In collaborative family health care both groups—the family and the interprofessional team—are critical to the activation and empowerment of patients.

The realities of medical practice, particularly the power hierarchies that can structure interactions, do not magically disappear. Yet ongoing attention to mutual respect and empowerment of all parties is a transforming process that can offset some of these barriers and create more satisfying and effective care relationships.

COLLABORATION WITH PATIENTS AND THEIR FAMILIES

Reynolds Price (1999), in an essay about illness and God, pointed to the importance of empowerment for patients and the role that family relationships can play in encouraging or discouraging healthy behaviors:

> I'm always shocked to be reminded how many people choose, quite early in their lives, to begin their deaths—and death is by no means always a mere cessation of heart and brain activity . . . a number of people choose lifelong mental and spiritual deaths in late adolescence, if not sooner—the curse of surrender to the backwash of time and the all but irreparable friction of trifling or too demanding human interactions. (p. 66)

A *collaborative* approach entails helping people with an illness choose life and active involvement in their social contexts and their options about care. Including families and meaningful social contexts expands options and possibilities for patients and clinicians.

The Family as Care Providers

Part of the role of the family psychologist on the primary care team is to help other professionals understand the power of the family in treating a patient. The move in the United States from hospital-based to ambulatory care has brought new emphasis on the family as care providers. The family is the first circle of health specialists to respond when a family member is sick or disabled, and they are the context of care for a majority of chronically ill individuals in this country (McDaniel et al., 1990). Almost every important health behavior is a family activity, or strongly influenced by the family (Doherty & Campbell, 1988). Family ghosts are often in the examination or hospital room each time a patient is seen. A patient may enter the hospital for some psychosomatic problem and be treated extensively and successively, only to return home and relapse because family members do not agree with the treatment plan. Conversely, some treatments for patients succeed precisely because the family is committed to providing what is needed for their loved one to heal.

Research on families and health documents the powerful influence of the family on health and illness and the benefits of family interventions (Campbell & Patterson, 1995), often delivered by psychologists. For example, Ewart, Taylor, Kraemer, and Agras (1991) demonstrated that couples communication training can lower blood pressure in couples in which one member has hypertension. In another study, Morisky et al. (1983) showed that family intervention improved compliance with blood pressure medication, resulting in reduced blood pressure and a 50% reduction in cardiac mortality. Other research has shown the cost-effectiveness of family psychoeducational programs for caregivers of patients with Alzheimer's or other incapacitating diseases (Mittelman, Ferris, Shulman, Steinberg, & Levin, 1996).

Research also documents how sharing power, and including patients and families as partners in health care, results in better health outcomes. For example, Fallowfield and colleagues, working in England (1994), documented the importance of effective communication when a physician discusses diagnosis and treatment options for women with breast cancer. Her research showed that all women desired information and participation in care but differed in their desire to make the final treatment decision with regard to breast conservation versus mastectomy. Some wished to make this decision; others chose to have their surgeon make it. Collaboration means that patients' perspectives are honored and partnerships are tailored to the needs and desires of each patient and family situation. The power involved in decision making is shared, and it is often the psychologist's role to help the team recognize how to collaborate with the patient and family in making these important decisions.

A Focus on Health as Well as Illness and Pathology

Primary care psychologists need to be trained to build on people's strengths to cope with illness or disorder. This focus is an important complement to the traditional pathology focus of biomedicine. It is helpful for health professionals to understand the culture and health beliefs of the patient and family, which are frequently very different than those of the medical culture (Rolland, 1994; Wright, Watson, & Bell, 1996). In general, clinicians must see patients and families not only as customers for services but also as "colleagues" or partners in the delivery of health care. Moves by managed-care companies to emphasize patient satisfaction in the job assessments of professionals make this a financial reality in much of American health care.

Making Families Part of the Health Care Team

In spite of the importance of incorporating the patient's significant relationships into the assessment and treatment of primary care problems, many physicians (and some mental health professionals) continue to view dealing with patient's family members as an irritating and unnecessary part of the job. Levine and Zuckerman (1999), in the journal *Annals of Internal Medicine*, suggested that the persistent tendency in medicine to equate families with trouble derives from Western medicine's almost exclusive focus on the individual. They argued for an "ethic of accommodation"—the need to negotiate care plans that recognize the capacities and limitations of family members. They suggested providing family members with timely information, training, compassionate recognition of their anxiety, guidance in defining their roles and responsibilities, and support for setting fair limits on the extent of personal sacrifice required to care for the patient. These are management strategies that may facilitate care but stop short of creating a process of shared inquiry or collaborative care. The family psychologist can assist a health care team in moving beyond a model that simply accommodates families to a collaborative model that incorporates family knowledge, beliefs, and resources while still respecting the patient's autonomy and confidentiality. Consider the following example:

> A beloved middle-aged, obese priest had a sudden seizure of unknown origin. He regained consciousness but suffered a debilitating stroke while in the hospital. The priest's physician had known him for years and was distraught over the sudden deterioration of this relatively young man. There was a history of family turmoil and abuse, demonstrated in a physical altercation on the hospital ward in which the police were called. At this point, the primary care physician requested a psychologist to consult with the family. For the month of hospitalization until his death, the psychologist[3] met two to three times a week with the family to discuss the series of health care decisions that had to be made, allow them to express their painful feelings, increase their sense of agency, begin the grieving process, and help them care for themselves and each other during this trying time. She also engaged the priest's religious family, some of whom came to family meetings and helped them as they tried to help the priest's parishioners deal with their loss. She consulted regularly with the primary care physician, to stay current with the priest's medical condition

---

[3]The psychologist for this case was Ellen Poleshuck, PhD.

and to allow him to discuss the stresses of caring for this dying man. (At one point, the physician reported a frightening nightmare in which the priest suddenly woke up and yelled disparaging comments at him.) When the priest died, the psychologist and the physician attended the funeral. The psychologist moved from a crisis intervention phase to medical family therapy that centered on grief but also addressed long-standing individual and family problems.

In this case, the psychologist did much more than simply accommodate a patient and his family or support a dying patient and his physician. The psychologist took initiative, helping determine who should be involved and facilitating that involvement. She provided the opportunity for the physician to articulate his feelings, so he could be more consciously present with the patient and family. By involving more people in the process, the psychologist also received assistance and support herself. Much of this work is the domain of excellent psychological training. Other aspects especially reflect the medical family therapy model.

MEDICAL FAMILY THERAPY

Medical family therapy is a biopsychosocial approach to psychotherapy for people with health problems that activates the inherent strength in each patient and family (McDaniel et al., 1992). Medical family therapy focuses on the role of illness in the emotional lives of patients and families. It is a metaframework (Breunlin, Schwartz, & MacKune-Karrer, 1992), an overarching perspective that attends to the biological and the psychosocial factors in any psychotherapy—cognitive–behavioral, psychodynamic, systems, and so on.

Agency and Communion

Medical family therapy has two primary goals: increasing (a) *agency* and (b) *communion* (Bakan, 1969). Taken together, agency and communion reflect individual autonomy in a relational context. Helgeson (1994), in a review of the research on agency and communion, concluded that both agency and communion are required for optimal health. Unmitigated agency, or unmitigated communion, is associated with increased morbidity.

Agency is the personal experience of power, the sense that one can make personal choices in dealing with illness and the health care system. It is a sense of activism about one's own life in the face of all that is uncertain when facing illness. Activating agency requires collaborating with the patient and asking questions such as: "What do you think caused your problem?", "Why do you think it started when it did?", "What kind of treatment should you receive?", "Has anyone else in your family faced an illness similar to this?", and "What might make healing now a struggle for you?"

Working to increase a patient's and family's sense of agency does not imply that psychological health will cure people of disease. When and how belief becomes biology has yet to be fully understood. They are interrelated, but to imply that patients directly cause their illnesses through emotional weakness, or can control their cures through emotional strength, is dangerous: Patients will blame themselves not only for their illness but also for their treatment failures. Psychologists must continue researching links between emotional and physical health and empower patients to do whatever they can to facilitate healing (Belar & Deardorff, 1995; Lovallo, 1997; McDaniel et al., 1992; Roth-Roemer, Kurpius, & Carmin, 1998). The second underlying goal for medical family therapy is communion. Serious illness or disability is an existential crisis that can isolate people from those who care for them, with significant health consequences (House, Landis, & Umberson, 1988). *Communion* refers to strengthening emotional and spiritual bonds that can be frayed by illness, disability, and contact with the health care system. It is the sense of being cared for, loved, and supported by a community of family members, friends, and professionals. It is a way of encouraging healthy interdependency.

Medical Family Therapy Techniques

Specific clinical techniques to facilitate agency and communion can be woven into any type of psychotherapy (see Exhibit 6.1). The central feature of medical family therapy is *biopsychosocial integration*, which involves recognizing the biological features of any psychosocial problem and the psychosocial aspects of any biological problem. This means interweaving psychosocial with health questions during an interview. Sometimes this can be accomplished by simply eliciting the illness story. Patients and families always have a story about their illness, their search for a diagnosis, their treatments, and their interactions with the health care system. This story builds the therapeutic alliance and provides information for assessing the patient and the system. It also promotes healing. Arthur Frank (1995) wrote poignantly about the importance of witnessing and testimony as a way to enhance agency, a sense of personal power:

> As wounded, people may be cared for, but as storytellers, they care for others. The ill, and all those who suffer, can also be healers. Their injuries become the source of the potency of their stories. Through their stories, the ill create empathic bonds between themselves and their listeners . . . But telling does not come easy, and neither does listening. Seriously ill people are wounded not just in body but in voice. They need to become storytellers in order to recover the voices that illness and its treatment often take away. (p. xii)

Recognize the biological features of any problem.
Elicit the illness story.
Respect defenses, diminish blame and guilt, and accept unacceptable feelings.
Ask about the family illness history and illness meanings.
Attend to developmental issues.
Help regain the family's identity.
Provide psychoeducation and support.
Increase the patient's and family's sense of agency.
Draw on individual and family strengths and resources.
Maintain communication.
Empathize.
Facilitate an open-ended termination.

As stories are presented, it is often evident that family members vary in their recollections and meanings about illness. These differences can lead to conflict, avoidance, and other disruptive patterns. Medical family therapy includes recognition of these differences and patterns as normal responses to abnormal crises. This is demonstrated clinically by respecting individual defenses, diminishing their blame and guilt, and accepting their unacceptable feelings. Members of a family are frequently in different places with regard to recognizing and accepting the illness. One member seems to deny the illness and advocate for life to go on uninterrupted, while another seems to focus solely on illness and the caregiving it requires.[4] Both positions are important for family functioning. Making space for each point of view without judgment often allows the family to reach consensus or understanding over time, moving from polarized positions to closer acceptance as a group. Family histories often contain illness stories that may illuminate preferred coping styles. People usually respond to an illness on the basis of their own experience or significant others' experience. If a woman's father died suddenly of a heart attack, she will respond differently to her husband's heart attack than if she had no cardiac disease in her family. As with other issues in psychotherapy, asking about previous experience with similar problems is revealing.

The individual and family's life cycle stage is also a factor in how the family is affected by illness (Rolland, 1994). Adolescents with diabetes, for example, are notorious for not taking good care of themselves. They are faced with a serious responsibility at the same developmental period in which they want to affirm their immortality, question authority, and increase acceptance with peers. The interaction of illness with life span developmental issues is always relevant. The goal, whenever possible, is to help the family tend to developmental challenges while also tending to the illness. Families frequently

---

[4]This process can also happen on health care teams, across specialists, where one professional presents a very optimistic prognosis while another is more pessimistic.

reorganize to care for the patient during the crisis, or diagnostic, phase of an illness. They may then become stuck in that way of functioning, perhaps becoming hypervigilant and neglecting other individual and family tasks. Medical family therapy works to help them regain the patient's and family's identities by reinstating important daily rituals, and holidays, but still include room to care for the illness and acknowledge emotional responses to the illness.

Many patients and families fear that their emotional reactions to an illness are signs of weakness or psychopathology. Medical family therapy provides psychoeducation and support to help patients and families recognize responses that are normative. Psychoeducational support groups (Campbell & McDaniel, 1997; McDaniel & Speice, 2001), videotapes, and self-help books can be useful adjuncts in this endeavor. More intensive psychotherapy is warranted when emotional symptoms are severely exacerbated by illness crises. An open-ended termination allows families to return to the psychologist for additional work or support as needed, such as when an illness reaches a new and difficult stage or a family experiences a new developmental challenge.

Treating a Broad Spectrum of People and Problems

Psychologists in primary care have the opportunity to use these skills with families who would never walk into a traditional mental health office. Many people find it less stigmatizing to receive treatment from a primary care physician than from a psychologist for common concerns such as anxiety, depression, or attention-deficit disorders. In addition, psychologists in the primary care setting expand treatment access for somatizing patients and those with serious emotional disturbance who refuse to use the traditional mental health treatment systems. These include somatizing patients; patients with serious emotional disturbance who refuse to use the traditional mental health treatment system; and patients with commonplace, biopsychosocial, primary care problems. A 10-year-old with asthma who wants to go to slumber parties is in conflict with her parents, who fear asthma attacks at other families' homes. The physician recognizes that the child wants to be "normal" while the parents want to protect their child from a dangerous illness. This is a family that will benefit from a physician's early intervention, support, and education. The intervention may disclose further conflict, such as parental disagreement about their daughter's treatment, that might mirror other marital discord. If the primary care level of intervention is not sufficient, both physician and family will benefit from a psychologist's expertise in parent–child behavior and negotiation skills. Other common examples for intervention include couples with sexual apprehension after a husband's heart attack, or adult children negotiating care of an elderly parent.

GUIDELINES FOR SUCCESSFUL
INTERPROFESSIONAL COLLABORATION

With regard to the skills necessary for partnering with other professionals, it is important to acknowledge that it is possible to provide decent patient care when professionals simply *tolerate* each other. With uncomplicated patients, this may be appropriate. We suggest that *cooperation* reflects providers' efforts to recognize each other's care and adapt plans accordingly. In contrast, *collaboration* involves the shared inquiry and treatment plan previously described. The more complex and difficult the patient, the more important it is that professionals move along the continuum from tolerating each other, to cooperating, to full collaboration.

Pediatrician Ellen Perrin (1999), calling for a model of collaboration between pediatricians and psychologists, distinguished professional collaboration from *help*. She wrote:

> The difference between "collaboration" and "help" is that in a collaboration the participants have the same goal, relatively equal status and power, but different skills and knowledge that contribute to attaining the goal. Helpers, on the other hand, have the same goal, but they have. . .generally less power and status. Collaboration works best when two partners approach the effort with the idea that each has knowledge and skills and opportunities that the other needs, and wants to achieve a goal that both hold in common. Each member of the collaboration should gain something in the process, and the product should be better than either of its separate parts can provide. (p. 58)

Overcoming Barriers to Collaboration

If cooperation involves respect and accepting differences, collaboration is a process of using those differences to more effectively achieve a common goal. There are, however, many barriers to professional collaboration, including the sociopolitical differences afforded the different health care professions. Unfortunately, most education of health and mental health professionals occurs in separate silos, where each profession is socialized to believe that they are the good ones, the chosen ones, and the rest are bad. . .or at least limited.

Although each profession has a proud history, there is a well-developed hierarchy of status and responsibility within medicine. A nurse holds a different status than a physician, a pediatrician different from a cardiac surgeon, and a social worker different than a psychologist. These status differentials are overtly supported through pay scales or insurance reimbursement, resulting in differential personal incomes for different professionals. Resentment about these differences can stymie collaboration. Advocacy at the national level, and the development of personal relationships at the local level, can allow professionals to work through, or avoid, these professional turf battles.

Collaboration within health care systems requires this same awareness. When professionals partner together respectfully, they do not pretend that status differences are absent. They recognize the perceived and actual differences, but they learn enough about each other's culture and language to lean on one another.

Learning about culture, even professional cultures, requires interest and time spent in that culture, with members of that culture. Clinical education and internship experiences can help foster increased understanding (Hepworth & Jackson, 1985; McDaniel & Campbell, 1997; Seaburn et al., 1996). Clinicians in practice can make efforts to increase collegial relationships to learn how to respond to cultural differences (Bray & Rogers, 1995, 1997).

Cultural differences between physicians and psychologists reflect different training experiences, values, and theoretical differences. Psychologists and physicians use specialized language and may have different views on health and healing, use of time, and concern with confidentiality. Physicians, for example, are generally trained to locate pathology, and remove or cure it, all in a brief period of time. Psychologists are allowed longer sessions, and they work with patients over time to change behavior as well as established beliefs or patterns of interaction. Psychologists are trained to work with patients, so that all communications are privileged and confidential. Physicians also support confidentiality but extend this privilege to sharing information with a larger health care team. Without an understanding of these differences in culture and working styles, attempts to work together can result in mutual blaming and power struggles.

Once differences among professionals are acknowledged, clinicians can find ways to use their unique strengths in caring for patients. Communication is central in this process. It should include:

- the nature of referral or collaboration,
- the mechanism of communication (chart notes, phone calls, etc.),
- the role of each clinician with the patient and family,
- the nature of confidentiality,
- regular recognition when a colleague does good work, and
- a plan about how to give constructive negative feedback and resolve disagreements.

These guidelines highlight the importance of clear boundary and role definitions in the development of a common mission. Basic to this process is comfort with one's own professional role and competence and an understanding of how one's role fits with responsibilities of other professionals. Training together can offer useful opportunities to learn these relationships and practice working together (Bray & Rogers, 1995, 1997; Gawinski, Edwards, &

Speice, 1999; Hepworth, Gavazzi, Adlin, & Miller, 1988; McDaniel & Campbell, 1997; Patterson, Scherger, Bischoff, & McIntosh-Koonitz, 1998).

The Case for Collaborative Practice in Primary Care

Collaboration requires a change in paradigm for the physician and the psychologist. What is the evidence that it matters? Collaborative care has been demonstrated in randomized controlled trials to produce better outcomes with problems such as depression, somatization, health behavior changes (e.g., tobacco and other substance use, exercise, etc.), and caregiving coping (British Family Heart Study, 1994; Katon et al., 1995, 1996; Mittelman et al., 1996; Morisky et al., 1983; Smith, Monson, & Ray, 1986; Smith, Rost, & Kashner, 1995). It is often these collaborations that produce clinical innovation with patients that are currently underserved or difficult to treat (Campbell & McDaniel, 1997). In addition, collaboration provides reciprocal support for the stressful work of caring for complex patients.

A family physician colleague, John Cordes, reminded us of how these factors come together in daily collaborative practice:

> Recently, a pregnant patient, Mary, came for a "routine prenatal visit" during which her boyfriend Alan, the baby's father, suddenly emerged from the waiting room. I had not met him before, so was curious as I introduced myself and attempted to get to know him. Mary had just moved out of their apartment and back to her mother's house due to escalating tensions in the couple's relationship. Alan made it clear that he wanted Mary and their baby back, and wanted me to help him convince Mary to return. In a brief conversation, Alan and Mary described concerns about parenting, and how their fears about past experiences were leading them to argue about their future.
>
> During the conversation, I stepped out of the room and found my colleague, a family therapist, and seized the window of opportunity that had presented itself in this encounter. Both partners were willing to talk, and the therapist was able to meet with them briefly and have them agree to return for a longer visit later that week. In the meantime, I was able to meet with another scheduled patient and then return briefly with Mary and Alan. Both seemed pleased to have had the opportunity to speak with the therapist and me, and were looking forward to their next visit with the therapist. The outcome is still uncertain, but having had a therapist so immediately available was a powerful reinforcer for getting this couple into therapy. It helped me feel that I wasn't alone with their care (J. C. Cordes, personal communication, March 10, 2000).[5]

---

[5]Dr. Cordes provided this account as part of a continuous quality improvement survey of collaboration experience in Jeri Hepworth's family practice clinic.

This example reflects the advantages of having psychologists available on site in a primary care office. In this case, the physician realized that the family stress was so high that the intervention would require a degree of involvement and expertise that he could not offer at that time. The couple was in crisis and wanted some help as soon as possible. The opportunity to have a psychologist partner meet with the family immediately, even for a short time, was a timely and effective intervention.

Models of Collaboration

Most collaborative relationships, however, do not occur in the same physical location (see chap. 7, this volume, for a discussion of collaboration in independent practice; see also Bray & Rogers, 1995, 1996.) Michael Glenn (1987), and later Seaburn et al. (1996), have noted that coordination of care is easier when clinicians have more contact with one another. Glenn described a continuum of collaborative practice settings, from the traditional model, to the collaborative-but-traditional model, to the collaborative model. The traditional model involves the typical referral patterns in which clinicians practice separately in different locations and have limited contact with one another through initial referral and termination letters and occasional telephone consultations. The collaborative-but-traditional model involves closer consultation in which the psychologist and the referring physician both work in the same hospital or ambulatory setting. Even though the two professionals work at the same site, this model maintains the separation of physical and psychosocial concerns. Although the clinicians are geographically available to each other, the referral and communication patterns are traditional, like those clinicians who work off site. The collaborative model changes the practice paradigm and makes use of geographic availability to construct comprehensive, coordinated, biopsychosocial treatment plans between primary care clinicians and psychologists to share the care of complex, time-intensive patients. The collaborative model should be obvious to patients so that they identify both the psychologist and the physician as their clinicians, and recognize that they work together.

Benefit to Professionals

Along with the importance of collaborating with patients and families to increase their sense of agency and communion, it is also critical—amidst all this stress and strain of changing health care systems, changing political climates, symptomatic patients and families, and challenging work systems—for health professionals to attend to their own sense of agency and communion. It is easy to become burned out and depleted and lose a sense of effectiveness and satisfaction at work. This is where a good multidisciplinary team of colleagues can function like a supportive family does in private life: to provide feedback and support when the responsibilities of professionals seem overwhelming. It is not uncommon in primary care settings for psychologists to provide primary support and advice regarding self-care to the other members of the team. Sometimes this role is formalized, as when psychologists lead a support or consultation group (Balint, 1957; Botelho, McDaniel, & Jones, 1990).

Although psychologists may provide important support to the team, it is also true that this is often a two-way street: Other professionals on the team may provide valuable support and consultation to the psychologist. In addition, it is valuable to seek support from psychologists outside one's own setting, to provide perspective and understanding. None of us is wise to function in today's health care arena without carefully attending to our own needs.

CONCLUDING COMMENTS

Collaboration is an alternative to the traditional use of power in health care relationships. Rather than ignoring or just accommodating families, psychologists on health care teams have the opportunity to incorporate family knowledge, beliefs, and resources into patient care. Working together as professionals can result in clinical innovation and better outcomes that benefit patients and families. Collaboration can also provide support and stimulation that benefit us as professionals. It is possible to be independent and effective on our own, but as a team of professionals, patients, and family members, we are greater than the sum of our parts.

REFERENCES

American heritage dictionary (2nd college ed.). (1991). Boston: Houghton Mifflin.

Bakan, D. (1969). *The duality of human existence*. Chicago: Rand McNally.

Bakhtin, M. M. (1997). Freudianism: A critical sketch. In P. Morris (Ed.), *The Bakhtin reader* (pp. 38–48). London, Arnold. (Original work published 1927)

Balint, M. (1957). *The doctor, his patient, and the illness*. New York: International Press.

Belar, C. D., & Deardorff, W. W. (1995). *Clinical health psychology in medical settings: A practitioner's guidebook*. Washington, DC: American Psychological Association.

Bloch, D. (1993). The "full-service model": An immodest proposal. *Family Systems Medicine, 11*, 1–7.

Bloch, D. (1994). Dreaming of elephants. *Family Systems Medicine, 12*, 1–3.

Botelho, R., McDaniel, S. H., & Jones, J. E. (1990). A family systems approach to a Balint-style group: A report on a CME demonstration project for primary care physicians. *Family Medicine, 22*, 4293–4295.

Bray, J. H., & Rogers, J. C. (1995). Linking psychologists and family physicians for collaborative practice. *Professional Psychology: Research and Practice, 26*, 132–138.

Bray, J. H., & Rogers, J. C. (1997). The linkages project: Training behavioral health professionals for collaborative practice with primary care physicians. *Families, Systems, & Health, 15*, 55–63.

Breunlin, D. C., Schwartz, R. C., & MacKune-Karrer, B. (1992). *Metaframeworks: Transcending the models of family therapy*. San Francisco: Jossey-Bass.

British Family Heart Study. (1994). Randomised controlled trial evaluating cardiovascular screening and intervention in general practice: Principal results of British Family Health Study. *British Medical Journal, 308*, 313–320.

Campbell, T., & McDaniel, S. H. (1997, Summer). Branching out: A randomized trial of collaborative family healthcare for distressed high utilizers of the medical system. *American Family Therapy Academy Newsletter*, 7–9.

Campbell, T. L., & Patterson, J. (1995). The effectiveness of family interventions in the treatment of physical disorders. *Journal of Marital and Family Therapy, 21*, 545–583.

Candib, L. (1995). *Medicine and the family*. New York: Basic Books.

Doherty, W. J., & Campbell, T. L. (1988). *Families and health*. Beverly Hills, CA: Sage.

Ewart, C. K., Taylor, C. B., Kraemer, H. C., & Agras, W. S. (1991). High blood pressure and marital discord: Not being nasty matters more than being nice. *Health Psychology, 10*, 155–163.

Fallowfield, L., Hall, A., Maguire, P., Baum, M., & Hern, R. (1994). Psychological effects of being offered choice of surgery for breast cancer. *British Medical Journal, 309*, 448.

Frank, A. (1995). *The wounded storyteller: Body, illness, and ethics*. Chicago: University of Chicago Press.

Freud, S. (1962). Further remarks on the defence—Neuro-psychoses. In J. Strachey (Ed. & Trans.), *The standard edition of the complete psychological works of Sigmund Freud* (Vol. 3, pp. 159–185). London: Hogarth Press. (Original work published 1893)

Freud, S. (1962). Sexuality in the aetiology of the neuroses. In J. Strachey (Ed. & Trans.), *The standard edition of the complete psychological works of Sigmund Freud* (Vol. 3, pp. 261–286). London: Hogarth Press. (Original work published 1898)

Friedrich, W. N. (1997). Facing yourself in your work: A young man with head and neck cancer. In S. McDaniel, J. Hepworth, & W. Doherty (Eds.), *The shared experience of illness* (pp. 120–127). New York: Basic Books.

Gawinski, B., Edwards, T., & Speice, J. (1999). A family therapy internship in a multidisciplinary healthcare setting: Trainees' and supervisor's reflections. *Journal of Marital and Family Therapy, 25*, 469–484.

Glenn, M. (1987). *Collaborative health care: A family-oriented model*. New York: Praeger.

Guggenbuhl-Craig, A. (1971). *Power in the helping professions*. Woodstock, CT: Spring.

Helgeson, V. S. (1994). Relation of agency and communion to well-being: Evidence and potential explanations. *Psychological Bulletin, 116*, 412–428.

Hepworth, J., Gavazzi, S., Adlin, M., & Miller, W. (1988). Training for collaboration: Internships for family therapy students in a medical setting. *Family Systems Medicine, 6*, 69–79.

Hepworth, J., & Jackson, M. (1985). Health care for families: Models of collaboration between family therapists and family physicians. *Family Relations, 34*, 123–127.

House, J. S., Landis, K. R., & Umberson, D. (1988, July 19). Social relationships and health. *Science, 241*, 540–545.

Katon, W. (1985). Somatization in primary care. *Journal of Family Practice, 21*, 257–258.

Katon, W., Robinson, P., Von Korff, M., Lin, E., Bush, T., Ludman, E., et al. (1996). A multifaceted intervention to improve treatment of depression in primary care. *Archives of General Psychiatry, 53*, 924–932.

Katon, W., Von Korff, M., Lin, E., Walker, E., Simon, G. E., Bush, T., et al. (1995). Collaborative management to achieve treatment guidelines: Impact on depression in primary care. *Journal of the American Medical Association, 273*, 1026–1031.

Levine, C., & Zuckerman, C. (1999). The trouble with families: Toward an ethic of accommodation. *Annals of Internal Medicine, 130*, 148–152.

Lovallo, W. J. (1997). *Stress and health: Biological and psychological interactions.* Thousand Oaks, CA: Sage.

McDaniel, S. H., & Campbell, T. L. (1997). Training health professionals to collaborate. *Families, Systems & Health, 15*, 253–259.

McDaniel, S. H., Campbell, T. L., & Seaburn, D. (1990). *Family-oriented primary care: A manual for medical providers.* New York: Springer-Verlag.

McDaniel, S. H., & deGruy, F. (1996). Relational disorders in primary care. In F. Kaslow (Ed.), *Handbook on relational diagnosis* (pp. 126–136). New York: Wiley.

McDaniel, S. H., Hepworth, J., & Doherty, W. J. (1992). *Medical family therapy: A biopsychosocial approach to families with health problems.* New York: Basic Books.

McDaniel, S. H., Hepworth, J., & Doherty, W. J. (1997). *The shared experience of illness: Stories of patients, families, and their therapists.* New York: Basic Books.

McDaniel, S. H., & Speice, J. (2001). What family psychology has to offer women's health: The examples of conversion, somatization, infertility treatment, and genetic testing. *Professional Psychology: Research and Practice, 32*, 44–51.

Mittelman, M. S., Ferris, S. H., Shulman, E., Steinberg, G., & Levin, B. (1996). A family intervention to delay nursing home placement of patients with Alzheimer disease: A randomized controlled trial. *Journal of the American Medical Association, 276*, 1725–1731.

Morisky, D. E., Levine, D. M., Green, L. W., Shapiro, S., Russell, R. P., & Smith, C. R. (1983). Five-year blood pressure control and mortality following health education for hypertensive patients. *American Journal of Public Health, 73*, 153–162.

Patterson, J., Scherger, J., Bischoff, R. J., & McIntosh-Koonitz, L. (1998). Training for collaboration: Suggestions for the joint training of mental health clinicians and family practice residents. *Families, Systems & Health, 16,* 147–157.

Pequegnat, W., & Bray, J. (1997). Family and HIV/AIDS: Introduction to the special section. *Journal of Family Psychology, 11,* 3–10.

Perrin, E. (1999). The promise of collaborative care. *Developmental and Behavioral Pediatrics, 20,* 57–62.

Price, R. (1999). *Letter to a man in the fire.* New York: Scribner's.

Rolland, J. (1994). *Families, illness and disability.* New York: Basic Books.

Roth-Roemer, S., Kurpius, S. R., & Carmin, C. (Eds.). (1998). *The emerging role of counseling psychology in health care.* New York: Norton.

Seaburn, D. B., Lorenz, A. D., Gunn, W. B., Gawinski, B. A., & Mauksch, L. B. (1996). *Models of collaboration: A guide for mental health professionals working with health care practitioners.* New York: Basic Books.

Smith, G. R., Monson, R. A., & Ray, D. C. (1986). Psychiatric consultation in somatization disorder: A randomized controlled study. *New England Journal of Medicine, 314,* 1407–1413.

Smith, G. R., Rost, K., & Kashner, T. M. (1995). A trial of the effect of a standardized psychiatric consultation on health outcomes and costs in somatizing patients. *Archives of General Psychiatry, 52,* 238–243.

Suchman, A. (1997). A model of empathic communication in the medical interview. *Journal of the American Medical Association, 277,* 678–682.

Sullivan, H. S. (1953). *The interpersonal theory of psychiatry.* New York: W. W. Norton.

Wellisch, D. K. (1995). A family systems approach to coping with cancer. In R. Mikesell, D. D. Lusterman, & S. H. McDaniel (Eds.), *Integrating family therapy: Handbook of systems theory and family psychology* (pp. 389–404). Washington, DC: American Psychological Association.

Wood, B. L. (1995). A developmental biopsychosocial approach to the treatment of chronic illness in children and adolescents. In R. Mikesell, D. D. Lusterman, & S. H. McDaniel (Eds.), *Integrating family therapy: Handbook of systems theory and family psychology* (pp. 427–455). Washington, DC: American Psychological Association.

Wright, L., Watson, W., & Bell, J. (1996). *Beliefs: The heart of healing in families and illness.* New York: Basic Books.

7

PRIMARY CARE PSYCHOLOGY IN INDEPENDENT PRACTICE

W. DAVID DRISCOLL AND EUGENE P. McCABE

Is it possible to collaborate effectively with other health professionals when each practices in separate locations? In this chapter we describe one such example, the independent practice of Family Psychology Associates (FPA), which has collaborated intensively with other health professionals in Rochester, New York, since 1985. The practice is composed of four psychologists, including ourselves. An important goal of the practice is to provide "one-stop shopping" for physicians seeking mental health services for their patients (McDaniel, Campbell, & Seaburn, 1990). Understanding that practicing physicians need convenient access to appropriate psychological services for their patients, we at FPA respond regularly to their consultation and triage requests in addition to referrals for direct intervention. These consultations may result in referrals to the practice but often involve referring patients to appropriate professionals and services outside of our practice. We are less concerned that the service be provided by our office and more concerned that patients receive appropriate service in the community at large.

Our practice is guided by a set of core assumptions:

- The psychologists apply psychological knowledge and skill through a variety of channels as part of a larger health care team (Hepworth & Jackson, 1986).
- Ecological models of epistemology guide the psychologists in developing intervention and collaboration strategies (Bateson, 1971; Watzlawick & Weakland, 1977).
- Biopsychosocial formulations are effective in conceptualizing assessment and treatment strategies (Engel, 1977, 1980; McDaniel, 1995; Wynne, 1961).
- The psychologists incorporate a wide range of theoretically diverse intervention techniques (Lazarus, 1971, 1976).
- The psychologists place a high value on collaboration with other primary care health professionals (McDaniel, Hepworth, & Doherty, 1992; Seaburn, Lorenz, Gunn, Gawinski, & Mauksch, 1996).

In this chapter we use the experience of FPA psychologists to illustrate off-site collaboration. We cover the following issues:

- practice structure and associated infrastructure,
- relationship patterns with collaborating physicians,
- range of interventions possible within collaborative care relationships,
- patient relationships in a collaborative care model,
- integrating support staff into a collaborative care model,
- relationships with payors, and
- financial aspects of collaborative practice.

FAMILY PSYCHOLOGY ASSOCIATES

Structural Overview

At the practical level, the structure of professional relationships within our practice is critical to the health and stability of the practice. The business arrangements within the practice are designed to reflect balance and equality among the psychologists. Structurally speaking, each psychologist operates his or her own practice. There are no long-term contracts, because we believe professionals should be happy and satisfied in the practice and free to leave when they choose. This is a shared financial risk that we absorb to maintain the health of the practice model. The infrastructure necessary to support collaborative practice is significant, expensive, and most reasonable to support when shared by like-minded colleagues. The practice structure resembles more closely that of practicing physicians than that of most of our psychologist colleagues. In addition to individually dedicated office space and shared waiting room and reception space, our infrastructure includes one part-time office manager and one part-time accounts manager. Communication is maintained through multiple-line phone systems with voicemail backup, a full-time personal answering service, and a personal pager for each psychologist. Rapid and direct contact is possible to any of the psychologists at any time. After-hours coverage is shared on a rotating basis. The offices are equipped with Internet access, full dictation capability, fax service, electronic billing, and reception services during normal business hours. The office can be opened at any time for urgent or emergency patient contact.

The purpose of FPA's infrastructure is to free the psychologists from nonprofessional responsibilities and to increase the availability and efficiency of collaborative interactions. Collaborating with practicing physicians is a labor-intensive style of practice that is demanding of psychologists' time. We estimate that there is approximately 15 min spent in collaborative professional activity for every 60 min of billable direct contact in the office. Beyond this variable, frequency of appointments for each treatment episode is lower, necessitating a high volume of referrals and turnover of patients to be viable. This is another factor that contributes to increased overhead.

At present, the psychologists contribute to the support of the practice in direct relationship to the level of their professional activity. Our experience has shown us that there is a direct relationship between practice volume and overhead costs. This relative financial contribution is calculated annually to track fairly the actual expenses of the practice and has hovered around 25%. Income derived from professional activities outside the practice is not included in any overhead costs to the psychologist. The founding psychologist is compensated for managing the day-to-day operation of the practice and overseeing the functioning of the support staff. The benefits of efficiencies of functioning are shared by everyone, as are the burdens of the expense. Financial incentives are aligned with the professional balance we are striving to maintain.

Based on approximate annual office volume of between 3,000 and 4,000 encounters among four part-time providers, expenses in 2002 were approximately $68,000—one third for space ($23,000); one third for support personnel ($23,000); and one third for supplies, equipment, postage, telephones, and answering services ($22,000).

In describing our practice, we focus on groups with which we interact regularly to provide care: practicing physicians, patients, support staff, and payors. Within each of these core groups the key processes we consider important in collaborative practice are access and communication, intervention, documentation, and evaluation and follow-up.

Physicians and Nurse Practitioners

Access and communication with physicians is a cornerstone of collaboration. The outcome of this process is a well-informed and unified team of providers who support patients and each other in achieving mutual treatment goals. The primary objective is to establish safe and respectful relationships with colleagues that are congruent with sound therapeutic principles. In a developmental sense, these relationships require investment of professional time and effort for later functional returns. For example, when contacted by a physician about an urgent case, we find a way to make room for the patient even when our schedules are full. This contact is coupled with rapid and concise mutual feedback that initiates dialogue, provides timely information to both professionals, and cultivates an ongoing professional relationship with the practicing physician. The dividends from these relationships include improved patient outcomes and additional referrals from physicians and colleagues. This process also tends to improve the quality and reliability of communication between patients and their team of providers. It allows the physician, psychologist, or both, to be identified as the patient's primary link(s) to the treatment system.

When dealing with new physician relationships, we routinely make collateral contacts within the first three visits, either by phone, in writing, or by voicemail. We state briefly the reason for referral, summarize the patient or family background, and include our initial assessment. We typically include plans for treatment and ask the physician or nurse practitioner for input, further background, and agreement to the plan. We try to convey timelines and general expectations for treatment. This initial plan includes actions that each of us is expected to implement, such as medications, school consults, or family meetings.

We now present a case example that highlights communication among a primary care physician, psychologist, an adolescent and his family, and his school. Successful collaboration was key to engaging this young man in treatment.

> John, a 14-year-old, was initially treated by his pediatrician, Dr. S., because of chronic and increasing family conflict, which escalated as John approached adolescence. Dr. S. had managed John's attentional problems (with associated learning disabilities) throughout childhood while coaching his parents around difficult management issues. John was a bright and articulate youngster who presented in a mature manner. He provided cogent explanations for how family conflicts occurred, which usually involved irrational overreactions by parents, both of whom were professionally employed and had busy schedules. Although John's advanced verbal abilities enabled him to succeed academically without much effort, John's work ethic was a frequent focus of conflict with parents. They were frustrated that John was not achieving his potential and also not assuming normal household responsibilities. John was frequently in conflict with his father, while his mother attempted to moderate this conflict.
>
> Dr. S. ultimately referred the family to his favorite adolescent psychologist, Dr. M., who involved himself with the family immediately,

seeing John and his parents both together and separately. In sessions, John was open and expressive, yet his parents remained highly reactive, especially father, who would frequently get stuck in debates about details of situations. The parents complained that John was disrespectful to them at home, challenging their authority and defying their directives. There was frequent discussion of whether John was responsible for his behavior in light of his learning and attentional deficits. How much could he be expected to accomplish independently, and how much direction could he tolerate now that he was a blossoming adolescent? Developmentally speaking, the emergence of John's autonomy was conflicting with his needs for support and supervision. His parents' anxiety over the resolution of these issues resulted in chronic levels of conflict and tension. Otherwise, the marital relationship appeared healthy and stable.

Dr. S. and Dr. M. discussed John frequently, as they shared office space part of the week. John also manifested the typical adolescent reaction to medications, with considerable ambivalence and inconsistent compliance. Eventually, Dr. S. and Dr. M. met jointly with the family and conferred on both medical management and family behavioral issues. These meetings served multiple purposes, because ongoing debates about the medical issues could be quickly resolved. The family also witnessed adults working together and communicating clearly while maintaining respect for each other and for competing perspectives. John's need for independence was balanced with guidelines and management strategies for adolescence. Dr. M contacted John's school to obtain updated academic information and to clarify the level of support services needed.

During his junior year, John suddenly developed Type I diabetes. He was hospitalized briefly at that time and quickly became an astute and highly informed diabetic patient. In the context of this medical crisis, family conflicts subsided, but then re-emerged, with medical management of John's diabetes becoming the new focus for family control battles. During this period there were regular meetings among the family, Dr. S., and Dr. M.

The nurse practitioner from the hospital endocrinology clinic that regularly communicated with John's pediatrician oversaw the coordination of John's diabetic management. She was in regular contact with Dr. S. about significant laboratory results and associated management strategies. Family visits were held at Dr. S.'s office, with Dr. M. present on the days he was on site. Billing for visits alternated between Dr. S. and Dr. M. During this initial stage, John had to make one visit to the emergency room due to a critical reaction, but several other crises were averted by rapid contact with either Dr. M. or Dr. S. by phone or in person. The parents frequently would benefit from brief phone contact at the height of a conflict when they were asserting extreme reactions, such as threatening to send John away to a boarding school. The family cycle of conflict continued, but the amplitude and the frequency of the conflicts declined.

In this family, the conflicts divided the members and accelerated normal levels of separation, resulting in considerable "splitting." John, as a verbal and articulate adolescent, capitalized on differences between authority figures that could have infected the pediatrician–psychologist relationship if such close and regular communication were not their routine. In addition, the complications of complex and chronic medical management were quickly and effectively addressed as part of the resolution of adolescent autonomy. There were no additional hospitalizations. The family expressed enormous gratitude and satisfaction with the process despite the fact that conflicts continued. They recognized that they had learned to process their conflicts without risking John's physical health in the management of his diabetes. Dr. S. and Dr. M. continue to monitor the family's functioning through occasional joint family meetings.

Other physician colleagues with whom we regularly consult might have more traditional forms of contact with us. It is common to have a physician call to discuss cases where no referral is contemplated, because we have a knowledge base that is valued and helpful to our medical colleagues. The phone conversation might concern appropriate resources in the community for a particular patient, a referral source for a teenager with a suspected eating disorder, or a school program for a dyslexic child. We extend efforts to interact with physicians by maintaining frequent contact and find that this results in regular reciprocal contacts. At times, in urgent situations, we take a call from a physician in the middle of a session. Most patients accept this rather graciously, because they know the same type of urgency would be extended for them if needed. One local pediatrician stated thankfully that we were the only psychologists he could contact immediately, even when in session, as a tribute to our understanding his practice needs. This type of immediate access to colleagues is standard practice among physicians and is not taught to psychologists in training. Indeed, treatment sessions are often held as sacrosanct, contributing to the view that the therapeutic process is more important than anything with which a physician colleague could be dealing.

The range of possible interventions involving physicians depends on the psychosocial skills of the referring physician, the developmental level of the relationship between the psychologist and physician, the qualities of the case, and the institution or agency involved. Maturity of the professional relationship is a primary factor in determining what interventions are possible with a physician colleague. With a long-standing collegial relationship, a lot can be accomplished quite easily; with newer physician colleagues, careful assessment of the process is necessary. For example, to successfully refer patients for specialist assessment (e.g., substance abuse, neurodevelopmental, psychiatric) more extensive physician–psychologist communication is required in less mature relationships. Although this principle may seem obvious, we continue to experience it as critical and easy to overlook in the rush of a busy practice day. We always need to gauge the maturity of the collegial relationship accurately before proceeding with interventions, just as we would with patients' professional colleagues.

First, the physician may realize it is useful to avoid becoming involved in advising the patient about a problem, in preparation for referral to therapy. In these cases, no intervention with the physician is necessary; the referral is "clean." On occasion, a physician has started some counseling efforts with a patient and then refers the patient because of lack of progress. In such cases it is critically important to communicate with the physician and maintain some continuity with the physician's efforts. This may mean acknowledging the previous treatment and investigating with the patient and physician additional strategies that would be appropriate at this point in the sequence of interventions. Whatever we do supports and extends the prior treatment; it is a follow-up to previous efforts that were preliminary and formative in the care of this patient. Again, this process is common between primary physicians and their medical specialist colleagues.

Another level of intervention involves coordinating communication and relationships among other professionals who may be involved with a patient, such as school personnel, agency professionals, or employers. In our experience, psychologists can increase their value to physicians and improve patient outcomes by effectively coordinating and managing these interactions. A prime example of this is the evaluation of treatment for attentional disorders in children whose behavior so often varies greatly across settings (Barkley, 1998). Frequently, parents and family do not see a severe problem, but within the school context the youngster is experiencing and creating significant problems. Without input from school sources, our clinical assessments mean less. In another example, follow-up with family and spouse needs to be actively considered to assess outcomes with depressed patients.

Medication management is one common area of collateral contact between psychologists and physicians. In spite of some current professional efforts suggesting that certain psychologists are qualified to advise on the selection and administration of psychotropic medications, we prefer to leave that in the domain of our physician colleagues, including psychiatrists. We make referrals when we suspect a patient might benefit from medication, and we stand ready to help gauge medication response. In our experience, respecting this boundary between psychologists and physicians results in the most effective professional relationships and outcomes for patients.

Documentation is usually the last activity on which psychologists wish to expend time and effort. It is often deferred in the course of a busy practice day. However, in addition to standard requirements and professional expectations for documentation, we have found that that there are important clinical applications for documenting our work. First, psychologists need to remember that the patients they see continue to be patients of the physicians while we are involved and probably long afterward. Hence, informing physicians about treatment developments is more than a courtesy; they need to know what is happening in the psychologist's care so that when a treatment situation arises, either psychiatric or medical, they are adequately prepared to respond. We have found that physicians prefer to have some form of written communication in their charts at the outset of treatment, updates during the course of treatment, and a summary at termination. Hence, in addition to the usual informal communications, we provide regular brief written documents outlining progress.

Documentation has other purposes as well. It can be useful to have written notes of a session distributed to participants in order to ensure more reliable follow-through. Sometimes it is helpful to have patients themselves take responsibility for documenting these notes and distributing them, as a form of independence and responsibility for care. At times, we have used audio- or videotapes of a session to document important activities and to assist patients in follow-through. We include all phone messages in the chart and document repeated attempts to contact patients or other parties. We try to record all important phone numbers with the release of information. Of importance is that we try to communicate with and document agency personnel their cooperative and helpful actions, sending copies of thank you notes to appropriate supervisory personnel.

We use a treatment plan format to summarize our assessment and treatment plan and a basic SOAP note (symptoms, observations, assessment, and plan) to document ongoing contact. We allocate additional time for intake assessments in order to complete the initial clinical and clerical tasks. Often, initial treatment planning is only partially completed after the first session because additional data are needed from various sources. Therefore, we obtain release-of-information forms during our initial contact. At this time, we make it clear that patients are free to deny permission for contact with collateral professionals. Although a rare occurrence, when patients are reluctant to permit contact with important collateral sources, we often take a wait-and-see attitude, accepting their initial reluctance as a possible sign of anxiety or lack of trust that becomes a focus of treatment. We may ultimately need to decide whether we can responsibly treat the patient with no collateral contact.

The process of follow-up and evaluation illustrates the essential elements of our contextual–ecological model of treatment. To have meaningful follow-up, it is necessary to obtain input from various sources in different contexts. In our clinical experience, as well as in results from local surveys, physicians consistently point out that psychologists are deficient in providing follow-up information on patients. This has been physicians' primary complaint about psychologists in our community. We find that when we make contact with physicians they are open and grateful. In situations where progress is not positive, we have been reluctant to inform physicians but have found that they understand these developments, because they occasionally fail with patients as well. Sometimes, we conclude that the patient or family is not ready for change or that the match between patient and psychologist is not a good one. We find that physicians are receptive to honest and direct feedback even when it is disappointing. Also, physicians can benefit from our experiences with families and patients. For example, when we discover that a family does not make decisions unless the father is present, then the pediatrician can improve the effectiveness of future professional contacts by including the father in critical decisions.

Patients and Families

Conceptualizing clinical intervention as a collaborative enterprise with patients assures that the initial "joining" is successfully achieved. Madsen (1999) and others have articulated the clinical aspects of this approach in discussing the "accountable ally" position of the therapist. Use of the relationship is a central factor in all of our interventions. We devote substantial effort to establishing a supportive and mutually responsible relationship with patients and families that will foster future collaborative efforts (Freedman & Combs, 1996; White & Epston, 1990). Knowledge of general patterns of previous therapeutic relationships can be helpful here. At the outset, we try to determine what kinds of relationships have been successful and unsuccessful. One goal is to create a facilitative environment in which patients' resources can be identified and mobilized for problem resolution. The initial stages of this intervention often include focused effort at disabusing patients of traditional expectations for therapy and consultation. We often have to demonstrate our belief in a family's resources by acknowledging their accomplishments, resiliency, and persistence (Cade & O'Hanlon, 1993; O'Hanlon & Wilk, 1987; Seaburn, Landau, & Horwitz, 1995). In addition, we recognize the importance of developmental and biological factors that often represent specific challenges. In this process, we tend to lower patients' expectations of the therapist as a "magic bullet" who will unilaterally effect change. Instead, as with other professionals, we attempt to share responsibility with patients within a framework of collaboration.

In our initial discussions with patients, we focus on the pragmatics of intervention. For example, it is not uncommon to have an initial consultation that ends without a scheduled date for follow-up. We sometimes send patients and families home to consider the situation as they see it after the initial consultation and request that they get back to us with their planned direction. It might occur during the session that we would leave the room and ask the patient to consider a particular topic without us present. In contrast to orthodox family systems treatment (Minuchin, 1974), we offer the patient a choice in deciding with us who should attend. We are clear when we feel therapy will be handicapped by a member's absence, but we invite the perspective of the patient as well.

These approaches signify the presence of a collaborative spirit in the quest of common therapeutic goals, an approach that parallels our relationship with the patient's physician. Within our relationships with patients, documentation can include the use of written materials as adjuncts to other therapeutic interventions. For example, it is common for us to summarize important content from a session and give it to a patient. This can trigger a more systematic follow-up on recommendations and conclusions agreed on during the session. Sometimes we give a pad and pencil to patients for them to jot down important aspects of our discussion. At times, it is even useful to include a tape recorder as part of a session. These aides can be particularly helpful when working with families in which one or more members has some form of learning difficulty or with patients for whom organizational problems often arise. Such patients often have parallel problems in therapy, where communications can be misunderstood and not executed because of information-processing problems that transcend therapeutic issues. Use of these learning aides can compensate for weaknesses and variations while also communicating the collaborative nature of our work. In addition, we sometimes use written notes to patients after the session to encourage a reflective response to material discussed in the sessions. Narrative therapists (Freedman & Combs, 1996) have advocated this technique for some time. We often encourage patients to journal and to write letters on important and emotionally intense subjects. When we model writing as a clinical intervention, we provide a form of support and implicit suggestion for such self-monitoring strategies.

In our model, we consider patient feedback to be a continuous process that is subject to individual considerations, including the nature of the case and timing of the questions. When we ask for feedback from patients during treatment, we explicitly express to the patient the collaborative nature of our relationship with him or her. Many patients are surprised by a question about process and evaluation, but once they answer, they have already experienced an important aspect of treatment: sharing responsibility for outcome. A particular challenge of our collaborative model comes with the evaluation of medication responses. Physicians and patients often look to treating psychologists as the professionals in the best position to facilitate this evaluation. Although we accept this as a natural extension of our collaborative model, we are careful to maintain our physician colleagues as the final arbiters of any medication judgments and decisions.

Support Staff

If we are to be successful in implementing a collaborative model of primary care psychology practice, it is essential to incorporate office staff who are the gatekeepers of communication among all the other parties involved. It is vital that the staff understand the general nature of our model and are able to incorporate it into their daily interactions. In addition to standard levels of courtesy and respect toward patients, we encourage staff to extend a welcome to patients and colleagues both in phone contacts and in person. This may include offering opportunities to inquire about insurance issues, clarifying upcoming appointments, and arranging specific times for phone contacts with clinicians. Responding to requests for service when a psychologist is backlogged is a critical skill in this area. We encourage office staff to inform interested patients of the current delay in availability and to help them identify alternatives. This frequently is a time-consuming process and often involves the psychologist directly, but it is crucial in establishing a standard of collaborative practice that focuses primarily on the needs of the patient. It also communicates a readiness to work with other colleagues in the community, a feature of practice that has secondary reciprocal benefits in the long term. Indeed, physicians will use our expertise as a triage resource when they are stuck and cannot find an appropriate referral source. We view this as a legitimate form of collaboration. Although time consuming, the positive impact on the professional relationship is important. The support staff are also informed about developing and urgent situations that might require immediate response. They are trained to discern critical situations and inform us quickly. We have found that patients can develop meaningful and effective relationships with support staff who are open to contact and personally available. Indeed, when these characteristics accrue, patients feel more comfortable coming to the office and are more likely to seek contact when necessary.

Cultivating relationships with support staff from physicians' offices is also paramount to ensure appropriate access and to facilitate sharing of information. It usually is unnecessary to bother a physician with specifics of a situation because one has developed a trusting relationship with the office manager. In the case of insurance issues, informing them of no-shows, as well as routine checks, the office manager or nurse can often supply the information without interrupting the physician. Although it is inappropriate to include support staff directly in intervention, we have found that there is a "normalizing effect" for patients when support staff are comfortable enough to gently engage patients through the transitions of arriving, checking in, and departing. Indeed, it is sometimes helpful for them to join in a superficial conversation at the front desk to relieve tension, especially at the initial contact. Alternately, it is important for office staff to recognize that certain patient situations should be ignored and boundaries respected, for example, when children are unruly in the waiting room. Initial selection of office staff with good interpersonal skills provides a solid foundation for positive response to on the job training and feedback.

Evaluation and follow-up become important aspects of the office staff's responsibility. For example, when a patient fails to keep an appointment, the staff follows up. Depending on the nature of the case, we either send a letter that indicates the missed appointment and copy the physician or, if there is significant risk involved, follow up with a phone call.

Payors

It is not immediately apparent, but collaborative relationships among patients, physicians, and psychologists quite often involve a fourth party: the payor, most often an insurance company. In the difficult climate that predominates in some of today's health care markets, it is often challenging for psychologists to approach this topic without becoming subject to intense emotionality and vigorous debate. Nonetheless, from our perspective, the issues exist within the context of existing contemporary realities and how we have coped with them. Of note is that we have approached relationships with our major payors from a collaborative relationship model as we have other important contextual relationships in our practice. We recognize that the relationship is one of mutual need: The payors and primary physicians need psychologists to provide specialty services to their subscribers and patients, patients need help, and psychologists need fair reimbursement for their professional services. In a concrete sense, we have been active at the community level in our local major Independent Practice Association (physicians group), where we enjoy equal organizational status with our physician colleagues. This status resulted from years of collaboration with payors, physicians, and delivery systems to solve significant local mental health issues in the community. As the relationship has evolved, psychology in our community has earned significant representation both within the IPA and one major health maintenance organization (HMO).

The operating philosophy in these organizational relationships has been for psychologists to achieve parity with physician colleagues in whatever processes are under consideration. This compelling position has resulted in many positive changes for psychology in our community, including more openness about the care being provided, and has been balanced by earning representation and parity with community physicians. In our judgment, the time has passed to discuss whether psychology should have become involved in the health care payor systems. We are part of the health system and believe that professional collaboration can help the system function as effectively as possible.

Communication with payors is an activity that transcends all levels of interactions within the practice. At a clinical level, payment arrangements are part of the therapeutic contract. As patients choose to consider using their health insurance to cover their mental health services, they accept another partner into the relationship. Choosing this option is typically seamless and has no significant consequences. Patients receive services, payors are billed, and professionals receive reimbursement. The complexity of this relationship can vary widely and affect significantly the services provided. At the outset of treatment there is often a decision to be made about whether a service will be covered. As professional participants in HMOs we are responsible for representing our services accurately and helping to educate patients about their coverage. Although most problems we treat are straightforward, we often need to clarify other situations. In our region, marital therapy, family therapy, long-term psychotherapy, off-site services, and initial psychoeducational testing are some services that are covered only when specific criteria are met. Confronting the need for patients to pay directly for these services often raises their anxieties. Experience has shown us that as we and our staff are viewed as honest in these dealings by our patients, patients begin to develop trust and respect. If one begins to compromise—by selective reporting, massaging documents, or otherwise misrepresenting the relationship—seeds of distrust can infect the therapeutic process.

At an individual level, it is our experience that payors appreciate honest and open dealings with us. Responding nondefensively to routine and contractual requests for information reduces anxieties and provides a foundation for effective collaboration when difficult problems confront us. Some examples of these problems include patients who cannot afford needed treatment and are at risk for more intense and expensive services later and patients who exhaust benefits before treatment has been completed. In our practice, with the ongoing focus on collaboration, we resolve most of these challenges with a positive outcome with payors.

At an organizational level, each member of the practice has participated to some degree in relationships with the payors through committee work, peer review, and problem solving activities. One clear example of this collaborative process was when a local HMO consulted the mental health panel to address physician concerns about appropriate patient access to mental health services. A mental health professional database was thus developed that could be accessed by practicing physicians seeking services for their patients.

The relationship between the psychologists in our practice and our major payors around intervention issues is generally positive, with contact occurring on an as-needed basis. Thus far in the development of the relationship, practice standards for intervention have not been promulgated by the payors. They rely on the joint professional determinations of the primary care physicians and psychologists. The payors vary in the amount of information they require at different stages of treatment and how this information is collected and reviewed. In one case, a brief summary form is reviewed before approval of additional treatment that is being recommended. In another case, clinical information is collected prospectively only when the professional is designated as requiring regular reviews. This occurs with all new psychologists for the first 2 years, psychologists with a pattern of utilization significantly different from that of their peers, and in cases where there have been problems identified in the care of patients.

It is likely that this pattern of minimal involvement with payors in regard to intervention issues is attributable to the collaborative processes in our practice. As we communicate regularly and professionally throughout our practice relationships, outcomes are positive, problems are minimized, patients are satisfied, and treatments are relatively brief. All are popular results with payors. Exceptions certainly exist where refractory problems and difficult patients present challenges to all systems involved. We try to address these problems early in their development in a proactive manner, which usually leads to positive resolution. There are some situations where patients prefer no communication with payors. Although they are informed of anticipated communication with payors before treatment begins, they also may choose to limit communication with other systems, or ultimately receive services on a fee-for-service basis without involvement of any outside parties in their treatment.

As noted earlier, the documentation necessary to interact with third-party payors consists of billing records, treatment plans, and copies of past communications. There are significant expectations for treatment documentation from both major payors in our community. In one case, these standards were promulgated by the payor and imposed on the community. In the other case, the standards were developed and approved through a process that involved the payor and representative mental health professionals in the community. In fact, both standards are similar and resemble closely standards for other health care systems. The monitoring of compliance with these documentation procedures consumes significant resources of office staff time.

The relationship with payors changes when we begin to consider the issues of evaluation and follow-up in independent practice. At the patient level, there is no formal process for examining issues regarding termination of treatment or evaluating process and outcome. Although this could be desirable, incentives do not exist to support this process.

Evaluating patient outcome and follow-up occurs only in cases that have presented unique difficulty or have involved inpatient treatment. Alternately, evaluation and follow-up processes are integrated into the credentialing and quality-assurance activities of the payors in the community. Payors maintain a database of information on each provider. This database includes demographics, patient complaints, chart review results, site visit results, and specialty designations. The IPA is refining a data analysis tool to rate the efficiency of providers. Combined, this information is used to gauge ongoing provider quality and is the basis for recredentialing decisions that occur biennially. Ad hoc reviews of psychologist performance can occur anytime there is immediate cause for concern about professional functioning. We have participated in the refinement and implementation of these processes through organizational involvement with payors as described earlier, and we believe they are valuable, fair and, most important, consistent with processes used for our physician colleagues.

CONCLUSIONS

Collaboration, as a model of independent practice in primary care psychology, incorporates a variety of processes, which stem from core beliefs in the value of community-oriented and interactional perspectives in mediating change. Conceptualizing the role of the psychologist as a member of a treatment team within the context of a community of health care professionals provides a foundation for acting flexibly in a broad range of roles that are helpful to patients and ultimately useful in promoting a prosperous and enduring practice. Embracing this conceptualization of independent practice enables the psychologist to broaden professional roles, continue to act in the best interest of the patient, demonstrate competence, and heighten appeal for future services. Expanded roles include arranging for supplementary services, including physicians and patients in treatment partnerships, and participating in community-based professional activities.

We have described a collaborative approach to practice based on a biopsychosocial model. We believe that the epistemological beliefs about the nature of human functioning and the purpose of independent practice in human services drives this model and is largely responsible for the success of our practice. The community orientation underlying our work has evolved into mutually beneficial relationships with colleagues, patients, and payors. Implementation of this approach is time consuming and practical only when considering long-term goals and practice development criteria. We believe it is helpful to look for unifying aspects of functioning across disciplines and to treat other providers as partners with a shared goal: improved health and functioning of our patients and the community.

REFERENCES

Barkley, R. A. (1998). *Attention-deficit hyperactivity disorder: A handbook for diagnosis and treatment* (2nd ed.). New York: Guilford Press.

Bateson, G. (1971). *Steps to an ecology of mind.* New York: Ballantine.

Cade, B., & O'Hanlon, W. (1993). *A brief guide to brief therapy.* New York: Norton.

Engel, G. L. (1977). The need for a new medical model: A challenge for biomedicine. *Science, 196,* 129–136.

Engel, G. L. (1980). The clinical application of the biopsychosocial model. *American Journal of Psychiatry, 137,* 535–544.

Freedman, J., & Combs, G. (1996). *Narrative therapy: The social construction of preferred realities.* New York: Norton.

Hepworth, J., & Jackson, M. (1986). Health care for families: Models of collaboration between family therapists and family physicians. *Family Relations, 34,* 123–127.

Lazarus, A. (1971). *Behavior therapy and beyond.* New York: McGraw-Hill.

Lazarus, A. (1976). *Multi-modal behavior therapy.* New York: Springer.

Madsen, W. C. (1999). *Collaborative therapy with multi-stressed families: From old problems to new futures.* New York: Guilford Press.

McDaniel, S. H. (1995). Collaboration between psychologists and family physicians: Implementing the biopsychosocial model. *Professional Psychology, 26,* 117–122.

McDaniel, S. H., Campbell, T. L., & Seaburn, D. (1990). *Family-oriented primary care: A manual for physicians.* New York: Springer-Verlag.

McDaniel, S., Hepworth, J., & Doherty, W. (1992). *Medical family therapy: A biopsychosocial approach to families with health problems.* New York: Basic Books.

Minuchin, S. (1974). *Families and family therapy.* Boston: Harvard University Press.

O'Hanlon, W., & Wilk, J. (1987). *Shifting contexts: The generation of effective psychotherapy.* New York: Guilford Press.

Seaburn, D., Landau, J., & Horwitz, S. (1995). Core techniques in family therapy. In R. Mikesell, D. Lusterman, & S. McDaniel (Eds.), *Integrating family therapy* (pp. 5–26). Washington, DC: American Psychological Association.

Seaburn, D., Lorenz, A., Gunn, W., Gawinski, B., & Mauksch, L. (1996). *Models of collaboration: A guide for working with health care practitioners.* New York. Basic Books.

Watzlawick, P., & Weakland, J. (Eds.). (1977). *The interactional view.* New York: Norton.

Wynne, L. C. (1961). *The study of interfamilial alignments and splits in exploratory family therapy.* New York: Family Service Association of America.

8

MAKING IT IN THE REAL WORLD: DIVERSE MODELS OF COLLABORATION IN PRIMARY CARE

NANCY B. RUDDY AND CAROLYN S. SCHROEDER

Primary care clinicians have responsibility for providing comprehensive, continuous care in the context of the family and the community. To meet this charge, they must collaborate and consult with professionals from many other health disciplines. As noted in other chapters of this volume, psychology professionals have unique skills and expertise to offer the primary care health team. It is, however, often difficult for psychologists to make the transition to this medical setting. In this chapter we present some of the practical issues that must be considered when psychologists are planning to work with primary health care professionals. We present various models of medicine–psychology collaboration and discuss the pros and cons of psychologists collaborating with medical professionals. We also review practical ideas on how to foster a successful collaborative health care team, and we describe the innovative roles taken by psychologists in primary care settings.

KINDS OF MEDICINE–PSYCHOLOGY COLLABORATION

A variety of models are used by psychologists and physicians to work together to enhance patient care (Doherty, 1995; Drotar, 1995; Glenn, 1987;

Seaburn, Lorenz, Gunn, Gawinski, & Mauksch, 1996). The models reflect a continuum from relatively independent care to highly integrated, collaborative care.

The most common model is the specialist–generalist model, in which the psychologist, as the specialist, provides consultation, diagnosis, and treatment of the patient, independent of the physician's work. The psychologist's practice is completely separate, and the referral of the patient provides the only link between the two professionals. This can result in little communication or collaboration. Geographic proximity is not necessary in this model but is often helpful in establishing a referral relationship.

Next on the continuum is a consultation model of working together. The physician maintains primary responsibility for patient care, while the psychologist provides information or advice. The consultation can be ongoing in the context of clinical care or delivered in case conferences. The professional receiving the information is responsible for its implementation with the patient. Geographic location is generally unimportant in this model.

On the farthest end of the continuum, physicians and psychologists jointly carry responsibility for patient care in a collaborative team model. They share their relevant expertise and make treatment decisions together. Geographic colocation is important in this model to facilitate communication and allow for on-the-spot consultation.

The traditional model of independent, separate practices that are linked primarily by referral is currently the normative model. It emphasizes autonomy, can discourage collaboration, and can limit the psychologist's team role. Time constraints and schedule conflicts often make direct conversation very difficult. Nonbillable collaboration time may conflict with clinical productivity and financial goals. In addition, mental health professionals may be reluctant to accept complex patients or certain types of insurance, fearing financial drain. It unfortunately is often these very patients with whom primary care providers need the most assistance.

Independent-practice models usually limit collaboration to postreferral. This is problematic in a number of ways.

1. Many patients in need of mental health consultation will not agree to a referral. Primary care providers get "stuck" with patients whose needs far exceed their expertise, available time, or desire to provide a certain type of care, potentially compromising the quality of care. With these patients, physicians may need assistance with the process of making the referral. Primary care physicians sometimes inadvertently create patient dependence in the early stages of problem management. This complicates the referral because patients may feel abandoned or betrayed when referred and thus have difficulty making a connection to the mental health provider. In addition,

it is common for the psychologist to spend a great deal of time and effort toward helping many patients reformulate their problem from a purely biomedical conceptualization to a biopsychosocial conceptualization. Data have been collected that indicate that simply meeting the mental health provider at the time of the referral can enhance a patient's follow-through significantly (D. Waxman, personal communication, March 19, 1997).

2. Psychologists may make inappropriate assessments or treatment recommendations if they are unaware of the physician–patient relationship history. Familiarity with the physician and good prereferral communication minimize the likelihood that a psychologist will make unhelpful recommendations or become triangulated between the physician and the patient.

3. Physicians might not recognize patients in need of psychological services. Psychologists on site can elevate awareness of these issues.

4. Psychologists who do not work directly with physicians do not have the opportunity to educate them about available services. Often, psychologists are aware of community resources that can be helpful to patients who might never accept a referral for treatment by a psychologist.

Many psychologists have settled on a hybrid of the completely separate and more collaborative models. One such hybrid is a *geographically adjacent practice* (e.g., in the same building or office park). This maintains the psychologist's autonomy while increasing accessibility and opportunities for communication. Medical providers typically will make referrals to psychologists in the vicinity, for patient convenience. Over time, with physician and psychologist commitment, such an arrangement may grow into a more structured relationship, and the providers may develop a means of sharing care more fully.

The second type of hybrid is a *space sharing*, or *landlord–tenant* relationship, in which it is typical for a psychologist to rent space from a primary care provider. Each professional maintains independent practices in that there can be little communication about shared patients (e.g., charting is separate), and they do not coordinate schedules. Although geographic proximity reduces logistical barriers to collaboration and opens the door for prereferral collaboration, the lack of a formal structure or agreement about collaboration may interfere with the collaborative efficiency and quality. In addition, the "renter" may sacrifice some autonomy, and he or she may or may not have a voice in office decisions that affect him or her (Hurley, 1995).

Some primary care providers and psychologists take space sharing to the next level: a truly collaborative relationship. *True collaboration* implies shared responsibility for patient care and a flexible hierarchy depending on relevant expertise. Although psychologists can be paid in a fee-for-service manner, they may be an employee of the physician, or of a third entity of which the physician is also an employee (e.g., a hospital-owned practice). Although employee status reduces autonomy, it also reduces some of the pressure on provision of billable services and may allow for greater creativity in the types of services offered (e.g., groups, call-in lines, etc.; Schroeder & Mann, 1991). Psychologists can be available to assist prereferral and in crisis situations. They sometimes may be able to see a patient with the primary care provider, to facilitate a referral, or to provide consultation. On-the-spot assistance helps primary care providers resolve situations during the patient's visit rather than processing their options after the opportunity has passed.

It is clear that no one model has all of the answers or is perfect for all situations. Each clinician must examine his or her own values, work preferences, and style of patient care to determine the best arrangement. A large part of the decision will depend on how much one values practicing collaboratively. In the following section we address the advantages and disadvantages of collaboration and present research results on the impact of collaboration.

PROS AND CONS OF COLLABORATION

There are many advantages to collaboration. First, it creates shared responsibility for patient care, which may reduce burnout and stress, especially with challenging, complex cases. This may lead to improved work satisfaction for both primary care providers and psychologists (Seaburn et al., 1996). Second, working collaboratively in primary care gives the psychologist a good source of referrals and the opportunities for long-term follow up. In fact, many psychologists working in primary care have noted a change in their practice patterns (Schroeder, 1996). Patients tend to treat the psychologist more like a primary care professional—they return for care periodically, as needed, rather than engaging in psychotherapy and terminating when their issues are "resolved." In addition, Wright and Burns (1986) pointed out that more clients are seen for less time, because clients generally present with less debilitating disorders in primary care.

Collaboration has many advantages for physicians as well. A large proportion of primary care office visits have a psychosocial component (Cassata & Kirkman-Liff, 1981; Regier, Goldberg, & Taube, 1978). Collaboration allows the physician to share responsibility in difficult cases, to get advice on providing basic counseling or behavioral interventions, and to learn about relevant community resources. If the psychologist is available for prereferral collaboration, then the physician can get assistance with patients who would not follow up on a mental health referral. A great deal of therapeutic work often goes into preparing patients for mental health referral, and physicians benefit greatly from assistance in this process. An alumni survey of a residency program that offered on-site collaborative care indicated that many alumni missed the ease of making referrals and getting consultation they had experienced while in this setting (S. McDaniel, personal communication, April, 2000).

A major advantage of close collaboration between psychologists and primary care providers is the potential to enhance patient care by integrating psychosocial care into traditional medical care (Haley et al., 1998). Research has indicated that integrated psychosocial care enhances recovery from acute illness (Mumford, Schlesinger, Glass, Patrick, & Cuerdon, 1984), health promotion and disease prevention (Doherty & Campbell, 1988), chronic illness management (Rinaldi, 1985), and depression treatment (Katon & Gonzales, 1994; Katon et al., 1995). At the very least, collaboration with primary care clinicians facilitates the use of some psychotropic medications, because most psychologists currently do not prescribe medications.

Integrated mental health services also appear to result in an overall cost savings (Finney, Riley, & Cataldo, 1991; Jones & Vischi, 1979; Mumford et al., 1984). On the basis of their review of the literature, Seaburn et al. (1996) concluded the following:

1. When mental health services are provided for appropriate patients, such as high utilizers of patient care, there is a reduction in nonpsychiatric medical utilization.
2. The most significant cost reductions can be seen in the lowered use of hospitalization. This is the case both for individuals with chronic physical illness and for those with psychiatric illness.
3. The most significant cost reductions in outpatient care occur with patients who receive brief to moderate treatment. The cost-offset effects are seen less often in outpatient care for individuals with severe or chronic mental illness or those with comorbid medical and psychiatric illness (Seaburn et al., 1996, p. 84).

Despite the advantages, collaboration is not a bed of roses. Along with the loss of some independence, psychologists and primary care clinicians must put time and effort into developing a collaborative relationship. This includes managing challenges associated with cultural differences across medicine and mental health and those related to the myriad issues that can develop in the primary care clinician–psychologist–patient triad. In addition, psychologists who practice in a medical setting may find themselves professionally isolated (McDaniel, Hepworth, & Doherty, 1992). Developing a sense of professional identity can be particularly difficult in a context away from professional peers, with all the demands implicit in a medical setting (Seaburn et al., 1996). The pre-existing tensions between medicine and psychology can leave a collaborating psychologist feeling like a bit of a traitor to the profession. Some of these dynamics are related to the larger issues of power and control in the U.S. health care system. Some psychologists have had prior bad experiences with physicians, making them hesitant to believe they could work with a physician on equal footing.

THE SEEDS OF SUCCESSFUL COLLABORATION

If a psychologist weighs the pros and cons and decides to pursue the development of a collaborative relationship, how can he or she maximize the likelihood for success? Drotar (1993) identified three factors that set the stage for successful collaboration: (a) the collaborators share professional beliefs and expectations that collaboration is necessary and helpful (b) collaborators have the basic skills of collaboration, and (c) the setting supports collaboration.

Seaburn and colleagues (1996) identified six "key ingredients" for collaboration. First, and foremost, the collaborators must have a good *relationship*. They noted that collaborative relationships rarely "click" immediately and that potential collaborators go through the same stages in developing their collaborative relationship that they do in the development of all relationships. Second, collaborators should have a *common purpose*. Third, collaborators should ideally *share similar paradigms*, or theories of change. Although consistent paradigms are not necessary in the context of mutual respect and good communication, thinking about the world in the same way makes collaboration much easier. Fourth, there must be clear communication. Fifth, *proximity of providers* eases collaboration but is not necessary or sufficient for collaboration to occur. Finally, collaborators should recognize the importance of their *business relationship*.

How does one create a practice that embodies these critical characteristics? We next offer a step-by-step guide. We also refer readers to the American Psychological Association Primary Care Task Force's article that reviews practical tips for psychologists as they begin to practice in primary care settings (Haley et al., 1998).

Setting the Stage for Collaboration: Self-Assessment

The first step in developing a collaborative relationship with another primary care clinician is to examine one's own values and reasons behind the desire for collaboration. What do you hope will happen as a result of the collaboration? Having your own goals in mind will serve as a guide and as motivation when the path is not easy. Self-examination of one's own biases about the medical culture and physicians also can be helpful. Ideas and issues with medicine may be rooted in personal experiences, the experiences of family and friends, or common stereotypes. Seaburn et al. (1996) encouraged would-be collaborators to examine their family-of-origin experiences related to illness and interaction with health care providers, the social currents and beliefs they bring to collaborative relationships, critical life events that may have precipitated the desire to collaborate, and professional socialization issues relevant to collaboration (e.g., theoretical framework, importance of connection to one's own "discipline of origin"). Training in psychosocial issues related to physical health and illness (or being willing to seek such training) is of crucial importance in making a decision to move into the health care setting.

Finding a Practice Partner

The second step is finding the right practice partner(s). Current referral sources are a good place to begin the search. Colleagues may also be able to give you recommendations of primary care clinicians who might be interested in collaborating with a psychologist. Obviously, the ideal physician or nurse practitioner makes many mental health referrals and sees the psychosocial issues of patients as appropriate and critical areas for intervention.

Approaching Physicians to Collaborate

The third step is to approach a prospective collaborative practice. Because time pressures are so intense in medical practice, it is important that your initial pitch is practical, results oriented, and brief. Upfront commitment to working together should be minimized until both parties have had a chance to know each other better and to think through the ramifications of beginning a collaborative practice. In the process of learning more about the practice, it is helpful to assess the primary care clinician's previous experiences with mental health practitioners and his or her level of knowledge about psychologists. Often, primary care clinicians are relatively naive about psychology training and practice (just as most psychologists are naive about medical and nursing training and practice). Negative stereotypes abound on both sides of the mental health–medicine fence (McDaniel & Campbell, 1986). A lack of information is not problematic as long as both people are open to learning about the other's expertise and challenges.

Negotiating a Collaborative Relationship

The fourth step, after finding physicians or nurse practitioners who are open to collaboration, is to negotiate various aspects of the relationship. The viability of a collaborative partnership will depend greatly on the negotiations that take place before providers make any commitments. Financial arrangements (e.g., rent, billing, compensation for nonbillable services, salary, etc.) and logistical details (e.g., access to support staff; record keeping; space; and management of phone calls, scheduling, records, and emergencies) must be agreed on up front, with contingencies for review and change over time. It is important (Hurley, 1995) that any contracts and business agreements be reviewed by an attorney before plans are finalized.

Beyond business arrangements, it is helpful to discuss how collaborative partners will communicate with one another regarding patient care. Clarity about when and how to communicate can enhance patient care, both by ensuring that health and mental health practitioners are aware of all relevant issues and by reducing potential conflicts among members of the treatment team. How often, and in what form, will the physician and psychologist communicate with one another (e.g., "hallway consults," chart notes, phone calls, letters, meetings)? Communication will vary across cases and time, but some agreement about what is minimally sufficient can prevent problems. Often, communication after the first few sessions, and when the patient is terminating therapy, is sufficient in relatively simple cases (Seaburn et al., 1996).

Bray and Rogers (1995) outlined one model for precollaboration negotiation and education. They worked with 10 pairs of rural psychologists and physicians to enhance their collaborative relationships, particularly regarding substance abuse. They provided two training sessions timed 6 months apart. The first session focused on the diagnosis and treatment of substance abuse problems and making successful referrals. The pairs discussed cultural differences across medical and mental health treatment environments and assessed their practice styles with regard to orientation toward psychosocial aspects of care, using case scenarios to plan how to work best together. In the second training session, the pairs discussed their level of success implementing the model, and what changes were necessary to increase successful collaboration. Eight of the 10 pairs were able to maintain some level of collaboration. The most successful collaborators had worked together previously, worked in geographic proximity, or had at least one person who put a great deal of effort into making the collaboration happen. Bray and Rogers's results highlight the extent to which relationship quality, geographic proximity, and a desire to work together are essential elements, even in the context of training and a structure that supports collaboration.

Preparing to Work in a Medical Setting

If your collaborative work is to be on site in a medical practice, it is helpful to be prepared for the some of the cultural differences across mental health and medicine (McDaniel, Campbell, & Seaburn, 1990). Recently, some health psychology programs have developed specific training programs for working in primary care. While this training area grows, most psychologists find they must undergo on-the-job training to be successful in primary care.

To begin, the languages of medicine and mental health are quite different. Psychologists often may not understand the terms and abbreviations that physicians use; and physicians may be unfamiliar with some of the more esoteric psychological terms. Some psychologists have found it helpful to keep a notebook of unfamiliar medical terms and invest in a good medical dictionary. Most important is the willingness to ask your health colleague to explain a term or disease process.

Time management and pace are very different across the disciplines and settings. Psychologists have traditionally seen patients for an hour at a time, with weeks between appointments. It is common that prospective patients are expected to wait weeks for an appointment. Primary care physicians generally have about 10–15 minutes to spend with a patient. In this time, they must assess the presenting problem, negotiate a treatment plan, arrange for follow-up and, often, screen for a variety of other potential issues. Physicians are expected to make room on their schedules for acutely ill patients, resulting in occasional double-bookings and extensions of their workdays.

In part because of the time pressures, medicine tends to focus on results rather than process. Psychologists may feel that medical providers don't give enough attention to emotional issues, while medical providers may feel that psychologists never get to the point. Psychologists working in primary care have to learn to be flexible and recognize that brief contacts within a long-term relationship can provide effective treatment.

Finally, different norms about confidentiality can result in frustration and interfere with good communication. Physicians tend to share information with health care colleagues much more freely, seeing all providers involved in a patient's care as part of the team and therefore having a need to know about the patient. Psychologists are trained to share information only with written consent and even then to share only what they feel another person needs to know. Physicians may feel the psychologist is being secretive or not respecting the relationship they have with the patient (which almost always predates the relationship between the patient and psychologist!). Psychologists may feel unsure what it is appropriate or inappropriate to share with their physician colleagues. Discussion with the patient can help the psychologist to decide what can and cannot be shared.

Beginning to Collaborate

How does one make the transition from the idea to the reality of collaboration? The metaphor of traveling in a foreign country is appropriate for the experience of psychologists beginning to practice in medical settings. One can avoid mistakes and adjustment difficulties in exactly the same way one does when in a different culture while traveling: with respectful curiosity and an ethnographic approach. A psychologist entering a medical setting needs to keep an open mind and allow for time to understand this new culture. McDaniel, Campbell, and Seaburn (1995) and Seaburn et al. (1996) have borrowed the concept of the mental health practitioner as a "missionary" from Doherty (1986). They note that missionary zeal can result in inadvertently offending medical providers or in frustration for the psychologist attempting to make changes prematurely. They have drawn a parallel between the stereotypic American tourist (the "ugly American") who boorishly applies American cultural norms in other countries and the overzealous mental health professional who attempts to "convert" medical providers to their more psychosocially oriented form of patient care (the "ugly collaborator").

Recognizing that both psychologists and physicians have relevant expertise can help avoid this situation. Respecting the culture of medicine, and attending to how one's insecurities affect interactions, can also minimize problems. Psychologists may feel they have little to offer in the context of life-and-death medicine, and physicians may feel relatively inept at managing patients' emotional reactions to situations. Open communication about the impact of collaboration can ease these tensions. Psychologists also benefit from consulting with other mental health professionals who have worked in medical settings. It is important to continue to engage in professional activities in one's discipline of origin. These activities can provide information, support, and a sense of professional identity that can be threatened when working in a non-mental health setting.

There are also practical approaches a psychologist can use to ease his or her transition. It is very helpful to have an overall picture of how a medical practice works and to understand the different roles of office staff. Shadowing office staff—including support staff, nurses, nurse practitioners, and physicians—helps to clarify the challenges of each role as well as the background of each person. This is also a great way to get to know others in the office and to show that you value everyone's unique contributions. Before shadowing someone, talk with him or her about how you can learn from him or her without interfering with the work. It might also be helpful to talk with him or her about how to introduce you to patients.

Ask questions! Psychologists will often be faced with unfamiliar situations that can be uncomfortable. More information can ease this discomfort. Be aware that there is an appropriate time and place for questions, and respect the provider's time. It can be helpful to keep a notebook of questions that can be addressed at an appropriate time.

When approached for consultation, always ask medical providers how much time they have and to clarify their desired outcome. "How can I help you?" rather than "What can I teach you?" helps avoid frustrating interactions (Seaburn et al., 1996). Often, medical providers do not desire, neither do they have time for, a discourse on the psychological sequelae of the presenting situation. They want to know what to do, what not to do, and who can help them with the patient. Make recommendations in protocol form, with a decision tree, if–then format. An excellent resource that models this form of communication is *Family Oriented Primary Care: A Manual for Medical Providers* (McDaniel et al., 1990). Each chapter ends with a very pragmatic protocol, or how-to section that clarifies and emphasizes the major points of each chapter. These protocols are a great source of ideas for collaborative recommendations.

Although Pace, Chaney, Mullins, and Olson (1995) focused on a consultation model, their suggestions also apply to working in close collaboration. They noted that a successful consultation must begin with an evaluation of the reason for referral, both "stated and unstated." They encouraged consultants to talk with the referring provider before seeing the patient in order to better understand these questions and who the "customer" for the referral is (whether it is the patient, the physician, a nurse, a family member, etc.). In addition, this preconsultation discussion can increase the odds that the health professional and psychologist have a shared understanding of the problem and questions and help the psychologist understand how the doctor–patient relationship may be relevant to the referral. Second, they emphasized the importance of assessing and establishing a therapeutic relationship with both the patient and his or her family. Third, they recommended including the perspectives of other professionals who provide care to the patient but may not be directly involved in the referral. They noted that consultations are far more likely to be successful when all members of the treatment team agree on roles, goals, problem definition, and ideas for intervention. Finally, they stated that the consultant should educate the referring provider and treatment team about empirically based intervention strategies that are specific and practical. It is very helpful to keep all of the systems of care (patient, family, referring provider, and treatment team) in mind throughout the consultation. The more agreement there is among these parties, the more likely it is that suggestions will be seen as potentially helpful and, therefore, adopted.

Maintaining a Collaborative Practice

Like any other relationship, collaborative relationships need ongoing care and attention to thrive. Collaborative partners should schedule periodic meetings, or "check-in" times, when they can process their successes and failures and the experience of working with one another. Such processing also should occur whenever there is a conflict or particularly difficult clinical situation. The stresses and frustrations of difficulties in patient care can easily become fodder for relationship problems.

Psychologists' relationships with other office personnel also need attention. Over time, the psychologist often becomes part of the practice. It is helpful to negotiate the psychologist's role in processing practice issues before they arise. One role can be that of a systems consultant, who helps the practice members work through conflicts and provides staff education regarding management of difficult office situations. It is obviously important to think through potential problems before consulting on office conflicts. Psychologists may also find that office staff with personal problems seek them out for an empathic ear. Just as in any other work setting, the psychologist must tread the line between being a supportive friend and triage agent versus being a therapist. It is important to learn to set friendly but firm boundaries.

Psychologists may notice changes in their clinical practice when they work on site with other primary care clinicians. Working on site reduces many barriers to mental health services, especially if the psychologist, rather than the patient, initiates contact on referral. Patients who might not have the motivation or wherewithal to find a therapist elsewhere will come to see a therapist in their primary care provider's office. Although lowering these barriers facilitates preventative care, it can result in patients who are less advanced in their readiness to change. These patients have little insight or motivation regarding the links between their problems and life stresses or emotional problems. Psychologists may need to adjust their joining and assessment techniques appropriately (e.g., using a slower pace) to be helpful to these patients. On initial contact with some patients, it may become clear that it is the physician, not the patient, who wants the patient to be in treatment. Under these circumstances, consultation with the physician to care for the patient and prepare for future referral may be the best option. Patients who need psychotherapy but are not yet ready or able to accept referral are often a great challenge and frustration.

Working in a primary care setting gives the psychologist ample opportunity for creativity and innovation, particularly when not under fee-for-service productivity pressures. Patients who are in an early stage of readiness to change, or not amenable to traditional therapy, may benefit from other types of psychological services, such as psychoeducational or support groups. Patients who would never consider seeing a psychologist might attend a smoking cessation group or a psychoeducational group for a chronic illness.

It can be helpful initially to present services in a consultative capacity (Wynne, McDaniels, & Weber, 1986). This reduces the commitment needed by the patient to initiate treatment. It also gives the psychologist a mechanism by which to refer out patients whose needs can be better met in another setting. In addition, one to two sessions of consultation with a psychologist is sufficient for many patients who present in primary care. This approach lowers barriers, such as stigma and fear, that prevent patients from obtaining needed psychological services.

One of the most exciting aspects of working in primary care is being on the "front lines" of medical care. There are many patients who simply will not avail themselves of traditional mental-health based services. Regier et al. (1978) estimated that 15% of primary care patients had a diagnosable mental health condition, but only 3% sought treatment in a mental health setting. Nine percent of the patients received treatment from their primary care physician. Collaborating with primary care physicians clearly gives psychologists a new venue for reaching many more people in need.

PUTTING IT ALL TOGETHER: EXAMPLES OF COLLABORATIVE PRACTICES IN THE "REAL WORLD"

There are few published works that describe specifics of collaborative practices. Most publications describe collaboration in hospital-owned or academically based practices, in which both the physician and psychologists are employees. Many articles outline research projects that occurred in the context of a collaborative practice but say little about how the practice evolved or its strengths and foibles (e.g., Riekert, Stancin, Palermo, and Drotar, 1999).

The few publications that describe collaborative practices in community primary care settings indicate that psychologists are most likely to develop collaborative practices with family physicians and pediatricians. Cunningham (1995) described her experiences working in the private practice of three full-time pediatric gastroenterologists. She was an employee of the practice, using her fee-for-service income to cover overhead, salary, and benefits. The financial arrangements were renegotiated yearly. Over a 6-month period, she received 94 referrals, with the most common medical presentations being functional encopresis and recurrent abdominal pain. Psychological reasons for referral included nonadherence to treatment regimens, possible depression, toileting problems, behavioral problems, school avoidance, family conflicts, and feeding problems. Cunningham provided psychological services through parent groups, a children's library with relevant videotapes, psychological testing, individual psychotherapy, behavioral plans, parent guidance, and school consultation. Collaboration with the physicians and nurse practitioner occurred through personal interactions, chart notes, and memos.

Carolyn S. Schroeder has described her collaborative practice with pediatricians over 25 years in a number of publications (Schroeder, 1979, 1997, 1999). From 1973 to 1982, the work of the psychologists at Chapel Hill Pediatrics was part of an interdisciplinary training program at the University of North Carolina. This practice involved provision of prevention services (developmental screening, parent education groups, telephone consultations, and brief face-to-face contacts with parents) as well as consultation to the pediatricians. Because these services were provided as part of a training program, there was no charge for them. The training involved students from psychology, social work, nursing, and pediatrics. The population seen was primarily "well child" and only about 17% of the clients with whom they had contact were referred for more in-depth assessment and treatment.

In 1982, Schroeder joined the pediatric practice on a full-time basis. Given her long-term collaborative relationship with the pediatricians and the parents in the practice, this was a relatively easy transition. It did, however, involve negotiating office renovation and a financial arrangement in which Schroeder formed an independent corporation and shared in overhead costs. The prevention and early-intervention services continued to include students and some faculty from the university and were free to the patients. The psychology staff provided these services on a pro bono basis. The preventative services initially included developmental screening, 2-hours/week call-in time for parents to ask questions regarding development and child management, and groups for parents with children from preschool age to adolescence. They were eventually expanded to include a free library of books and handouts on a wide range of developmental–management issues and ongoing groups for parents of infants and toddlers. By the mid-1980s, a fee was charged for the parent groups. The pediatricians agreed to pay for costs incurred by infant and toddler groups so that they could be free to patients.

Clinical services in this practice include individual and family assessment and treatment for a full range of developmental and psychosocial problems, issue-specific groups for parents and children, and consultation with the schools. Funding for services was provided from a variety of sources. For example, insurance companies provided funding for a patient with attention-deficit hyperactivity disorder in part because of the collaborative nature of the practice. A psychiatrist (who was also a developmental pediatrician) was added to the practice when psychotropic medication became a more viable treatment option.

The pediatric clinic's role as the county medical evaluation center for children who had been neglected and abused provided an opportunity to provide services to sexual abuse victims. The pediatricians advocated an expansion of funding to include psychological assessments. The local Department of Social Services also funded the psychologists to provide group treatment for sexually abused children and their parents. The clinic ultimately received a grant from the National Institute of Mental Health to study factors that influenced the accuracy of children's testimony. The practice became involved in training social service workers, mental health workers, physicians, judges, and lawyers across the state about the assessment and treatment of sexual abuse. Reviewing cases and providing expert testimony also became a source of revenue for the practice. This helped fund talks to community groups and allowed the psychologists to spend time with the schools to develop sex education programs.

Funding, in addition to fee-for-service revenue, was always an important consideration in compensating for the unfunded services such as prevention, curbside consultation with the pediatricians and nurses, collaboration time, and clients who could not pay. In addition to the previously mentioned funding sources, the Pediatrics Department of the University of North Carolina at Chapel Hill funded the psychologists to train pediatric residents 1 day a week on developmental and management issues. This contract had the added benefit of demonstrating the importance of psychologists in primary care, and many of the residents went on to establish collaborative relationships with psychologists in their own practices.

Despite the long-term success of this collaboration, a number of events occurred in the past several years that have made collaboration more difficult and the activities and services of the practice less varied. In the early to mid-1990s, managed care began to have a major impact on the revenues of both the pediatricians and the psychologists. Because of different reimbursement schedules, the pediatricians were providers for a number of plans that did not provide sufficient reimbursement for the psychologists. Therefore, children, mostly preschoolers, on those plans had to be referred to the community mental health center or did not receive treatment. This decrease in early identification and intervention of preschool children has contributed to an increase in the number of older children referred for more serious emotional and behavioral problems.

Practice patterns changed significantly when the psychologists physically moved out of the primary care setting into an adjacent building because of an increased need for space by the medical staff. Although neither the pediatricians nor the psychologists wanted to increase geographic distance, we hoped that, because of our long-term relationship and commitment to working collaboratively, collaboration would not decrease. We planned to have regular joint staff meetings; publish a joint newsletter; continue the telephone consultation hours in the primary care setting; and keep one office in the primary care office for on-site consultation with parents, research, and training. It is interesting that many of the parents seemed pleased to be seen in a quieter, more private setting than the primary care office. The 2-minute walk between buildings, however, has not been made by either the pediatricians or the psychologists on a regular basis. The lack of a daily presence in the pediatric office has decreased the referral rate. The Chapel Hill experience indicates that next door is too far away for close collaboration. Being physically removed from the primary care setting decreased the opportunities to maintain old relationships as well as develop new ones, particularly with the addition of new pediatric and psychology staff. Although both the psychology and pediatric practices are doing well, they are doing less together to meet the needs of the primary care patient population and the community. This decreased collaboration to meet the population needs has moved the psychologists more to a parallel or independent practice in which collaboration and communication is limited to the individual referral.

Schroeder (1997) described how three other psychologists instituted and maintained collaborative pediatric–psychology practices. Although each practice had evolved along its own path, there were consistencies in common presenting problems (negative behavior, attention-deficit hyperactivity disorder, school problems, and anxiety and depression). Each of the psychologists noted some of the professional cross-cultural issues described earlier, including differences in pace and rapid turnover of clients within brief therapeutic contacts. The psychologists shared the general conclusion that collaborating with pediatricians was both rewarding and, at times, exhausting.

Family medicine has also proven fertile ground for collaborative clinical care, teaching, and research (Campbell, McDaniel, & Seaburn, 1992; Seaburn et al., 1996). Family medicine emphasizes the biopsychosocial model (Engel, 1977) and the importance of family as the context in which health and illness occurs. Family physicians learn about multidisciplinary care and collaboration during their training, and a behavioral science curriculum is a mandated part of residency.

Multiple articles have described provision of mental health services in family medicine residencies (Seaburn et al., 1993). Because all residencies must have a behavioral health faculty member, that person often provides clinical services and consultation as well as direct teaching. Academic family medicine centers have also served as training sites for mental health providers who desire to practice or teach in an academic medical environment (Gawinski, Edwards, & Speice, 1999). Such academic settings are fertile ground for research on the impact on patient care, provider experiences, and training of integrating mental health services into primary care.

Little has been written about psychologist–family physician collaboration outside of academic settings. Nancy B. Ruddy worked in a semirural private family practice for 5 years. Her experience paralleled that of practitioners in academic settings. There were initial adjustments to be made by all involved, and a few surprises (e.g., arriving to find seven intakes scheduled on her first day at the practice). However, with good communication and persistence, the practice relationship eventually developed into a very rewarding means of providing patient care. In part because of the rural setting, a wide variety of clinical presentations were seen, ranging from multiple personality disorder (Ruddy, Farley, Nymberg, & Hayden, 1994) to depression, anxiety, marital problems, adjustment disorders, and domestic violence (Ruddy & McDaniel, 1995). Many patients stated directly that they would not have sought treatment outside of their physician's office. They said they followed through on the referral only because the services were on site, and their trusted physician seemed to have a great deal of faith in the psychologist's ability to be helpful.

Because of productivity demands in a fee-for-service environment, some of the more innovative modes of treatment (which were not reimbursable) were not practical. For example, it was helpful to attend medical appointments with patients, but this often was impossible because of scheduling concerns. However, sharing space gave the psychologist and physicians the opportunity to discuss cases easily and reduced both providers' anxiety about particularly difficult cases. Physicians regularly joined psychotherapy sessions for an update on issues relevant to medical care. In addition, the psychologist was able to help patients work through anxieties about medical procedures and conditions because she was able to attend portions of medical appointments. Finally, the psychologist and physicians were able to discuss their perceptions of the efficacy of psychotropic medications for patients and determine when referral to a psychiatrist was necessary. When Ruddy moved to a fully academic job to teach others to collaborate in primary care, many of the patients who had been seen expressed dismay that her practice arrangement was an anomaly. As one patient said, having psychologists and physicians practice together "just makes sense."

CONCLUSION

Psychologists have much to offer to primary care physicians who are particularly willing to collaborate on the high percentage of patients who present with psychosocial concerns. How one approaches this work is key to making a successful transition to working in primary care; flexibility, respectfulness, pragmatism, curiosity, and a sense of humor are all critical characteristics. Psychologists interested in working in primary care need to do homework to determine whether this work is a good fit for them personally and professionally. To succeed, primary care psychologists must learn about this "new land" and its challenges, find an appropriate practice, and develop and maintain a good collaborative relationship. All of this work can be well worth the trouble when it results in an ongoing collaborative relationship.

REFERENCES

Bray, J. H., & Rogers, J. C. (1995). Linking psychologists and family physicians for collaborative practice. *Professional Psychology: Research and Practice, 26,* 132–138.

Campbell, T. L., McDaniel, S. H., Seaburn, D. B. (1992). Family systems and medicine: New opportunities for psychologists. In T. J. Akamaten (Ed.), *Family Health Psychology.* New York: Hemisphere.

Cassata, D. M., & Kirkman-Liff, B. L. (1981). Mental health activities of family physicians. *Journal of Family Practice, 12,* 683–692.

Cunningham C. (1995). Collaborative psychological practice in pediatric gastro-enterology: Clinical issues and professional opportunities. In D. Drotar (Ed.), *Consulting with pediatricians: Psychological perspectives* (pp. 173–185). New York: Plenum.

Doherty, W. J. (1986). A missionary at work: A family therapist in a family medicine department. *Family Therapy Networker, 10,* 65–68.

Doherty, W. J. (1995). The whys and levels of collaboration. *Family Systems Medicine, 13,* 275–281.

Doherty, W. J., & Campbell, T. L. (1988). *Families and health.* Newbury Park, CA: Sage.

Drotar, D. (1993). Influences on collaborative activities among psychologist and pediatricians: Implications for practice, training, and research. *Journal of Pediatric Psychology, 18,* 158–172.

Drotar, D. (1995). *Consulting with pediatricians: Psychological perspectives.* New York: Plenum.

Engel, G. (1977). The need for a new medical model: A challenge for biomedicine. *Science, 196,* 126–129.

Finney, J., Riley, A., & Cataldo, N. (1991). Psychology in primary health care: Effects of brief targeted therapy on children's medical care utilization. *Journal of Pediatric Psychology, 16,* 447–461.

Gawinski, B. A., Edwards, T. M., & Speice, J. (1999). A family therapy internship in a multidisciplinary healthcare setting: Trainees' and Supervisors' Reflections. *Journal of Marital and Family Therapy, 25,* 469–484.

Glenn, M. L. (1987). *Collaborative health care: A family oriented model.* New York: Praeger.

Haley, W. E., McDaniels, S. H., Bray, J. H., Frank, R. G., Heldring, M., Johnson, S. B., et al. (1998). Psychological practice in primary care settings: Practical tips for clinicians. *Professional Psychology: Research and Practice, 29,* 237–244.

Hurley, L. K. (1995). Developing a collaborative pediatric psychology practice in a pediatric primary care setting. In D. Drotar (Ed.), *Consulting with pediatricians: Psychological perspectives.* New York: Plenum.

Jones, K., & Vischi, T. (1979). Impact of alcohol, drug abuse, and mental health treatment on medical care utilization. *Medical Care, 17,* 1–82.

Katon, W., & Gonzales, J. (1994). A review of randomized trials of psychiatric consultation–liaison studies in primary care. *Psychosomatics, 35,* 268–278.

Katon, W., VonKorff, M., Lin, E., Walker, E., Simon, G., Bush, T., et al. (1995). Collaborative management to achieve treatment guidelines: Impact on depression in primary care. *Journal of the American Medical Association, 273,* 1026–1031.

McDaniel, S. H., & Campbell, T. L. (1986). Physicians and family therapists: The risks of collaboration. *Family Systems Medicine, 4,* 4–8.

McDaniel, S. H., Campbell, T. L., & Seaburn, D. B. (1990). *Family oriented primary care: A manual for medical providers.* New York: Springer-Verlag.

McDaniel, S. H., Campbell, T. C., & Seaburn, D. (1995). Principles of collaboration between health and mental health providers in primary care. *Family Systems Medicine, 13,* 283–298.

McDaniel, S. H., Hepworth, J., & Doherty, W. J. (1992). *Medical family therapy: A biopsychosocial approach to families with health problems.* New York: Basic Books.

Mumford, E., Schlesinger, H., Glass, G., Patrick, C., & Cuerdon, T. (1984). A new look at evidence about reduced cost of medical utilization following mental health treatment. *American Journal of Psychiatry, 141,* 1145–1158.

Pace, T. M., Chaney, J. M., Mullins, L. L., & Olson, R. A. (1995). Psychological consultation with primary care physicians: Obstacles and opportunities in the medical setting. *Professional Psychology: Research and Practice, 26,* 123–131.

Regier, D., Goldberg, I., & Taube, C. (1978). The de facto U.S. mental health and addictive disorders service system. *Archives of General Psychiatry, 35,* 685–693.

Riekert, K. A., Stancin, T., Palermo, T. M., & Drotar, D. (1999). A psychological behavioral screening service: Use, feasibility, and impact in a primary care setting. *Journal of Pediatric Psychology, 24,* 405–414.

Rinaldi, R. (1985). Positive effects of psychosocial interventions on total health care: A review of the literature. *Family Systems Medicine, 3,* 417–426.

Ruddy, N. B., Farley, T., Nymberg, J., & Hayden, K. (1994). A case for collaboration: Treating multiple personality disorder in a primary care setting. *Family Systems Medicine, 12,* 327–338.

Ruddy, N. B., & McDaniel, S. H. (1995). Domestic violence in primary care: The psychologist's role. *Journal of Clinical Psychology in Medical Settings, 2,* 49–69.

Schroeder, C. S. (1979). Psychologist in a private pediatrics office. *Journal of Pediatric Psychology, 1,* 5–18.

Schroeder, C. S. (1996). Psychologists and pediatricians in collaborative practice. In R. J. Resnick & R. H. Rosensky (Eds.), *Health psychology through the life span: Practice and research opportunities* (pp. 109–131). Washington, DC: American Psychological Association.

Schroeder, C. S. (1997). The changing practice paradigm in pediatric settings. In R. J. Illback, C. Cobb, & H. Joseph, Jr. (Eds.), *Integrated services for children and families: Opportunities for psychological practice* (pp. 221–255). Washington, DC: American Psychological Association.

Schroeder, C. S. (1999). Commentary: A look to the past and a view to the future. *Journal of Pediatric Psychology, 5,* 447–452.

Schroeder, C. S., & Mann, J. (1991). A model for clinical child practice. In C. S. Schroeder & B. N. Gordon (Eds.), *Assessment and treatment of childhood problems: A clinician's guide* (pp. 375–398). New York: Guilford Press.

Seaburn, D. S., Gawinski, B. A., Harp, J., McDaniel, S. H., Waxman, D., & Shields, C. (1993). Family systems therapy in a primary care medical setting: The Rochester experience. *Journal of Marital and Family Therapy, 19,* 177–190.

Seaburn, D. S., Lorenz, A. L., Gunn, W. B., Gawinski, B. A., & Mauksch, L. B. (1996). *Models of collaboration.* New York: Basic Books.

Wright, L., & Burns, B. J. (1986). Primary mental health care: A "find" for psychology. *Professional Psychology: Research and Practice, 17*, 560–564.

Wynne, L. C., McDaniels, S. H., & Weber, T. T. (Eds.). (1986). *Systems consultation: A new perspective for family therapy*. New York: Guilford Press.

168   RUDDY AND SCHROEDER

9

THE AIR FORCE EXPERIENCE: INTEGRATING BEHAVIORAL HEALTH PROVIDERS INTO PRIMARY CARE

PAUL G. WILSON

Integrating behavioral health providers into primary care can be a complex undertaking. The U.S. Air Force sought to understand this complexity and discover whether the generally positive outcomes experienced in the civilian sector held true in the Air Force, an environment that has both differences with and similarities to primary care settings in the civilian sector. In this chapter I give background information about what came to be know as the *Tinker project*, including the rationale for undertaking the project, the goals the Air Force hoped to obtain by undertaking the project, and information about the project setting. I then present findings from the project,

The views expressed in this chapter are those of the author only and should not be interpreted as the official position of the U.S. Air Force or the Department of Defense. I express appreciation to all individuals, too numerous to mention, who have been and are involved in efforts to integrate behavioral health into primary care within the U.S. Air Force. I extend special thanks to Col. Skip Moe, Dr. David Lombard, and Maj. Carol Copeland, whose collective efforts were instrumental to making the project happen.

along with lessons learned from the perspectives of patients, medical providers, and behavioral health providers.[1]

PROJECT RATIONALE

Patients, providers, and health care systems are recognizing that traditional health care, which tends to be guided by mind–body dualism, is overly constrictive and often not as effective as more holistic approaches. Furthermore, traditional health care, with its splitting of the behavioral health and physical health components of health conditions, does not match well with the human experience. Most conditions are influenced by factors in both behavioral and physical realms, and it is often difficult to discern which is most important.

Health care systems, including the Air Force Medical Service, have recognized that behavioral health problems are common in the people they serve and are consistently at the top of the list in terms of frequency and cost to the system. They have also recognized that the behavioral health component of problems primarily classified as physical in nature is often quite large. Because of these concerns, there has been increasing emphasis on improving the collaboration between behavioral health providers and medical providers.

There are many models for how collaboration can occur between behavioral health and medical providers. These models range from very minimal collaboration (e.g., sending a letter back to the referring provider) to full integration of services (i.e., the behavioral health provider functions as one of many health care providers in a common setting; Seaburn, Lorenz, Gunn, Gawinski, & Mauksch, 1996). The Air Force traditionally has been in the middle of the continuum. Our mental health clinics are under the auspices of the treatment facility (i.e., hospital or clinic) commander and are usually physically located within the hospital or clinic, although some are geographically separated. Thus, the opportunity for collaboration is easier than in some systems where behavioral health facilities are geographically separated or "carved out."[2] Whatever collaborative model is chosen, the overarching goal is to improve collaboration between behavioral health and medical providers so that health care is improved and costs are minimized.

---

[1]The study was named after the intervention site, Tinker Air Force Base in Oklahoma City, and I served as project manager for most of the project. This chapter expands on and summarizes previous reports on the Tinker project (Wilson, 2000a, 2000b, 2001).
[2]Although the Air Force does not technically carve out behavioral health services, a good portion of those services are outsourced, because many mental health clinics see only active-duty personnel, because the primary mission is to keep active-duty personnel fit, healthy, and ready for war or other operations. The hope of recapturing some of the outsourced care, bringing it back into the facility, is another reason the Air Force is interested in providing some kind of behavioral health services in primary care.

The Air Force decided to initiate the Tinker project for six main reasons:

1. Behavioral health problems are common and costly.
2. Most behavioral health problems are seen in primary care settings.
3. A large amount of the workload in primary care settings focuses on behavioral health.
4. Current treatment of behavioral health problems in primary care settings is not optimal.
5. There are barriers to providing behavioral health care in traditional behavioral health settings.
6. Previous studies have shown significant advantages for integrating behavioral health services into primary care.

PROJECT GOALS

The overall goal of the Tinker project was to increase collaboration not by merely colocating behavioral health providers with medical providers in a primary care setting but by having the behavioral health providers practice differently than they would in a traditional behavioral health setting. In the primary care setting they would be seen not as a specialty care service to which patients could be referred but as an integral part of a health care team providing integrated care to the beneficiary population.

There were four specific goals for the project: (a) provide greater access to behavioral health care, (b) increase early identification of behavioral health problems, (c) assess the cost impact to the system, and (d) gain experience for Air Force-wide implementation (e.g., patient and provider satisfaction, methods of practice, unique training needs). I next present details on how the project met each of these goals, along with how the project achieved other goals and how it gave the Air Force valuable information on how to proceed with a more complete, systemwide implementation.

PROJECT SETTING

Tinker Air Force Base was chosen as the intervention site largely because it was believed to be representative of an average Air Force Base in terms of size, population, and operational tempo. It is home to about 30,000 active-duty individuals and beneficiaries. About 16,000 of these people were in the study cohort because they were enrolled through Tricare Prime (the health maintenance organization for the Department of Defense) in the Family Medicine Clinic during the project. The Family Medicine Clinic offered family practice, pediatrics, and obstetrics–gynecology services and employed 17 professional staff, including 7 physicians, 8 physician assistants, and 2 nurse practitioners, along with a number of support personnel.

The project placed two active-duty behavioral health providers into the Family Medicine Clinic. One was a clinical psychologist with postdoctoral training in clinical health psychology, and the other was a social worker. In addition to the two behavioral health providers, the project provided a civilian on site to help with data collection and an active-duty mental health technician was assigned to the Family Medicine Clinic. The technician assisted with checking patients in, conducting group treatments and, after receiving training, performing biofeedback with patients in conjunction with the clinical psychologist. The formal study period of the project was from November 1997 through November 1998.

FINDINGS

Access to Behavioral Health Care

To assess access to behavioral health care, patient visits to the behavioral health providers in the Family Medicine Clinic and visits to behavioral health providers in the Mental Health Clinic were examined. Also examined were the type of beneficiaries served and the number of visits to behavioral health providers in the Family Medicine Clinic and Mental Health Clinic.

Before the initiation of the project, behavioral health care was provided through the Mental Health Clinic or by referral to civilian providers off base. The Mental Health Clinic only saw active-duty personnel; all other beneficiaries (e.g., spouses, children, retirees) were referred off base. Thus, any increase in the number of other beneficiaries seen by the behavioral health providers in the Family Medicine Clinic represented an increase in access for those patients. In fact, the behavioral health providers in the Family Medicine Clinic did increase access by seeing about 1,100 non-active-duty beneficiaries over the course of the project. In addition, they saw almost 500 active-duty personnel, representing increased access for those patients as well.

Another way of looking at access to care is to examine the number of patient visits per provider per month. More patient visits means more patients are accessing the system and being seen. Prior to the Tinker project, an average of about 73 patient encounters were accomplished by each behavioral health provider per month. All of these encounters were in the Mental Health Clinic. Over the course of the project, the behavioral health providers in the Mental Health Clinic averaged 61 visits per provider per month, whereas the behavioral health providers in the Family Medicine Clinic averaged 153 visits per provider per month. Thus, productivity per provider was 253% greater in the Family Medicine Clinic than in the Mental Health Clinic. It is interesting that the behavioral health providers in the Family Medicine Clinic saw almost as many active-duty personnel per provider as the behavioral health providers in the Mental Health Clinic. It is difficult to make a one-to-one comparison between visits to the Mental Health Clinic and those to the Family Medicine Clinic, as different types of patients and different types of cases may be seen in the two clinics. However, it is clear that more patient visits can be accomplished using the Family Medicine Clinic service delivery model.

Still another way to look at access is to consider access to behavioral health providers by medical providers. If medical providers can easily access behavioral health providers for consultation, then access to behavioral health care may increase for patients indirectly, through their medical provider. To assess this aspect of access, a loose accounting was kept of the number of "hallway consultations" provided by the behavioral health providers to the medical providers in the Family Medicine Clinic. Although the data were not kept consistently, it is known that the behavioral health providers had this kind of contact at least six times per day with the medical providers. A consistent comment from the medical providers was that they felt the increased access to behavioral health care was a critical success factor for the project. They felt that it improved clinic services and affected the way they personally delivered care to their patients, making it more holistic.

Early Identification of Behavioral Health Problems

The rate at which common behavioral health disorders were diagnosed was examined to see whether recognition of these problems increased over the course of the project. Increasing recognition of behavioral health problems is an important first step in treating the problems earlier on, thus costing the system less and decreasing suffering on the part of patients. Visits were analyzed for the primary diagnosis given and whether the diagnosis fit into one of eight general categories of behavioral health problems commonly seen in primary care settings: (a) alcohol problems, (b) depression, (c) anxiety, (d) pain, (e) somatization, (f) attention deficit/hyperactivity, (g) panic, and (h) posttraumatic stress. It was thought that focusing on these common problems would capture the majority of cases and simplify the analyses.

The percentage of total visits to the Family Medicine Clinic that had one of the eight common behavioral health diagnoses increased from 2.7% to 3.8% with the addition of one behavioral health provider and increased to 5.0% with the addition of another behavioral health provider (see Figure 9.1). Thus, recognition of these common behavioral health diagnoses increased 85%. It should be noted that focusing only on these eight common

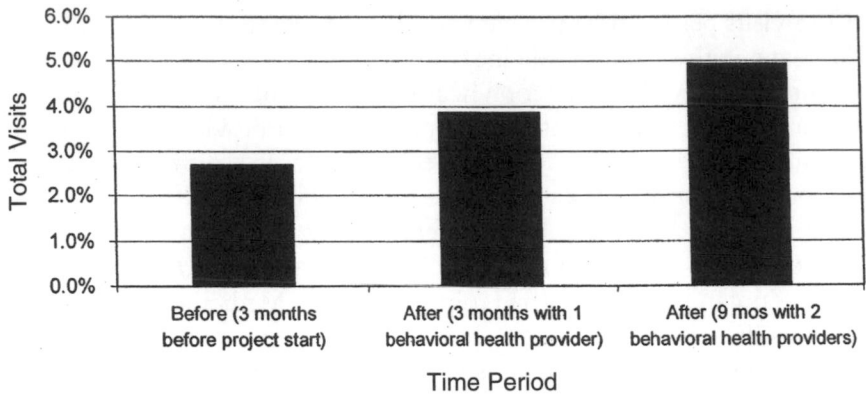

Figure 9.1. Percentage of total visits to the Family Medicine Clinic with selected behavioral health diagnoses, by time period.

diagnoses gives a conservative estimate of the increase in identifying these problems. Including all potential behavioral health diagnoses would have given an even larger estimate of the increase in early identification.

One may wonder what was responsible for the increased recognition: the medical providers, the behavioral health providers, or both. Looking only at common behavioral health diagnoses assigned by the medical providers, the diagnosis rate remained relatively stable from before the project (2.7%) to after the project (2.8% with the addition of one behavioral health provider, 2.2% with two behavioral health providers). The increased recognition, as measured by primary diagnosis assigned, was clearly due to the behavioral health providers and not the medical providers. It is interesting that although one might argue that the medical providers simply shifted the recognition of behavioral health problems to the behavioral health providers, verbal reports from the medical providers do not support this. The medical providers stated that they were more cognizant of behavioral health problems, not less. They stated that they changed their practice pattern so that when faced with a potential behavioral health problem they referred the patient to one of the behavioral health providers. It appears that the medical providers increased their recognition of behavioral health problems but did not assign a primary behavioral health diagnosis. Instead, they referred the patient to the behavioral health provider who provided the diagnosis. In any case, it is clear that recognition of behavioral health problems increased substantially.

Cost Impact

Cost impact for the project was assessed in two ways: (a) pharmacy costs to the Family Medicine Clinic and (b) resource utilization by "high utilizers." I delineate these and discuss them in turn.

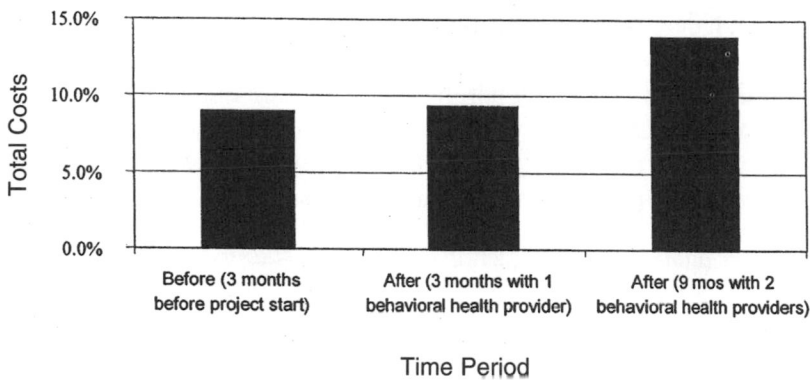

Figure 9.2. Percentage of total Family Medicine Clinic pharmacy costs spent on psychotropic medication, by time period.

Pharmacy Costs to the Family Medicine Clinic

Pharmacy costs were assessed to determine the potential influence the behavioral health providers had on prescribing practice in the clinic. The behavioral health providers discussed medication issues with medical providers within their scope of practice and comfort level, including the need for a medication evaluation, indications for specific medication regimens, and patient response to medication.

Pharmacy costs were broken out into two general categories: (a) psychotropic medications and (b) nonpsychotropic medications. As a way of determining the relative weight of changes in these two costs, and as a way of standardizing costs over time (e.g., controlling for inflation), Family Medicine Clinic pharmacy costs for psychotropic medications were examined as a percentage of total pharmacy costs. In this way, the relative costs of psychotropic and nonpsychotropic medications could easily be compared.

The percentage of total pharmacy costs spent on psychotropic medications increased from 9.0% to 9.3% with the addition of one behavioral health provider and increased to 13.9% with the addition of another behavioral health provider (see Figure 9.2). What this means is that the proportion of total costs spent on psychotropic medication went up while the proportion spent on nonpsychotropic medication went down. Thus, there was clearly an increase in psychotropic medication costs associated with the project. Nonpsychotropic drug costs also increased, but not as much.

It appears that the addition of the behavioral health providers may have increased pharmacy costs for psychotropic medication. It may be that the increase in the recognition and treatment of behavioral health problems, as documented in the preceding section, led to an increase in the use of psychotropic medications. Of course, these analyses do not take into account any cost savings due to more effective treatment of behavioral health problems.

For example, if depression is identified and treated more effectively, then the patient will do better and should need to visit the Family Medicine Clinic less often. Over and above any potential cost savings due to more effective treatment of behavioral health problems, one must consider the benefit of providing better treatment in terms of decreasing suffering—that is, even though it may cost more, if treatment alleviates suffering it is well worth it.

Resource Utilization by Patients Identified as "High Utilizers"

A cohort of *high utilizers* was formed by identifying patients with the highest number of visits to the Family Medicine Clinic who had remained at Tinker for a 2-year period spanning 1 year prior to the project through the year of the project (n = 734).[3] Of the 734 high utilizers, 60 saw a behavioral health provider during the year of the study, and 674 did not.

We (members of the research team) looked at resource utilization by examining what happened with patient visits by this select cohort of patients who had used the system the most. A comparison of the average number of visits in the year prior to the arrival of the behavioral health providers to the year of the project when the behavioral health providers were on staff revealed that high utilizers who saw a behavioral health provider significantly decreased their visits to medical providers in the Family Medicine Clinic from 25.6 (SD = 12.9) to 17.3 (SD = 14.5), $t(59)$ = –4.7, p = .0001. On average, these high utilizers were seen 8.3 fewer times by the medical providers, representing a decrease of 32%. This means that for every high-utilizing patient seen by a behavioral health provider, the medical provider gained more than eight appointment slots, or more than 2 hours of medical provider time per patient—time that is more expensive to the system than behavioral health provider time.

We were interested in seeing whether this decrease in medical provider utilization was due to a simple shifting of appointments to the behavioral health providers. In other words, perhaps the savings in medical provider appointments were offset by visits to the behavioral health providers. We know that this is not what happened. In fact, overall utilization of appointments, whether to a behavioral health provider or a medical provider, decreased by 18%. Including all visits to the Family Medicine Clinic, high utilizers who saw a behavioral health provider significantly decreased their visits over the year from 25.6 (SD = 12.9) to 20.9 (SD = 13.2), $t(59)$ = –2.5, p = .014. On average, they were seen for 4.7 fewer appointments over the course of the year.

It is important to note that this cohort was composed only of high-utilizing patients who had seen a behavioral health provider over the course of the project. There was little systematic effort to identify high-utilizing

---

[3]*High utilizers* were defined as those in the top 25% of the distribution of patient visits over the year prior to the project start. This amounted to those who had been seen 14 or more times in that year.

patients during the project, although the behavioral health providers did ask medical providers if they could be of assistance with their more problematic cases. As the project neared completion, a group treatment approach was started for the high-utilizing patients (and others) to specifically deal with the issues they were facing. It is possible that if a concerted effort had been made from the onset of the project to deal with the highest utilizing patients there may have been an even greater impact. However, the results seen are significant.

To put this in another context, consider what would happen if the results were extended to high-utilizing patients not seen by the behavioral health providers. If all of the high-utilizing patients had been seen by the behavioral health providers and had the same decrease in utilization, then we would expect the clinic to gain more than 1,500 hours of medical provider time, which translates into 80% of one full-time equivalent position. Over and above any hours spent by behavioral health providers dealing with these patients, the clinic would still gain more than 860 hours, or 40% of a full-time equivalent.

These analyses are rough at best and were done post hoc, so caution is advised in interpreting the results. There are many reasons that could explain the decrease in utilization that are not related to the behavioral health providers. In fact, there was a decrease in utilization for all patients, not just the highest utilizers. Unknown differences in patient characteristics between "normal" and high-utilizing patients make it difficult to interpret the findings. For example, it is not known whether some of the high-utilizing patients had "legitimate" reasons for using services so highly (e.g., postsurgical). Also, during the study period a new medical care system (Tricare) was introduced at Tinker that could have led to decreases in utilization through other means, such as demand management. With appropriate cautions given, it still remains that a decrease in utilization was seen that was potentially influenced by the behavioral health providers.

LESSONS LEARNED

There were a number of lessons learned from the project as a result of examining the experiences of the patients, medical providers, and behavioral health providers involved. I first describe opinions expressed by patients and medical providers concerning the behavioral health services provided in the Family Medicine Clinic and then turn the focus to lessons learned from the viewpoint of the behavioral health providers.

Patient Satisfaction

A convenience sample (all patients in 1 week) of 46 patients who had seen one or both of the behavioral health providers was given feedback forms to fill out after the behavioral health providers had been in the clinic for approximately 7 months. Thirty-three patients completed the forms. Respondents rated the behavioral health providers very highly both overall and in terms of helpfulness, with the average rating on both dimensions falling between "excellent" and "outstanding" (the highest rating possible). Respondent ratings for confidence in using services again and recommending the services to acquaintances were very close to the highest rating possible ("definitely"). In addition, 15 patients chose to write additional comments, and all the comments were positive.

It is clear that the patients sampled were highly satisfied with the care they received from the behavioral health providers. Although these results could have come from an unrepresentative sample, we (members of the research team) think this is unlikely and that the results are fairly representative of patients seen by the behavioral health providers. There was no effort to single out the most receptive patients, and a good percentage of those sampled returned the questionnaire, allowing more confidence in the results.

Medical Provider Satisfaction

All medical providers ($n = 17$) were surveyed by telephone in the 10th month of the study by myself; I was located at an Air Force base in another state. The overall ratings for the availability of the behavioral health providers, the quality of care delivered, professional knowledge, and communication and rapport with the medical staff were all close to the top of the rating scale ("outstanding"). The providers also felt the addition of the behavioral health providers much improved overall patient care in the clinic and had a positive impact on the care they personally provided their own patients. Most of the open-ended comments acknowledged the increased access to behavioral health care for both the patient and the provider and the belief that the providers were better able to treat the "whole patient." All 17 of the providers "strongly favored" (the highest rating possible) including behavioral health providers in similar settings in the future.

Advice for Behavioral Health Providers

There was a multitude of knowledge gained by the experiences of the behavioral health providers. This knowledge has been distilled into a series of lessons aimed toward behavioral health providers considering working in a primary care setting. Readers should keep in mind that these lessons may not apply to every setting.

There are two main lessons, with a number of sublessons, all of which are consistent with themes mentioned by others in the literature (e.g., Blount, 1998; Cummings et al., 1997; Seaburn et al., 1996). The following is a summary of the lessons learned. Each one is subsequently considered in turn.

1. Fit into the culture
   - Be flexible, respectful, and tolerant
   - Get to know the staff
   - Seek out those who are supportive
   - Clarify expectations
   - Be a generalist (but realize you can't do it all)
2. Keep it short and simple
   - Make yourself available
   - Get control of your schedule
   - Be brief, concise, and solution focused
   - Document differently

Fit Into the Culture

The first and most important step in trying to integrate oneself into the primary care setting is to recognize that the primary care environment is very different from the traditional behavioral health setting. The behavioral health provider has the responsibility to fit into this new culture.

Be flexible, respectful, and tolerant. Probably the most important concept to keep in mind is that the primary care setting is very different from the traditional behavioral health setting. Both have different cultures surrounding the provision of health care. Examples of these differences include the use of diagnoses (e.g., more general vs. more specific, the *International Classification of Diseases* (World Health Organization, 1990) vs. the *Diagnostic and Statistical Manual of Mental Disorders* [American Psychiatric Association, 1994]), the use of space (e.g., smaller, shared, brightly lit examination rooms vs. larger, individual offices with softer lighting), and the use of time (quick, brief, simple interactions with patients vs. slower, in-depth, complex discussions with patients). Although the primary care setting may need to make some adjustments to accommodate a behavioral health provider (e.g., creating space, changing patient care to include behavioral health aspects), the responsibility of adjusting to the new setting falls squarely on the shoulders of the behavioral health provider. The behavioral health provider is the "outsider" coming into the new culture and will need to remain flexible and tolerant of how things are accomplished in the primary care setting.

Get to know the staff. In some respect, all staff involved in the clinic have some influence over what happens there. The new behavioral health provider should proactively approach all staff, including clinic chiefs, managers, medical providers, nurses, administrative–medical technicians, and other support personnel with the attitude that there is something to learn from everyone. Because the behavioral health provider functions as another health care provider in the clinic and interacts frequently with other providers, it is especially important to get to know the other providers.

With this project, it worked well to meet informally with each provider individually (e.g., over a cup of coffee in the morning, over lunch) to get to know him or her as a fellow provider and to find out how one might be of assistance to him or her. It is crucial to learn about the provider's previous experience with behavioral health providers (e.g., Has he or she ever worked with a behavioral health provider? What was that like? What are his or her impressions of the role of behavioral health? etc.), because this can help ascertain who may be supportive and who may present barriers. Learning about the provider's current patient load and specific patients he or she thinks may benefit from behavioral health care helps identify how one may be of assistance.

In getting to know the provider staff one may encounter those who do not see a need to collaborate with the behavioral health provider. With the Tinker project, there were three such providers initially. These providers wanted to manage the cases themselves and did not see a need for a behavioral health specialist. Just as with any type of provider, there will be variability in the types of education, training, experience, philosophies, and personal preferences of the providers. One should be cognizant of these factors and work within (or sometimes around) them to ensure that good working relationships are maintained and good patient care is accomplished. After a short time, all of the providers who were initially resistant were using the behavioral health provider's services.

Seek out those who are supportive. With the Tinker project, the chief of the Family Medicine Clinic was a family practice physician who had had the opportunity to work with a behavioral health provider on staff during his residency training. He was very favorable to including behavioral health providers as part of the staff of the Family Medicine Clinic. His support of the project was crucial to acceptance by the other providers within the clinic. Because all family practice residencies are required to have a behavioral scientist on staff, family practice physicians in particular may be good people from whom to gain support when behavioral health providers offer their services as a new addition to a primary care setting. One should also seek out individuals who are influential in the clinic. This usually will include the clinic chief but may also include others who are respected and listened to by the other staff. As an outsider to the clinic, the behavioral health provider should get to know who these key personnel are and make efforts to win their support.

Clarify expectations. As part of getting to know the staff, one should clarify expectations of what the behavioral health provider will do. These expectations can be either professional or administrative in nature. For example, in the Tinker project there was an initial expectation that the behavioral health providers would advise other providers on the use of psychotropic medications. Although some states have recently given psychologists with training in psychopharmacology authority to provide medication consultation, this would have been overstepping the limits of competence for these behavioral health providers. This expectation was negotiated, and it was agreed that behavioral health providers would advise other providers on when it seemed that medication might be helpful but would not advise on specific medications or dosages.

Another expectation of a more administrative nature was the role of the behavioral health provider in relation to the Mental Health Clinic. In this project, the behavioral health providers were assigned to the Family Medicine Clinic, and their performance was overseen and judged by the Family Medicine Clinic. Although there was interaction with the mental health clinic, the providers were assets of the Family Medicine Clinic and were treated as such. The role of the behavioral health provider and his or her interaction with the Mental Health Clinic should be clarified from the outset.

Be a generalist (but realize you can't do it all). The primary care setting is usually where many different types of problems are seen and treated. If the treatment needed is beyond the scope of what the primary care setting can handle, the patient is referred out. In this project, the behavioral health providers undertook the same attitude. Most problems that were presented to the behavioral health providers were dealt with in the Family Medicine Clinic. When necessary, cases were referred to specialty clinics or to other systems of care. Cases requiring treatment longer than six to eight sessions were referred out.

Keep It Short and Simple

As noted above, there are a number of things one can do to fit into the culture of a primary care setting. Part of fitting in involves learning to work differently than one would in a traditional behavioral health setting, which is exemplified in the following dictums.

Make yourself available. One of the key ingredients of success for this project was the availability of the behavioral health providers and ease of access to them, which made it simple for the medical providers to use their services. Availability and ease of access were fulfilled in a number of ways. First, physical colocation made it easy for the medical providers to have "hallway consults" and to walk patients directly to the behavioral health provider when needed. Whenever possible, the behavioral health provider should be colocated within the primary care setting. If the behavioral health provider is a full-time asset, there will need to be permanent office space made available. If the behavioral health provider is a part-time asset, there may be spare office space available. Often there is space for other part-time assets (e.g., specialty consultants), and this may be shared. If possible, the behavioral health provider should be a full-time asset of the primary care setting. Being a full-time asset means that the behavioral health provider is a full member of the team and is available on a continual basis.

A second way to be available for the medical staff is to ensure prompt response to their needs. In this project, the behavioral health providers saw patients deemed to have "urgent" needs within 72 hours and those with "emergent" needs within 30 minutes. Referrals to the behavioral health providers were initially made formally, on consult request forms. However, this was soon seen as an unnecessary burden, and referrals were made informally, as "internal clinic referrals."

When medical providers wanted assistance from one of the behavioral health providers, they often would approach the behavioral health provider while the patient was still in their office, discuss the case briefly in the hallway ("hallway consult"), and then both would see the patient briefly. The behavioral health providers maintained time in their schedules to accommodate these kind of quick consultations. When seeing the patient with the medical provider, the behavioral health provider would introduce him- or herself and set up an appointment for assessment and treatment planning with the patient. After the behavioral health provider saw the patient, the medical record served as the primary communication vehicle and was sent back to the referring medical provider. Referrals from other clinics (e.g., internal medicine, physical therapy, mental health) were received occasionally and were accomplished by means of formal consult requests.

Still another way the behavioral health provider can be available is to serve functions other primary care team members serve. This may involve attending meetings (e.g., staff, team, continuing medical education) or serving on various committees (e.g., clinical guidelines, prevention, morale, etc.). The behavioral health providers in this project served on a number of committees and attended all staff, continuing medical education, and clinic team meetings, which helped them be seen as true team members.

Get control of your schedule. The scheduling of appointments to primary care settings across the Air Force are often handled by a central appointment desk. With the Tinker project, this was problematic. Some patients who should have seen a medical provider first were booked into behavioral health provider appointments, some appointments were double booked, and some patients were booked for more time than they needed. The behavioral health providers brought the problem to the attention of the clinic chief (who was very supportive of the project), who initiated changes in the scheduling system. Appointments to the behavioral health providers eventually were accessible only by the health care providers, which greatly reduced the confusion caused by using central appointment booking.

How the behavioral health providers used their time also changed during the project. The scheduling template for the behavioral health providers was initially set up with individual, marital, family, and biofeedback appointments scheduled for 40–50 minutes, and groups (stress management and weight management) were scheduled for 90 minutes. The scheduling template was eventually changed to only four types of appointments: (a) routine, lasting 10–30 minutes,; (b) today, lasting 20–30 minutes,; (c) biofeedback, using 10 minutes of provider time and 50 minutes of technician time, and

(d) groups (stress, weight, depression, and anxiety management, and a men's and women's group). The men's and women's groups evolved into high-utilizer groups that provided supportive treatment to patients who were identified by their medical providers as utilizing Family Medicine Clinic services frequently. Hallway consultations and urgent or emergent cases were seen during the "today" appointment slots, which were scheduled for 30 minutes every hour, meaning that a behavioral health provider was usually available within a short period of time. Thus, the medical providers usually had easy access to a behavioral health provider throughout the day, every day.

Be brief, concise, and solution focused. Primary care settings are very different environments than traditional behavioral health settings. Fitting into the culture of the primary care setting is a key to being an effective part of the primary care team. The behavioral health providers for this project had to change how they traditionally provided behavioral health services and learn new ways more fitting for the new environment. They had to change their interventions so they were briefer and more solution focused (sessions were set at 20–30 minutes and treatment was kept to 6–8 sessions). The focus initially was on dealing with depression, anxiety, attention-deficit/hyperactivity disorder, and marital problems. Diagnoses were kept at a general level (e.g., "depression" rather than "Major Depressive Disorder, Single Episode, In Partial Remission"). Feedback to the medical providers also was kept brief and straightforward. Whereas in-depth case conceptualization is valuable in a traditional behavioral health setting, it is unwieldy in the primary care setting. Feedback to the medical providers usually consisted of symptoms, diagnosis, treatment plan, and prognosis. Extensive psychometric assessment was also not accomplished by the behavioral health providers. In the primary care setting for this project, psychometric assessment was limited to occasional use of brief assessment tools (e.g., Zung Depression Scale, Beck Anxiety Inventory, SF-36, ADD-H Comprehensive Teacher/Parent Rating Scales [ACTeRs]).

Document differently. Documentation of care by the behavioral health providers was handled very differently in this setting compared to how it is handled in a traditional behavioral health setting. As mentioned already, feedback to the medical providers was usually brief, less inclusive, and problem-oriented and was usually accomplished by means of the medical record. The notes focused on symptoms, diagnosis, treatment plan, and prognosis. There was no duplicate record, as in traditional Air Force behavioral health settings. In addition, there were no separate Privacy Act forms or informed-consent documents. It was decided early on in the project that the Privacy Act form already in the medical record was sufficient. In addition, it was decided that a separate informed-consent document was not necessary and might be a barrier to behavioral health care (e.g., concern by patients that they had to sign a form to get "mental health treatment" and the associated stigma). However, patients were informed that they were seeing a behavioral health provider and that there were limits to confidentiality. Their understanding of these facts was documented in the initial intake note, along with the patient's understanding and acceptance of the treatment plan. Whether a specific informed-consent document is necessary in primary care settings is a contentious issue. Guidelines for providing behavioral health care usually necessitate a specific written document, but these guidelines are not typically geared to working in a primary care setting. Although informed consent to treatment is necessary, how to accomplish and document it is an issue that has not been fully resolved.

SUMMARY/NEXT STEPS

The Tinker project was designed to discover how the Air Force might take procedures instituted in the civilian sector and apply them to its unique environment. These procedures were aimed at increasing the collaboration between medical providers and behavioral health providers by integrating behavioral health services into a primary care setting. It was hoped that this collaboration would be a first step in showing how health care services in an Air Force setting could better integrate mind and body. The behavioral health providers did a wonderful job in taking on the challenges of practicing in ways very different from traditional practice. They more than met the challenge and have provided the Air Force with extremely valuable lessons about how to change business practices to include behavioral health services in primary care.

There were four specific goals for the project, and all of these goals were met. First, the project increased access to behavioral health care by making it available to non-active-duty beneficiaries, by increasing productivity, and by increasing access for medical providers to behavioral health consultation. Second, the project increased the recognition of behavioral health problems so they could be dealt with earlier. Third, the project found that pharmacy costs may increase slightly because of increased use of psychotropic medication but that costs may decrease in other ways, such as decreasing utilization in patients who use the system frequently. Fourth, the project garnered a tremendous amount of knowledge about how behavioral health providers could do this new kind of work in the Air Force system. It also showed that implementing this new service delivery model for behavioral health care can lead to high patient and medical provider satisfaction. The Tinker project was tremendously valuable in all of these respects.

The value of the Tinker project is being demonstrated today in the fact that the knowledge gained has been used as a stepping-off point for another project designed to disseminate a similar model of integrated care across the Air Force. This follow-on project, known as the *Behavioral Health Optimization Project*, has incorporated training in this new service delivery model at three major Air Force medical centers and uses a train-the-trainer model for assimilation of integrated primary health care across the Air Force. It already has been implemented at a large number of Air Force medical treatment facilities, and this number is increasing rapidly. The Behavioral Health Optimization Project is also providing standardized training and provision of care across all behavioral health providers in primary care in the Air Force.

Although there have been barriers to implementing a new service delivery model, teamwork by key people at all levels of the Air Force health care system—from executive management to individual provider—has overcome most of these barriers. There is now a synergism in the system that has coalesced into a solid movement toward integrated care as part of a larger movement focusing on prevention and the health of the entire beneficiary population. The Air Force is well on its way to changing how behavioral health care, and health care in general, is provided within it.

REFERENCES

American Psychiatric Association. (1994). *Diagnostic and statistical manual of mental disorders* (4th ed.). Washington, DC: Author.

Blount, A. (1998). Introduction to integrated primary care. In A. Blount (Ed.), *Integrated primary care: The future of medical and mental health collaboration* (pp. 1–43). New York: W. W. Norton.

Cummings, N. A., Cummings, J. L., & Johnson, J. N. (Eds.). (1997). *Behavioral health in primary care*. Madison, CT: Psychosocial Press.

Seaburn, D. B., Lorenz, A. D., Gunn, W. B., Gawinski, V. A., & Mauksch, L. B. (1996). *Models of collaboration: A guide for mental health professionals working with health care practitioners*. New York: Basic Books.

Wilson, P. G. (2000a). The Tinker project—Part I: Major outcomes. *The Air Force Psychologist, 18*(1), 23–26.

Wilson, P. G. (2000b). The Tinker project—Part II: Lessons learned. *The Air Force Psychologist, 18*(3), 5–9.

Wilson, P. G. (2001). *The Tinker project: Integrating behavioral health providers into primary care*. Unpublished manuscript.

World Health Organization (1990). *International classification of diseases and related health problems* (10th rev.). Geneva: Author.

III

PRIMARY CARE PSYCHOLOGY FOR SPECIFIC POPULATIONS

10

BEHAVIORAL AND DEVELOPMENTAL PROBLEMS OF CHILDREN IN PRIMARY CARE: OPPORTUNITIES FOR PSYCHOLOGISTS

MAUREEN M. BLACK AND LAURA NABORS

Almost 25 years ago, Regier, Goldberg, and Taube (1978) provided convincing evidence that most of the mental health care for children in the United States was provided in primary care facilities by providers trained in primary care and not in mental health clinics by providers trained in mental health. Although most of the mental health care they described consisted of brief counseling, prescriptions for psychotropic medications, and referrals for mental health services, this limited level of care was more than most children with behavioral or developmental problems received from mental health specialists (Kelleher & Long, 1994). Primary care providers are even more likely to assume responsibility for children's mental health services in today's health care delivery environment, especially in the current era of managed care with limited referral resources (Kelleher, Scholle, Feldman, & Nace,

Preparation of this chapter was partially supported by Grant MCJ-240301 from the Maternal and Child Health Research Program of the U.S. Department of Health and Human Services, and by the Lanata–Piazzon Partnership.

2000; Schroeder, 1999; Starfield, 1992). This pattern raises concerns, because there are many children in primary care with both unrecognized and recognized, but untreated, psychosocial problems. The Surgeon General's 1999 report on mental health raised concerns that primary care providers did not pay enough attention to children's mental health problems (U.S. Department of Health and Human Services, 1999). Rates of behavioral and developmental problems vary from 18% to 25% (Costello et al., 1988; Kelleher, McInerny, Gardner, Childs, & Wasserman, 2000; Kelleher & Rickert, 1994; Lavigne et al., 1996) and extend throughout the pediatric age range, including preschoolers. Rates of identification of behavioral and developmental problems have historically been low, leading some professionals to label behavioral and developmental problems the "hidden morbidity" in pediatric care (Costello et al., 1988; Horwitz, Leaf, Leventhal, Forsyth, & Speechley, 1992).

Parents from all socioeconomic levels worry about their children's behavior and development, with their specific concerns reflecting the unique challenges in their families or communities (Hickson, Altemeier, & O'Connor, 1983; Stickler, Salter, Broughton, & Alario, 1991). The unrecognized and unmet mental health needs of children are problems of national concern. Children with unmet behavioral and developmental needs are not only less able to benefit from educational and other community services but also at increased risk for developing serious psychiatric illnesses (Szilagyi & Schor, 1998), for becoming high users of the general health care system (Janicke, Finney, & Riley, 2001), and for becoming involved in the juvenile justice system (Timmons-Mitchell et al., 1997). In this chapter we examine strategies for psychology professionals to collaborate with primary care providers with the goal of preventing the "hidden morbidity" of behavioral and developmental problems and promoting the mental health of America's children.

BARRIERS TO PSYCHOSOCIAL SERVICES IN PRIMARY CARE

There are many barriers to the provision of psychosocial services in primary care. First, the demands on primary care providers, imposed primarily by managed care, leave insufficient time to address psychosocial issues. Pediatricians spend an average of 14 minutes with each patient (Ferris et al., 1998), which is hardly enough time to care for acute medical needs; screen for general medical issues; and provide basic preventive services, such as immunizations. Second, pediatricians have a training mandate to prioritize children's physical health and may not regard behavioral and developmental issues as within their range of expertise (Lavigne et al., 1998; Sharpe, Pantell, Murphy, & Lewis, 1992). All pediatricians should have received training in children's behavior and development; however, their hands-on, clinical exposure varies. Some pediatricians are very competent dealing with these is-sues, whereas others are uncomfortable or unfamiliar with behavioral issues, particularly around sensitive ones, such as sexuality or substance use (Blum, 1987; Perrin, 1999; Sharpe et al., 1992). Although there are many systematic procedures for gathering information about children's behavior and develop-ment (Stancin & Palermo, 1997), these procedures are not routinely used in primary care. Third, children and families may be reluctant to report behav-ioral and developmental problems to their pediatrician (Horwitz, Leaf, & Leventhal, 1998; Marks, Malizio, & Hoch, 1983), particularly if the prob-lems involve sensitive issues (Turner et al., 1998) or if their pediatrician does not initiate discussion on behavioral and developmental issues (Wissow, Roter, & Wilson, 1994). Finally, without adequate resources to deal with children's behavioral and developmental problems, some pediatricians feel that it is frustrating or unethical to raise behavioral and developmental issues (Perrin, 1998).

Most pediatricians work diligently to overcome these barriers but find that even if children's behavioral and developmental issues are identified within primary care settings there are substantial barriers to referral and treat-ment. In addition to the constraints of time, training, expertise, and level of comfort, the reimbursement system makes it extremely difficult for pediatri-cians to refer children to mental health providers or to be reimbursed for treating children's behavioral and developmental problems themselves (Kelleher & Rickert, 1994; Kelleher, Scholle, et al., 2000). Because many insurance plans separate mental health from physical health, reimbursement plans differ. For mental health providers to be reimbursed, the child must have a psychiatric diagnosis, based on the *Diagnostic and Statistical Manual of Mental Disorders* (*DSM–IV*; American Psychiatric Association, 1994). Many of the problems identified among children in primary care interfere with their school and family interactions but may not be severe enough to warrant a *DSM–IV* diagnosis.

PSYCHOLOGY–PEDIATRIC COLLABORATION

In the 1960s, both pediatricians and psychologists recognized the mer-its of increasing collaborations between the two disciplines (Kagan, 1965; Wilson, 1964; Wright, 1967). The field of pediatric psychology was born in the scientist–practitioner model to address behavioral and developmental issues in children's health and illness (Wright, 1967). Journals in pediatrics and psychology (e.g., *Pediatrics*, *Journal of Developmental and Behavioral Pedi-atrics*, *Journal of Pediatric Psychology*, and *Journal of Clinical Child and Adoles-cent Psychology*) include many excellent examples of collaboration between pediatricians and psychologists in research, training, and clinical services. However, most of the collaboration occurs in medical centers; there are fewer examples of collaboration in primary care or in community settings, where most children receive primary care services (for exceptions, see Evers-Szostek, 1997; Schroeder, 1999).

MODELS OF COLLABORATION

Drotar (1995) outlined four models of collaboration between pediatricians and psychologists. The most common model of collaboration is the psychologist as tertiary provider. In this model, pediatricians assume responsibility for identifying children with behavioral and developmental problems and referring them to psychologists. The level of collaboration between pediatricians and psychologists varies, but each one maintains an independent practice. The second model is one of consultation and often occurs in multidisciplinary teams in medical centers. One provider (often the pediatrician) assumes primary responsibility for the patient and the other provider (often the psychologist) provides consultation. The third model, interdisciplinary, also occurs in medical centers, but it is a closer collaboration than the second model because the two providers share responsibility, rather than one assuming primary responsibility. Interdisciplinary teams, rather than multidisciplinary teams, often function through shared responsibility, and billing is done as a team. The final model of collaboration is focused at the level of the practice or the community, not on individual patients. In this model, pediatricians and psychologists work together to define the needs and intervention options for the community. This type of collaboration may lead to beneficial programs that reduce children's behavioral and developmental problems (Black & Krishnakumar, 1998), but it does not fit within insurance reimbursement plans.

The Psychologist as Tertiary Provider

There are many successful examples of psychology as a tertiary or referral service for children with behavioral and developmental problems, particularly among children with chronic illnesses (Roberts, 1992); that is, when primary care pediatricians suspect that a child is experiencing developmental or behavioral problems, they refer the child to a psychologist, usually located in a separate practice. The field of psychology has a long tradition of using scientific methods to validate treatments (Routh, 1982), and there are many published examples of empirically validated treatments delivered in tertiary settings (e.g., Kazdin, Bass, Ayers, & Rodgers, 1990; Spirito, 1999).

The Psychologist as Consultant

Schroeder (1999) is a well-recognized pioneer in the integration of psychological services into primary care. She began her work as part of an interdisciplinary training program for trainees in psychology, social work, pediatrics, and nursing at the University of North Carolina. Consistent with the second model of collaboration described by Drotar (1995), the pediatricians maintained primary responsibility for the patients, and the interdisciplinary trainees provided consultation through developmental screening, parent groups, telephone consultation, brief parent meetings, and consultations with pediatricians. These services were designed to prevent behavioral and developmental problems and were offered at no fee (Schroeder, 1999). Perrin (1999) also noted that the consultative model works well within a pediatric practice, as long as external funding is available.

Over time, Schroeder (1999) noted that the move from a consultative model to a separate-provider model introduced multiple threats to the effectiveness of psychological services for children (see chap. 8, this volume).

In addition to challenges from managed care practices that made referrals difficult, challenges arose when the psychologists no longer shared space with the pediatricians (Schroeder, 1999). Although space within the pediatric practice was often tight and noisy, the proximity had many advantages. Not only were psychologists available to see or schedule patients as soon as concerns were detected, but also they frequently engaged in informal "curbside consults" with pediatricians regarding research, prevention, and training. In addition, the presence of psychologists in the pediatric practice often reduced the stigma associated with psychological services, promoted access to psychological providers, and prompted parents to raise questions about their children's behavior and development.

The Psychologist as Interdisciplinary Team Member

Children with special health care needs and chronic illnesses present unique challenges to health care providers and often require the expertise of providers from different disciplines working together (Drotar, 1995). The benefits of interdisciplinary care have been well documented in areas such as developmental disabilities (Yerbury, 1997), asthma (Weinstein, Chenkin, & Faust, 1997), oncology (Melamed, 1995), diabetes (Saunders, Miller, & Cates, 1989), child abuse (Kolbo & Strong, 1997), and failure to thrive (Black, Feigelman, & Cureton, 1999). The role of psychology in interdisciplinary teams is broad, extending from preventive services to education to diagnostic and therapeutic care.

In the past, reimbursement often went to interdisciplinary teams through Medicaid contracts; however, reforms in health care reimbursement have changed that pattern. Managed-care companies often insist on the accountability of individual providers (Seid, Sadler, Peddecord, & Kurtin, 1997) rather than the accountability of interdisciplinary teams. Although there are merits to ensuring that individual providers are accountable, the separation of managed-care plans into physical and behavioral components has introduced a major barrier into the provision of interdisciplinary services for children with special health care needs. If psychologists are forced to rely on *DSM–IV* diagnostic codes to bill for interdisciplinary services, then they have no way to bill for the preventive and educational services they provide. Thus, children with special health care needs are often denied the services that enable them to function, unless they have a psychiatric diagnosis. This restrictive reimbursement practice has dismantled many interdisciplinary teams and replaced the provision of services to children with special health care needs with a less effective, although financially viable, single-provider model of care.

The Psychologist as Community Collaborator

In the community-collaborator model, psychologists work with pediatricians and other colleagues to develop programs to prevent or treat children's behavioral and developmental problems (Black & Krishnakumar, 1998). Programs that offer the most promise are those that are based on sound psychological principles, use empirically validated strategies, involve families, are developmentally and culturally sensitive, and are integrated into existing educational or health care systems in the community. Strategies such as inviting community members to participate on advisory boards, helping communities identify and overcome environmental stressors, and facilitating support and connections among community members can promote community collaboration and contribute to the development of culturally relevant programs (Isaacs-Shockley, Cross, Bazron, Dennis, & Benjamin, 1996; Wandersman & Nation, 1998). *Fourteen Ounces Of Prevention* (Price, Cowen, Lorion, & Ramos-McKay, 1988) describes successful prevention programs that have been developed and evaluated by psychologists in collaboration with community partners.

Diagnostic Codes

One of the challenges to primary care has been the necessity of using *DSM–IV* diagnostic codes to describe children's behavioral and developmental problems. The codes in the *DSM–IV* are more serious and less prevalent than the range of behavioral and developmental problems frequently seen among children in primary care. To address this problem, the American Academy of Pediatrics, in collaboration with other professional organizations, including the Society of Pediatric Psychology, developed the *Diagnostic and Statistical Manual for Primary Care (DSM–PC), Child and Adolescent Version* (Wolraich, Felice, & Drotar, 1996; Wolraich, 1997).

The *DSM–PC* was developed on the basis of the philosophy that the quality of children's environments should be incorporated into an assessment of their symptoms, because the environment could alter a child's vulnerability to behavioral and developmental problems. Thus, there is a "Situations" section of the *DSM–PC* that addresses 12 potentially stressful situations: (a) Challenges to Primary Support Group (e.g., divorce), (b) Changes in Caregiving (e.g., parental physical illness), (c) Functional Changes in Family (e.g., birth of a sibling), (d) Community or Social Challenges (e.g., religious discrimination), (e) Educational Challenge (e.g., parental illiteracy), (f) Parent/Adolescent Occupational Challenges (e.g., unemployment), (g) Housing Challenges (e.g., homelessness), (h) Economic Challenges (e.g., poverty), (i) Inadequate Access to Health and/or Mental Health Services, (j) Legal System or Crime Problem (e.g., incarceration of parent), (k) Other Environmental Situation (e.g., witness of violence), and (l) Health-Related Situations (e.g., chronic health condition; Drotar, 1999). In addition, providers are encouraged to include both risk and protective factors in their assessment of the impact of environmental conditions on children's behavior and development.

The *DSM–PC* also includes Child Manifestations or symptoms. There are 10 behavioral clusters: (a) Developmental Competency (e.g., speech and language); (b) Impulsive/Hyperactive or Inattentive Behaviors; (c) Negative/Antisocial Behaviors (e.g., aggression); (d) Substance Use/Abuse; (e) Emotions and Moods (e.g., symptoms of anxiety); (f) Somatic and Sleep Behaviors; (g) Feeding, Eating, Elimination Behaviors; (h) Illness-Related Behaviors (e.g., nonadherence to medical recommendations); (i) Sexual Behaviors; and (j) Atypical Behaviors (e.g., bizarre behavior). Each behavioral cluster is divided into three categories. The first category, *developmental variations*, includes behaviors that parents may describe as worrisome but are within the range of normalcy for the child's age and level of development. The second category, *problems*, includes behaviors that are serious enough to affect the child's functioning at home or at school but not serious enough to warrant a psychiatric diagnosis. The third category, *disorders*, includes problems that meet *DSM–IV* criteria. This classification system enables providers to determine when a child's behavior should be monitored and when it is of enough concern to warrant referral.

The *DSM–PC* provides developmental guidelines to indicate how symptoms are typically manifested among children of differing ages. In addition, information is provided to help clinicians identify alternative causes (e.g., medical conditions) and comorbid and associated conditions (Drotar, 1999).

The *DSM–PC* offers potential advantages to all primary care providers, because it classifies behavioral and developmental problems before they reach the level of psychiatric diagnoses, thereby extending the focus of care to prevention and early intervention. However, it is unclear how managed-care companies will view the *DSM–PC* codes, because implementation is likely to lead to more children being identified and more requests for reimbursement (Rappo, 1997). Although the *DSM–PC* has been presented to pediatricians at national meetings and in training sessions, it has not been adopted by most pediatric practices, and there are many unanswered questions regarding training and implementation (Drotar, 1999).

Managed Care

Most insured patients are enrolled in managed-care plans that include "carve-outs" for mental or behavioral health problems—that is, separate plans (and providers) are responsible for mental and behavioral health services. Kiesler (2000) argued that carve-outs arose partially because the demand for behavioral and mental health services was unpredictable and therefore not amenable to a capitated system. He also alleged that psychologists, trained in individual treatment models, were unprepared to deal with capitation or population-based treatment models.

Separation of physical and behavioral provider systems has introduced an artificial dichotomy into treatment, particularly for children with chronic illnesses. Not only is there a link between the quality of functioning within the families of children with chronic illnesses and children's adjustment to their illness (Drotar, 1997), but also, in many cases, children's physical and behavioral problems have common origins (MacLean, Perrin, Gortmacher, & Pierre, 1992).

Although the merits of integrated physical and behavioral systems may eliminate carve-outs (Kiesler, 2000), psychologists will need to renegotiate their roles within managed health care systems. Just as pediatricians predict that pediatric care will often be delivered by nonphysicians, such as pediatric nurse practitioners (Nazarian, 1995), it is likely that in some states, particularly where they are not enough doctoral-level psychologists, psychological care will be delivered by master's-level therapists, under the supervision of doctoral-level psychologists. In addition, psychologists will have to be prepared to use and defend empirically supported interventions and to examine the efficacy of innovative methods of prevention and treatment, including short-term therapy, group therapy, and other nontraditional alternatives (Finney, Riley, & Cataldo, 1991). Accountability and quality control are central concepts that include clinical outcomes, financial responsibility, and patient satisfaction (Seid et al., 1997). Although change can be stressful for providers trained in one method of providing services, change also provides opportunities for new and innovative services.

HEALTH CARE NEEDS OF LOW-INCOME CHILDREN

Despite America's wealth and industrial leadership, approximately 43 million people in the United States have been classified as medically underserved (Hawkins & Rosenbaum, 1993). Estimates of the number of children with unmet health care needs range from 4.7 million to 14.2 million, primarily related to poverty and the lack of health insurance (Hawkins & Rosenbaum, 1993; Newacheck, Hughes, Hung, Wong, & Stoddard, 2000; Szilagyi & Schor, 1998). The creation of the State Child Health Insurance Program in 1997, as Title XXI of the Social Security Act, was designed to offer health insurance to approximately 3 million uninsured children (Ullman, Bruen, & Holahan, 1998). This program extends coverage to children whose family income is below 200% of the federal poverty level, are not eligible for other Medicaid programs, and do not have other forms of insurance. In 2002, coverage was extended until children reach 18 years of age.

With the passage of the State Child Health Insurance Program, it and Medicaid have become primary agencies for children's health care. Over half of all Medicaid recipients are children, and the rate is increasing rapidly (Ullman et al., 1998). Yet little is known about performance measures for children enrolled in Medicaid. Recent evidence has shown that monitoring focuses on immunization rates, with approximately half the states also focusing on chronic conditions, primarily asthma (McManus, Graham, Fox, Mercil, & Irwin, 2000). Although some attention has been directed to children with mental health diagnoses, most states have focused on care for children who have been hospitalized for specific mental health disorders. As with most managed-care organizations, more attention has been directed to cost and utilization, and less attention has been directed to measuring satisfaction and quality of life, particularly for less severe forms of behavioral and developmental problems (Simpson & Fraser, 1999). The large databases maintained by many managed-care organizations provide opportunities for psychologists to develop and evaluate quality-of-care measures directed to children's behavioral and developmental services. There is much work to be done to ensure that some of the most vulnerable children in this country receive adequate services to avoid or ameliorate behavioral and developmental problems.

WHAT DO FAMILIES WANT FROM PRIMARY PROVIDERS?

The health problems confronting children of the 21st century are vastly different from those that confronted previous generations of children (Haggerty, 1995). Not only have social problems replaced infectious diseases as being major contributors to children's morbidity, but also families have changed. In some communities, single-parent and multigenerational families have replaced the traditional two-parent, mother-and-father families. In addition, diversity in ethnicity, gender roles, education, and economic resources contribute to the confusion regarding the role of families in children's health care (Knitzer, 1993; Sue, 1992).

Families need to be involved as partners in treating their children's problems (Epstein et al., 1993) rather than viewed solely as contributing to the child's presenting problems. Although families' desire for assistance with their children's behavioral and developmental problems has been well documented (Young, Davis, Schoen, & Parker, 1998), it is not clear what strategies work best. Schultz and Vaughn (1999) sampled parents in an urban primary care clinic and found that they were more likely to endorse a need for information about behavioral and developmental issues than about general medical topics. Although the majority reported that they would feel comfortable asking their pediatrician about parenting issues, only half had initiated questions about parenting or wanted more time with the pediatrician. In contrast, over 85% requested that universal information on parenting be available through videotapes or pamphlets to take home.

The evaluations that have been conducted on patient materials suggest that patients gain knowledge from handouts (Gibbs, Waters, & George, 1989) and alter both their knowledge and parenting behavior from culturally sensitive videotapes (Black & Teti, 1997). The development and evaluation of these materials are clearly within psychology's domain, particularly because it is often necessary to search for external funds from research or service organizations to support these efforts.

OPTIMAL STRATEGIES FOR PSYCHOLOGY TO COLLABORATE IN PRIMARY CARE

Pediatric primary providers are likely to continue to provide developmental and behavioral services within their practices. In fact, primary care providers will probably be called on to provide more behavioral services, particularly if the pattern of reimbursement changes from a dual system of physical and behavioral providers to a single integrated system or if the DSM–PC codes are adopted for reimbursement. The call for collaboration between pediatricians and psychologists remains strong (Perrin, 1998, 1999; Schroeder, 1999). What is needed are innovative strategies for collaboration within primary care settings.

First, parity is needed between physical and behavioral systems of health care services. The separation is particularly damaging to children with chronic illnesses and special health care needs. Although an integrated system may require psychologists to consider capitated services and to alter their methods of service provision, it should enhance the quality of services to children and provide a more professionally cohesive system for psychologists and their colleagues.

Second, it is important to learn from the examples of colleagues who are successfully integrated into primary care practices. Schroeder (1999) described the Task Force on Primary Care, sponsored by the Society of Pediatric Psychology. Task force members noted several common features, including close collaboration with pediatricians, quick turnover of patients, and long-term relationships with families punctuated by brief therapeutic contacts. Psychologists in primary care benefit by interacting with one another, and they, their colleagues, and patients benefit from the exploration of new models of care.

Third, although some children will continue to require long-term therapy, it is unlikely that long-term psychotherapy will be the standard of care (Kiesler, 2000). Because managed-care companies are guided by fiscal responsibility and demand accountability, they are often looking for short-term, relatively inexpensive options. Consistent with the models of practice described by the Task Force on Primary Care (Schroeder, 1999), psychologists have to be prepared to provide brief therapeutic encounters. To meet these needs, additional models of behavior change methods and adaptation of existing treatment modalities that can be applied in primary care settings and to children from diverse backgrounds are needed (Tarnowski, 1991). Short-term treatment with follow-up visits is one way to provide cost-effective services (Finney et al., 1991). Kiesler (2000) described the need for psychologists to develop models of "good enough treatment" whereby managed-care companies pay for short-term treatment designed to deal with specific issues. As Mohl (1998) wrote, patients who want assistance with longer term issues, such as improved self-esteem or relationships, are advised that such therapy is on their "nickel" and not included in managed-care reimbursement plans.

Fourth, psychologists should focus on innovative strategies for screening and early intervention. Psychologists with a solid background in research are well qualified to develop psychometrically reliable and valid methods of screening children for behavioral and developmental problems that could be incorporated into primary care. For example, Riekert, Stancin, Palermo, and Drotar (1999) described an innovative procedure in which psychologists developed a behavioral screening service for use in a large, urban, primary care clinic. Without seeing the child (or presumably generating a bill), psychologists score, review, and interpret the behavioral rating scales to produce a report for the primary care providers. Primary care providers use the information to inform their decisions on which children should be referred for mental health services. This type of service should increase the identification of children with behavioral and developmental problems and lead to more appropriate referrals for behavioral and developmental services.

In another example, psychologists and other providers have used the technological advances of multimedia to develop videotape or computerized materials that can be used to introduce preventive messages into primary care and to screen children and adolescents about behavioral and developmental issues (Black & Ponirakis, 2000; Gardner, Kelleher, & Pajer, 2002; Paperny, 1997). Not only are youth more likely to endorse sensitive behaviors when questions are presented on a computer rather than in a face-to-face interview (Turner et al., 1998), but also computerized information can be gathered and delivered quickly, usually while patients are waiting. In addition, computerized information can be used to develop databases to enhance clinical practice. Again, once children with behavioral problems are recognized, it is more likely that pediatricians will refer them to psychologists.

Many psychologists who are involved in prevention and early intervention define their roles beyond the provision of individual services. For example, in a recent review of 177 programs aimed at preventing behavioral and developmental problems in children, Durlak and Wells (1997) reported remarkable success. Children in the intervention groups obtained scores that were 59%–82% higher than the scores of children in the control groups. Home-visiting programs, often designed using psychological principles, can be integrated into primary care settings. There have been immediate benefits, such as better adherence to feeding recommendations among adolescent mothers (Black, Siegel, Abel, & Bentley, 2001), as well as benefits extending 15 years, including reductions in child abuse and neglect, crime, welfare use, substance abuse, and increased workforce participation (Olds et al., 1997).

Fifth, psychologists need to add economic indicators to their evaluations, to publicize their successes, and to advocate for their services with policymakers and managed-care companies. Although these are not traditional roles that have been incorporated into training programs for psychologists, they are necessary to ensure the future of the profession. As both Perrin (1999) and Schroeder (1999) have noted, although pediatric primary care providers value collaboration with psychologists, they cannot assume financial responsibility for their psychologist colleagues. Thus, psychologists have to look for creative opportunities to attract external funds to support their activities. Relying on standard fee-for-service models is unlikely to enable psychologists to provide the education and preventive services that children need to avoid behavioral and developmental problems, regardless of how beneficial the services are or how well they are integrated into the primary care practice.

Medicaid's move into the responsibility for children's health care provides an opportunity for psychologists to develop and evaluate performance measures. If Medicaid is going to be fiscally responsible, then performance measures for children's mental health must extend beyond the current practice of targeting services for hospitalized children (McManus et al., 2000).

Sixth, psychologists who collaborate with pediatricians in primary care settings have to be prepared to deal with the multiple challenges inherent in a busy primary care practice. Armstrong et al. (1999) described the integration of neurocognitive evaluations into primary care services for children infected with HIV. Evaluations are conducted in the primary care site, usually in conjunction with medical visits. As Schroeder (1999) also noted, sharing clinical space in a busy primary site facilitates immediate collaboration with pediatricians and enables psychologists to ensure that their procedures are timely and consistent with the other demands of the visit. However, space in primary care sites is often tight and can be a source of tension, because pediatric contacts with children are usually briefer than the relatively lengthy testing and therapy procedures used by psychologists. Psychologists have to be willing to compromise on their time requirements, and space allocation should be addressed early in the negotiation process (Armstrong et al., 1999).

Seventh, psychology trainees need to be prepared for the changing marketplace. By incorporating primary care experiences into formal training, future psychologists and pediatricians will be better prepared to work together. Trainees should also be exposed to expanded roles of psychology, such as program evaluation, community consultation, or Web-based education or prevention. Psychology trainees will benefit by learning to conduct program evaluations that include issues of diversity, empirically supported outcomes, and fiscal responsibility.

Eighth, psychologists can play an important role by helping pediatricians serve as gatekeepers to identify children with behavioral and developmental problems. For example, when pediatricians ask parents about behavioral issues and reveal their genuine interest in their responses, parents are more likely to raise concerns (Felt & O'Connor, 2003; Wissow et al., 1994). In addition, the DSM–PC provides a focus for training pediatricians to inquire about children's behavioral and developmental problems. Although some psychologists may anticipate that pediatricians will use these skills to provide behavioral services themselves, Drotar (1999) argued that, given the existing demands on pediatricians and the large number of children with unrecognized behavioral and developmental problems, most pediatricians will refer children with behavioral problems to psychologists. Pediatricians who have been trained by psychologists are likely to be more familiar with the contributions of psychologists, thus facilitating collaboration.

Finally, there is an urgent need for research in the integration of psychological services into primary care (Starfield, 1992). Research and practice share a bidirectional relationship, with each area contributing to and informing the other (Kutash & Robbins-Rivera, 1995). At the population level, we need to know how changes in managed care and access to services are affecting children's behavioral and developmental health care. At the family level, we need to understand how environmental and situational changes are influencing children's behavior and development and to identify how risks and protective factors alter those relationships. At the service delivery level, we need to know what strategies are effective in preventing or ameliorating behavioral and developmental problems.

Information generated by research can be used to direct resources toward prevention or empirically validated intervention services. For example, Lavigne et al. (1999) showed that although the prevalence of disruptive disorders among preschool-age children in primary care is high, if prevention is a goal, then screening should focus on risk factors associated with family problems and negative affect. Screening that focuses exclusively on disruptive disorders will identify children with identified problems but will not identify those at risk.

CONCLUSIONS

Pediatric primary care providers have regular and ongoing contact with children, particularly during infancy and preschool years. In their role as sentinels in the identification and treatment of problems that can undermine children's health and well-being, pediatricians have extended the boundaries of primary care far beyond the traditional domain of children's physical health. In the 1970s, Haggerty, Roghmann, and Pless (1975) introduced the "new morbidity," representing the social challenges to children's well-being, including problems associated with poverty, disparities in access to services, child abuse, parental mental illness, and other areas. As pediatricians have expanded their levels of service to embrace this expanded mandate, they have discovered the "hidden morbidity" associated with the high rate of psychosocial problems present among children in primary care (Costello et al., 1988; Haggerty, 1995). The mandate to recognize and treat children's behavioral and developmental problems places new challenges on pediatric primary care practices. However, through innovative models of collaboration with psychologists who have expertise in research, evaluation, and theories of behavior and development, primary care providers can uncover the "hidden morbidity" and continue in their mission to promote children's health and well-being, including the prevention and amelioration of children's behavioral and developmental problems.

REFERENCES

American Psychiatric Association. (1994). *Diagnostic and statistical manual of mental disorders* (4th ed.). Washington, DC: Author.

Armstrong, F. D., Harris, L. L., Thompson, W., Semrad, J. L., Jensen, M. M., Lee, D. Y., et al. (1999). The Outpatient Developmental Services Project: Integration of pediatric psychology with primary medical care for children infected with HIV. *Journal of Pediatric Psychology, 24,* 381–391.

Black, M. M., Feigelman, S., & Cureton, P. (1999). Evaluation and treatment of children with failure-to-thrive: An interdisciplinary perspective. *Journal of Clinical Outcomes Management, 6,* 60–73.

Black, M. M. & Krishnakumar, A. (1998). Children in low-income, urban settings: Interventions to promote mental health and well-being. *American Psychologist, 53,* 635–646.

Black, M. M., & Ponirakis, A. (2000). Computer-administered interviews with children: Methodological, developmental, and ethical issues. *Journal of Interpersonal Violence, 15*, 682–695.

Black, M. M., Siegel, E., Abel, Y., & Bentley, M. E. (2001). Home and videotape intervention delays early complementary feeding among adolescent mothers. *Pediatrics, 107*, 67.

Black, M. M., & Teti, L. O. (1997). Promoting mealtime communication between adolescent mothers and their infants through videotape. *Pediatrics, 99*, 432–437.

Blum, R. (1987). Contemporary threats to adolescent health in the United States. *Journal of the American Medical Association, 257*, 3390–3395.

Costello, E. J., Edelbrock, C., Costello, A. J., Dulcan, M. K., Burns, B. J., & Brent, D. (1988). Psychopathology in pediatric primary care: The new hidden morbidity. *Pediatrics, 82*, 415–424.

Drotar, D. (1995). *Consulting with pediatricians: Psychological perspectives*. New York: Plenum.

Drotar, D. (1997). Relating parent and family functioning to the psychological adjustment of children with chronic health conditions: What have we learned? What do we need to know? *Journal of Pediatric Psychology, 22*, 149–165.

Drotar, D. (1999). The *Diagnostic and Statistical Manual for Primary Care (DSM–PC)*, Child and Adolescent Version: What pediatric psychologists need to know. *Journal of Pediatric Psychology, 24*, 369–380.

Durlak, J. A., & Wells, A. M. (1997). Primary prevention mental health programs for children and adolescents: A meta-analytic review. *American Journal of Community Psychology, 25*, 115–152.

Epstein, M. H., Nelson, C. M., Polsgrove, L., Coutinho, M., Cumblad, C., & Quinn, K. (1993). A comprehensive community-based approach to serving students with emotional and behavioral disorders. *Journal of Emotional and Behavioral Disorders, 1*, 127–133.

Evers-Szostek, M. (1997). Psychological practice in pediatric primary care settings. In L. Vandecreek, S. Knapp, & T. Jackson (Eds.), *Innovations in clinical practice: A sourcebook* (Vol. 16, pp. 325–335). Sarasota, FL: Professional Resources Press.

Felt, B. T., & O'Connor, M. E. (2003). Use of the child development review increases residents' discussion of behavioral problems. *Ambulatory Pediatrics, 3*, 2–8.

Ferris, T. G., Saglam, D., Stafford, R. S., Causino, N., Starfield, B., Culpepper, L., & Blumenthal, D. (1998). Changes in the daily practice of primary care for children. *Archives of Pediatric and Adolescent Medicine, 152*, 222–223.

Finney, J. W., Riley, A. W., & Cataldo, M. F. (1991). Psychology in primary health care: Effects of brief targeted therapy on children's medical health utilization. *Journal of Pediatric Psychology, 16*, 447–461.

Gardner, W., Kelleher, K. J., & Pajer, K. A. (2002). Multidimensional adaptive testing for mental health problems in primary care. *Medical Care, 40*, 812–823.

Gibbs, S., Waters, W. E., & George, C. F. (1989). The benefits of prescription information leaflets. *British Journal of Clinical Pharmacology, 27*, 723–739.

Haggerty, R. J. (1995). Child health 2000: New pediatrics in the changing environment of children's needs in the 21st century. *Pediatrics, 96,* 804–812.

Haggerty, R. J., Roghmann, K., & Pless, I. B. (1975). *Child health and the community.* New York: Wiley.

Hawkins, D. R., & Rosenbaum, S. (1993). *Lives in the balance: The health systems of America's medically underserved populations: A special report.* Washington, DC: National Association of Community Health Centers.

Hickson, G. B., Altemeier, W. A., & O'Connor, S. (1983). Concerns of mothers seeking care in private pediatric offices: Opportunities for expanding services. *Pediatrics, 66,* 619–624.

Horwitz, S. M., Leaf, P. J., & Leventhal, J. M. (1998). Identification of psychosocial problems in pediatric primary care. *Archives of Pediatric Adolescent Medicine, 152,* 367–371.

Horwitz, S. M., Leaf, P. J., Leventhal, J. M., Forsyth, B., & Speechley, K. N. (1992). Identification and management of psychosocial and developmental problems in community-based primary care pediatric practices. *Pediatrics, 89,* 480–485.

Isaacs-Shockley, M., Cross, T., Bazron, B. J., Dennis, K., & Benjamin, M. P. (1996). Framework for a culturally competent system of care. In B. A. Stroul (Ed.), *Systems of care for children's mental health: Creating a system of care in a changing society* (pp. 23–39). Baltimore: Brookes.

Janicke, D. M., Finney, J. W., & Riley, A. W. (2001). Children's health care use: A prospective investigation of factors related to care-seeking. *Medical Care, 39,* 990–1001.

Kagan, J. (1965). The new marriage: Pediatrics and psychology. *American Journal of Diseases of Children, 110,* 272–278.

Kazdin, A. E., Bass, D., Ayers, W. A., & Rodgers, A. (1990). Empirical and clinical focus of child and adolescent psychotherapy research. *Journal of Consulting and Clinical Psychology, 58,* 729–740.

Kelleher, K. J., & Long, N. (1994). Barriers and new directions in mental health services research in the primary care setting, *Journal of Clinical Child Psychology, 23,* 133–142.

Kelleher, K. J., McInerny, T. K., Gardner, W. P., Childs, G. E., & Wasserman, R. C. (2000a). Increasing identification of psychosocial problems: 1979–1996. *Pediatrics, 105,* 1313–1321.

Kelleher, K. J., & Rickert, V. I. (1994). Management of pediatric mental disorders in primary care. In J. Miranda, A. A. Hohmann, C. C. Attkinson, & D. B. Larson (Eds.), *Mental disorders in primary care* (pp. 320–346). San Francisco: Jossey-Bass.

Kelleher, K. J., Scholle, S. H., Feldman, H. M., & Nace, D. (2000). A fork in the road: Decision time for behavioral pediatrics. *Journal of Developmental and Behavioral Pediatrics, 21,* 133–135.

Kiesler, C. A. (2000). The next wave of change for psychology and mental health services in the health care reform. *American Psychologist, 55,* 481–487.

Knitzer, J. (1993). Children's mental health policy: Challenging the future. *Journal of Emotional and Behavioral Disorders, 1,* 8–16.

Kolbo, J. R., & Strong, E. (1997). Multidisciplinary team approaches to the investigation and resolution of child abuse and neglect: A national survey. *Child Maltreatment: Journal of the American Professional Society on the Abuse of Children, 2,* 61–72.

Kutash, K., & Robbins-Rivera, V. (1995). Effectiveness of children's mental health services: A review of the literature. *Education and Treatment of Children, 18,* 443–477.

Lavigne, J. V., Arend, R., Rosenbaum, D., Binns, H. J., Christoffel, K. K., Burns, A., & Smith, A. (1998). Mental health service utilization among young children receiving pediatric primary care. *Journal of the American Academy of Child and Adolescent Psychiatry, 37,* 1175–1183.

Lavigne, J. V., Gibbons, R. D., Arend, R., Rosenbaum, D., Binns, H. J., & Christoffel, K. K. (1999). Rational service planning in pediatric primary care: Continuity and change in psychopathology among children enrolled in pediatric practices. *Journal of Pediatric Psychology, 24,* 393–403.

Lavigne, J. V., Gibbons, R. D., Christoffel, K. K., Arend, R., Rosenbaum, D., Binns, H. J., et al. (1996). Prevalence rates and correlates of psychiatric disorders among preschool children. *Journal of the American Academy of Child and Adolescent Psychiatry, 35,* 204–214.

MacLean, W. E., Jr., Perrin, J. M., Gortmacher, S., & Pierre, C. B. (1992). Psychological adjustment of children with asthma: Effects of illness severity and recent stressful life events. *Journal of Pediatric Psychology, 17,* 159–171.

Marks, A., Malizio, J., & Hoch, J. (1983). Assessment of health needs and willingness to utilize health care resources of adolescents in a suburban population. *Journal of Pediatrics, 102,* 456–460.

McManus, M. A., Graham, R. R., Fox, H. B., Mercil, C. M., & Irwin, C. E. (2000). How far have state Medicaid agencies advanced in performance measurement for children. *Archives of Pediatric and Adolescent Medicine, 154,* 665–671.

Melamed, B. G. (1995). The interface between physical and mental disorders: The need to dismantle the biopsychosocialneuroimmunological model of disease. *Journal of Clinical Psychology in Medical Settings, 2,* 225–231.

Mohl, P. C. (1998). Medical necessity: A moving target. *Psychiatric Services, 49,* 1391.

Nazarian, L. F. (1995). A look at the private practice of the future. *Pediatrics, 96,* 812–816.

Newacheck, P. W., Hughes, D. C., Hung, Y.-Y., Wong, S., & Stoddard, J. J. (2000). The unmet health needs of America's children. *Pediatrics, 105,* 989–997.

Olds, D. L., Eckenrode, J., Henderson, C. R., Kitzman, H., Powers, J., Cole, R., Sidora, K., Morris, P., Pettit, L. M., & Luckey, D. (1997). Long-term effects of home visitation on maternal life course and child abuse and neglect. *Journal of the American Medical Association, 278,* 637–643.

Paperny, D. M. N. (1997). Computerized health assessment and education for adolescent HIV and STD prevention in health care settings and schools. *Health Education & Behavior, 24,* 54–70.

Perrin, E. C. (1998). Ethical questions about screening. *Journal of Developmental and Behavioral Pediatrics, 19,* 350–352.

Perrin, E. C. (1999). Collaboration in pediatric primary care: A pediatrician's view. *Journal of Pediatric Psychology, 24,* 453–458.

Price, R. H., Cowen, E. L., Lorion, R. P., & Ramos-McKay, J. (1988). *Fourteen ounces of prevention: A casebook for practitioners.* Washington, DC: American Psychological Association.

Rappo, P. D. (1997). Use of *DSM–PC* and implications for reimbursement. *Journal of Developmental and Behavioral Pediatrics, 18,* 175–177.

Regier, D. A., Goldberg, I. D., & Taube, C. A. (1978). The de facto US mental health services system: A public health perspective. *Archives of General Psychiatry, 35,* 685–693.

Riekert, K. A., Stancin, T., Palermo, T. M., & Drotar, D. (1999). A psychological behavioral screening service: Use, feasibility, and impact in a primary care clinic. *Journal of Pediatric Psychology, 24,* 405–414.

Roberts, M. C. (1992). *Vale dictum:* An editor's view of the field of pediatric psychology. An overview. *Journal of Pediatric Psychology, 17,* 785–805.

Routh, D. (1982). Pediatric psychology as an area of scientific research. In J. Tuma (Ed.), *Handbook for the practice of pediatric psychology* (pp. 251–289). New York: Wiley.

Saunders, R. B., Miller, B. B., & Cates, K. M. (1989). Pediatric family care: A interdisciplinary team approach. *Children's Health Care, 18,* 53–58.

Schroeder, C. S. (1999). Commentary: A view from the past and a look to the future. *Journal of Pediatric Psychology, 24,* 447–452.

Schultz, J. R., & Vaughn, L. M. (1999). Learning to parent: A survey of parents in an urban pediatric primary care clinic. *Journal of Pediatric Psychology, 24,* 441–445.

Seid, M., Sadler, B., Peddecord, K., & Kurtin, P. (1997). *Accountability: Protecting the well-being of America's children and those who care for them.* Alexandria, VA: National Association of Children's Hospitals and Related Institutions.

Sharpe, L., Pantell, R. H., Murphy, L. O., & Lewis, C. C. (1992). Psychosocial problems during child health supervision visits: Eliciting, then what? *Pediatrics, 89,* 619–623.

Simpson, L., & Fraser, I. (1999). Children and managed care: What research can, can't, and should tell us about impact. *Medical Care Research and Review, 56,* 13–36.

Spirito, A. (1999). Empirically supported treatments in pediatric psychology. *Journal of Pediatric Psychology, 24,* 87–174.

Stancin, T., & Palermo, T. M. (1997). A review of behavioral screening practices in pediatric settings: Do they pass the test? *Journal of Developmental and Behavioral Pediatrics, 18,* 183–194.

Starfield, B. (1992). *Primary care: Concept, evaluation and policy.* New York: Oxford University Press.

Stickler, B. B., Salter, M., Broughton, D. D., & Alario, A. (1991). Parents' worries about children compared to actual risks. *Clinical Pediatrics, 30,* 522–528.

Sue, S. (1992). Ethnicity and mental health: Research and policy issues. *Journal of Social Issues, 48,* 197–205.

Szilagyi, P. G., & Schor, E. L. (1998). The health of children. *Health Services Research, 33,* 1001–1039.

Tarnowski, K. J. (1991). Disadvantaged children and families in pediatric primary care settings: I. Broadening the scope of integrated mental health service. *Journal of Clinical Child Psychology, 20,* 351–359.

Timmons-Mitchell, J., Brown, C., Schulz, S. C., Webster, S. E., Underwood, L. A., & Semple, W. E. (1997). Comparing the mental health needs of female and male incarcerated juvenile delinquents. *Behavioral Sciences & The Law, 15,* 195–202.

Turner, C. F., Ku, L., Rogers, S. M., Lindberg, L. D., Pleck, J. H., & Sonenstein, F. L. (1998, May 8). Adolescent sexual behavior, drug use, and violence: Increasing reporting with computer survey technology. *Science, 280,* 867–783.

Ullman, F., Bruen, B., & Holahan, J. (1998). *The State Children's Health Insurance Program: A look at the numbers.* Washington, DC: Urban Institute.

U.S. Department of Health and Human Services. (1999). *Mental health: A report of the Surgeon General.* Rockville, MD: U.S. Department of Health and Human Services, Substance Abuse and Mental Health Services Administration, Center for Mental Health Services, National Institutes of Health, National Institute of Mental Health.

Wandersman, A., & Nation, M. (1998). Psychological contributions to understanding toxicity, resilience, and interventions. *American Psychologist, 53,* 647–656.

Weinstein, A. G., Chenkin, C., & Faust, D. (1997). Caring for the severely asthmatic child and family: I. The rationale for family systems integrated medical/psychological treatment. *Journal of Asthma, 34,* 345–352.

Wilson, J. L. (1964). Growth and development of pediatrics. *Journal of Pediatrics, 65,* 984–991.

Wissow, L. S., Roter, D. L., & Wilson, M. E. (1994). Pediatrician interview style and mothers' disclosure of psychosocial issues. *Pediatrics, 93,* 289–295.

Wolraich, M. L. (1997). *Diagnostic and statistical manual for primary care (DSM–PC) child and adolescent version:* Design, intent, and hopes for the future. *Journal of Developmental & Behavioral Pediatrics, 18,* 171–172.

Wolraich, M. L., Felice, M. E., & Drotar, D. (Eds.). (1996). The classification of child and adolescent mental diagnosis in primary care: *Diagnostic and Statistical Manual for Primary Care (DSM–PC) Child and Adolescent Version.* Elk Grove, IL: American Academy of Pediatrics.

Wright, L. (1967). The pediatric psychologist: A role model. *American Psychologist, 22,* 323–325.

Yerbury, M. (1997). Issues in multidisciplinary teamwork for children with disabilities. *Child: Care, Health & Development, 23,* 77–86.

Young, K. T., Davis, K., Schoen, C., & Parker, S. (1998). Listening to parents: A national survey of parents with young children. *Archives of Pediatric and Adolescent Medicine, 152,* 255–262.

11

PSYCHOLOGISTS IN WOMEN'S PRIMARY CARE AND OBSTETRICS–GYNECOLOGY: CONSULTATION AND TREATMENT ISSUES

HELEN L. COONS, DIANA MORGENSTERN, EILEEN M. HOFFMAN, MEG I. STRIEPE, AND CATHY BUCH

Coping with overwheming stress. Ms. L. is a 52-year-old Caucasian woman who was seen by her internist for a persistent cough. The physician expressed concern that Ms. L. had not had a physical in 2 years and because she appeared extremely tired. Ms. L. became tearful as she acknowledged how stressful it was to work in an unsatisfying job; provide for two teenagers as a single mother; and care for her elderly father, who has Alzheimer's disease.

After prescribing an antibiotic for an infection, the internist introduced Ms. L. to a primary care psychologist, who worked with Ms. L. over a 3-month period. The psychologist treated her moderate depression using cognitive–behavioral techniques, which reduced her depressive symptomatology, and focused on identifying strategies to reduce her complicated family- and work-related stress. As her mood improved, Ms.

We thank Susan H. McDaniel for her comments on drafts of this chapter.

L. was invited to consider asking others for assistance at home and to evaluate her satisfaction with her middle-management position. Ms. L. agreed to ask her sister and brother to each help one night a week and on the weekends to give her some respite, she was encouraged to begin walking three times a week when her siblings were caring for their father, and she began to consider her own personal and professional needs. As a result of interdisciplinary, collaborative care, Ms. L. secured additional help for her father not only from both of her siblings but also from a community agency that provided respite to caregivers. She also spent more time with her children and friends; enjoyed regular exercise, which improved her mood, sleeping habits, and energy level; experienced a decline in her overall stress level; and helped her manage bothersome menopausal symptoms. Follow-up sessions with the psychologist also included Ms. L.'s siblings to discuss the possibility of moving their father to a nursing home.

Women's "health is a complex function of the interaction of economic, political, cultural, biological, psychological, physiological, spiritual and familial factors" (American Psychological Association, 1996, p. 22; Heldring, 1998). The challenging range of issues affecting Ms. L.'s[1] health and well-being underscore the need for interdisciplinary approaches to prevention, diagnosis, and treatment in primary care (Hoffman, Maraldo, Coons, & Johnson, 1997). In this chapter we discuss the rationale for integrating health psychology services into women's primary care and obstetrics–gynecology, and then we present examples of gender-specific assessment and treatment interventions used by psychologists in these settings. Throughout the chapter, *health psychology services* refers to both mental health and behavioral medicine interventions.[2] Primary care focuses on the health and well-being of adolescent girls through elderly women who are seen in internal medicine and family practice, as well as obstetrics–gynecology. Obstetrics–gynecology is considered a primary care setting because of the significant portion of women—especially those in their reproductive years—who frequently receive all of their health care from these providers. In this chapter we emphasize how psychologists can work effectively and collaboratively in primary care settings to address women's biopsychosocial needs across the life span and to promote optimal health and mental health outcomes.

---

[1]The six cases included in this chapter were either created by us, or multiple cases were heavily disguised and then combined to illustrate the varied roles of psychologists providing collaborative care to women and family members in primary care settings.
[2]We do not use the label *behavioral health* to refer to mental health or health psychology services, because the term fails to recognize the importance of problems such as violence, poverty, homelessness, discrimination, and so on, which are significant correlates of mental health and psychosocial concerns among women and are not simply a function of women's behavior per se.

INTEGRATION OF HEALTH PSYCHOLOGY SERVICES INTO WOMEN'S PRIMARY CARE

Integrating health psychology services into women's primary care has several benefits. First, women routinely disclose mental health and psychosocial concerns during visits to primary care providers. Primary care providers are, as a consequence, de facto addressers of complex mental health problems (Gleid & Kofman, 1995). In addition, women are frequently reluctant to follow through on referrals to mental health professionals. This may be because women prefer to receive care in their providers' offices (Curbow, Khoury, & Weisman, 1998) or because of the lack of parity between health and mental health benefits. Furthermore, women may be more willing to speak with a mental health professional who is introduced as a "member of the team" by their trusted primary care provider. Locating health psychology services within medical settings also reduces geographic, cultural, and linguistic barriers for women living in both inner-city and rural areas. Care within women's own neighborhoods or communities may be perceived as more accessible and associated with less stigma than traditional psychiatric settings. "One-stop" care also decreases the need for additional scheduling that is often complicated by competing family, work, school, or community commitments, and it may increase patient satisfaction with care (Curbow et al., 1998).

Interdisciplinary teams may be most effective in recognizing and addressing the complex interplay among biological, psychosocial, behavioral, and sociocultural factors that affect the diagnosis, treatment, and course of women's health concerns. Over 60% of primary care visits do not result in a confirmed physical diagnosis. Undetected biomedical problems, psychosocial issues, or both, may consequently be contributing to the patient's decisions to seek care (Pollak, Cummings, Dorken, & Henke, 1995). On the other hand, because many physical complaints are dismissed by practitioners or seen as psychological in nature, misdiagnosis and misunderstanding are likely to occur (Commonwealth Fund, 1993; Klonoff & Landrine, 1997). This may especially be the case when physical disorders present with psychological symptoms, when mental health and psychosocial concerns underlie physical complaints, or when women are coping with the physiological and psychosocial sequelae of chronic or life-threatening medical conditions and their treatments. In the following section we present a broad overview of the consultation and treatment issues commonly addressed by psychologists in the primary care of women.

Consultation and Treatment Issues in Women's Primary Care

In this section we discuss routine clinical problems seen among women of all ages in primary care settings: psychosocial stressors; mood, anxiety, and other mental health disorders; health promotion and prevention; chronic medical conditions; anxiety about diagnostic and treatment procedures; and concerns about sexual functioning (see Zerbe, 1999).

Psychosocial Stressors

To promote health and mental health outcomes in primary care, psychologists must appreciate the nature and complexity of demands women face on a daily basis as well as the relational, social, cultural, and economic contexts of their lives. Although a comprehensive discussion of the psychosocial challenges experienced by women is not the focus of this chapter, we briefly highlight two types of stressors that are particularly common among women seen in primary care: (a) gender-based demands associated with multiple roles and (b) potential victimization throughout the life span.

Multiple roles. Women simultaneously cope with responsibilities associated with their family, work, and community. Psychosocial assessment of their relationships, roles, and expectations is essential to understand the range of factors affecting their physical and emotional well-being. For example, over 60% of women in the United States are employed in full- or part-time positions (Misra, 2001). Unsatisfying or demanding jobs are associated with acute stress reactions (e.g., anxiety, sleep disturbance, headaches) and chronic health problems (e.g., depression, coronary artery disease) as well as greater use of prescription and nonprescription drugs (Swanson, Piotrokowski, Puryear Keita, & Becker, 1997). The relationships between work demands and women's health underscore the importance of careful assessment of the sources of occupational stress. Simply asking for a job title during the clinical encounter does not provide the information necessary to explore options for making the patient's current position less stressful, improve stress management skills, address gender or racial discrimination in the workplace, or invite the patient to consider alternative employment.

Well over half of women with children under age 18 work outside the home (Swanson et al., 1997). Consequently, women return home for a "second shift" to care for dependent children as well as grandchildren, older parents, or other relatives, many of whom have special care needs related to illness and disability. In fact, approximately 9% of the 2,850 women who participated in the Commonwealth Fund 1998 Survey of Women's Health were caring for a sick or disabled family member (Commonwealth Fund, 1998). Forty-three percent of the female caregivers in this study provided more than 20 hours of care per week (Misra, 2001). As the case of Ms. L. illustrates, managing work and family demands with inadequate support can contribute to physical symptoms and emotional distress.

As caregivers, women frequently place their own physical and emotional concerns secondary to the needs of other family members. As a consequence, routine exercise, reasonably balanced diets, adherence to medication regimens, and making and keeping appointments for preventive and primary health care (e.g., Pap smears, mammograms, blood pressure screening, etc.) all too often become low-priority tasks in a long list of demands. As in the case of Ms. L. primary care psychologists frequently work with women to treat their depression, help them evaluate their needs and priorities, improve their time management skills, enhance their problem-solving skills and their use of social and practical support, and increase their access to community resources, to ensure that they also take care of their own well-being.

Victimization across the life span. Women are more likely than men to be victims of childhood sexual abuse, rape/sexual assault, domestic/partner violence, and elder abuse (see Koss, Goodman, Browne, Puryear Keita, & Felipe Russo, 1994, for a review of the prevalence of male violence against women across the life span). All forms of victimization are associated with increased physical health, mental health, psychosocial problems, and health care utilization and costs (Commonwealth Fund, 1998; Koss, Bailey, Herrera, & Lichter, 2000; Misra, 2001). These findings underscore the need for routine screening of all women for history of or current sexual, physical, or emotional abuse.

Eisenstat and Bancroft (1999) noted that

> in addition to being at increased risk for physical injury or death, victims of *domestic violence* [italics added] are also at risk for complications of pregnancy and childbirth, gynecologic problems, sexually transmitted diseases and HIV, chronic somatic disorder, exacerbation of chronic medical conditions, non-compliance with medical treatment, depression, anxiety disorders, and suicide, eating disorders, alcoholism, and substance abuse. All of these conditions in turn lead to the increased use of medical services and resources. (p. 886)

The case of Ms. S., presented next, demonstrates how psychologists evaluate women who are experiencing ongoing partner violence and provide crisis, short-, and long-term treatment to prevent or decrease the adverse sequelae of trauma.

> *Coping with partner violence.* Ms. S. is 38-year-old married Latina who was seen by her nurse practitioner for pain in her ribcage and shoulder. She also reported marked depression, insomnia, decreased energy and appetite, tearfulness, social withdrawal, and decreased concentration. Although she was reluctant to try an antidepressant, she returned to the primary care clinic when her symptoms became worse following more "stress at home." When the provider became concerned about the location and nature of Ms. S.'s injuries, she asked about her marriage and specifically screened for any hitting, punching, or kicking in the relationship. Ms. S. acknowledged that her partner had punched her twice in the ribs, threatened her with a knife, and repeatedly called her demeaning names. He also controlled her access to any money for food or personal items. The provider gave Ms. S. a clear message that she did not

deserve to be physically or emotional hurt or controlled and introduced her to the psychologist on the primary care team. The psychologist then met with Ms. S. to further assess and treat her depression and posttraumatic stress disorder (PTSD); provide education about partner violence; help her clarify the factors affecting her desire to stay in the relationship (e.g., emotional attachment, economic need, need for housing, cultural beliefs, etc.); develop a safety plan; provide referrals to a 24-hr, bilingual domestic violence hotline and shelter; and arrange a follow-up appointment in 1 week. The nurse practitioner and psychologist worked collaboratively with Ms. S. for several months to treat her depression and to support her while she identified her needs and options.

The treatment of women who have experienced childhood sexual abuse and sexual assault involves examination of the impact of the trauma on their mood, self-care, self-esteem, relationships, sexual functioning, and so on (Courtois, 1988). The repercussions of sexual abuse and assault often leave women feeling depressed, overwhelmed by the symptoms of PTSD, and suffering from eating and body image problems. Others self-medicate with alcohol, street drugs, or prescribed medication to avoid painful memories and feelings. Flashbacks associated with PTSD are common among women who have been victimized and may interfere with their sleep, concentration, sexual functioning, and capability of responding to effective interventions (Foa & Meadows, 1997; Maltz, 1991). Psychologists treat women who are facing these issues in collaboration with primary care providers as well as with community-based agencies that offer support groups for survivors of sexual abuse, rape crisis counseling, or both. The case of Ms. G., presented later in this chapter, illustrates the collaborative care provided to a woman with a history of childhood sexual abuse who found gynecologic procedures highly distressing.

Mood, Anxiety, and Other Mental Health Disorders Among Women in Primary Care

Women are more likely than men to be diagnosed with major depression, dysthymia, panic disorder, PTSD, eating disorders, and somatization disorder (Margo & Margo, 1999; Misra, 2001; Zerbe, 1999). For example, women are at increased risk for depression when they have a history of victimization, live in poverty, are homeless, abuse drugs or alcohol, are coping with a chronic or life-threatening physical condition, or have inadequate support while caring for a disabled or ill family member (Mazure, Keita, & Blehar, 2002). Screening women at any age for these treatable mental health problems is becoming a standard part of primary care practice (Zerbe, 1999). Psychologists can contribute to accurate differential diagnoses in primary care settings to prevent underdiagnosis of physical conditions (e.g., thyroid disease, multiple sclerosis, lupus, pancreatic cancer) that may present with psychological symptoms (e.g., anxiety or depression) and to avoid extensive diagnostic testing to evaluate physical symptoms (e.g., heart palpitations or dizziness) that may be a function of mental health problems (e.g., panic disorder) or psychosocial issues (e.g., stress-related headaches; Klonoff & Landrine, 1997; Zerbe, 1999).

Health care providers are far more likely to prescribe antidepressants and anxiolytics to women than to men (Hamilton, Jensvold, Rothblum, & Cole, 1995). Psychologists must consequently have a working knowledge of psychopharmacology to work effectively and collaboratively in the primary care of women. They need to know when to refer patients for a medication consultation, and they need to be prepared to discuss the benefits and side effects of a host of medications with women across the life span. Women who are pregnant or postpartum and breastfeeding, for example, frequently have serious concerns about taking medications, whereas some individuals are reluctant to take antidepressants that cause weight gain or affect their sexual functioning. Others fear side effects or becoming substance dependent. Psychologists must also recognize iatrogenic effects of medications that mirror psychological symptoms (e.g., the decreased appetite and low sexual desire caused by some selective serotonin reuptake inhibitors vs. depression). They also need to appreciate possible sex and gender differences in psychopharmacology (i.e., in pharmacokinetics and pharmacodynamics) as a function of the class of drug, timing in the menstrual cycle, and patient age (Hamilton et al., 1995). For example, older women and women with systemic complications (e.g., impaired renal function) caused by chronic or life-threatening disease may metabolize drugs more slowly, which may result in higher blood levels of medications and, consequently, more side effects. Psychologists must also collaborate with providers to assess patients' response to medications and recommend a medication consult with a psychiatrist when indicated.

Primary care psychologists routinely clarify when psychosocial and socioeconomic issues must be addressed, irrespective of whether a woman is taking an antidepressant or an anxiolytic agent. Psychotropic medication alone is unlikely to adequately resolve ongoing problems with depression, PTSD, panic and eating disorders, or chronic pain when victimization, substance abuse, life-threatening medical problems, or other complicated underlying issues are present. The next case, that of Ms. R., illustrates how failure to address past or ongoing psychosocial stressors that contribute to poor self-care, physical and mental health problems, and increased or underutilization of health care can further compromise women's health and quality of life.

Coping with depression, fear, and anticipatory grief. Ms. R. is a 67-year-old Hindi woman who was seen for a routine pelvic examination by the same physician assistant who has cared for her for years. Ms. R. tearfully disclosed that her husband of 50 years was recently diagnosed with metastatic lung cancer. Ms. R. reluctantly shared that she was terrified that she would wake up beside her life partner and find him dead. She acknowledged marked symptoms of depression and anxiety, including depressed mood, initial and middle insomnia, a 20-lb weight loss, and emotional withdrawal from her husband. Ms. R. had not told her husband, adult children, or friends about her fear of her husband's death or her concerns about her own well-being after his death. She hesitantly agreed to start taking an antidepressant and to meet the primary care psychologist, who joined the patient and provider in the consultation room. Collaborative care over six sessions supported Ms. R. in disclosing her fear to her husband, encouraged her to find additional ways to express her anticipatory grief, restored her sleep cycle, improved her mood and nutrition, and allowed her and her husband to experience considerable emotional intimacy during their time together.

Health Promotion in Women

A major goal of psychologists working in women's primary care is to facilitate decision making and behavior that will minimize health problems and promote well-being. For example, individuals may benefit from problem-solving strategies to find time for exercise and to eat reasonably well in order to reduce weight, blood pressure, blood sugar, and stress. In addition, interventions in primary care frequently focus on reducing substance use and abuse. According to a 1993 National Household Survey on Drug Abuse, approximately 50% of all women ages 15–44 have used illicit drugs at least one time in their lives, and 4 million women took prescription drugs for nonmedical purposes during the year prior to the study (National Institute on Drug Abuse, 1995). An alarming 24% of women also smoke, in spite of the well-known associations between cigarette use and coronary artery disease, stroke, pulmonary problems, lung cancer, early menopause, osteoporosis, increased risk for cervical cancer, higher rates of low birth weight and infant mortality, and increased risks for complications with concomitant hormonal contraceptive use. Research on gender differences in the initiation, maintenance, and treatment of substance (e.g., caffeine, cigarettes, alcohol, street drugs) use and abuse has significant clinical implications when working with women in primary care (Center for Substance Abuse Treatment, 1994; Gritz, Nielsen, & Brooks, 1996; National Institute on Drug Abuse, 1995). To maximize the chances of successful cessation, treatment strategies must address women's concerns about weight gain, withdrawal symptoms, modulation of mood (i.e., anxiety, irritability, depression, loneliness, etc.), memories of abuse, changes in relationships and social networks, risk of relapse, and so on.

Chronic and Life-Threatening Conditions

Women across the life span routinely cope with a host of chronic or life-threatening medical conditions with psychosocial sequelae. A significant proportion of women seen in primary care also live with multiple physical problems. According to the Commonwealth Fund 1993 Survey on Women's Health, among older women (ages 65–85), 31% had one illness, 27% had two illnesses, and 24% were coping with three or more. Women in their 30s and 40s, however, also deal with the challenges associated with multiple medical conditions. For example, individuals with lupus, most commonly diagnosed in younger women, may develop fatigue, arthritis, renal problems, and cardiac complications. All of these diagnoses have physical and psychosocial consequences that affect women's quality of life.

Primary care psychologists play a central role in assessing and treating the impact of chronic or life-threatening medical conditions on women and their families (Nicassio & Smith, 1995). Comprehensive evaluation in women's primary care includes ongoing assessment of the consequences of the disease and treatment for physical functioning; psychosocial concerns; and relationships with family, friends, and coworkers. Mood, body image, sexual functioning, responsibilities and relationships at home and work, finances, quality of life, and the needs of family members are all frequently affected.

Psychologists routinely assess the affective and cognitive status of women coping with chronic or life-threatening problems. Depression, anxiety, sleep disturbances, altered sexual functioning, and other changes in mental status may reflect: (a) physiological consequences of the disease (e.g., due to changes in metabolic functioning); (b) iatrogenic effects of commonly used medications (e.g., a corticosteroid, such as prednisone), anesthesia, or surgery; (c) emotional distress associated with coping with the illness and treatment; and (d) an interaction of these complex processes. Careful differential diagnosis by the interdisciplinary team is essential to prevent misdiagnosis of treatable problems and clearly has important implications for the type(s) of intervention recommended (Belar & Geisser, 1995).

Clinical experience and some data suggest several potential crisis points across the disease course that underscore the need to view psychosocial assessment and treatment as an ongoing process. Examples of possible crisis points include initial symptom presentation, undergoing diagnostic tests, receiving initial and follow-up diagnoses, developing new symptoms, hospitalizations, recurrence of symptoms, changes in or additional treatment, decreased ability to complete activities of daily living or to meet responsibilities at home or work, changes in family support and income, and the transition to advanced and terminal disease.

Psychologists in primary care are likely to have increased contact with women during the difficult times throughout the course of an illness and often provide interventions aimed at reducing or preventing adverse sequelae. As the following case of Ms. V., patients may benefit from additional information about the disease and treatment, an opportunity to acknowledge their fears and concerns about the future, pain management techniques, problem solving to enhance their adherence to treatment, discussing concerns about their disclosure of physical conditions to children or coworkers, and support to ask providers questions they fear may have uncertain or upsetting answers. Psychological adaptation to a chronic or life-threatening illness is also a reciprocal process among women and their family members. Spouses, partners, adult children, and other individuals may consequently be interviewed as well to assess the interactional nature of adaptation in the family system and to address the impact of the disease and treatment on relatives.

> *Coping with chronic pain.* Ms. V. is a 37-year-old married Hmong mother from Cambodia with five children. During a recent visit with her family physician, she described a persistent, dull pain in her joints. She came into the family practice clinic frequently and appeared depressed and isolated, and she was quite reluctant to take anti-inflammatory medication or try physical therapy. The physician suggested to Ms. V. that she might benefit from learning about pain management techniques and referred her to the primary care psychologist on the team. Results from the comprehensive pain management evaluation indicated that Ms. V.'s pain syndrome was complicated by her depression and past history of emotional trauma. The psychologist suggested that she participate in a 12-session group for Hmong women with health problems. The group was cofacilitated by a family physician, a psychologist, a medical assistant who could translate, and a family practice resident. Ms. V. agreed to try the group, and during the course of the sessions she met and received support from other women with similar cultural backgrounds; developed an understanding of the relationships among her physical symptoms, past trauma and current stress, and her depression; and learned several strategies (e.g., relaxation with guided imagery, activity–rest schedules, and physical therapy techniques) to reduce her pain level. (See Striepe & Coons, 2002, for a detailed description of this group.)

Preparing Women for Diagnostic and Treatment Procedures

Primary care psychologists routinely help prepare women for diagnostic and treatment procedures. Evaluation of common medical conditions in females involves repeated intrusive procedures such as pelvic, rectal, and breast examinations as well as transabdominal and intravaginal ultrasounds. Although tolerable to most individuals, these procedures can be highly distressing for women with histories of childhood sexual abuse or sexual assault. Furthermore, diagnostic, surgical, and treatment procedures, such as breast biopsy, lumpectomy, laparoscopy, colposcopy, colonoscopy, urodynamics, hysterectomy, mastectomy, abortion, pelvic exteration, radiation therapy, and chemotherapy are frequently painful, distressing, or both. Women coping with infertility may also undergo examinations to evaluate their Fallopian tubes (i.e., a hystosalpingogram) and the inside of their uterus (i.e., a hysteroscopy), frequent intravaginal ultrasounds, ongoing injections of hormones, and laparoscopic surgery, as well as surgical procedures necessary for assisted-reproductive technologies (ART). As the case of Ms. G., presented next, suggests, primary care psychologists have a role in preparing women for medical procedures to minimize anxiety and pain and to increase their sense of control before, during, and after the examination. Depending on the type of diagnostic or treatment procedure, interventions can involve identification of the patient's needs, education, relaxation techniques through focused breathing or distraction techniques, guided imagery, biofeedback, systematic desensitization or hypnosis, support, and so on. When possible and appropriate, patients' partners or friends are often helpful coaches during labor and procedures related to fertility and other medical domains.

> *Distressing procedures.* Ms. G. is a 38-year-old African American woman who became tearful during a pelvic examination. The gynecologist stopped the procedure and asked Ms. G. about her reaction. She acknowledged that she had been sexually abused several times as a teenager by an older relative. The provider introduced her to the psychologist working with the primary care team. They met to assess the impact of the abuse on her mood, self-esteem, functioning in relationships and at work, body image, and sexual functioning. Education about the impact of sexual trauma was offered, and treatment focused on decreasing her depressive symptoms, diffusing her flashbacks and frightening dreams, improving her sleep, and helping her to find ways to be sexually intimate with her partner that did not trigger memories of the abuse. Ms. G. also learned techniques to reduce her anxiety prior to and during pelvic examinations, which increased her sense of control and comfort during the procedure. Ms. G., the gynecologist, and the psychologist met together to discuss how she would know if she were ready for the examination as well as strategies that would be helpful to make the procedure less distressing. Ms. G. decided to sit up during the examination so that she could see and readily talk with the provider, and she asked her husband to be the coach during the procedure. Ms. G. was eventually able to separate the examination from the abuse, and she reframed the procedure as one of many positive ways she could take care of her body as an adult woman.

Facilitating Adherence to Care and Treatment

Women coping with acute and chronic conditions need to adhere to treatment recommendations for weeks, months and, frequently, years. Adherence to treatment regimens for a host of conditions is essential to prevent increased morbidity, debilitating complications, hospitalizations, or life-threatening sequelae. For example, women with diabetes often need to maintain dietary restrictions and take oral or injected hypoglycemics that lower blood sugar in order to prevent heart attacks, limb loss, or blindness from diabetic retinopathy. Likewise, women with HIV/AIDS who choose to take complex antiretroviral regimens must adhere to strict medication schedules to reduce their viral load, improve their immune function, and minimize the development of opportunistic infections and drug-resistant diseases.

Although adherence to ongoing treatment for most chronic and life-threatening conditions is challenging for women and men (Dunbar-Jacob, Burke, & Puczynski, 1995), women may face additional barriers. For example, they are more likely to be uninsured or underinsured and consequently may have difficulty paying for medications. Others may believe that medications should be avoided because of culturally based traditions about healing, or they may maintain that drugs are harmful as a result of past public health tragedies affecting women (e.g., the use of DES from 1945 to 1971, thalido-mide). Many women are also entirely focused on the care of others in their family and place their health needs second. There are other problems for women with HIV/AIDS, who may be unwilling to bring their medications home if they have not disclosed their HIV status to their family members or partner because they fear rejection. Psychologists play an important role in facilitating problem solving in women to reduce barriers and enhance adher-ence to treatment and care. This is especially true for women with develop-mental difficulties and enduring mental illness (e.g., schizophrenia). These disorders compromise women's abilities to adhere to directions for even simple medication or dietary regimens essential for successful outcomes.

Additional Consultation and Treatment Issues in Women's Primary Care Settings

Several additional issues common among women in primary care set-tings require specialized, collaborative consultation and treatment skills. Psy-chologists may, for example, evaluate women concerned about premenstrual syndrome to assess whether they have depressive symptoms that are exacer-bated in the late luteal phase of the menstrual cycle or if changes in mood are specific to this time period. A careful interview regarding affective function-ing, interpretation of symptoms, and sociocultural beliefs about menstrua-tion, followed by symptom monitoring for 2–3 months, is necessary for dif-ferential diagnosis and appropriate treatment (Derry, Gallant, & Woods, 1997).

It is not surprising that primary care psychologists working in family medicine and obstetrics–gynecology routinely care for women and couples dealing with pregnancy-related issues. Clinical consultation may occur prior to conception, during each of the trimesters, and during the postpartum pe-riod (McDaniel, Campbell, & Seaburn, 1990). For example, psychologists often see women and couples who are dealing with fertility problems. Al-though many new options exist for increasing the likelihood of pregnancy and successful delivery for women facing infertility, these individuals (and their partners) must also deal with the benefits, risks, and discomforts associ-ated with using ovulatory stimulants, make decisions about the number of eggs implanted during in vitro fertilization, address concerns about donor eggs and/or insemination, consider the possible use of a gestational carrier, and confront other complex issues that arise from new ART (McDaniel, 1994;

McDaniel & Speice, 2001; Pasch & Dunkel-Schetter, 1997). They may also have to decide whether to try to conceive again after reproductive failure or multiple pregnancy losses, contend with growing financial strains associated with ART, and face decisions about the possibility of adoption or remaining childless.

As described next, in the case of Ms. B., women who experience pregnancy complications or are particularly anxious about childbirth may require substantial support from the interdisciplinary team. Couples who suffer a preterm or term loss (e.g., miscarriage, fetal demise) may be overwhelmed and need intensive support throughout the grieving process, prior to considering another pregnancy and throughout subsequent pregnancies. Other women may experience postpartum complications such as depression, anxiety, or psychosis and require comprehensive, interdisciplinary treatment that may include medication, psychotherapy, and support from professionals as well as from other women who have had similar sequelae. Individuals may also have to cope with unexpected neonatal health problems and the death of their children. Women, their partners, and other family members benefit greatly from the information, support, and treatment provided by primary care psychologists during these painful and challenging times.

> *Pregnancy complications*. Ms. B. is a 28-year-old Caucasian lesbian whose first child was delivered vaginally after extended labor and fetal distress. Although she was excited about having a second child, she was extremely worried about the possibility of going through another difficult delivery. Her obstetrician referred her to the team psychologist for evaluation and treatment. Sessions focused on clarifying her concerns about the delivery; identifying questions she wanted to ask her provider about another vaginal birth and epidural; and improving her relaxation skills to decrease stress, muscle tension, fatigue, and discomfort during childbirth. She actively practiced relaxation and guided-imagery techniques to reduce her anxiety before and during labor, and her partner came in for a session so that she could prompt Ms. B. to use a range of coping strategies. The psychologist also gave the obstetrician brief information about Ms. B.'s guided imagery for her labor and delivery chart so that she too could invite the patient to use the techniques during labor.

Psychologists also work with women to decrease bothersome symptoms associated with menopause, such as weight gain, hot flashes, irritability, and insomnia. Women who are perimenopausal, have surgically induced menopause, or are receiving treatment for breast cancer frequently cope with menopausal symptoms while they continue to work; take care of young or adult children, aging parents, or other relatives (e.g., grandchildren); adjust to their changing body image; deal with a life-threatening condition; and address a host of life transitions. Clinical assessment includes vasomotor, cognitive, affective, sexual, and relational changes during the peri- and postmenopausal periods (Zerbe, 1999). Many women respond to information about the underlying physiological causes of their symptoms, whereas others benefit from therapeutic strategies, medication, or both, to stabilize their mood and sleep.

Women with chronic gynecologic conditions also benefit greatly from comprehensive, interdisciplinary evaluation and treatment. Herpes, chronic yeast infections, polycystic ovarian syndrome, pelvic pain, vulvodynia, and so on, often adversely affect women's mood; self-esteem; body image; and comfort with emotional, physical, and sexual intimacy. Although relatively little research has focused on the types of psychosocial interventions that would most benefit women with these distressing physical problems, clinical experience suggests that treatment can improve women's well-being.

Sexual Functioning and Dysfunction

Primary care psychologists are also asked to assess and treat women with sexual concerns. Recent estimates suggest that 43% of women and 31% of men suffer from sexual dysfunction (Laumann, Palk, & Rosen, 1999). Lack of sexual desire is the most common sexual complaint among women (Laumann et al., 1999; Rosen & Leiblum, 1995). Changes in sexual functioning may be (a) a direct consequence of a medical problem (e.g., pelvic surgery), (b) related to the vaginal drying that often accompanies menopause, (c) symptoms of depression, (d) a side effect of medications (e.g., selective serotonin reuptake inhibitors), (e) associated with psychosocial or relational issues, or (f) a combination of these factors (Maurice, 1999; Regan, 1999). For example, among older women, sexual functioning is greatly affected by illness and the lack of a sexual partner (Mooradian & Greiff, 1990).

Primary care psychologists treat sexual concerns using individual, couples, and group therapy. Gender-specific care includes educating women about the female response cycle (Basson, 1999), including how it differs from a physiological-based male response cycle. Treatment focuses on clarifying attitudes toward sexuality, improving sexual knowledge (e.g., sexual anatomy and physiology), clarifying gender role expectations, and learning effective communication skills (e.g., being able to tell a partner how one would like to be touched) (Striepe & Feldman, 2000). The treatment of sexual problems in women requires coordinating care with primary care providers who can address biomedical concerns and assist in the management of underlying mental health problems.

GROUPS IN WOMEN'S HEALTH AND MENTAL HEALTH

Primary care psychologists routinely facilitate monthly treatment and support groups for women in primary care settings. Groups may be time limited or ongoing, may or may not include family members, and are often coled by members of the interdisciplinary primary care team. Clinical experience and research in several areas of women's health indicate that groups that focus on coping with medical and psychosocial concerns are effective adjuncts to medical treatment. Gender- and culture-specific groups, such as the one described in the case of Ms. V., typically validate women's experiences, facilitate disclosure of distressing experiences, enhance social and informational support, improve problem-solving skills and self-esteem, and consequently promote physical and emotional well-being.

INTERDISCIPLINARY COLLABORATION IN WOMEN'S PRIMARY CARE

Clinical practice in women's primary care and obstetrics–gynecology provides consistent, challenging, and poignant opportunities to enhance the well-being of women and their family members by actively supporting their empowerment and resilience. Psychologists in these settings also routinely provide "curbside consultations" with colleagues in regard to psychosocial and behavioral issues; attend interdisciplinary team meetings regarding or with patients and families; link patients to community-based services; participate in the training of residents, medical students, psychology interns, and other allied health providers; conduct collaborative research; and participate in continuous quality improvement initiatives to enhance prevention and treatment outcomes.

To function effectively in women's primary care and obstetrics–gynecology, psychologists must have the appropriate interdisciplinary training in clinical psychology, clinical health psychology, women's studies, family systems theory and therapy, and public health. In addition, they must have extensive knowledge of biomedical and clinical practice issues in women's health prevention, diagnosis, and treatment as well as the culture of primary care settings (Hoffman et al., 1997). As the American Psychological Association's (1996) Research Agenda for Psychosocial and Behavioral Factors in Women's Health suggested:

> Major changes are needed in approaches to education and training in the health professions if we are to produce health scientists and professionals with the knowledge, skills, and sensitivity required to generate and apply new knowledge concerning the health needs of women from all ethnic groups over the life cycle and in diverse social and cultural contexts. In particular, a comprehensive approach is required that both critiques traditional approaches and provides innovative and exciting alternatives, and that is responsive to women's diverse sociocultural contexts and identities. (p. 21)

This perspective is particularly true for primary care psychologists who want to develop the clinical competencies necessary to provide interdisciplinary, collaborative care on behalf of women and their families.

REFERENCES

American Psychological Association. (1996, February). *Research Agenda for Psychosocial and Behavioral Factors in Women's Health: Recommendations from the Advisory Committee of the Psychosocial and Behavioral Factors in Women's Health.* Washington, DC: Author.

Basson, R. (1999, October). *Use of an alternative model of women's sexual response cycle to address low sexual desire.* Paper presented at the New Perspectives in the Management of Female Sexual Dysfunction Conference, Boston.

Belar, C. D., & Geisser, M. E. (1995). Roles of the primary care psychologist in the management of chronic illness. In P. M. Nicassio & T. Smith (Eds.), *Managing chronic illness: A biopsychosocial perspective* (pp. 33–57).Washington, DC: American Psychological Association.

Center for Substance Abuse Treatment. (1994). *Practical approaches in the treatment of women who abuse alcohol and other drugs.* Rockville, MD: U.S. Department of Health and Human Services, Public Health Service.

Commonwealth Fund. (1993). *Commonwealth Fund survey of women's health.* New York: Author.

Commonwealth Fund. (1998). *Commonwealth Fund survey of health concerns across a women's lifespan: 1998 survey of women's health.* New York: Author.

Courtois, C. (1988). *Healing the incest wound: Adult survivors in therapy.* New York: W. W. Norton.

Curbow, B., Khoury, A., & Weisman, C. S. (1998). Provision of mental health services in women's health centers. *Women's Health: Research on Gender, Behavior, and Policy, 4,* 71–91.

Derry, P. S., Gallant, S. J., & Woods, N. F. (1997). Premenstrual syndrome and menopause. In S. J. Gallant, G. Puryear Keita, & R. Royak-Schaler (Eds.), *Health care for women: Psychological, social, and behavioral influences* (pp. 203–220). Washington, DC: American Psychological Association.

Dunbar-Jacob, J., Burke, L. E., & Puczynski, S. (1995). Clinical assessment and management of adherence to medical regimens. In P. M. Nicassio & T. Smith (Eds.), *Managing chronic illness: A biopsychosocial perspective* (pp. 313–349). Washington, DC: American Psychological Association.

Eisenstat, S. A., & Bancroft, L. (1999). Domestic violence. *New England Journal of Medicine, 341,* 886–892.

Foa, E. B., & Meadows, E. A. (1997). Psychosocial treatments for post-traumatic stress disorder: A critical review. In J. Spence (Ed.), *Annual review of psychology* (pp. 449–480). Palo Alto, CA: Annual Reviews.

Gleid, S., & Kofman, S. (1995). *Women and mental health: Issues for health reform.* Background paper prepared for The Commonwealth Fund Commission on Women's Health.

Gritz, E. R., Nielsen, I. R., & Brooks, L. A. (1996). Smoking cessation and gender: The influence of physiological, psychological and behavioral factors. *Journal of the American Women's Medical Association, 51,* 35–42.

Hamilton, J. A., Jensvold, M. F., Rothblum, E. D., & Cole, E. (1995). *Psychopharma-cology from a feminist perspective*. New York: Haworth.

Heldring, M. (1998). Integrated primary care for women. In A. Blount (Ed.), *Integrated primary care* (pp. 247–260). New York: W. W. Norton.

Hoffman, E., Maraldo, P., Coons, H. L., & Johnson, K. (1997). The women-centered health care team: Integrating perspectives from managed care, women's health and the health professional workforce. *Women's Health Issues, 7*, 362–374.

Klonoff, E. A., & Landrine, H. (1997). *Preventing misdiagnosis of women: A guide to physical disorders that have psychiatric symptoms*. Thousand Oaks, CA: Sage.

Koss, M. P., Bailey, J. A., Herrera, V. M., & Lichter, E. L. (2000, October). *Depression, PTSD, and health problems in survivors of male violence: Research and training initiatives to facilitate recovery*. Invited paper presented at the American Psychological Association Summit on Women and Depression, Wye River, MD.

Koss, M. P., Goodman, L. A., Browne, A., Puryear Keita, K., & Felipe Russo, N. (1994). *No safe haven: Male violence against women at home, at work, and in the community*. Washington, DC: American Psychological Association.

Laumann, E. O., Palk, A., & Rosen, R. (1999). Sexual dysfunction in the United States. *Journal of the American Medical Association, 281*, 537–544.

Maltz, W. (1991). *The sexual health journey: A guide for survivors of sexual abuse*. New York: HarperCollins.

Margo, G. M., & Margo, K. L. (1999). Somatization in the primary care setting. *Women's Health in Primary Care, 2*, 344–350.

Maurice, W. L. (1999). *Sexual medicine in primary care*. St. Louis, MO: Mosby.

Mazure, C. M., Keita, G. P., & Blehar, M. C. (2002). *Summit on women and depression: Proceedings and recommendations*. Washington, DC: American Psychological Association.

McDaniel, S. H. (1994). Within-family reproduction technologies as a solution to childlessness due to infertility: Psychological issues and interventions. *Journal of Clinical Psychology in Medical Settings, 1*, 301–308.

McDaniel, S. H., Campbell, T. L., & Seaburn, D. B. (1990). *Family oriented primary care: A manual for medical providers*. New York: Springer-Verlag.

McDaniel, S. H., & Speice, J. (2001). What family psychology has to offer women's health: The examples of conversion, somatization, infertility treatment, and genetic testing. *Professional Psychology: Research and Practice, 32*, 44–51.

Misra, D. (Ed.). (2001). *Women's health data book: A profile of women's health in the United States* (3rd ed.).Washington, DC: Jacobs Institute of Women's Health and the Henry J. Kaiser Family Foundation.

Mooradian, A. D., & Greiff, V. (1990). Sexuality in older women. *Archives of Internal Medicine, 150*, 1033–1038.

National Institute on Drug Abuse. (1995). *NIDA notes: Articles on women, gender differences, and drug abuse* (Report No. NN0013). Rockville, MD: Author.

Nicassio, P. M., & Smith, T. (1995). *Managing chronic illness: A biopsychosocial perspective*. Washington, DC: American Psychological Association.

Pasch, L. A., & Dunkel-Schetter, C. (1997). Fertility problems: Complex issues faced by women and couples. In S. J. Gallant, G. Puryear Keita, & R. Royak-Schaler (Eds.), *Health care for women: Psychological, social, and behavioral influences* (pp. 187–202).Washington, DC: American Psychological Association.

Pollak, M. S., Cummings, N. A., Dorken, H., & Henke, C. J. (1995). Effect of mental health treatment on medical costs. *Mind/Body Medicine, 1,* 7–11.

Regan, P. C. (1999). Hormonal correlates and causes of sexual desire: A review. *Canadian Journal of Human Sexuality, 8,* 1–16.

Rosen, R. C., & Leiblum, S. R. (1995). Treatment of sexual disorders in the 1990s: An integrated approach. *Journal of Consulting and Clinical Psychology, 63,* 877–890.

Striepe, M. I., & Coons, H. L. (2002). Women's health in primary care: Interdisciplinary interventions. *Families, Systems and Health, 20,* 237–251.

Striepe, M. I., & Feldman, J. (2000, October). *Women's sexual health and family medicine: Diagnosis and intervention.* Paper presented at the North Central Regional Meeting of the Society of Teachers of Family Medicine, Madison, WI.

Swanson, N. G., Piotrokowski, C. S., Puryear Keita, G., & Becker, A. B. (1997). Occupational stress and women's health. In S. J. Gallant, G. Puryear Keita, & R. Royak-Schaler (Eds.), *Health care for women: Psychological, social, and behavioral influences* (pp. 147–159).Washington, DC: American Psychological Association.

Zerbe, K. J. (1999). *Women's mental health in primary care.* Philadelphia: W. B. Saunders.

12

SERVING OLDER ADULTS: CLINICAL GEROPSYCHOLOGY IN PRIMARY CARE

WILLIAM E. HALEY

Throughout this book, the case has been made that psychological services should increasingly be made available in primary care health care settings. Psychological services delivered in primary care settings offer access to many patients of all ages who would not seek out treatment in the mental health sector and can provide a better overall quality of care because of the integration of psychological and medical services.

For a number of reasons, primary care is probably even more important as a setting for older adult populations, and psychologists must be prepared for some unique problems encountered in the assessment and treatment of older primary care patients. In this chapter I review three topics: (a) the need for clinical geropsychology in primary care settings, (b) special issues faced by psychologists in working with older patients, and (c) important issues for the future of geropsychology in primary care.

THE NEED FOR CLINICAL GEROPSYCHOLOGY IN PRIMARY CARE

Several issues point to the special importance of psychological services in primary care for older adults. These include high levels of need, low levels of utilization of mental health services, high rates of use of general medical services, and projected growth of the older adult population, factors that I review in detail below.

Older Adults Need Psychological Services But Rarely Receive Them

Although it is often assumed that older adults are lonely, isolated, and incapable of coping successfully with stress, the majority of community-dwelling older adults are independent, maintain their social activities and social networks, and have lower rates of most mental disorders than younger adults (Cohen, 1992). Many older individuals in the current cohort over age 65 have coped successfully with dramatic social change and events such as the Great Depression and World War II, and they were raised in an era when self-reliance was taught and expected. Older adults are often found to cope with stress as well as, if not more successfully than, younger individuals, which is due in part to the benefits of life experience (Aldwin, 1994; Rowe & Kahn, 1998). Increasing attention has been paid to the study of successful aging (Rowe & Kahn, 1998), and there is evidence that future cohorts of older people may experience aging even more benignly than current elders because of improved education, financial status, and lifestyle.

However, substantial numbers of older adults do experience psychological difficulties. Of community-dwelling elders, 7%–12% have a diagnosable mental disorder (George, 1992), and up to 27% of older medical patients have clinically significant subdysthymic depression (Mossey, Knott, Higgins, & Talerico, 1996). In addition to the mental disorders that are common in younger patients, older individuals are at increased risk for cognitive impairment, including delirium and dementia, both of which can best be diagnosed and treated with inclusion of psychological approaches. Left untreated, mental disorders among older primary care patients are associated with greater amounts of disability, higher utilization of health care services, and lower quality of life (Callahan et al., 1994; Penninx et al., 1998; Unutzer et al., 1997). In addition, elderly women with less education, low income, or minority status are even more likely to suffer with a high burden of illness (Bierman & Clancy, 2001). Many older primary care patients without a mental disorder could also use psychological services to improve their coping with age-related issues such as chronic disability and facing mortality (Knight, 1996).

Older Adults Rarely Use Conventional Mental Health Services

It has been repeatedly observed that older adults are underserved in mental health settings. This appears to be due to some combination of attitudes and knowledge of older people, system barriers, and ageism on the part of service providers (Lebowitz & Niederehe, 1992). Robb, Haley, Becker, Polivka, and Chwa (2003) found that older adults prefer to receive mental health services in collaboration with their primary care physicians and are much less likely than younger persons to seek psychological services for problems such as depression, anxiety, and stress.

Older patients often receive inadequate mental health care in the general medical sector. It has been estimated that 50%–70% of older adults who commit suicide have major depression and that 75% of these individuals have seen a primary care physician in the month before the suicide who did not detect or treat the depression (Koenig & Blazer, 1990). Older depressed patients seen in primary care settings in health maintenance organizations (HMOs) are at particular risk for underservice and were found to be less likely than younger patients to receive appropriate medications (Bartels, Horn, Sharkey, & Levine, 1997). Bartels et al. (1997) also found that nearly 50% of older depressed patients seen in primary care HMO settings were prescribed benzodiazepines (a class of drug that can be particularly problematic for older patients) rather than antidepressant medications. Inadequate physician training and the increasing time pressures to treat patients quickly are factors that make mental disorders particularly difficult for primary care physicians to detect and treat successfully (Bartels et al., 1997; Callahan et al., 1994).

Older Adults Utilize Vast Amounts of Health Care Services

Because older adults are especially likely to have multiple chronic diseases, they utilize far more health care services than younger persons. Individuals over age 65 accounted for more than 192 million physician visits in 1995, representing 22% of total physician visits, in a year in which they represented 13% of the population (National Center for Health Statistics, 1997). Older adults averaged 6.8 physician visits per year, more than double the rate per person of the U.S. population as a whole. Older adults also averaged 2.1 days per year in hospitals, more than triple the rate for the overall population. Undetected and untreated mental disorder appears to be particularly costly in older adults. Unutzer et al. (1997) found that older depressed patients had about 50% higher health care costs than nondepressed elders, a finding that was consistent even after controlling for objective disease, age, and other important factors. Depressed older adults had higher utilization rates for all services studied, including inpatient admissions, outpatient medical visits, laboratory costs, and emergency room visits. Of note is that less than 1% of health care costs in this sample were accounted for by specialty mental health services. Because there is evidence that treatment of depression in older patients leads to reduced hospitalization rates (Flaherty et al., 1998), the importance of effectively diagnosing and treating mental disorders in the elderly to cut costs is clear.

Older Adults Will Be an Increasing Proportion of the Population and Health Care Services

The "graying of America" has profound implications for psychologists interested in providing services in health care settings. Whereas only 4% of the U.S. population was over age 65 in the year 1900, during the year 2000 about 13% of the population—about 35 million Americans—was over age 65 (Federal Interagency Forum on Aging Related Statistics, 2000). With the projected growth of the "baby boomers" into older age groups in the years ahead, projections suggest that by the year 2030, 21.8% of the U.S. population will be over age 65 (Federal Interagency Forum on Aging Related Statistics, 2000). Of particular importance in discussing the importance of the aging population is the increase in survival to very advanced age. Gerontologists speak of older adults as including the "young-old" (65–74), "old-old" (75–84), and the "oldest-old" (85 and above). In particular, survival beyond the age of 85 is associated with higher risk of a number of diseases and types of disability, as well as nursing home placement. The fastest growing population group in the United States comprises individuals over age 85, the "oldest old"—currently 2% of the U.S. population—who use by far the most health services. For these reasons, the Medicare budget is projected to more than double in constant dollars by the year 2020 (Schneider & Guralnik, 1990).

Advantages to Providing Psychological Services to Older Adults in Primary Care Settings

Provision of psychological services in medical settings has the potential to ease many of the barriers to providing mental health services to older adults in conventional mental health settings. Older patients with multiple, complex medical problems often need medical, psychological, and social services, which can be provided in the primary care setting.

Such an approach reduces stigma, allowing the older patient to be seen for mental health and behavioral health concerns without having to self-identify as "mentally ill," a common concern when older patients are referred to a psychiatric setting. In addition, practice in primary care allows coordination of medical and psychological care and for mutual learning on the part of medical and psychological providers. Team approaches and interdisciplinary comprehensive care in geriatrics have been found to lead to improved functional and quality-of-life outcomes for older patients across a large number of studies (Stuck, Siu, Wieland, Adams, & Rubenstein, 1993; Zeiss & Steffen, 1996).

SPECIAL ISSUES IN SERVING OLDER ADULTS IN PRIMARY CARE: ROLES FOR PSYCHOLOGISTS

Although many of the issues professionals face in working with primary care patients are common across patients seen in primary care throughout the life span, some concerns are especially important with older patients. I briefly review the areas where primary care psychologists must be particularly attuned to special issues with older adults and offer suggestions for the special roles psychologists can play.

Comorbidity and Complexity

One important issue is the presence of multiple medical and psychological problems, or *comorbidity*. Older patients whom I have seen commonly have in excess of a dozen different medical diagnoses and up to 30 medications. With multiple medications comes an increased likelihood of dangerous drug side effects or interactions. For example, Wilcox, Himmelstein, and Woolhandler (1994) found that 24% of individuals over age 65 were receiving at least one medication whose use is contraindicated in older adults. Also, a new report found that 1 in 5 elderly people are prescribed potentially inappropriate medications (Zhan et al., 2001). Medication issues are particularly problematic in older adults because of age differences in tolerance of side effects, longer drug half-lives, and problems with adherence to multiple medications (Haley, 1996). Complexity is further introduced with the presence of multiple psychosocial issues. One older patient had a medical problem list that included hypertension, peripheral neuropathy, gastritis, esophagitis, peptic ulcer, anemia, polypharmacy, and folate deficiency and psychosocial–behavioral problems that included chronic alcohol abuse, confusion, noncompliance, and family conflict (Haley, 1999). Key intervention in this case included uniting the team to insist that the family caregiver (the patient's daughter) control the patient's access to alcohol, to enforce abstinence. Both the psychological and medical reasons for abstinence were presented in a united way, and the patient's cognitive impairment was emphasized as a factor requiring control of drinking by the family.

Comorbidity forces clinical teams to focus on the most salient problems that are vital to the patient's quality of life. Psychotherapy must be strategic in addressing problems that are both important and that have a reasonable likelihood of change. With complex cases, the psychologist can play a key role in case formulation, focusing on a central problem that may yield improvement in multiple areas.

Cognitive Impairment

Although individuals of all ages present with a variety of mental disorders, with older patients, Alzheimer's disease and other forms of dementia are particular concerns. Physicians and other primary care health providers often have insufficient knowledge about dementia. The presentation of dementia is complicated, because patients often maintain social skills and hide their disorders unless cognitive assessment and interview of an informant are included. This is an important role for psychologists. Because dementia may either coexist with depression, or be confused with depression (Zarit & Zarit, 1998), psychological assessment is vital to proper diagnosis of dementia. A particular need for health care providers in primary care settings is to improve their detection of dementia and their referral and provision of information to caregiving families during early stages of dementia. Failure to properly diagnose dementia or refer families for necessary services may lead to years of unnecessary delays in receiving needed legal and social services (Barrett, Haley, & Powers, 1996).

Dementia patients utilized an average of $6,209 per year of Medicare dollars in 1992, nearly double the rate of Medicare beneficiaries as a whole. Most Alzheimer's patients are not managed by neurologists or other specialists in dementia; internal medicine was the most common physician provider for these patients, perhaps in part because of the high levels of comorbidity common in dementia (Weiner, Powe, Weller, Shaffer, & Anderson, 1998).

Key roles for psychologists in patients with dementia include cognitive assessment, which can be used to inform family and team members about neuropsychological deficits (MacNeill & Lichtenberg, 1999) and guide determinations of legal competency (Moye, 1999), and developing treatment plans for behavior management problems and family caregiver issues (Zarit & Zarit, 1998). Over the last 10 years, medications have become available for the treatment of Alzheimer's disease that have been demonstrated to improve cognitive functioning (Fillit, 1999). Cognitive assessment is critical in assessing what may be relatively subtle effects of these medications. Pharmacological approaches, behavioral management, and family support all have shown indications of facilitating cost savings by delaying disability and institutionalization (Fillit, 1999; Mittelman, Ferris, Shulman, Steinberg, & Levin, 1996; Shields, King, & Wynne, 1995).

Depression, Anxiety, Substance Abuse, and Suicide

In general, the present cohort of older adults has lower rates of major depression than middle aged and young adults, but older adults have rather high rates of milder depressive symptomatology, which typically are related to difficulties adapting to impairments in physical health (Koenig & Blazer, 1990). Depression in older adults is often misdiagnosed because of its comorbidity with medical problems and presentation to medical settings. Suicide is also a major concern for older adults, because the group with the highest suicide rates in the United States is White men over age 65 (Koenig & Blazer, 1990). White men over age 65 had a suicide rate of 46 per 100,000 population members, a figure more than 2.5 times the rates for older Black men, more than 6 times the rates for older White women, and about 21 times the rate for older Black women (U.S. Senate, 1991).

Anxiety disorders have been less commonly addressed than depression in older adults, but they are quite common in older patients and are often complicated by such issues as comorbidity, possible aggravation by medications, and potential for dependence on anxiolytic medications (Zarit & Zarit, 1998; Zhan et al., 2001). Another disorder that is frequently ignored is alcohol abuse in the elderly. Older adults are especially sensitive to the effects of alcohol, and problem drinking may be hidden despite close links to other health and psychological problems (Smyer & Qualls, 1999). For two thirds of older problem drinkers this is a chronic problem, but for the other one-third alcohol abuse begins in late life and has a particularly good prognosis for successful treatment (Zarit & Zarit, 1998). For these and other mental disorders, the psychologist's role is not only to assess and treat the patient but also to educate other health professionals, who may have a limited awareness of the value of treating mental disorders in older patients.

Family Issues

Family issues are particularly important for older adults, who often receive assistance from family members when they develop disability and accompany older adults to their medical sessions (Shields et al., 1995). Caregiving roles can vary from occasional assistance to the "36-hour day" (Mace, Rabins, & McHugh, 1999) of caring for a relative with Alzheimer's disease. The stress experienced by caregivers increases their risk for depression, negative health behaviors, and use of psychotropic medication (Haley & Bailey, 1999). Caregivers clearly desire and require special assistance beyond the medical care given to the patient to deal with the heavy responsibilities of care.

Consideration of caregiving issues leads to important implications for medical care. For example, open communication of the diagnosis of Alzheimer's disease may be very helpful to the caregiver in understanding that patient behavior problems are unintentional, giving families a socially acceptable way to explain the patient's behavior to others, and allowing families to plan ahead. Focus on the patient–caregiver unit also recognizes that the quality of care the patient receives may be dependent on the caregiver's reaction to the strain of caregiving. Shields et al. (1995) provided a framework for assessing and intervening at different levels with families and health care systems. Health care professionals should be aware of the variety of behavior management and pharmacological options available and be prepared to refer families for supportive services.

End-of-Life Issues

Psychologists who work with terminally ill older adults can be of special value not only by providing direct counseling but also in helping patients and families communicate more effectively with other health care providers (see King, 2001, and Shields et al., 1995, for case examples). Such communication is typically handled poorly, and many older adults with terminal illness suffer unnecessarily and without their wishes and concerns being adequately addressed (SUPPORT Principal Investigators, 1995).

Cummings (1998) provided an example of an innovative program to address problems related to bereavement (which is a risk factor for increased mortality and health care utilization) in older adults. Through an HMO plan, widowed individuals were identified, and 85% received services through aggressive yet sensitive outreach. The intervention included 14 group sessions and was found to substantially reduce health care costs (Cummings, 1998). Psychologists can be useful not only in working with terminally ill patients and helping their families cope with bereavement but also in helping team members cope with loss (Rosen, 1990; Shields et al., 1995).

Special Settings and Systems of Care

Because of the high prevalence of disability found in older adults, and the high expenses associated with hospitalization, many older adults receive care in such settings as home health, subacute care units, or nursing homes. Although only 5% of individuals over age 65 reside in nursing homes, these residents have very high rates of cognitive impairment and mental disorders (Smyer & Qualls, 1999). Psychologists' roles can include direct services such as assessment and intervention, consultation and attention to organizational issues, and training staff to deliver behavioral interventions (Shields et al., 1995; Smyer & Qualls, 1999).

Adaptations to Assessment Procedures

As noted above, psychologists in primary care settings have the opportunity to provide specialized expertise in assessment of cognitive and behavioral functioning. Physicians often value testing that can quantify patient progress during psychotherapy, helping to turn what may seem to be a rather abstract type of intervention into something with demonstrable effectiveness. A recent volume (Lichtenberg, 1999) provides a comprehensive guide to assessment of older adults.

Assessment procedures must be used carefully with older adults; for example, one must ensure that appropriate test norms are available to support the validity of tests with diverse older adults. Research indicates that even simple screening tests are strongly influenced by race, age, and education (Crum, Anthony, Bassett, & Folstein, 1993). Many older adults with less than an 8th grade education are likely to be misclassified without the use of age- and education-adjusted norms, with older patients from racial–ethnic minority groups particularly likely to be misdiagnosed without attention to normative data (Murden, McRae, Kaner, & Bucknam, 1991). Clinicians have an obligation to remain current in their understanding of the appropriateness of assessment tools with older patients depending on the purpose of the assessment.

Adaptations to Intervention Procedures

A growing literature has documented the effectiveness of psychotherapy with older adults. In general, older patients respond as well to psychotherapy as younger individuals, but they benefit from certain differences in approach, such as use of problem-focused, short-term approaches and attention to family and life experiences particular to a given age cohort (Knight, 1996; Shields et al., 1995). Two areas that have received special attention to date include (a) treatment of geriatric depression and (b) psychosocial interventions for family caregivers of a person with dementia.

Scogin and McElreath (1994) conducted a meta-analysis of treatments for depression in older adults and found that older patients showed benefits from psychotherapy similar to those of younger patients. Several recent studies have also demonstrated the value of psychotherapy tailored to the needs of medically ill older adults who might be seen as difficult candidates for conventional psychotherapy. Mossey et al. (1996) found that interpersonal psychotherapy could be successfully administered to frail older patients during home visits in the aftermath of hospitalization, with significant improvements in depression compared with standard care. Arean and Miranda (1996) tailored cognitive–behavioral treatment to a multicultural group of medically ill older adults seen in primary care settings and observed successful reductions in depression. Combined antidepressant medication and interpersonal psychotherapy led to far lower relapse rates in elderly patients with major depression when compared with patients who received medication or psychotherapy alone (Reynolds et al., 1999). Adaptations such as provision of case management services, psychotherapy delivered directly to patients' homes, and use of psychoeducational models have met with particular success with older patients.

Focusing on family caregivers has also proven particularly beneficial. Results of a meta-analysis of interventions for family caregivers showed that individual and family interventions for caregivers are also highly effective (Knight, Lutzky, & Macofsky-Urban, 1993). A protocol to train caregivers to better manage depression in dementia patients has been found to have significant effects in decreasing both dementia patient and family caregiver depression compared with control groups (Teri, Logsdon, Uomoto, & McCurry, 1997). In another major study, a comprehensive package of caregiver interventions, including support groups, individual and family counseling, telephone support, and in-home counseling, has been demonstrated to improve caregiver depression and to delay placement of the patient in a nursing home by 329 days compared with usual care (Mittelman et al., 1995, 1996). Thus, caregiver interventions show promise not only in helping the patient and family member but also in cost savings.

IMPORTANT ISSUES FOR THE FUTURE OF GEROPSYCHOLOGY IN PRIMARY CARE

Training Issues in Geropsychology

Psychologists should gain the training necessary to work successfully with older adults in medical settings. Psychologists and other psychotherapists have been found to have negative biases in treating both younger and older patients with medical problems (James & Haley, 1995). Few psychologists have had specialized training in geropsychology, and clinicians increasingly have developed an interest in geropsychology after establishing a professional career focused on other areas. Such clinicians should seek specialized training related to aging and should not deceive themselves into thinking that their own experience of aging, or expertise in other areas of clinical practice, will prepare them for practice in clinical geropsychology. Qualls (1998) summarized the suggested areas of competency for clinicians interested in geropsychology, and a brochure from the American Psychological Association (1997) provides a useful overview for psychologists interested in working with older patients.

Reimbursement

Medicare is the predominant health insurer for older adults and provides good coverage for most psychological services. The American Psychological Association has been particularly active and effective over the past few years in working to ensure that local Medicare carriers provide proactive guidance on their documentation requirements and avoid capricious shifts in policy about covered services. However, psychologists who work with older adults must stay well informed in order to bill Medicare appropriately and to remain aware of the complex and puzzling regulations that sometimes make it difficult for providers to be certain that reimbursement will be provided for legitimate psychological services. Medicare reimbursement rules change frequently and require continued vigilance by providers in order to avoid having claims rejected (Hartman-Stein & Ergun, 1998). For example, Medicare currently covers only 50% of the costs of outpatient mental health services but covers 80% for inpatient services (Smyer & Qualls, 1999). Medicare reimbursement for initial interviews and psychological testing is also 80%. Some psychologists find it difficult to be reimbursed even for appropriate services to patients with dementia, and such necessary services as staff consultation and training are not currently reimbursable (Zarit & Zarit, 1998).

Managed care is an increasing force that affects psychologists not only in the general health care sector but also in Medicare (Smyer & Qualls, 1999). This is of particular concern, because Ware, Bayliss, Rogers, Kosinski, and Tarlov (1996) found that poor, chronically ill older adults were especially at risk for poor outcomes with managed care. Managed-care Medicare programs may also have little incentive to provide services that delay nursing home placement, because these costs are typically paid by Medicaid (Bartels & Colenda, 1998). Managed-care programs may arbitrarily limit access to skilled geropsychology providers (Hartman-Stein & Ergun, 1998). It is of note that many managed-care programs have dropped their Medicare coverage over the past several years, returning older patients to fee-for-service plans.

Because of these concerns, psychologists must become more involved in lobbying efforts to improve Medicare benefits and to ensure that regulations are written and enforced fairly. The American Psychological Association has a number of initiatives underway aimed at helping psychologists understand Medicare, improving regulations, and expanding coverage for psychological services.

Role Issues for Psychologists

Psychological practice with older adults in primary care medical settings can be extremely rewarding. Such work provides the opportunity to collaborate with physicians and other health care providers and to teach them about the benefits of attending to psychological aspects of care for older patients. Collaborative care in geriatrics also allows psychologists to learn a great deal about the interaction of medical and psychological issues in older persons. The ability to work in primary care settings may be a key to the survival of many psychologists as the health care system evolves and may also be the only way to access many older patients who need psychological services.

Psychologists have great opportunities to provide services for older adults, but currently psychologists are underutilized in geriatric settings. Psychologists need to work to join innovative comprehensive geriatric programs, because such programs frequently use nurses, social workers, and case managers to assess depression and alcohol abuse, conduct cognitive screening, and develop treatment plans. One recent book on enhancing primary care services for older adults (Netting & Williams, 1999), for example, made no reference to involvement of psychologists. Psychologists will increasingly have to demonstrate "added value" (Lichtenberg, 1998) in medical settings in order to be viable alternatives to less expensive health care providers.

There seems little doubt that psychologists can develop greater roles in health care settings that serve older adults. In particular, psychologists' expertise in assessment, behavioral interventions, and research provide skills that are less common in other providers who also address psychosocial issues. As demonstrated in this chapter, psychological intervention has already been widely demonstrated to be effective with older patients, and evidence for possible cost savings in treating older patients appears promising. Although I have reviewed a number of unique challenges in working with older patients, psychologists with skills and experience in such areas as neuropsychological assessment, consultation, treatment planning, and interdisciplinary teamwork can find many examples of the application of these roles in geropsychology (e.g., Lichtenberg, 1998). Perhaps the greatest challenge for psychologists is to find ways to market their services and make the practice of clinical geropsychology financially feasible. Psychologists who have been successful in private practice in geriatric behavioral health care (Hartman-Stein, 1998) have found opportunities in medical settings, nursing homes, and home care, and several companies, such as Senior Psychology Services, have developed innovative and successful business approaches to packaging and providing psychological services. As the population of older adults increases in the years ahead, this is likely to be an area of great opportunity for psychologists with the clinical and entrepreneurial skills needed both to serve older adults and to gain access to this growing population.

REFERENCES

Aldwin, C. M. (1994). *Stress, coping, and development: An integrative perspective.* New York: Guilford Press.

American Psychological Association. (1997). *What practitioners should know about working with older adults* [Brochure]. Washington, DC: Author.

Arean, P., & Miranda, J. (1996). The treatment of depression in elderly primary care patients: A naturalistic study. *Journal of Clinical Geropsychology, 2,* 153–160.

Barrett, J. J., Haley, W. E., & Powers, R. E. (1996). Alzheimer's disease patients and their caregivers: Medical care issues for the primary care physician. *Southern Medical Journal, 89,* 1–9.

Bartels, S. J., & Colenda, C. C. (1998). Mental health services for Alzheimer's disease: Current trends in reimbursement and public policy, and the future under managed care. *American Journal of Geriatric Psychiatry, 6*(Suppl. 1), S85–S100.

Bartels, S. J., Horn, S., Sharkey, P., & Levine, K. (1997). Treatment of depression in older primary care patients in health maintenance organizations. *International Journal of Psychiatry in Medicine, 27,* 215–231.

Bierman, A. S., & Clancy, C. M. (2001). Health disparities among older women: Identifying opportunities to improve quality of care and optimize functional health outcomes. *Journal of the American Medical Women's Association, 56,* 155–160.

Callahan, C. M., Hendrie, H. C., Dittus, R. S., Brater, D. C., Hui, S. L., & Tierney, W. M. (1994). Improving treatment of late-life depression in primary care: A randomized clinical trial. *Journal of the American Geriatrics Society, 42,* 839–846.

Cohen, G. D. (1992). The future of mental health and aging. In J. E. Birren, R. B. Sloane, & G. D. Cohen (Eds.), *Handbook of mental health and aging* (2nd ed., pp. 893–914). New York: Academic Press.

Crum, R., Anthony, J., Bassett, S., & Folstein, M. (1993). Population-based norms for the Mini-Mental State Examination by age and educational level. *Journal of the American Medical Association, 269,* 2386–2391.

Cummings, N. A. (1998). Approaches to preventive care. In P. E. Hartman-Stein (Ed.), *Innovative behavioral healthcare for older adults* (pp. 1–17). San Francisco: Jossey-Bass.

Federal Interagency Forum on Aging Related Statistics. (2000). *Older Americans 2000: Key indicators of well-being.* Washington, DC: Author.

Fillit, H. (1999). Improving the quality of managed care for patients with mild to moderate Alzheimer's disease. *Drug Benefit Trends, 11,* 6–11.

Flaherty, J. H., McBride, M., Marzouk, S., Miller, D. K., Chien, N., Hanchett, M., et al. (1998). Decreasing hospitalization rates for older home care patients with symptoms of depression. *Journal of the American Geriatrics Society, 46,* 31–38.

George, L. K. (1992). Community and home care for mentally ill older adults. In J. E. Birren, R. B. Sloane, & G. D. Cohen (Eds.), *Handbook of mental health and aging* (2nd ed., pp. 793–813). New York: Academic Press.

Haley, W. E. (1996). The medical context of psychotherapy with the elderly. In S. Zarit & B. Knight (Eds.), *A guide to psychotherapy and aging: Effective clinical interventions in a life-stage context* (pp. 221–239). Washington, DC: American Psychological Association.

Haley, W. E. (1999). Psychotherapy with older adults in primary care medical settings. *In Session: Psychotherapy in Practice, 55,* 991–1004.

Haley, W. E., & Bailey, S. (1999). Research on family caregiving in Alzheimer's disease: Implications for practice and policy. In B. Vellas & J. L. Fitten (Eds.), *Research and practice in Alzheimer's disease* (Vol. 2, pp. 321–332). Paris: Serdi.

Hartman-Stein, P. E. (1998). Hope amidst the behavioral healthcare crisis. In P. E. Hartman-Stein (Ed.), *Innovative behavioral healthcare for older adults* (pp. 201–214). San Francisco: Jossey-Bass.

Hartman-Stein, P. E., & Ergun, M. (1998). Marketing strategies for geriatric behavioral healthcare. In P. E. Hartman-Stein (Ed.), *Innovative behavioral healthcare for older adults* (pp. 179–199). San Francisco: Jossey-Bass.

James, J. W., & Haley, W. E. (1995). Age and health bias in practicing clinical psychologists. *Psychology and Aging, 10,* 610–616.

King, D. A. (2001). The case of the "expendable" elder: Family therapy with an older depressed man. In S. H. McDaniel, D. D. Lusterman, & C. L. Philpot (Eds.),

Casebook for integrating family therapy: An ecosystemic approach (pp. 157–168). Washington, DC: American Psychological Association.

Knight, B. G. (1996). Overview of psychotherapy with the elderly: The contextual, cohort-based, maturity-specific-challenge model. In S. Zarit & B. Knight (Eds.), *A guide to psychotherapy and aging: Effective clinical interventions in a life-stage context* (pp. 17–34). Washington, DC: American Psychological Association.

Knight, B. G., Lutzky, S. M., & Macofsky-Urban, F. (1993). A meta-analytic review of interventions for caregiver distress: Recommendations for future research. *The Gerontologist, 33,* 240–248.

Koenig, H. G., & Blazer, D. G. (1990). Depression and other affective disorders. In C. K. Cassel, D. E. Rissenberg, L. B. Sorenson, & J. R. Walsh (Eds.), *Geriatric medicine* (2nd ed., pp. 473–490). New York: Springer-Verlag.

Lebowitz, B. D., & Niederehe, G. (1992). Concepts and issues in mental health and aging. In J. E. Birren, R. B. Sloane, & G. D. Cohen (Eds.), *Handbook of mental health and aging* (2nd ed., pp. 3–26). New York: Academic Press.

Lichtenberg, P. A. (1998). *Mental health practice in geriatric health care settings.* New York: Haworth.

Lichtenberg, P. A. (Ed.). (1999). *Handbook of assessment in clinical gerontology.* New York: Wiley.

Mace, N. L., Rabins, P. V., & McHugh, P. R. (1999). *The 36-hour day: A family guide to caring for persons with Alzheimer disease, related dementing illnesses, and memory loss in later life* (3rd ed.). Baltimore: Johns Hopkins University Press.

MacNeill, S. E., & Lichtenberg, P. A. (1999). Screening instruments and brief batteries for assessment of dementia. In P. A. Lichtenberg (Ed.), *Handbook of assessment in clinical gerontology* (pp. 417–441). New York: Wiley.

Mittelman, M. S., Ferris, S. H., Shulman, E., Steinberg, G., Ambinder, A., Mackell, J., et al. (1995). A comprehensive support program: Effect on depression in spouse–caregivers of AD patients. *The Gerontologist, 35,* 792–802.

Mittelman, M. S., Ferris, S. H., Shulman, E., Steinberg, G., & Levin, B. (1996). A family intervention to delay nursing home placement of patients with Alzheimer's disease: A randomized controlled trial. *Journal of the American Medical Association, 276,* 1725–1731.

Mossey, J. A., Knott, K. A., Higgins, M., & Talerico, K. (1996). Effectiveness of a psychosocial intervention, interpersonal counseling, for subdysthymic depression in medically ill elderly. *Journal of Gerontology: Medical Sciences, 51A,* M172–M178.

Moye, J. (1999). Assessment of competency and decision making capacity. In P. A. Lichtenberg (Ed.), *Handbook of assessment in clinical gerontology* (pp. 488–528). New York: Wiley.

Murden, R. A., McRae, T. D., Kaner, S., & Bucknam, M. E. (1991). Mini-Mental State Exam scores vary with education in Blacks and Whites. *Journal of the American Geriatrics Society, 39,* 149–155.

National Center for Health Statistics. (1997). *Health, United States, 1996–97 and injury chartbook.* Hyattsville, MD: Author.

Netting, F. E., & Williams, F. G. (Eds.). (1999). *Enhancing primary care of elderly people*. New York: Garland.

Penninx, B. W. J. H., Guralnik, J. M., Ferrucci, L., Simonsick, E. M., Deeg, D. J. H., & Wallace, R. B. (1998). Depressive symptoms and physical decline in community-dwelling older persons. *Journal of the American Medical Association, 279,* 1720–1726.

Qualls, S. H. (1998). Training in geropsychology: Preparing to meet the demand. *Professional Psychology: Research and Practice, 29,* 23–28.

Reynolds, C. F., Frank, E., Perel, J. M., Imber, S. D., Cornes, C., Miller, M. D., et al. (1999). Nortriptyline and interpersonal psychotherapy as maintenance therapies for recurrent major depression: A randomized trial in patients older than 59 years. *Journal of the American Medical Association, 281,* 39–45.

Robb, C., Haley, W. E., Becker, M. A., Polivka, L. A., & Chwa, H. (2003). Attitudes toward mental health care in younger and older adults. *Aging and Mental Health, 7,* 142–152.

Rosen, E. J. (1990). *Families facing death: Family dynamics of terminal illness*. New York: Lexington.

Rowe, J. W., & Kahn, R. L. (1998). *Successful aging*. New York: Pantheon.

Schneider, E. L., & Guralnik, J. M. (1990). The aging of America: Impact on health care costs. *Journal of the American Medical Association, 263,* 2335–2340.

Scogin, F. R., & McElreath, L. (1994). Efficacy of psychosocial treatments for geriatric depression: A quantitative review. *Journal of Consulting and Clinical Psychology, 62,* 69–74.

Shields, C. G., King, D. A., & Wynne, L. C. (1995). Interventions with later life families. In R. H. Mikesell, D. D. Lusterman, & S. H. McDaniel (Eds.), *Integrating family therapy* (pp. 141–158). Washington, DC: American Psychological Association.

Smyer, M. A., & Qualls, S. H. (1999). *Aging and mental health*. Malden, MA: Blackwell.

Stuck, A. E., Siu, A. L., Wieland, G. D., Adams, J., & Rubenstein, L. Z. (1993). Comprehensive geriatric assessment: A meta-analysis of controlled trials. *The Lancet, 342,* 1032–1036.

SUPPORT Principal Investigators. (1995). A controlled trial to improve care for seriously ill hospitalized patients: The Study to Understand Prognosis and Preferences for Outcomes and Risks of Treatments (SUPPORT). *Journal of the American Medical Association, 274,* 1591–1598.

Teri, L., Logsdon, R. G., Uomoto, J., & McCurry, S. M. (1997). Behavioral treatment of depression in dementia patients: A controlled clinical trial. *Journal of Gerontology: Psychological Sciences, 52B,* P159–P166.

Unutzer, J., Patrick, D. L., Simon, G., Grembowski, D., Walker, E., Rutter, C., & Katon, W. (1997). Depressive symptoms and the cost of health services in HMO patients aged 65 years and older: A 4-year prospective study. *Journal of the American Medical Association, 277,* 1618–1623.

U.S. Senate Special Committee on Aging. (1991). *Aging America: Trends and projections*. U.S. Department of Health and Human Services. Washington, DC: Author.

Ware, J. E., Bayliss, M. S., Rogers, W. H., Kosinski, M., & Tarlov, A. R. (1996). Differences in 14-year health outcomes for elderly and poor chronically ill patients treated in HMO and fee-for-service systems. *Journal of the American Medical Association, 276,* 1039–1047.

Weiner, M., Powe, N. R., Weller, W. E., Shaffer, T. J., & Anderson, G. F. (1998). Alzheimer's disease under managed care: Implications from Medicare utilization and expenditure patterns. *Journal of the American Geriatrics Society, 46,* 762–770.

Wilcox, S. M., Himmelstein, D. U., & Woolhandler, S. (1994). Inappropriate drug prescribing for the community-dwelling elderly. *Journal of the American Medical Association, 272,* 292–296.

Zarit, S. H., & Zarit, J. M. (1998). *Mental disorders in older adults: Fundamentals of assessment and treatment*. New York: Guilford Press.

Zeiss, A. M., & Steffen, A. M. (1996). Interdisciplinary health care teams: The basic unit of geriatric care. In L. L. Carstensen, B. A. Edelstein, & L. Dornbrand (Eds.), *The practical handbook of clinical gerontology* (pp. 423–450). Thousand Oaks, CA: Sage.

Zhan, C., Sangl, J., Bierman, A., Miller, M., Friedman, B., Wickizer, S., et al. (2001). Potentially inappropriate medication use in the community-dwelling elderly: Findings from the 1996 medical expenditure panel survey. *Journal of the American Medical Association, 286,* 2823–2829.

13

PSYCHOLOGICAL PRACTICE IN RURAL PRIMARY CARE

JAMES H. BRAY, MICHAEL F. ENRIGHT, AND IRENE EASLING

Psychological practice in rural America continues to be an arena in which the needs of the populace outweigh the available services (Morris, 1997). In rural areas, the lack of specialists places increased pressures on primary care physicians to diagnose and treat a broad spectrum of biomedical and psychosocial problems. In addition, with the increase in managed health care, patients with mental health problems are more likely to receive treatment from a primary care provider than a mental health specialist (Bray, 1996; Sturm, Camp, & Wells, 2001). Of special importance is the role of human behavior in the genesis of poor health. Lifestyle and behaviors that affect good health, such as smoking, alcohol abuse, family violence, teen pregnancy, accidents and occupational injuries, occur at high rates in rural areas (Blazer et al., 1985; Wagenfeld, 1990). Consider, for example, the following case.

Micah, a 52-year-old cook, abruptly left a remote hunting camp in the middle of the night after experiencing "spells" consisting of nausea, vom-

This chapter is based in part on a presentation given at the National Institute of Mental Health conference "Rural Mental Health Research: From Research to Practice," Oxford, Mississippi, April 1997.

iting, dizziness, and numbness in her hands and feet. She presented the
next morning at the office of her internal medicine specialist, who assessed her for stroke and seizure and ordered a routine blood screen. Then
he referred her to the consulting psychologist (whose office was in the
next building) for further assessment and intervention. Micah described
a work environment in which she was the only woman in a hunting
camp 20 miles from the nearest road. The camp was accessible only by
horse, and Micah's duties involved rising at 4:00 a.m. to prepare break-
fast, working on camp chores all day, and retiring after 10:00 p.m., when
all of the guests had eaten and were in bed. Micah described her boss as
a "tough old boot" who was prone to "hollering" when things didn't go
his way. Upon further questioning, Micah revealed that she had recently
been divorced from an abusive alcoholic, and she found herself working
for a man who treated her much like her ex-husband had. A condition
that initially presented at a primary care office looking suspiciously like a
transient ischemic attack resolved with education, insight, and helping
Micah to understand her stressors and take responsibility for her life and
work environment.

This example highlights differences in the context of providing rural
health care services and issues that face rural psychologists. It is unfortunate
that mental health providers in rural practice are often isolated from the
primary care medical system (Bray & Rogers, 1995). Thus, in rural America,
the professionals trained to assess and treat psychosocial problems may not
be readily available to medical professionals and their patients who need
these services. The example of Micah illustrates how psychological interventions can be useful in treating patients in rural primary care settings. In this
chapter we review the literature on rural mental health and mental health
problems in primary care and discuss practice models for treatment of mental
health problems in primary care and training issues. We also address research
issues for mental and behavioral health in primary care, with a special emphasis on rural life.

RURAL MENTAL AND BEHAVIORAL HEALTH

Part of the problem with studying rural psychological practice is the
difficulty in defining rural. The U.S. Bureau of Census defines rural populations as all territory, population, and housing units located outside of urbanized areas or urban clusters. It contains both place and nonplace territory.
Urban is defined as all territory, population, and housing units located within
an urbanized area or an urban cluster. These urban areas are defined as core
census block groups or blocks that have a population density of at least 1,000
people per square mile and surrounding census blocks that have an overall
density of at least 500 people per square mile (U.S. Bureau of the Census,
1995, 2001).

More than one quarter of the U.S. population resides in nonurban areas, and nearly all states have distinct rural populations. These rural Americans experience incidence and prevalence rates of mental illnesses and substance abuse that are similar to (Blazer et al., 1985; Wagenfeld, Murray, Mohatt, & DeBruyn, 1994) or greater than (Eggebeen & Lichter, 1993) their urban counterparts. They also experience chronic shortages of mental health providers and services, which significantly affects the organization and delivery of mental health care. Rural residents are also less likely than their urban counterparts to have access to inpatient mental health services (Morris, 1997).

Little research has focused specifically on mental and behavioral health in rural primary care settings. Most of the research relating to the prevalence of mental disorders in primary care has focused on urban areas (Philbrick, Connelly, & Wofford, 1996). Residents of rural areas are sometimes assumed to have better mental health than their urban counterparts, because rural life is perceived as quiet and stress free (Eggebeen & Lichter, 1993). However, there are some rural types of stress, such as higher poverty rates, substandard housing, and poorer employment prospects (Eggebeen & Lichter, 1993), and the ongoing farm crisis continues to have had a serious negative impact on the mental and behavioral health of rural residents (Fitchen, 1986; Wagenfeld, 1990). Also, rural areas have a higher proportion of people at risk of poor mental health, such as the elderly and the chronically ill, and there are usually deficiencies in both the level and quality of mental health services available in rural areas (Human & Wasem, 1991; Wagenfeld, 1990).

In the early 1980s, rural–urban differences in the prevalence of nine psychiatric disorders were studied in the Piedmont Health Survey (Blazer et al., 1985), a part of the multisite Epidemiological Catchment Area collaborative program sponsored by the National Institute of Mental Health. At that time, major depressive episodes and drug abuse and dependence were found to be more prevalent in the urban county, and alcohol abuse and dependence was more common in the rural areas. However, when demographic variables (age, gender, race–ethnicity, and education) were controlled for, major depressive disorders were found to be twice as frequent in the urban area, whereas no disorder was significantly more prevalent in rural areas. These findings point to the importance of differentiating between specific psychiatric disorders and of controlling for demographic factors when studying urban–rural differences in psychiatric morbidity.

This study also found that, on average, rural residents perceive their overall health to be not as good as that of their urban counterparts. This may be due to the fact that rural residents are older and may also reflect their lower propensity to complain of psychological suffering compared with a perception of somatic problems (Blazer et al., 1985). Rural residents are also more satisfied with their social relationships and more likely to have a religious affiliation. In contrast, Eggebeen and Lichter (1993), using data from the National Survey of Families and Households, found that rural adults of all ages consistently rated their health more poorly than did nonrural residents. With the exception of middle-aged residents, rural residents were more likely to have depressive symptoms and to rate themselves as less happy than those who lived in suburbia or fringe areas (i.e., nonmetropolitan counties adjacent to a metropolitan county).

Rost, Smith, and Taylor (1993) argued that stigma associated with psychiatric disorders can be an obstacle to mental health care, especially in rural areas. They examined rural–urban differences in stigma associated with depressive symptoms and seeking treatment for such disorders. On average, rural and urban participants perceived that neither negative nor positive characteristics were attributed by their communities to persons with depressive symptoms. However, rural participants with a history of depressive symptoms perceived more stigma attached to seeking treatment than did those in urban areas. Because of this perception, the authors suggested that attention be paid to improving the public image in rural areas of seeking treatment for depression.

MENTAL DISORDERS AND RURAL PRIMARY CARE

Several studies have concluded that the prevalence of mental disorders in rural areas is as high or higher than that in urban areas (Blazer et al., 1985; Paykel, Abbott, Jenkins, Brugha, & Meltzer, 2000; Yuen, Gerdes, & Gonzales, 1996). Two studies of mental health problems in rural areas have reported a range of problems and prevalence rates. Philbrick et al. (1996) found that 34% of rural respondents met the criteria for one or more mental disorders. Mood disorders (or depressive disorders) were the most prevalent category reported (21.7%), followed by anxiety disorders (12.3%), somatoform disorders (11.1%), probable alcohol abuse or dependence (6.0%), and eating disorders (2.0%). Respondents with mental health diagnoses had significantly lower functional status and higher utilization of professional services, even after the investigators controlled for demographic variables. In comparison, Barrett, Barrett, Oxman, and Gerber (1988) found a prevalence rate of 26.5% for all mental disorders among adult patients. The rate for depressive disorders was 10.0%, and the rate for disorders without depression 5.3%. In addition, 11.2% of patients were considered to have disorders with significant depressive symptoms that could not be assigned to a specific depressive disorder category. Patients ages 65 and older were more likely to have episodic depression than younger patients were but were less likely to show characterologic depression, less mixed anxiety and depression, and less generalized anxiety. There was a much higher prevalence of masked/suspected depression among patients ages 45 and older than among patients under age 45. Women had higher rates than men for each depressive disorder, although the rate differences varied across disorders. Although direct comparisons between urban and rural patients was not reported in either study, these researchers concluded that the prevalence of mental disorders in rural primary care practices is as high as that in urban practices.

Yuen et al. (1996) examined the use of mental health services in two rural group model HMOs and found that linkage between primary care providers and mental health providers was an important factor in determining the amount and kind of mental health care received by patients. More specifically, they reported that primary care patients who had less available mental health services, who had higher rurality, and who utilized sites that had weaker linkages with mental health services were more likely rely on primary care providers overall for mental health services and had more mental health hospitalizations. These findings point to the need for increased linkages between primary care providers and mental health providers in rural, underserved populations.

LACK OF RECOGNITION OF MENTAL HEALTH PROBLEMS BY PRIMARY CARE PHYSICIANS

Despite the high prevalence of certain mental disorders in rural primary care settings (Philbrick et al., 1996), primary care physicians often overlook these needs and focus on diagnosis and treatment of physical health symptoms (Eisenberg, 1992). Estimated rates of failure by primary care physicians to detect psychiatric disorders range from one half to two thirds (deGruy, 1996; Higgins, 1994). It is important to note that non-psychiatric physicians write over 50% of the prescriptions for psychotropic medications in the United States (deGruy, 1996). However, patients usually benefit when primary care providers and psychologists have collaborative working relationships in terms of more accurate diagnoses and treatments. Consider the following example.

> Anton, a 42-year-old national park law enforcement officer, was referred for immediate evaluation after presenting at the office of a family physician on an emergency basis from his post in a remote mountain station. Anton came to the psychologist's office with a referral note that stated he was "suffering from sleep problems, tachycardia, weepy—history of hyperventilation." He had a bag with samples of an antidepression agent and prescriptions for both anxiolytic and soporific medicines. He had been seen for a full 15 minutes. The physician, sensing he needed a more thorough workup, requested a psychological consult "stat." Anton's psychological history revealed that, as the chief ranger responsible for "critical incident stress debriefing" for his park, he had been involved with numerous traumas in which loss of life was common. He had been required to investigate the suicide of another ranger (who was also a close friend) the week before. Since the time of the suicide investigation, Anton

had experiences increasing episodes of panic and symptoms of posttraumatic stress disorder. He was also feeling guilt at not being able to "handle" his emotions, because so many of his colleagues relied upon him to be strong in a crisis. The isolation of his extremely rural post had further exacerbated his sense of hopelessness and failure. Close collaboration between primary care and psychology professionals resulted in an expeditious recovery involving education, psychotherapy, and a brief course of medication.

Unlike the physician in this example, physicians frequently fail to recognize mental disorders for patients with physical disease and those presenting with physical symptoms, especially "nonspecific" symptoms such as fatigue and multiple pains. Furthermore, patients consistently underreport personal distress to physicians. In a study of primary care in rural counties of California, Good and her colleagues (Good, Good, & Cleary, 1987) found that only 20%–30% of patients with emotional distress, family problems, and/or behavioral problems reported them to their primary care providers. It may also be possible that because primary care providers are not trained to target these concerns, their patients' complaints are simply ignored.

Primary care providers in rural areas play a greater role in the management of depression than their metropolitan counterparts (Rost, Humphrey, & Kelleher, 1994). There are 10 times as many psychiatrists per capita in metropolitan statistical areas than in nonmetropolitan statistical areas, and there are twice as many psychologists as psychiatrists in nonmetropolitan statistical areas (American Psychological Association, Office of Rural Health, 2001).

Rural patients with depression seem to experience poorer outcomes than depressed urban patients. Rost, Wherry, Williams, and Smith (1992) found that 68% of primary care patients with major depression in rural areas continued to have the disorder 5 months later. On the other hand, 40% of urban patients with major depression had improved after 1 month (Popkin, Callies, & Mackenzie, 1985), 70% were in remission after 6 months (Schulberg, McClelland, & Gooding, 1987), and 59%–64% were in remission 2 years later (Wells, Burnam, Rogers, Hays, & Camp, 1992). These differences may be due to the fact that treatment for depression requires close follow-up to be optimal.

In a cross-sectional survey in nonmetropolitan Arkansas counties, 43 randomly selected primary care physicians were asked about their treatment preferences and barriers to caring for patients who had problems with depression (Rost et al., 1994). The respondents estimated that an average of 19.7% of the patients in their practice had experienced problems with depression during the previous year. Medication alone was considered to be the best treatment for depression by 44.2% of the respondents, 30.2% preferred to prescribe medication and refer patients to mental health professionals for counseling, and 25.6% chose to prescribe medication and conduct counseling themselves. The greatest obstacles to treatment were patients' failure to recognize depression and physicians' lack of time to provide assessment and care.

Rost and her colleagues (1993, 1994) think that patients' failure to recognize depression may be more of a problem in rural areas because of lower educational levels. In addition, the rural physicians in the study saw an average of 150 patients each week, compared with an average of 99 patients seen by urban physicians (American Medical Association Center for Health Policy Research, 1991). Also, rural family physicians have to handle psychiatric emergencies without support from mental health professionals and community hospitals with appropriate facilities for suicidal patients. The rural physicians unfortunately were reimbursed at lower rates, but they spent considerably more time treating depressed patients (Rost et al., 1994). Payment in rural practices is usually based on the unit of a visit and is low compared with specialist fees. This disparity makes it difficult to recruit and keep expert professionals in rural areas (Ormel & Tiemens, 1995; Pion, Keller & McCombs, 1997).

To examine the process and outcomes of rural family practice patients diagnosed with major depression, Rost, Williams, Wherry, and Smith (1995) conducted a 5-month follow-up study of patients with major depression. Although 63% of the patients obtained a prescription for one or more antidepressants during the 5-month study period, only about 12% of them received pharmacological treatment in accordance with the 1993 Agency for Health Care Policy and Research guidelines. More than two thirds (68.4%) of the patients met the criteria for major depression at follow-up. Those whose treatment met Agency for Health Care Policy and Research guidelines showed more improvement than the other study patients did. Most physicians in Rost et al.'s (1994) study had recently referred one or more depressed patients to specialty care. However, the severe shortage of mental health professionals in the rural area and the resulting long waiting lists generally discouraged referrals from primary care physicians. When referrals were made, primary care physicians complained about the lack of specialist feedback. Rost et al. (1994) believe this further hindered collaborative treatment.

Rosenthal and his colleagues (Rosenthal, Shiffer, Lucas, & DeMaggio, 1991) reviewed 138 referrals from rural family physicians in the Rural Health Research Network of Western New York to psychotherapists. The physicians considered 59% of the referrals successful, and 70% of the patients were satisfied with the referral. The only factor significantly related to the physicians' evaluation of success was postreferral feedback initiated by the psychotherapist. A number of other variables—including success of referral outcome, number of preparatory or follow-up visits to the physician, physician's knowledge about the psychotherapy process, patient economic status, and insurance coverage—were not significantly related to referral success. Patient attendance at more than one therapy session was associated with the number of prereferral physician visits, distance to the therapist's office, and referral by a physician who included counseling in his or her practice. These studies support the need for mental health services in primary care settings and for quick, reliable feedback between collaborating professionals.

PRACTICE MODELS

With the increase in managed health care and integrated health care systems, rural primary care physicians have experienced added pressures to diagnose and treat a broad spectrum of biomedical and psychosocial problems (Sturm et al., 2001). However, rural psychologists are not regularly trained to work with primary care physicians, and they often have limited access to the general health care system. Increased collaborative practice between mental health practitioners and physicians is one method of meeting the multiple needs of primary care patients in rural areas (Bray, 1996; Bray & Rogers, 1995, 1997; McDaniel, Hepworth, & Doherty, 1992). The following is an example of successful collaboration.

> Tonya, a 35-year-old registered nurse who worked in a rural health clinic, presented to a rural psychologist with symptoms typical of depression. Tonya complained of a sudden onset of weight gain, fatigue, and impairment in sleep onset latency. She reported that she wept frequently for "no reason." She feared that she would lose her job if she could not "get control" of her emotions. Upon referral to a family physician, laboratory tests including a complete blood count, thyroid panel, and a free thyroxine index uncovered a previously undetected hypothyroid condition that responded favorably to thyroid supplements. This simple, routine intervention would have been impossible without close collaboration between primary care and psychological, and Tonya's care would have been extended, costly, and complicated.

Two common dimensions have been identified in emerging rural collaborative practice models (Bray & Rogers, 1995). The first dimension is the physical structure of the physician's practice; the second dimension is the function of the physician's practice. The structure of the physician's practice can cover a wide range of options for collaboration. One model is a self-contained, comprehensive physician practice in which the doctor treats and manages the entire range of biopsychosocial problems. It also includes a model in which two professionals in independent practice (a physician and a psychologist) with mutually exclusive medical and psychosocial skills collaborate on patient care. Another model currently in use is two professionals in independent practice where the physician has some psychosocial management skills but refers patients with psychosocial problems to the psychologist

(Enright & Blue, 1989). Finally, it includes a model in which two colleagues work together in the same office and make referrals to each other and conduct joint interviews (Bray, Enright & Rogers, 1997; Bray & Rogers, 1995; Dym & Berman, 1986). The functional aspects of the collaboration range from (a) informal and formal consultation to (b) limited referral where the patient maintains a relationship with the physician and sees the psychologist for a particular concern to (c) comanagement of the patient with cotherapy during conjoint sessions (Bray & Rogers, 1995; McDaniel, Campbell, & Seaburn, 1990).

In addition, deGruy (1996) suggested having a primary care provider in a behavioral health setting as a consultant. He maintained that this model may be an effective practice method to manage and treat patients with comorbid disease. This would seem especially applicable in rural areas where there is a shortage of psychiatrists. This model underscores the importance of primary care providers becoming familiar with behavioral health practice styles and systems so they can work effectively in these contexts.

A government-sponsored project examined linking health and mental services. The project was a joint program of the U.S. Bureau of Community Health Services and the National Institute of Mental Health (Wagenfeld, 1990). One hundred community health centers in underserved areas received grants to establish linkages with mental health facilities. In rural areas it was found that the provision of mental health and consultation services on site was more effective than referrals to mental health centers (Burns, Burke, & Ozarin, 1983). The lack of funding at the end of the grant prevented continuation of the linkage program (Wagenfeld, 1990).

To meet the needs of rural primary care patients with mental health problems, both physical health providers and mental health providers need additional specialized training. Research indicates that primary care providers need additional training in the recognition and treatment of mental health problems (deGruy, 1996). Both types of health providers need to learn how to collaborate to take care of the unmet needs of rural patients (Pion et al., 1997; see also chap. 4, this volume, for further information about training for psychologists).

To better understand the effects of focused training, a demonstration project was undertaken to evaluate a collaborative practice model between rural psychologists and family physicians (Bray & Rogers, 1995, 1997). The purpose of this "Linkage Project" was to demonstrate that collaborative practices between psychologists and family physicians in rural areas could be developed to enhance the assessment and treatment of alcohol and other drug abuse and other behavioral problems. James H. Bray was a trainer for the program, and Michael F. Enright participated as a collaborating psychologist. The goals of the project were to facilitate linkages between family physicians and psychologists in rural areas; educate psychologists and family physicians regarding models of collaborative practice and treatment of alcohol and other drug abuse problems; increase the knowledge base of participating providers about alcohol and other drug abuse identification, treatment, and prevention; and enhance the level of service and treatment options for patients with alcohol and other drug abuse problems.

Ten pairs of psychologists and family physicians were recruited in rural Texas and Wyoming to participate in the project. The two groups met in their respective states for a day of initial training on collaborative practice and were monitored for 5 months by program staff. The professionals then participated in another day of training and debriefing on the process of their collaborative practice.

CASE EXAMPLES FROM THE LINKAGE PROJECT

The following are two examples of collaborative cases treated by participants in the Linkage Project (Bray & Rogers, 1995). In the first case, the physician and psychologist worked in the same building. A 40-year-old White woman was evaluated by the physician during a routine medical visit. The physician suspected that the woman was intoxicated and evaluated her using the methods taught in the training session. He determined that she had a history of alcohol abuse and depression. The patient was reluctant to acknowledge her drinking problem or seek treatment. The psychologist was consulted and came to the physician's office to see the patient. He conducted a further examination of the patient, and he too determined that the woman had a current drinking problem. In the joint meeting, he recommended that the patient receive counseling for her drinking and depression. The professionals then worked together with the patient to help her with her problems. This joint treatment included both separate and conjoint sessions with the patient. The physician reported that having the psychologist readily available helped to accurately diagnose the patient's problems and engage her in treatment.

In the second case, a man consulted his physician for a routine visit. The physician performed an examination and determined that the patient had an elevated liver function test. She discussed this with the patient, and the patient admitted that he had had a drinking problem in the past but had quit drinking. Because of the elevated liver function test and other clinical signs, the physician suspected that the patient was continuing to abuse alcohol. She consulted with the psychologist, and he evaluated the patient. The patient had a long history of alcohol abuse and had been in and out of treatment several times. The patient initially refused additional treatment and indicated that he could handle the problem on his own. Later, he returned to the physician because his driver's license had been suspended, and he needed a physician's approval to reapply for another license. This served as motivation for the patient to enter treatment with the psychologist. The physician told the patient that he would help the patient reapply for his driver's license if he would continue in treatment. The patient was treated with Naltroxin by the physician and was provided outpatient psychotherapy by the psychologist. The patient improved for a time but relapsed after several months. The patient wanted to see only the physician. However, the physician refused to treat the patient unless he continued psychotherapy with the psychologist. Joint treatment was begun again, and the patient was able to stop drinking again. The joint sessions focused on how the patient's medical and psychological problems were linked, informing each professional about developments in their treatment with the patient and reinforcing the ongoing treatment. Continued booster sessions were planned for the patient.

In each of these cases, the proximity, in terms of location and accessibility of the physician and psychologist, enhanced the ability of the team to collaborate in the treatment process. The availability of the psychologist to the physician's practice also improved the likelihood of a referral and collaborative practice for the patient's benefit. In both cases, the physicians felt that a simple referral to see the psychologist would not have been successful. The ability of the psychologist to quickly assess the situation and work with the physician to develop a rationale and motivation for the patient to continue in treatment were important factors in the successful outcomes of these cases. Obviously, in most cases this type of proximity and availability is not feasible. However, these cases illustrate the importance of the collaboration between the professionals for the effective treatment of alcohol and other drug abuse problems.

The Linkage Project was successful in linking providers and in enhancing the level and quality of collaborative practice between physicians and psychologists. The predominant changes in the collaborative relationship was from self-contained, independent practitioners to independent practices with mutually exclusive skills and from no relationship to limited referral and some consultation between professionals. In most cases, this type of arrangement was a step forward, but the training did not result in fully integrated forms of practice, with the exception of one pair who already shared offices prior to the training. The goals of the project were accomplished, at least to some limited degree, and support the continued examination of this model of practice in rural settings. The participants indicated that collaboration enhanced the effectiveness of each professional, reduced professional isolation, and resulted in better diagnosis and treatment of medical and psychosocial problems. Participants reported that the linkage improved their own sense of efficacy and satisfaction in working with patients with alcohol and other drug abuse problems. In addition, through the collaboration patients were provided enhanced treatment options for their problems. The results of this project suggest that collaboration and linkage between physicians and psychologists in rural America can be effected and that such linkages are beneficial for professional practice. Although the Linkage Project focused on rural practitioners, it appears that many of the basic parts of this model of training are applicable to both rural and urban settings.

CONCLUSION

We close with a comment by Frank deGruy (1996):

> Since most mental health care occurs in the primary care setting, we have had a profoundly unbalanced mental health research agenda. At this time, the single most effective strategy for improving the mental health of the people of this country and one of the most effective strategies for improving the overall health of these same people would be to make a significant investment in primary care mental health research. (p. 306)

It is also imperative that this research includes a focus on the unique needs of rural Americans. A Pew Commission-sponsored report, entitled "Critical Challenges: Revitalizing the Health Professions for the 21st Century" (O'Neil & The Pew Health Commission, 1998), made a number of suggestions which include the main points covered in this chapter. Foremost in these recommendations are that key areas of training must be integrated across professional communities, through increased sharing of clinical training resources and inclusion of more cross-teaching and more exploration of the various roles played by professionals. The report also recommended that educators create a training programs based on related discipline clusters and create multiskills and interdisciplinary core curricula. These recommendations are wise counsel for health professions in general but represent a blueprint for success for meeting both the primary care and mental health needs of rural citizens in the years ahead.

REFERENCES

American Medical Association Center for Health Policy Research. (1991). *Socioeconomic characteristics of medical practice 1990/1991*. Washington, DC: American Medical Association Socioeconomic Monitoring System.

American Psychological Association, Office of Rural Health. (2001). *Rural graduate training programs* [On-line]. Retrieved April 1, 2002, from http://www.apa.org:80/rural/gradcombo.html

Barrett, J. E., Barrett, J. A., Oxman, T. E., & Gerber, P. D. (1988). The prevalence of psychiatric disorders in a primary care practice. *Archives of General Psychiatry, 45,* 1100–1106.

Blazer, D., George, L. K., Landerman, R., Pennybaker, M., Melville, M. L., Woodbury, M., et al. (1985). Psychiatric disorders: A rural/urban comparison. *Archives of General Psychiatry, 42,* 651–656.

Bray, J. H. (1996). Psychologists as primary care practitioners. In R. J. Resnick & R. H. Rozensky (Eds.), *To your health: Psychology across the lifespan* (pp. 89–100). Washington, DC: American Psychological Association.

Bray, J. H., Enright, M. F., & Rogers, J. (1997). Collaboration with primary care physicians. In J. Morris (Ed.), *Practicing psychology in rural settings: Hospital privileges and collaborative care* (pp. 55–65). Washington, DC: American Psychological Association.

Bray, J. H., & Rogers, J. C. (1995). Linking psychologists and family physicians for collaborative practice. *Professional Psychology: Research and Practice, 26,* 132–138.

Bray, J. H., & Rogers, J. C. (1997). The Linkages Project: Training behavioral health professionals for collaborative practice with primary care physicians. *Families, Systems, & Health, 15,* 55–63.

Burns, B. J., Burke, J. D., & Ozarin, L. D. (1983). Linking health and mental health services in rural areas. *International Journal of Mental Health, 12,* 130–143.

deGruy, F. (1996). Mental health care in the primary care setting. In M. S. Donaldson, K. D. Yordy, K. N. Lohr, & N. A. Vanselow (Eds.), *Primary care: American's health in a new era* (pp. 285–311). Washington, DC: National Academy Press.

Dym, B., & Berman, S. (1986). The primary health care team: Family physician and family therapist in joint practice. *Family Systems Medicine, 4,* 9–21.

Eggebeen, D. J., & Lichter, D. T. (1993). Health and well being among rural Americans: Variations across the life course. *Journal of Rural Health, 9,* 86–98.

Eisenberg, L. (1992). Treating depression and anxiety in primary care: Closing the gap between knowledge and practice. *New England Journal of Medicine, 326,* 1080–1084.

Enright, M. F., & Blue, B. A. (1989). Collaborative treatment of panic disorders by psychologists and family physicians. *Psychotherapy in Private Practice, 7,* 85–89.

Fitchen, J. (1986). When rural communities collapse: Implications for mental health. *Rural Community Health Newsletter, 13,* 5–9.

Good, M. J. D., Good, B. J., & Cleary, P. D. (1987). Do patient attitudes influence physician recognition of psychosocial problems in primary care? *Journal of Family Practice, 25,* 53–59.

Higgins, E. S. (1994). A review of unrecognized mental illness in primary care. *Archives of Family Medicine, 3,* 908–917.

Human, J., & Wasem, J. (1991). Rural mental health in America. *American Psychologist, 46,* 232–239.

McDaniel, S. H., Campbell, T. L., & Seaburn, D. (1990). *Family-oriented primary care: A manual for physicians.* New York: Springer-Verlag.

McDaniel, S. H., Hepworth, J., & Doherty, W. J. (1992). *Medical family therapy.* New York: Basic Books.

Morris, J. (1997). (Ed.). *Practicing psychology in rural settings: Hospital privileges and collaborative care.* Washington, DC: American Psychological Association.

O'Neil, E. H., & The Pew Health Commission. (1998, December). *Recreating health professional practice for a new century: The fourth report of The Pew Health Professions Commission*. San Francisco: Pew Health Professions Commission.

Ormel, J., & Tiemens, B. (1995). Recognition and treatment of mental illness in primary care. *General Hospital Psychiatry, 17*, 160–164.

Paykel, E. S., Abbott, R., Jenkins, R., Brugha, T. S., & Meltzer, H. (2000). Urban–rural mental health differences in Great Britain: Findings from the National Morbidity Survey. *Psychological Medicine, 30*, 269–280.

Philbrick, J. T., Connelly, J. E., & Wofford. A. B. (1996). The prevalence of mental disorders in rural office practice. *Journal of General Internal Medicine, 11*, 9–15.

Pion, M. G., Keller, P., & McCombs, H. (1997). *Final report of the Ad Hoc Rural Mental Health Provider Work Group*. Rockville, MD: U.S. Department of Health and Human Services.

Popkin, M. K., Callies, A. L., & Mackenzie, T. B. (1985). The outcome of antidepressant use in the medically ill. *Archives of General Psychiatry, 42*, 1160–1163.

Rosenthal, T. C., Shiffer, J. M., Lucas, C., & DeMaggio, M. (1991).Factors involved in successful psychotherapy referral in rural primary care. *Family Medicine, 23*, 527–530.

Rost, K., Humphrey, J., & Kelleher, K. (1994). Physician management preferences and barriers to care for rural patients with depression. *Archives of Family Medicine, 3*, 409–414.

Rost, K., Smith, R., & Taylor, J. L. (1993). Rural–urban differences in stigma and the use of care for depressive disorders. *Journal of Rural Health, 9*, 57–62.

Rost, K., Wherry, J., Williams, C., & Smith, G. R. (1992, October). *Major depression in rural primary care practices: Treatment and outcomes*. Paper presented at the National Institute of Mental Health International Research Conference on Mental Health Problems in the General Health Care Sector, Washington, DC.

Rost, K., Williams, C., Wherry J., & Smith, R. (1995). The process and outcomes of care for major depression in rural family practice settings. *Journal of Rural Health, 11*, 114–121.

Schulberg, H. C., McClelland, M., & Gooding, M. A. (1987). Six-month outcomes for medical patients with major depressive disorders. *Journal of General Internal Medicine, 2*, 312–317.

Sturm, M. R., Camp, P., & Wells, K. B. (2001). Effects of cost-containment strategies within managed care on continuity of the relationship between patients with depression and their primary care providers. *Medical Care, 39*, 1075–1085.

U.S. Bureau of the Census. (1995). *Urban and rural definitions*. Washington, DC: U.S. Government Printing Office.

U.S. Bureau of the Census. (2001). *Urban and rural classification: Census 2000. Urban and rural criteria* [On-line]. Retrieved April 1, 2002, from http://www.census.gov/population/www/censusdata/ur-def.html

Wagenfeld, M. O. (1990). Mental health and rural America: A decade review. *Journal of Rural Health, 6*, 507–522.

Wagenfeld, M. O., Murray, J. D., Mohatt, D. F., & DeBruyn, J. (Eds.). (1994). *Mental health and rural America: An overview and annotated bibliography 1978–1993*. Washington, DC: U.S. Government Printing Office.

Wells, K. B., Burnam, M. A., Rogers, W., Hays, R., & Camp, P. (1992). The course of depression in adult outpatients: Results from the Medical Outcomes Study. *Archives of General Psychiatry, 49*, 788–794.

Yuen, E. J., Gerdes, J. L., & Gonzales, J. J. (1996). Patterns of rural mental health care: An exploratory study. *General Hospital Psychiatry, 18*, 14–21.

14

CHRONIC ILLNESS MANAGEMENT IN PRIMARY CARE: THE CARDINAL SYMPTOMS MODEL

ROBERT G. FRANK, KRISTOPHER J. HAGGLUND, AND JANET E. FARMER

The last century has witnessed a significant evolution in the understanding of the causes of illness and disability among Americans. One hundred years ago, the primary threats to health were poor sanitation and lack of safe drinking water. In the 21st century, chronic conditions have replaced infectious diseases as a main threat to health (Frank, 1999; Hoffman, Rice, & Sung, 1996). Hoffman et al. (1996) defined *chronic conditions* a as "a general term that includes both chronic diseases and impairments" (p. 1473). More than 100 million Americans are affected by chronic health conditions (Hoffman et al., 1996). Most individuals with these conditions are not disabled, but they face increasing obstacles that may lead to disability or "recurrent exacerbations, higher health costs, more lost days from work than others, and the risk of long term-term limitations and disabilities" (Hoffman et al., 1996, p. 1477).

Chronic health conditions also engender significant health care cost. For example, in the Medicare program, 14% of the beneficiaries account for 76% of all medical expenditures (Gluck & Hanson, 2001). Although individuals with limitations in one or more activities of daily living account for less than 17% of the Medicare beneficiaries, they account for almost 50% of the expenditures. Health care costs are almost doubled for individuals with two or more chronic health conditions (Pope & Tarlov, 1991). Similar patterns are observed in the Medicaid program and, in response to fiscal crises and the absence of improved health care delivery models, many states have begun to cut benefits for people with disabling chronic conditions (Smith, Ellis, Gifford, Ramesh, & Waching, 2002). The U.S. health care system evolved to treat acute disorders and continues to approach most disorders from this perspective. Routine health services typically comprise a 15-minute interaction with a primary care provider who focuses on acute health problems (Wagner, Austin, &Von Korff, 1996), and there is no organized system necessary for the management of chronic health conditions (Bodenheimer, 1999). The emphasis of the health delivery system on acute disorders can lead to mismanagement of many conditions; exacerbation of the condition; and failure to utilize many strategies, such as education, that may alter the course of the disorder. This design places individuals with chronic conditions at risk to be treated inadequately and face higher out-of-pocket expenses (Hoffman et al., 1996), and it contributes to the high costs of care for people with chronic illnesses.

Effective management of chronic illness requires emphasis on partnerships between health care professionals and consumers and should include:

- a focus on activities that promote health and physiological reserve through exercise, nutrition, social activities, and sleep;
- routine interactions among consumers, health care providers, and other systems of care;
- use of explicit protocols that encourage healthy lifestyles;
- monitoring of physical and emotional status as affected by symptoms; and
- managing the impact of the illness on the individuals' roles, emotions, and interpersonal functioning (Wagner et al., 1996).

In addition, providers need adequate time for these patient encounters and access to information about chronic health conditions. Although many health care systems purport to address these issues, most evidence suggests that few systems, including primary care, focus on comprehensive care and self-management (Institute of Medicine [IOM], 2001; Wagner et al., 1996). A recent IOM report of health care quality in the United States noted that one of the greatest challenges to the health care system is the delivery of effective care to individuals with chronic health care conditions (IOM, 2001).

CHRONIC CARE AND PRIMARY CARE

Behavioral factors can significantly affect the development of chronic health conditions. Behavioral factors such as unhealthy diet, lack of exercise, tobacco use, alcohol and drug use, and risky sexual behaviors cause or contribute significantly to the development of chronic illness and premature death in the United States. In fact, the 10 leading causes of death in the United States are attributable to behavioral factors. Psychologists have developed a range of clinical and educational services to reduce these risky behaviors. Curtailing risky behaviors is fundamental to preventing the onset or exacerbation of chronic health conditions (Center for the Advancement of Health, 1999).

The impact of these behaviors on disease has facilitated the recognition of psychologists as primary care providers (American Psychological Association, 1996; Haley et al., 1998). Most often, within primary care settings, psychologists have served as direct service providers or as teachers of primary care physicians (Frank, 1999). In these roles, psychologists have been recognized as integral to primary care delivery. The participation of psychologists in primary care teams addresses the most common definition of primary care preferred by the IOM in 1994: "the provision of integrated, accessible health care services by clinicians who are accountable for addressing a large majority of personal health care needs, developing a sustain partnership with patients, and practicing in the context of family and community" (p. 1).

As Frank (1999) noted, the IOM definition applies to more than psychologists working in primary care and other health settings. For example, many psychologists providing care within rehabilitation settings participate in teams that meet the criteria established by the IOM. By extension, the same criteria may be applied to psychologists who participate in teams that address chronic health conditions ranging from diabetes, to hypertension, to cancer, to spinal cord rehabilitation. Such teams provide coordinated, comprehensive, integrated care.

Applying the principles of primary care to chronic health conditions can improve health delivery, because there is a great need for comprehensive, coordinated care that is tailored to patient needs and that focuses on health promotion and disability prevention. Frank (1997) proposed such an approach to care for people with disabling and chronic illness and labeled it the *Cardinal Symptom model*. Central to the Cardinal Symptom model is the concept that comprehensive health care is more effectively provided by a team of trained providers than by any single provider. This approach also integrates assessment and intervention for psychological and behavioral problems that determine the long-term health and functioning of people with chronic illnesses.

In the next sections of this chapter, we review current chronic care management approaches and examine two vectors driving change in the health care system: (a) increases in federal health spending and (b) increases in consumer health knowledge and expectations. We then propose that an approach to health care for chronic conditions that is drawn from rehabilitation and the "cardinal symptoms" offers a model of integrated primary care that will improve health care delivery in the United States.

CHRONIC CARE PROGRAMS

Effective management of chronic health conditions requires access to information, consistent implementation of behavior change programs addressing psychological needs, access to experts, and effective information systems (Wagner et al., 1996). The most successful efforts to meet these criteria in the management of chronic health conditions have been through *disease management programs*. Bodenheimer (1999) described disease management as "the latest catch phrase in the ever evolving American health care spectacle" (p. 1202). Bodenheimer went on to say that

> Many primary care physicians are preoccupied with acute disorders and do not have organized systems tailored to the less urgent problems of chronic illness. Disease management programs can help by providing teams with trained health care personnel and organized systems of care. (p. 1202)

To date, the primary purpose of disease management programs has been the reduction of health care costs. There is some evidence that programs that address the most expensive conditions, such as diabetes, asthma, congestive heart failure, and depression, may have an impact on costs. For example, one company developed a diabetes disease management program for employers using managed-care interventions to control costs. The product is marketed as a pharmaceutical benefit service. The company identifies patients with diabetes through its 51 million-person pharmacy database. The patients are provided a self-assessment questionnaire and subsequently classified as either high- and low-risk patients. The lowest risk patients receive educational letters on critical topics such as food care and glucose testing. The physicians receive educational materials promoting practice guidelines of the American Diabetes Association. Patients may receive counseling during telephone conversations with personnel from the company's central office. In a study that involved 1,198 patients with Type I diabetes, the costs of health care before and after program implementation were examined. A 9% reduction in health care cost and a 20% decrease in the number of diabetes-related hospital days were found (Bodenheimer, 1999).

Pharmaceutical companies are interested in disease management because they recognize the huge potential market associated with chronic conditions. For example, prescription drugs constitute about 6% of health care spending. As noted previously, spending for chronic diseases accounts for approximately 50% of health spending. The enormous competition for the disease management market has led to a consolidation of programs to provide pharmaceutical benefit management. Currently, there are three leading companies in this niche. Although further consolidation is unlikely, intense competition is predicted to continue (Bodenheimer, 1999).

Disease management programs can be divided into two models. The first one, the *primary care model*, provides disease management within the context of an ongoing primary care relationship. In this approach, specialized teams work within a health maintenance organization (HMO) or other comprehensive health care program assisting primary care providers. Staff model HMOs, such as the Kaiser Permanente Health Care System and Group Health Cooperative, are leaders in developing in-house disease management programs (Bodenheimer, 1999). These programs can provide information resources, traveling experts within the HMO delivery system, and educators. Group Health in Washington state has designed a special primary care service by forming teams consisting of two physicians, a mid-level practitioner, a registered nurse, and three medical assistants. Each team provides care to a designated group of patients. As in many chronic illness delivery systems, there is extensive reliance on the use of nonphysician practitioners, practice guidelines, prevention protocols, and self-management programs (Bodenheimer, 1999; Wagner, 1998).

The second, alternative model to the primary care program for disease management is the *carve-out model*. This is the approach that has been pursued most aggressively by the pharmaceutical industry. In this model, the pharmaceutical benefits managers provide employers expert management for specific chronic diseases. Patients are often identified through the company's database, and specialized care is provided only to the carved-out diagnosis. There is limited or no contact with the comprehensive primary care system or other delivery systems. The entire focus is on symptoms within one chronic disorder.

Carved-out systems have been criticized for separating primary care from the carved-out condition. An alternative model, which is considered a *carve-in* rather than a carve-out, is offered by Diabetes Treatment Centers of America. This company provides nurses, dieticians, and health educators to work within a health organization and communicate with primary care clinicians to improve care only for diabetes. They report reducing glycated hemoglobin by 10% which resulted in a 26% reduction in health care costs for patients with diabetes (Bodenheimer, 1999).

These chronic care management programs have focused attention on individuals with specific, high-cost conditions, but there is substantial room for continued improvement in the system of care. Before we discuss the potential use of primary care principles to enhance the care of persons with chronic illness, it is important to consider two important forces driving changes in the health care system more generally: (a) increases in federal health spending and (b) increases in consumer health knowledge and expectations. Without fundamental changes in the nature of health care delivery for persons with chronic illnesses, these two trends will exacerbate the fragmentation in the current health care delivery system and reduce its ability to deliver adequate health care (IOM, 2001).

FUNDING CHRONIC CARE MANAGEMENT

Commercial purchasers have become sensitive to the cost incurred by chronic conditions. The federal government, one of the primary purchasers of health care, has demonstrated inconsistencies in its approach to chronic care. Medicare provides health insurance for nearly 40 million people age 65 and over and for certain disabled individuals (Gluck & Hanson, 2001). Medicare plays a critical role in the payment of services for individuals with chronic health conditions. Understanding Medicare's history and evolution is fundamental to appreciating the health care for America's elderly, many of whom are afflicted with chronic health conditions.

Medicare is the second largest federal social welfare program. It is an open-ended entitlement program that provides a defined benefit package. As a mandatory-spending program, allocations do not need to be reauthorized annually. There is no means testing; individuals meeting criteria are eligible for inclusion in the program (CRS Library of Congress, 1999).

The traditional Medicare program is fee-for-service, allowing consumers provider choice. The benefit package is less generous than the average employer package. Currently, only 13% of Medicare beneficiaries are enrolled in managed-care plans. The Balance Budget Act of 1997 included several features designed to increased participation in Medicare + Choice program that manages health care. Despite initial increases in participation, enrollment in Medicare + Choice. has slowed in the last 4 years (Henry J. Kaiser Family Foundation, 2002).

Medicare covers about 56% of all health care costs for its beneficiaries, with other insurers and out-of-pocket spending accounting for the remainder. Individuals with more health care needs, however, incur greater out-of-pocket expenses (Maxwell, Moon, & Segal, 2001; cited in Gluck & Hanson, 2001). Services are covered unevenly. For example, there is no outpatient drug coverage and no coverage for hearing aids. Part A of the program, which covers hospital services of Medicare, has faced shortfalls from the beginning. Solvency projections vary on the basis of economic assumptions for the model, but all projections suggest the fund is solvent until 2010–2020. To bring Part A for fiscal solvency through 2022, outlays must be reduced by 18% or revenue increased by 22% (CRS, 1998).

Modifying the Medicare program has proved complex. The payroll taxes now levied are already considered high, making additional increases unlikely. Moreover, the problems with insufficient funding will increase in the near future. In 2011, the first baby boomers (those born in 1946–1964) will begin to turn 65. In 1997, there were 3.9 workers per Medicare beneficiary. By the year 2010, there will be only 3.6, and by 2030 this number will be reduced to 2.3. In 1998, Medicare outlays represented 11.8% of the total governmental outlays. This number will increase by 2008, which is when the Congressional Budget Office estimates Medicare will comprise 16.8% of all federal spending (CRS Library of Congress, 1999). It is clear that current rates of spending in Medicare are unsustainable. Moreover, a relatively small portion of Medicare beneficiaries account for the majority of spending. The fact that 10% of Medicare beneficiaries account for 70% of all medical expenditures will lead policymakers to look toward chronic health conditions for further savings. As federal policymakers consider revisions in Medicare, they will consider initiatives in the private sector.

Children also experience chronic health conditions and disabilities that are costly to the public sector. About 18% of all U.S. children experience a chronic health condition that requires health and related services beyond those needed by most children, and approximately 6% have significant limitations in daily functioning (Newacheck et al., 1998). Children with special health care needs account for 70%–80% of all child medical expenditures, and their average medical costs are five to six times higher than those of healthy children (IOM, 2000; Newacheck & Taylor, 1992).

Funding for children's health care comes from multiple sources, but the primary source of public health insurance is Medicaid, which enrolls approximately 1 out of every 5 children (U.S. Bureau of the Census, 2000). Substantial financial support is also provided by other public programs, such as the State Children's Health Insurance Program, the Individuals with Disabilities Education Act, the Maternal and Child Health Bureau (Title V), and mental health programs for children with developmental disabilities (IOM, 2000). These funding programs developed in piecemeal fashion, resulting in fragmentation of care and a high need for care coordination to help families navigate the system of care (DuPlessis, Inkelas, & Halfon, 1998). Managed-care organizations have demonstrated some potential to promote integrated services for children with special health care needs, but cost containment efforts in managed-care organizations have raised concerns about their willingness to support adequate health care services for this group (Fox, McManus, & Austrian, 2000; Rosenbach & Young, 2000). In the midst of this complex and changing system of care, primary care physicians have experienced increasing demands to serve children with serious chronic conditions. However, many physicians report a lack of training in chronic care management as well as a lack of time and reimbursement for extended office visits (Leslie, Sarah, & Palfrey, 1998).

THE CHANGING INFORMATION ECONOMY

Over the last 10 years, there has been a fundamental change in the nature of the U.S. economy. Information and access to information is now a primary commodity that defines economic growth. The rapidity of the shift from an economy focused on goods and services to an economy focused on information has been stunning. For example, since 1990, sales for *Encyclopedia Britannica* have declined more than 50%. The decline in sales parallels the growth of Encarta, a Microsoft product, which provides encyclopedia information as part of the Microsoft product line. Microsoft Encarta licensed the Funk and Wagnall's encyclopedia that had been previously sold in vendors such as grocery stores. The Encarta product has been marketed for $50. In contrast, a traditional sales force sold the storied *Encyclopedia Britannica* for $2,000 per edition. The growth in consumer access to information, without middlemen such as sales forces, is in stark contrast to the historic model used by the *Encyclopedia Britannica* leadership. The *Encyclopedia Britannica* leadership failed to understand the fundamental shift associated with the initiation of the information economy (Evans & Wurster, 1997).

The information economy has altered the structure of businesses, including health care organizations. Organizations typically enable the rich exchange of information among key individuals in the hierarchy. Substantially less information is available to individuals lower on the hierarchy. This process results in an asymmetry of information, limiting the ability of individuals lower in the hierarchy to make knowledgeable decisions. At the same time, individuals higher in hierarchy are often overwhelmed by inputs of information, so that meaningful pursuit of change within one vector is difficult. Moreover, recent changes in Internet standards have created universal standards of communication. This has allowed electronic mail to become a universal messenger across levels of organizations and differing strata of society. Information is now available with less regard to role, function, or title. An Internet-aided communication pattern is described as *hyperarchy*. It allows the transmission of information to all levels of an organization. Availability of information is no longer a defining organizational characteristic.

The information economy has profound implications for product delivery systems. Already, new products such as Amazon.com, eBay, and portable electronic medical records have heralded the profound changes readily foreseeable in the near future. New methods for delivering products will lead to alterations in what constitutes a product. For example, in the current U.S. economy, many products are cross-subsidized and delivered as a unified whole. For example, newspapers include news articles as well advertising. Classified advertising provides about 20% of the revenue for the average newspaper but only 10% of the costs.

The information economy will lead to the unbundling of services that were traditionally linked. In this process, value will be ascribed to certain portions of the service chain. Vertically integrated products that rely on cross-subsidization between service steps will challenge this new model. Currently, many products are packaged so that those that are more cost-efficient subsidize more costly subproducts. The linking of products in this manner allows economies of scale to be created so that products can be distributed. When these products are unbundled, costly products may not be viable, as a lack of cross-subsidization will not allow that product to stand on its own.

Over the last 50 years, American business has adhered to the principle of product loyalty. Extensive marketing campaigns have been developed to identify brands and ensure that consumers develop an understanding of the quality the brand connotes. This concept of "branding" has become so pervasive in U.S. society that is has extended far beyond the production of products to include conceptual and service areas, such as the hospitals and health care. Yet the information economy challenges traditional concepts of branding. As the vertical integration of products is altered, the overall brand value of the integrated product will become less apparent. Consumers switch their loyalty to the software products that allow access to information rather than the overall service. As vertically integrated products are dismantled, the value chains within those products are unbundled. These value chains can be fragmented into multiple businesses. Each fragment will have a unique economy of scale. Some fragments, lacking the cross-subsidization previously available, will flounder. Others, especially those able to develop the critical mass needed to support the product, will flourish. This ability to develop critical mass will define the outcome of each product fragment.

As value chains are unbundled, customers face complex choices. They need to choose previously known dominant brands or learn about entirely new areas. When faced with such complex choices, consumers historically have chosen one of two strategies. They have either chosen the dominant brand (i.e., "Massachusetts General Hospital" vs. Dr. Smith, expert in pain management, who practices independently), or they have chosen a search vehicle that narrows the choice of formats into specific channels. This model, much like staying with a favorite TV channel, reduces the complexity of the choices and allows more refined discrimination among a narrower array of alternatives. This process creates a multitude of new business and opportunities for the providers of health care services.

As value chains are unbundled, new branding opportunities develop for parties that neither produce nor deliver the service. These new participants serve as channels, limiting the array of choices so that consumers can make finer discriminations. In industries such as banking it has been apparent that the creation of multiple channels has reduced the bargain power of many sectors of consumers. There are simply too many channels to allow any consumer group to gain substantial leverage. Consequently, bargaining power diminishes as customers chose to switch rather than bargain. As has been witnessed in the phone industry, producers will create incentives for switching that will further enhance the likelihood of consumers moving from producer to producer with no long-term product or brand loyalty (Evans & Wurster, 1997).

HEALTH CARE AND THE INFORMATION ECONOMY

During the last 10 years, health care delivery systems in the United States have undergone profound change (Frank, 1999; Frank & VandenBos, 1994). The rapid implementation of market-driven delivery systems following the failure of the Clinton health care reform plan increased the rate of change and led to myriad health system models. The merger frenzy among health care systems that dominated the late 1990s appears to have subsided. The resulting diversity of health care system models has clouded the consequences of changes resulting from the shift from a controlled health market to a market-driven health care system (Bingaman, Frank, & Billy, 1993). Reactions to payor dominance, mergers, and the influence of the new information economy have resulted in a confusing array of health delivery systems with no apparent national or state health policy direction.

It is now clear that changes wrought by the onset of the information economy will also affect health care. Parallels can be drawn to changes in other traditional industries. Consumers have shown a willingness to switch health plans, regardless of perceived allegiances to health providers, to gain a few dollars in savings. Consumers have expressed high levels of dissatisfaction with many aspects of the current evolution. They continue to be concerned with continuity of care. As the health care industry continues to change, it is likely consumers will continue to emphasize concerns regarding health problems they perceive as the most salient. Consumers have indicated their strong preferences for "patient rights," including the right to choose providers who are knowledgeable and committed to the care of their problems (Blendon, Benson, Brodie, Altman, & James, 2000). Indeed, there has been remarkable consensus among all types of voters on the issue of patient rights to select providers and have more control over their own health care (Blendon et al., 2000).

Transition to the information economy has already led to the unbundling of many services within the health care delivery system, for example, the differentiation between inpatient and outpatient services, delineation of intensive care services from general hospital services, and so on. Future unbundling of traditional services will lead competitors to pick off parts of the value chain, leaving components that have previously been cross-subsidized stranded by the burden of high cost. This process has been apparent in the reduction of support for psychology services in rehabilitation as the payment system was restructured, changing the bundling.

Products that are dependent on a vertically integrated value chain will be at significant risk. The escalating cost of care of chronic health conditions assures that payors will focus on reducing care. Similarly, the consumer revolution assures that consumers will look for health care systems that focus on effective and compassionate care of chronic health care symptoms. Traditional primary care models have focused on the provision of continuous comprehensive health care to the consumer but, as noted earlier, this approach is designed for short-term interactions focusing on acute health care problems. Consumers are concerned with how chronic health issues affect their ability to undertake daily activities. The routine focus of primary care systems on acute-care issues, combined with the interest of consumers and the reduction of health care costs, argues the need for a more effective model addressing consumer and cost concerns.

We have described three factors that will alter delivery systems for individuals with chronic health conditions. First, although primary care systems enhance health outcomes and improve cost-effectiveness and access to health care (Starfield, 2000), traditional primary care systems are not the most efficient systems for individuals with chronic or debilitating health conditions (Wagner et al., 1996). Second, escalating cost factors will require that service delivery systems be highly cost-effective. Over the next 10 years, the largest payor for chronic health services, Medicare, will face significant shortfalls as the baby boomers begin to utilize services in 2011. Last, fundamental changes in the information economy will echo in health care. Consumers, aided by an abundance of information and the ability to discuss their concerns and share information and outcomes, will pressure health care delivery systems, particularly those associated with chronic care, to modify their standards. Consumer concerns will emphasize a patient's right to choose providers, places of service, and, most fundamentally, to participate fully in his or her health care.

Traditional primary care systems, designed to manage acute illness, will be hard pressed to meet the demands of the fully enfranchised chronic-care patient. These consumers will demand the knowledge and specialized care provided by specialists (Donohoe, 1998) but also seek the continuity of care provided by primary care. Although primary care espouses education and self-management of disease conditions, this goal is seldom achieved (Fox & Gruman, 1999; Wagner et al., 1996). Consumers with chronic health conditions will seek: (a) education to manage their conditions, (b) individualized programs supported by professional collaborators, and (c) continuity of care (Fox & Gruman, 1999).

Most existing health care delivery systems are not capable of providing the comprehensive, specialized services future consumers will seek. Primary care systems provide the continuity of care and the comprehensive services, but most are not designed to provide the education and collaborative services needed for individuals with chronic health conditions. Appointment frequency and length is often inadequate for the chronic conditions. Individuals with chronic health conditions need more time with providers and routine assessment of clinical, behavioral, and psychological conditions. Primary care practices frequently lack the expertise in nutrition, pharmacy, and social systems needed for effective management of chronic health conditions. Moreover, the substantial ongoing shift created by movement to the information economy is likely to fundamentally alter the way patients interact with health care systems. The new, "informed" consumer will increasingly demand higher level information and involvement in health care services. Consumers will educate each other through Internet connections. In the area of chronic care, the role of practitioners, including physicians, will change. Consumers using the Internet will be highly informed and turn to practitioners as expert consultants. No longer "patients," consumers will focus on partnering with practitioners as equals in addressing their chronic health conditions. Informed consumers will seek more preventive services and be more likely to carefully evaluate the cost–benefit balance of suggested treatments.

Future health delivery systems will need to merge attractive aspects of the current primary care system with components of the specialty system to serve these informed consumers. Opinion polls indicate that the U.S. public desires health care providers who are familiar with their history and able to communicate with them (Donohoe, 1998). Individuals with chronic conditions also require providers able to collaborate and provide tailored programs, and continuity of care.

A single provider cannot supply the extensive services required by individuals with chronic conditions. Effective treatment requires a range of skills from medicine to psychological expertise. A model for this type of care currently exists in the field of rehabilitation and has existed for more than 50 years. In this model, a team of coordinated individuals provides care to individuals with catastrophic disability (Frank, 2001). The model of care used by rehabilitation teams offers a way to address the demands of managing chronic conditions and the rapid evolution of health care systems. Merging the rehabilitation team model with the primary care model yields the type of delivery system needed for individuals with chronic health conditions.

THE CARDINAL SYMPTOM MODEL

The Cardinal Symptom model (Frank, 1997) recognizes that individuals with chronic health conditions tend to define their care around the symptoms that are creating disability. The consumer identifies the health symptoms that present the greatest personal concern to him or her. By focusing on the consumer's perception of health concerns, the delivery of health care services yields cost-effective care. For example, a person with Chronic Obstructive Pulminary Disease may believe his pulmonary physician is the most critical provider. His pulmonary doctor may already provide most of his health care. In the Cardinal Symptom model, the consumer–patient works with his or her health insurance company to find a provider who can offer comprehensive, continuous care driven by the symptom system most salient to the consumer–patient.

For individuals with disabling conditions, the practitioner may be a physiatrist or other member of the rehabilitation team. The diversity and comprehensive nature of care available within the rehabilitation team assures coverage for all health care symptoms and continuity of care.

Within the Cardinal Symptom model, focused, continuous, comprehensive care is provided to the patient's most impairing symptoms. The rehabilitation team handles acute health care problems. When this proves infeasible, as in the current U.S. health care system, consultation is requested from primary care providers.

The Cardinal Symptom model presents a substantial shift from the most dominant current models of health care practice. It is interesting, however, that the Cardinal Symptom model meets many of the parameters common to the provision of services in the information economy. As health care moves to the hyperarchy model, patients will become active information-seeking consumers. As they do so, they will look for expert systems to serve as "channels " or "brand" managers. To achieve the constellation of services necessary, modifications will occur in virtually all health delivery systems. The traditional health system chain will be fragmented, creating unique products such as information, support groups, and health services determined by Cardinal Symptom clusters. In this evolving model, information will become a product that is unique. These information products will likely be channeled within larger health delivery systems and sold as unique and separate products. Each health system channel will require an information product as well as service delivery products.

The demands of caring for individuals with chronic conditions and disabilities call for innovative approaches to health care practice. One that integrates disease management into primary care is the Missouri Partnership for Enhanced Delivery of Services (MO-PEDS). An ongoing research demonstration project funded by the Robert Wood Johnson Foundation and modeled after a similar program at Boston Children's Hospital (Silva, Sofis, & Palfrey, 2000), MO-PEDS is designed to enhance the ability of primary care physicians to provide comprehensive, coordinated, family-centered care in community settings. The primary care team consists of the child and family, the child's physician, a nurse practitioner, and a paid parent consultant. The nurse practitioner, known as the *Family Support Specialist*, conducts a comprehensive assessment of medical and nonmedical needs, produces a written health plan with information regarding care management for the family and physician, links the family to community resources, and helps the family coordinate across service and funding agencies to maximize care. The parent consultant encourages informal, family-to-family supports and provides feedback to physicians regarding ways to improve their practice for children with complex needs. A pediatric rehabilitation psychologist, Janet Farmer, developed and implemented this program in collaboration with primary care physicians and public agencies serving Missouri children and will also be examining evaluation data to determine the program's impact. This integrated health service delivery model allows identification of a range of child and family needs, and it has the flexibility to provide services that not only treat acute problems but also promote health and prevent disability.

To create a fully integrated system for individuals with chronic health concerns, community-based, primary care clinicians must remain involved in care. For example, MO-PEDS has enhanced the ability of the local primary care providers to be members of the teams that provides families with a resource for continuity across multiple specialists. Other models of Cardinal Symptom management that vary the role of the primary provider are possible:

1. The primary care clinician continues to play an oversight role but has a local team to coordinate care from specialists and for nonmedical needs. This has been adopted in various forms by managed-care organizations working with children with special health care needs and reflects the approach of MO-PEDS.

2. A single specialist provides primary and specialty care (e.g., well-child checks, management of cerebral palsy) but, because of distance from the patient's home community, retains the primary care provider as an integrated part of the service delivery system. The specialist would provide oversight care, but the primary care clinician would act as a resource for triaging acute exacerbations of the chronic illness, treating acute illness not related to the chronic illness, and referring patients and families to community resources for nonmedical needs. This scenario may apply only to rural areas where geographic distance limits families from accessing their specialists for many functions of primary care.

3. The primary care clinician provides medical treatment in collaboration with specialists, but a nonphysician provider is a primary resource for treatment of presenting problems (e.g., a neuropsychologist for a child with behavior and learning problems associated with severe traumatic brain injury).

THE PSYCHOLOGIST'S ROLE IN A CARDINAL SYMPTOM TEAM

The role of psychologists in Cardinal Symptom teams is essential but can vary in specific tasks according to the needs of patients and the setting. It is clear that psychologists can direct and coordinate these interdisciplinary teams. Through the emphasis on interpersonal processes in their training, psychologists are prepared to lead Cardinal Symptom teams, especially when the presenting problems focus on psychological manifestations of chronic disease, including adjustment to disability, adherence to medical treatment regimens, family support, and community reintegration. In addition, psychologists can provide direct care for psychological factors affecting chronic health.

In the Cardinal Symptom model psychologists are important providers, but they can also perform activities in addition to clinical care. Included among these activities are program management, outcome evaluation, and policy development. In this capacity, psychologists contribute to development of the health care systems and to improvements in clinical care. Through this program, psychologists have the opportunity to improve primary care delivery and influence health care systems.

The Cardinal Symptom model promotes comprehensive care. For people with chronic conditions, such access to primary–specialty care teams and flexible, integrated services may be the most cost-efficient way to enhance health and prevent disability. For psychologists, the Cardinal Symptom approach offers the opportunity to develop and lead health programs influencing the individual and the health care system.

REFERENCES

American Psychological Association, Committee for the Advancement of Professional Practice. (1996). *Primary Care Task Force Report*. Washington, DC: Author.

Bingaman, J., Frank, R. G., & Billy, C. L. (1993). Combining a global budget with a market driven system: Can it be done? *American Psychologist, 48*, 270–276.

Blendon, R. J., Benson, J. M., Brodie, M., Altman, D. E., & James, M. (2000). Health care in the upcoming 2000 election. *Health Affairs, 19*, 210–221.

Bodenheimer, T. (1999). Disease management—Promises and pitfalls. *New England Journal of Medicine, 340*, 1202–1205.

Center for the Advancement of Health. (1999). *Patients as effective collaborators in managing chronic conditions*. New York: Milbank Memorial Fund.

CRS Library of Congress. (1999, April). Medicare: An overview. Retrieved July 14, 2003, from http://www.kff.org/docs/sections/medicare/quickfacts.html

CRS Report to Congress. (1998, October). Medicare reform: Issues and options. Retrieved July 14, 2003, from http://www.kff.org/docs/sections/medicare/quickfacts.html

DuPlessis, H. M., Inkelas, M., & Halfon, N. (1998). Assessing the performance of community systems for children. *Health Services Research, 33*, 1111–1142.

Evans, P. B., & Wurster, T. S. (1997). Strategy in the new economics of information. *Harvard and Business Review, 75*(5), 71–82.

Fox, H. B., McManus, M. A., & Austrian, J. S. (2000). *An analysis of safeguards for children with special needs in states' Medicaid managed care contracts* (Issue Brief No. 4). Washington, DC: Maternal and Child Health Policy Research Center.

Frank, R. G. (1997). Lessons from the great battle: Health care reform 1992–1994. *Archives of Physical Medicine and Rehabilitation, 78,* 120–124.

Frank, R. G. (1999). We zigged when we should have zagged. *Rehabilitation Psychology, 44,* 36–51.

Frank, R. G., & VandenBos, G. R. (1994). Health care reform: The 1993–1994 evolution. *American Psychologist, 74,* 851–854.

Gluck, M. E., & Hanson, K. W. (2001). *Medicare chart book.* Menlo Park, CA: Henry J. Kaiser Family Foundation.

Haley, W. E., McDaniel, S. H., Bray, J. H., Frank, R. G., Heldring, M., Bennett Johnson, S., et al. (1998). Psychological practice in primary care settings: Practical tips for clinicians. *Professional Psychology: Research and Practice, 29,* 236–244.

Henry J. Kaiser Family Foundation. (2002). *Medicare at a glance.* Menlo Park, CA: Author.

Hoffman, C., Rice, R., & Sung, H. (1996). Persons with chronic conditions: Their prevalence and cost. *Journal of the American Medical Association, 276,* 1473–1479.

Institute of Medicine. (2000). *America's health care safety net: Intact but endangered.* Washington, DC: National Academy Press.

Institute of Medicine. (2001). *Crossing the quality chasm: A new health care system for the 21st century.* Washington, DC: National Academy Press.

Leslie, L. K., Sarah, R., & Palfrey, J. S. (1998). Child health care in changing times. *Pediatrics, 101,* 746–752.

Newacheck, P. W., Strickland, B., Shonkoff, J. P., Perrin, J. M., McPherson, M., McManus, M., et al. (1998). An epidemiologic profile of children with special health care needs. *Pediatrics, 102,* 117–123.

Newacheck, P. W., & Taylor, W. R. (1992). Childhood chronic illness: Prevalence, severity, and impact. *American Journal of Public Health, 82,* 364–371.

Pope, P., & Tarlov, A. (1991). A model for disability and disability prevention. In P. Pope & A. Tarlov (Eds.), *Disability in America: Toward a national agenda for prevention.* Washington, DC: National Academy Press.

Rosenbach, M. L., & Young, C. G. (2000). *Care coordination in Medicaid managed care: A primer for states, managed care organizations, providers, and advocates* (MPR Reference No. 8541–400). Cambridge, MA: Mathematic Policy Research.

Silva, T. J., Sofis, L. A., & Palfrey, J. S. (2000). *Practicing comprehensive care: A physician's manual for implementing a medical home for children with special health care needs.* Boston: Institute for Community Inclusion/UAP.

Smith, V., Ellis, E., Gifford, K., Ramesh, R., & Wachino, V. (2002). *Medicaid spending growth: Results from a 2002 survey.* Menlo Park, CA: Henry J. Kaiser Family Foundation.

Starfield, B. (2000). Is U. S. health really the best in the world? *New England Journal of Medicine, 284,* 483–485.

U.S. Bureau of the Census. (2000). *Health insurance detailed table #10* [On-line]. Retrieved July 17, 2001, from http://www.census.gov/hhes/hlthins/hlthin99/dtable10.html

Wagner, E. H. (1998). Chronic disease management: What will it take to improve care for chronic illness? *Effective Clinical Practice, 1,* 24.

Wagner, E. H., Austin, B. T., & Von Korff, M. (1996). Organizing care for patients with chronic illness. *Milbank Quarterly, 74,* 511–544.

IV

HEALTH SYSTEMS, POLICY, AND PRIMARY CARE PSYCHOLOGY

15

U.S. HEALTH POLICY AND PSYCHOLOGY

MARGARET HELDRING

U.S. health care is a complicated, contested, $1.2 trillion enterprise. It presents a significant public policy paradox: As American medicine consistently advances to higher levels of excellence, American health care systems spiral downward toward more fragmentation, unsustainable costs, and general dissatisfaction. This creates an obvious tension that underlies much of the conflict that characterizes health care policy and politics in the United States. Psychology is broadly affected by both state and federal policies, ranging from legislative battles over mental health parity to federally subsidized training opportunities for psychologists. When psychologists understand and participate in this public policy context in which they operate, the field of psychology benefits. Historically, however, professional psychology grew largely independently of public policy and politics. These were typically seen as irrelevant to most psychologists and to the academic roots of psychology. Now, as psychology is defined as a health profession as well as a mental health profession, the scope, applications, and functions of psychology are increasingly shaped by larger public factors such as state and federal laws and regulations. Thus, it is in the self-interest of the members of the psychology profession to be actively engaged in public policy.

There is an additional reason for psychologists to appreciate the political and social context in which they train and work to bring psychology's knowledge and insights into the policy process where solutions to social problems are sought: the ethical imperative to contribute to the public interest. Within health care, these include insurance coverage, access to quality mental health and substance abuse services, integrated primary care, and disaster response and preparedness. Beyond health care issues, psychologists are obliged to share their knowledge about, for example, children and the elderly, the dynamics of aging and racism, or the impact of violence or poverty. Each time the field of psychology brings its voice to bear on social concerns, everyone benefits. Psychologists cannot expect a "place at the table" in the absence of such contributions. For most people and groups in the United States, policymaking is more a potluck than a seated dinner.

In this chapter I discuss U.S. health policy from both historical and contemporary perspectives, especially as it applies to primary care psychology. Health care policies arise from both the private and public sectors. Private insurers (who function mostly for profit) and large employers are the dominant voices in the private sector. In the public sector, local, state, and federal governments all determine critical public health and health care policies by the passage of laws and regulations. However, the distinctions between public and private sector policies are not absolute. For example, the policies of Medicare, the federal program that provides health care for the elderly and some disabled people, often foreshadow or spill over into private sector policies, especially in the issue areas of reimbursement rates. In an optimal scenario, science informs policy, but knowledge must pass through economic and political lenses that often seem more like kaleidoscopes than binoculars. Policymakers rely on an idiosyncratic blend of data, anecdotes, compelling needs, political implications, and budget estimates as legislative decisions are made and policy crafted.

Many issues make up the domain of health policy. Access to care and insurance coverage, mental health, rural health, education and training, delivery systems, provider interests, special disease groups, technology, public health, culture, military systems, and health care financing are just some of the areas requiring constant review and action. Seldom do these align in a compatible way to build and sustain a comprehensive, efficient, and fair health care system. In fact, the opposite is true: These moving parts tend to bump up against each other, with the consequence that health policy in the United States is neither particularly prospective nor rational. Instead, health policy is reactive to crises, economic factors, special interests, evolving consumer preferences, and new bodies of knowledge.

The U.S. federal government has a duty to protect the public's health and ensure access to care for the most vulnerable people. However, its policies often clash with the preferences of state governments, which tend to resist federal mandates, standards, and regulations, primarily because of real or anticipated costs associated with compliance. The nation fluctuates between competing political forces with key questions left unanswered about the appropriate roles of government (the public sector) and market (the private sector), how to define health, and how to allocate limited financial resources. The private and public sectors seem unable to find a stable balance between their agendas or an effective marriage of their respective strengths. The private sector's capacity to be efficient and innovative in the development of new knowledge, treatments, and delivery systems often competes with the public sector's obligation to be inclusive and its tendency to be cautious. Special interest groups dominate the health care landscape, most with individualistic agendas that set up competitive rather than collaborative approaches to health care. Trust breaks down along the way, access to care is uneven, and dollars flow to less-than-optimal sources.

CURRENT ISSUES IN U.S. HEALTH CARE POLICY

The symptoms of a frayed system are plentiful. In 2000, the World Health Organization, noting that the United States spends more per capita on health care than any other nation, ranked the quality of its health care system 37th in the world and 72nd on indexes that reveal the overall health status of its population. In the same year, nearly 40 million people in the United States lacked health care insurance. This number tends to increase if the economy weakens, unemployment rises, and health care costs increase, factors that in 2001 were driven chiefly by hospital and pharmaceutical costs (Levit, Smith, Cowan, Lazenby, & Martin, 2002). Added pressures contribute to health care logjams and policy debates. These include the growing practice of shifting new costs to the consumer, dwindling state revenues to support Medicaid, and a doctor shortage in Medicare due to low reimbursements made to providers.

There are important policy issues in addition to insurance coverage. Recent years have seen considerable attention paid to disparities in health status among different racial and ethnic groups. The National Institutes of Health recently reported that U.S. minority populations have shorter overall life expectancies and higher rates of cardiovascular disease, cancer, infant mortality, birth defects, asthma, diabetes, stroke, adverse consequences of substance abuse, and sexually transmitted diseases than does the majority population of Whites. African American men suffer from heart disease at a rate 40% higher than that of White men and experience strokes at almost twice the rate of Whites (Murphy, 2000). HIV/AIDS is increasingly becoming a disease of people of color. In 1999, the rate of new AIDS cases per 100,000 reported in the United States was 66 among African Americans and 7.6 among Whites. Of newly affected women, approximately 64% were African American, 18% were White, and 18% were Hispanic (Centers for Disease Control and Prevention, 2000a, 2000b; Smedley, Stith, & Nelson, 2003). Since the early 1990s, gender has become an important variable in health care advocacy (Heldring, 1998). Gender differences in health care access, research, benefit packages, and costs have ignited grassroots groups (e.g., those that focus on breast cancer, contraception coverage, etc.) and required corrections in research protocols as well as clinical care.

Poverty is the single biggest predictor of health status, and rates of poverty fall disproportionately across race and ethnicity (Kennedy, Kawachi, Glass, & Prothrow-Stith, 1998). In 1999, 12% of the overall U.S. population lived in poverty; however, 23% of Hispanic Americans, 24% of African Americans, and 26% of American Indians and Alaska Natives were in poverty (U.S. Department of Health and Human Services, 2001). A thesis of this volume is that primary care is a "critical portal" to the detection, treatment, and prevention of mental health disorders. Cooper-Patrick et al. (1999) reported that members of racial–ethnic minority groups are more likely to seek help with mental health issues in primary care than elsewhere, and yet Borowsky et al. (2000) found that minority patients are among those at greatest risk of nondetection of mental health disorders in primary care.

Health consequences for the uninsured are significant. Uninsured children receive 30% less care than insured children for common illnesses (e.g., ear infections). More than 1 million low-income, uninsured children have special health care needs; they are four times less likely to have a usual source of care and twice less likely to have those needs met. Twenty-five percent of uninsured adults rely on expensive emergency room care compared with 6% of privately insured patients. Forty percent of uninsured adults have no regular source of care (Kaiser Family Foundation, Commission on Medicaid and the Uninsured, 2000). These statistics represent missed opportunities for preventive care or early intervention, important hallmarks of primary care. Uninsured men have 40% fewer prostate exams and uninsured women 60% fewer mammograms. Uninsured Americans are hospitalized at least 50% more often than the insured for "avoidable hospital conditions" such as pneumonia, diabetes, and hypertension. Without health care insurance, diseases progress to greater degrees of severity. The uninsured have a 70% increased likelihood of being diagnosed with late-stage colorectal cancer and a 250% likelihood of being diagnosed with late-stage melanoma.

Today, the United States is the home not only of outstanding medical care and research but also a broken health care system and pervasive dismay among health professionals and patients. There is an absence of clear direction in health policy (O'Connor, 2001). The nation lacks shared goals that are backed by consensus and implemented cooperatively. The core elements of health care policy—access, cost, and quality—remain expensive challenges. At present, none are stable, and the shifting tensions among them have been perplexing and stressful for almost 100 years (Johnson & Broder, 1997; Starr, 1982).

HISTORICAL PERSPECTIVES ON U.S. HEALTH CARE POLICY

How did American health care get to this place? What have been important milestones in health policy history? Enduring principles, as much as recurring conflicts, characterize this history. The United States has a mandate to move forward and deliver on the original vision of equality and justice, striving to balance the many compelling needs and interests of a pluralistic democracy and learning to adapt to the enormous changes that population growth, diversity, and technology bring. Often, there is success. Passage of the 1965 and 1966 legislation that created Medicare and Medicaid and the 1996 Child Health Insurance Program (CHIP) are evidence that the United States has communal ties (expressed primarily through government) as well as individual goals (expressed primarily through the private sector). Many would argue that these acts of social justice reflect the deepest American values.

Progress in promoting equity in health policy has been uneven. In spite of a long history of trying to provide health care insurance to everyone, the United States has repeatedly failed to implement a rational system. Early advocacy for universal health care surfaced when President Theodore Roosevelt persuaded his Progressive Party to adopt national health insurance as part of its 1912 platform (Brazda, in press). Early support came from labor but expanded to include many people interested in social problems and convinced of the need to create a national system of social insurance. When this new coalition proposed universal health insurance, the American Medical Association, the American Hospital Association, and several business groups objected. Each feared government interference. The dynamics for the debate were drawn and persist today, with advocates of progressive ideology urging a role for government in order to assure a level of social security for citizens and more conservative voices and those wary of government regulation and price setting opposing state and federal oversight of medicine.

In 1934, President Franklin Roosevelt wanted health insurance included in the legislative package that created Social Security. Again worried about interference in professional practice, leading provider groups opposed the legislation, and final political negotiations left health insurance out of the final bill. Neglected domestic issues resurfaced after the nation recovered from the Depression and the end of World War II. In 1945, with health care costs at 4% of the gross domestic product, President Harry Truman announced that "we can afford to spend more on health." Yet he too was unable to build sufficient support for his vision of universal health care. Instead, in this postwar climate, the nation backed into employment-based insurance as a strategy to compensate workers at a time when salaries were frozen and businesses were looking for ways to attract and retain a competent workforce. Employment-based coverage has remained the dominant coverage mechanism, and today 80% of Americans receive such insurance. Although this arrangement has lasted more than 50 years, it carries risks and is not well understood by the public. For example, many employees believe health insurance is a benefit of employment, failing to realize that, in most cases, it comes out of their overall wages. In times of economic downturns, when employment is unstable, employees may be a "pink slip" (Shearer & Montezemelo, 2001) away from no coverage and, consequently, at significant risk for financial stress, if not catastrophe. Without insurance, people tend to postpone health care, and illnesses progress to more serious stages. Today, employment-based health insurance is tenuous, as the nature of work in America has changed. Rarely does anyone spend an entire working life with one employer; instead, frequent job changes and part-time or contract work disrupt coverage stability. In light of these factors, many argue for the natural demise of the employer-based insurance system and the design of something truly portable, preferably "owned" by individuals and families (Reinhardt, 1997).

Over time, health care costs rose dramatically as technology exploded onto the health care scene and employers saw their postwar workforce move into retirement with their expectation of supplemental insurance to Medicare. As costs rose, heightened anxiety among large employers prompted them to insist that the health insurers with whom they contracted to provide coverage benefits find ways to keep costs down. This led to managed care, a set of cost containment and control strategies (Ellwood & Etheredge, 1993). This "cure" for health care costs surfaced intensely in the 1980s. Not everyone was pleased with these strategies. Astute politicians such as former U.S. Senator Harris Wofford of Pennsylvania and former President Bill Clinton, campaigning for his first term in 1992, noticed this phenomenon, recognized the political potential as a populist issue, and placed health care on the national agenda.

Why has the employer-based system dominated since World War II? As America moved into a period of postwar prosperity, confidence in capitalism and market-based ideology grew, and support for government programs declined. Two critical dynamics drove health care policy: (a) health care professionals' objection to possible government interference in practice and (b) a belief that the private sector could manage health care more efficiently than the public sector. However, a stunning turnaround in perception began to emerge in the late 1990s. Groups historically opposed to government relinquished old fears and voiced new support for a system of universal coverage (American Academy of Family Physicians, 2001). It seemed that the onus of managed care was worse than the feared role of government. Although it remains a minority opinion to establish some kind of single-payor system such as a Medicare-for-all (Angell, 1999), many more voices encourage expansion of existing public programs or a hybrid of public programs and private options, subsidized as needed by tax credits (Pauly & Herring, 2000).

The United States still feels the fallout from Clinton's 1993–1994 failed effort to implement a cohesive system. His proposal failed because of poor political strategy, a complicated plan, and small business resistance to an employer mandate. These objections obstructed even preliminary legislative debate. No Congressional committee marked up the proposal. In the absence of legislative action and a clear public mandate for a particular policy or program, the nation once again defaulted to the market. With the exception of the 1997 CHIP, Congress and most political leaders—believing they represent public opinion—have subsequently avoided serious exploration of options to get to universal coverage. Incrementalism became the favored policy strategy for most, but that is perceived as too timid by others. In 2000, Presidential candidate Bill Bradley asked me to design a plan for nearly universal coverage. His policies proposed renewed investment in public health and a system of health care delivery that would reflect a biopsychosocial view of health. Bradley's agenda drew both respect and controversy but did not substantially outlive the end of his campaign, and once again the debate quieted temporarily. In 2002, the Robert Wood Johnson Foundation launched a multi-million dollar public awareness campaign about the plight of the uninsured in an attempt to move the issue to the front of the public's attention. This represents the most significant attempt in U.S. history by the nonprofit sector to shape health care policy on the question of insurance coverage.

What is conspicuously absent in this recurring drama is any substantial commitment to prevent disease and injury in the first place, promote health, and deliver care more effectively. This is where primary care psychology shows promise. It belongs on all agendas where such issues are debated.

CRITICAL ISSUES AND QUESTIONS IN NATIONAL HEALTH POLICY

As central as insurance coverage is, it is not the only issue at stake in national health policy. Fundamental questions and values need debating. For example, is it useful to find a common definition for the construct *health*? Should a ceiling be set on a national health care budget and funds for research, training, services, and public health be distributed from that (Marmor, White, Altenstetter, & Brown, 1994). Should the tax system be used to subsidize purchase of private health insurance or implement a Medicare-for-all system? How valid is the prevailing assumption that "too much" is spent on health care today? Should health care be viewed as a commodity or as a guaranteed benefit to which everyone is entitled?

National and state leaders have focused on the important issues of health care financing, quality, and delivery. The magnitude of this task has dominated public policy so entirely that the opportunity to step back to ask a larger question in health policy has been eclipsed: What are the nation's goals?

There is no fixed definition of *good health*. The notion of what is meant by good health fluctuates with cultural norms, emerging science, evolving medical practice, and rising public expectations (Sternberg & Fee, 1997). A generation ago, medical professionals had only the first glimpses of the effects of smoking on health. Most cancers were a nearly certain signal of imminent death. People rarely used seatbelts. There was limited understanding of depression and its damaging impact on health and quality of life. Society stigmatized people with serious mental illnesses such as schizophrenia, probably because it had so little to offer in the way of help; the antipsychotic medicines of today were still undergoing clinical trials. The nation stood on the frontier of organ transplantation and the ability to extend life, but people could not even imagine the potential for rehabilitation from spinal cord injuries. The challenge of HIV/AIDS had not yet been met, and people had not begun to comprehend what the growth in chronic illness would mean for a health care system evolved chiefly for the treatment of acute episodes of illness. People were learning that they could eradicate diseases such as polio with brilliant researchers and breakthrough vaccines, but the country was still several decades away from the epidemic of asthma that continues to be a challenge today. People knew that clean water and proper sanitation led to better public health and greater longevity, but the discovery that science, not just common sense, could prove that satisfying, close relationships are good for one's health or that prolonged (even if subtle) exposure to racism could explain higher prevalence rates of hypertension among African Americans (Krieger & Sidney, 1996; Krieger, Sidney, & Coakley, 1999) would have seemed as odd as the Internet would to our great-grandparents. Today, observational studies (Berkman, 1995) suggest that the death rate among people with weak social networks may be two to three times higher than the rates among those with strong networks. As science confirms psychosocial pathways to health, new opportunities will open up for primary care psychology. There will be opportunities for research, clinical practice, teaching and training, and consultation to public and private sectors. As this new knowledge is absorbed into mainstream health care, primary care psychologists can help shape collaborative models of care, cross-training curricula, and work to assure that resource allocations are properly made.

Along with growing research into the psychosocial pathways, there is currently a critical debate around the prominence of social determinants in health. How valid and powerful are racism, income inequality, and gender in influencing health? What portion of health status is properly attributed to individual behavior, psychological factors, genetics, access to care, and environment and social determinants (Auerbach & Krimgold, 2001).

Research opens up new knowledge. For example, researchers and ethicists are mapping out genetic blueprints and addressing the accompanying ethical issues (McDaniel & Speice, 2001). Others focus on social circumstances to find new perspectives on illness and injury as well as new opportunities to promote healthy people, families, and communities. Healthy People 2010 is an example—a federal initiative to improve health status among all Americans (U.S. Department of Health and Human Services, 2000). More members of the public and many scholars are drawn to alternative medicine such as acupuncture and homeopathic remedies. The neurosciences and neuropsychology are revealing how the brain and the immune system communicate and are, thereby, laying scientific foundations under the age-old intuition about the effect of stress and emotions on health (Ader, Felten, & Cohen, 2001). Along with America's growing demographic diversity comes greater sensitivity to culture and personal belief systems in health. American Indians, Harvard professors, the National Institutes of Health, and many personal anecdotes bring evidence about the efficacy of faith, prayer, and spirituality in health. Kwang, Wirth and Lobo (2001) reported the results of a study that looked at the effects of anonymous prayer on successful outcomes with *in vitro* fertilization. Baseline pregnancy rates for *in vitro* fertilization average 24%. Rates for the experimental group in this study were over 50%, and that for the control group was 26%.

These new avenues toward health are exciting, but they can be overwhelming as systems and the public work to accommodate new knowledge. We are repeatedly challenged on where to draw the line regarding what constitutes good health, or good enough health and health care. It is all in a constant state of movement, challenging our ability to build sturdy health care organizations on these shifting sands.

When new technology and knowledge combine with higher consumer expectations for health and health care, the results are potentially combustible. We seem to continually define health more broadly—to a point where our resources are strained and the competition among competing interests and special interest groups intensifies. It becomes harder to find a shared set of values and a compelling set of national goals.

What continues to obstruct the creation of a shared vision and strategy? Theory about health as much as ideology about financing of health care is one obstruction. Western medicine has competing models of health. The U.S. health care system has traditionally functioned within a biomedical model. In this model, the origins of disease are placed deep within cells and biochemistry. Health is whatever disease is not. On the basis of this model, the nation built its health care system around cure, treatment of disease, and provision of palliative care when cure was judged impossible. Prevention has been endorsed more in theory than practice (William L. Roper Partnership for Prevention, 2001). The fact that less than 2% of national health care expenditures go to prevention reflects this bias in approach to health and health care.

However, many people now find the biomedical model too narrow and offer an alternative, broader biopsychosocial model of health (Engel, 1977; McDaniel et al., 1995). In this model, the frame is widened to include behavioral, psychological, and social variables that are increasingly known to influence health and recovery from illness. Data about the actual causes of death (McGinnis & Foege, 1993) and the relationship between social support and health reinforce this model but raise new, formidable questions. If the biomedical model excludes too much, does a biopsychosocial one include too much? Are we inclined to medicalize social problems?

UPCOMING ISSUES IN NATIONAL HEALTH POLICY

Along with these historical challenges and unresolved issues come hopeful developments. Exciting opportunities in telehealth—the application of information technologies to health care—and advances in biotechnology hold great promise. Six years of debate about protections for patients have weakened managed care and provided incentives to health plans to open up provider networks and take at least symbolic steps in returning decision making to providers (Lesser & Ginsburg, 2000). States and the federal government look for ways to include coverage for prescription drugs in the Medicare program. Fewer children are uninsured than before CHIP. Former U.S. Surgeon General (1998–2002) David Satcher, M.D., released three landmark reports on mental health during his tenure. The first confirmed the legitimacy of mental health issues, the second outlined dramatically the racial and ethnic disparities in access to mental health care, and the third summarized the findings of a groundbreaking conference on mental health and primary care.

Satcher's first report made three primary conclusions: (a) mental health is fundamental to health, (b) mental health care should flow in the mainstream of health care, and (c) it is time to mend the destructive split between physical and mental health. In his second report, released in August 2001 at the Annual Convention of the American Psychological Association (APA), Satcher confirmed that "culture matters" (U.S. Department of Health and Human Services, 2001). His third report underscored the fact that the primary health care system is the nation's de facto mental health system.

PSYCHOLOGY, PSYCHOLOGISTS, AND HEALTH CARE POLICY

Satcher's reports create openings for psychologists to engage in public policy, even if they are relatively unaccustomed to national health policy. His reports are a call to action and provide the rationale to try to move policy in certain directions. However, psychologists need to recognize this and make important adjustments in order to meet the dual objectives of promoting the public welfare and advancing the profession. For example, there needs to be more academic curricula and training experiences that provide exposure to policy and political issues. These have traditionally been seen as irrelevant to clinical work, psychological research, and teaching. Curricula and training in psychology must expand to include cross-disciplinary experiences. Psychologists should view public service as a legitimate way in which to use their knowledge and skills.

Although the field of psychology is still learning to incorporate these perspectives, there is a long, successful history of psychologists working on behalf of psychology on state levels. For decades, psychologists have lobbied for state laws and regulations that promote the profession. Eligibility for third-party reimbursement, licensure, expanded scope of practice, hospital privileges, parity, and, most recently, prescriptive authority are issues many state psychological associations have pursued. Twelve states count psychologists as elected representatives to their state assemblies and legislatures (DeLeon et al., 2003).

On the national level, APA has matured into an effective voice on behalf of mental health, psychology as a health care discipline, patient protections, and psychology training and reimbursement issues. Professional psychologists are valued as consultants on social issues such as violence, racism, children's development, and aging. APA sponsors the Congressional Fellows Program, bringing several psychologists to Washington, DC, each year to gain firsthand experience in how policy is shaped. Several Fellows have transformed their career paths to remain in public policy and politics. Some serve on House and Senate staffs and committees. Three psychologists have been elected to the U.S. House of Representatives. I myself served as the first psychologist to direct major domestic policy for a Presidential campaign.

Psychologists serve in the executive branch of government as well, at agencies throughout the Departments of Health and Human Services and Education. In 1998, Susan McDaniel was the first psychologist to win a fellowship in the Bureau of Primary Care, and several psychologists, such as Robert Frank, Kris Hagglund, Suzanne Bennett-Johnson, and Danny Wedding, have won prestigious Robert Wood Johnson Fellowships. A psychologist was recently named the new president of the American Association for the Advancement of Science. These are all important and valuable avenues in which psychologists can expand their influence and contribute knowledge and skills to public policy.

From a public policy perspective, there are now three critical tasks for primary care psychology: (a) define and develop the knowledge base of primary care psychology; (b) educate and build partnerships with other primary care specialties, such as pediatrics, family medicine, and internal medicine and nursing, so that there is collaboration in policy as well as practice; and (c) as a partnership, interpret primary care psychology in clinical and economic terms for policymakers, purchasers of health care, and the general public. Psychology is health care, and primary care psychology is a place where important scientific and clinical issues will be resonant with national need.

REFERENCES

Ader, R., Felten, D. L., & Cohen, N. (Eds.). (2001). *Psychoneuroimmunology* (3rd ed., Vols. 1–2). New York: Academic Press.

American Academy of Family Physicians. (2001). *Assuring health care coverage for all.* Kansas City, MO: Author.

Angell, M. (1999). The American healthcare system revisited—A new series. *New England Journal of Medicine, 340,* 48.

Auerbach, J. A., & Krimgold, B. K. (Eds.). (2001). *Income, socioeconomic status, and health: Exploring the relationships.* Washington, DC: National Policy Association, Academy for Health Services Research and Health Policy.

Berkman, L. F. (1995). The role of social relations in health promotions. *Psychosomatic Medicine, 51,* 245–254.

Borowsky, S. J., Rubenstein, L. V., Meredith, L. S., Camp, P., Jackson-Triche, M., & Wells, K. B. (2000). Who is at risk of non-detection of mental health problems in primary care? *Journal of General Internal Medicine, 15,* 381–388.

Centers for Disease Control and Prevention. (2000a, September). *HIV/AIDS among Hispanics in the United States, HIV/AIDS Surveillance Report.* Atlanta, GA: Author.

Centers for Disease Control and Prevention. (2000b, September). *HIV/AIDS among U.S. women: Minority and young women at continuing risk. HIV/AIDS Surveillance Report.* Atlanta, GA: Author.

Cooper-Patrick, L., Gallo, J. J., Powe, N. R., Steinwachs, D. M., Eaton, W. W., & Ford, D. E. (1999). Mental health service utilization by African Americans and Whites: The Baltimore epidemiologic catchment area follow-up. *Medical Care, 37,* 1034–1045.

DeLeon, P. H., Hagglund, K. J., Ragusea, S. A., & Sammons, M. T. (2003). Expanding roles for psychologists in the 21st century. In I. B. Weiner (Series Ed.), G. Stricker, & T. A. Widiger (Vol. Eds.), *Handbook of psychology: Vol. 4. Clinical psychology* (pp. 551–568). New York: Wiley.

Ellwood, P., & Etheredge, P. (1993). The 21st century American health care system. *Health Care Strategy Management, 11,* 7–14.

Engel G. (1977). The need for a new medical model: A challenge for biomedicine. *Science, 196,* 129–136.

Heldring, M. (1998). Integrated health care for women. In A. Blount (Ed.), *Integrated primary care: The future of medical and mental health collaboration* (pp. 247–260). New York: Norton.

Johnson, H., & Broder, D. S. (1997). *The system: The American way of politics at the breaking point.* Boston: Little, Brown.

Kaiser Family Foundation, Commission on Medicaid and the Uninsured. (2000). *The uninsured and their access to health care—Uninsured facts.* Washington, DC: Kaiser Family Foundation.

Kennedy, B. P., Kawachi, I., Glass, R., & Prothrow-Stith, D. (1998). Income distribution, socioeconomic status, and self rated health: A U.S. multilevel analysis. *British Medical Journal, 317*, 917–921.

Krieger, N., & Sidney, S. (1996). Racial discrimination and blood pressure: The CARDIA study of young black and white adults. *American Journal of Public Health, 86*, 1370–1378.

Krieger, N., Sidney, S., & Coakley, E. (1999). Racial discrimination and skin color in the CARDIA study: Implications for public health research. *American Journal of Public Health, 88*, 1308–1313.

Kwang C. Y., Wirth, D. P., & Lobo, R. A. (2001). Does prayer influence the success of in vitro fertilization–embryo transfer? Report of a masked, randomized trial. *Journal of Reproductive Medicine, 46*, 781–787.

Lesser, C. S., & Ginsburg, P. (2000). Update on the nation's health care system: 1997–1999. *Health Affairs, 19*, 206–216.

Levit, K., Smith, C., Cowan, C., Lazenby, H., & Martin, A. (2002). Inflation spurs health spending. *Health Affairs, 21*, 172–181.

Marmor. T. R., White, J., Altenstetter, C., Brown, E. R., et al. (1994). Understanding the choices in health care reform. *Journal of Health Politics, Policy and Law, 19*, 499–541.

McDaniel, S. H., Campbell, T. L., & Seaburn, D. B. (1995). Principles for collaboration between health and mental health providers in primary care. *Family Systems Medicine, 13*, 283–298.

McDaniel, S. H., & Speice, J. (2001). What family psychology has to offer women's health: The examples of conversion somatization, infertility treatment, and genetic testing. *Professional Psychology: Research and Practice, 32*, 44–51.

McGinnis, J. M, & Foege, W. H. (1993). Actual causes of death in the United States. *Journal of the American Medical Association, 270*, 2207–2212.

Murphy, S. L. (2000). Deaths: Final data for 1998. *National Vital Statistics Report* (Vol. 48, No. 11, DHHS Publication No. 2000–1120). Hyattsville, Maryland: National Center for Health Statistics.

O'Connor, K. (2001). The buck stops nowhere: Why America's health care is all dollars and no sense. Seattle, WA: Hara Publishing.

Pauly, M., & Herring, B. (2000). *Cutting taxes for insuring: Options and effects of tax credits for health insurance.* Philadelphia: University of Pennsylvania.

Reinhardt, U. E. (1997). Employer-based health insurance: R.I.P. In S. H. Altman, U. E. Reinhardt, & A. E. Shields (Eds.), *The future U.S. healthcare system: Who will care for the uninsured?* (pp. 325–352). Chicago: Health Administration Press.

Shearer, G., & Montezemelo, S. (2001). *A pink slip away. . .Why Congress should subsidize health insurance coverage for laid-off workers.* Washington, DC: Consumers Union.

Smedley, B. D., Stith, A. Y., & Nelson, A. R. (2003). *Unequal treatment: Confronting racial and ethnic disparities in health care.* Washington, DC: The National Academy Press.

Starr, P. (1982). *The social transformation of American medicine*. New York: Basic Books.

U.S. Department of Health and Human Services. (2000). *Healthy people 2010: With understanding and improving health objectives for improving health* (2nd ed.). Washington, DC: U.S. Government Printing Office.

U.S. Department of Health and Human Services. (2001). *Mental health: Culture, race and ethnicity* [suppl.]. Washington, DC: U.S. Government Printing Office.

William L. Roper Partnership for Prevention. (2001). *What policymakers need to know about cost effectiveness*. Washington, DC: Author.

16

OUTCOME ASSESSMENT FOR RESOURCE ALLOCATION IN PRIMARY CARE

ROBERT M. KAPLAN, THOMAS L. PATTERSON, AND ERIK J. GROESSL

MENTAL HEALTH AND PRIMARY CARE

Changes in Primary Care

It has been estimated that approximately one half of all medical care visits are made to primary care physicians (Stafford et al., 1999). Primary care practice has faced major changes, including changes in demographic trends (Golini, 2001), changes in health care reimbursement (Blumenthal, 2001), and an increased emphasis on primary care education in medical school (Burke, Baron, Lemon, Losh, & Novack, 1994). The scope of primary care practice continues to expand, often beyond services that have been the core of primary care training (St. Peter, Reed, Kemper, & Blumenthal, 1999). The role of psychology in primary care remains to be defined.

A significant amount of mental health care is delivered in primary care settings, yet psychologists have played a surprisingly small role in providing evidence on the value of psychological interventions in primary care (Coyne, Klinkman, & Nease, 2002). In less than 10 years, primary care physicians doubled the number of prescriptions they wrote for antidepressant medications. The number now exceeds 15 million prescriptions per year (Hirschfeld, 1998). Although it is easy to argue that patients are better off with care provided by mental health providers, adequate evidence to support that argument is lacking. In this chapter we discuss measurement and analysis strategies that might be used to provide evidence for the benefits of behavioral interventions in primary care. We begin with a general overview of health care costs and the challenges of delivering mental heath services. Next, we consider the need for systematic evaluation of mental heath services in primary care settings. Specific approaches to quality-of-life assessment and cost-effectiveness analysis are then presented. We pay particular attention to the technical challenges of cost-effectiveness analysis for the evaluation of mental health services and to the application of standardized methodologies. In the final section of the chapter, we describe an example of cost-effectiveness analysis of screening for depression in primary care.

Changes in Mental Health Care

Like primary care, mental health care has undergone many changes in the last 20 years, some of which have resulted in cost reductions. During the 1990s, there was a substantial change in the way mental health care was delivered. For most patients, mental health care is now managed by for-profit "behavioral health" companies. These companies carved out a portion of the health insurance benefit by selling packaged mental health services at a low cost to health insurers or directly to employers. This relieved the health insurance companies of the responsibilities for mental health care (Iglehart, 1996) and resulted in a significant reduction in business for psychiatrists and psychologists. Instead of employing the services of psychiatrists, managed mental health companies rely heavily on the services of primary care physicians, social workers and, to some extent, psychologists (Meyer, 1993). These changes in policy have had profound effects on psychology. Psychiatrists have complained that the quality of patient care will suffer when nonpsychiatrists provide the care, yet there are simply no data available on whether patients fare better, worse, or the same with these new funding arrangements.

Psychiatrists were not the only professionals affected by the changes in the way mental health care was funded. Psychologists have felt crowded out by counselors with master's of social work and master's of family therapy degrees who might perform similar services for a lower wage. However, psychologists are beginning to play a bigger role in primary care medicine, and it is expected that this role will increase in the future (see chap. 14, this volume). However, to enhance this role, psychologists must be prepared to offer the data that support revisions in the health care system. As these changes take place, there is an increased need to assess outcomes.

WHAT ARE THE CHALLENGES?

Before discussing outcomes assessment, we must review a number of challenges for the analysis of health policy.

National Health Care Costs

Health care costs in the United States have grown exponentially since 1940. Although there was a temporary slowdown in the mid-1990s, the rate of increase began to accelerate again by the turn of the century. It has been estimated that health care in the United States consumed about 14% of the gross domestic product in 2002, while no other country in the world spends more than 10% (Heffler et al., 2001). Although the rate of growth has slowed, the Institute for the Future (2000) estimated that health care expenditures will increase at a rate of 6.4% annually and will account for 15.6% of the gross domestic product by 2010. Despite high expenditures, the U.S. system may not be producing exceptional health outcomes. Among 13 industrialized countries in one recent comparison, the United States ranked 12th when compared on 16 health indicators (Starfield, 2000). Therefore, improving health remains the top priority, but the challenge is to do so without continuing to increase expenses.

Opportunity Cost Problem

Although most provider groups understand that health care costs must be contained, few acknowledge that their own expenditures should be subject to evaluation. Successful lobbying to obtain reimbursement for a specific service may necessarily mean that another service is excluded. Suppose, for example, that the amount that can be spent on health care is fixed at $100 and that $3 of each $100 (3%) is devoted to behavioral health services. If psychologists are able to get $10 of each $100 spent on their services, then there will be less to spend on other, nonbehavioral health services. This is called the *opportunity cost problem*. Opportunity costs are the foregone opportunities that are surrendered as a result of using limited or fixed resources to support a particular decision. If more money is spent in one sector of health care, then by necessity, less is spent elsewhere. Therefore, an important question is "How do we decide which services should receive more and which should receive fewer resources?"

When confronted with the choice between two good programs, it is always tempting to support both. The difficulty is that it costs more to offer multiple programs. The cost of programs is represented in the fees for health insurance or the cost of health care to taxpayers. A society can choose to offer as many health programs as it wants; however, more programs require more funding, and health care consumers do not want higher fees for their health insurance or higher taxes.

Measures of Outcome

From a societal perspective, there is a need for measures that allow clinicians and policymakers to determine the efficacy of various treatments while taking into consideration costs, potential side effects that may result from treatments, and the dimensions of outcome that may or may not be improved by the treatments. Outcomes researchers have provided a variety of methods to quantify the benefits of health care interventions. In this section we review some of the concerns of outcome measurement, and then we examine methods that can be used for these evaluations.

What Populations Are We Considering?

Primary care physicians see a heterogeneous group of patients. In 1994, the top 10 diagnostic clusters represented less than half of all primary care visits (43.4%; Crews, Batal, Elasy, Casper, & Mehler, 1998). These diagnoses range from psychiatric diagnoses to sprains and strains; each disorder represents a unique set of symptoms, which last for varying lengths of time, and the treatment for each of these diagnoses has unique side effect profiles and widely divergent costs. These complexities suggest that outcome measures either must be specific to the disorder in question, which means that direct comparisons between disorders would be difficult, if not impossible, or be able to capture dimensions that are common to all of these disorders.

In addition to treating specific diagnoses, primary care physicians are cast in the role of providing preventive services such as dietary counseling and blood pressure management. It is well understood that the morbidity and mortality associated with chronic diseases such as cancer, heart disease, hypertension, HIV, and diabetes mellitus could be significantly reduced through lifestyle modifications. The Healthy People 2010 project suggests that reduction of morbidity and mortality is a shared responsibility of the individual, family, community, media, government, and health professionals (U.S. Department of Health and Human Services & Healthy People 2010 [Group], 2000). In fact, the majority of the average 18.1-min visit to primary care physicians can be taken up with attention to these matters (Stafford et al., 1999). It may appear that there are no immediate benefits from such activities, but quality preventive care might improve long-term outcomes. This suggests that primary care outcomes should consider measures that demonstrate long-term benefits such as quality-adjusted life years, a concept we describe later in this chapter.

Comorbidities and Side Effects

Measurement of outcome is complicated by patient comorbidities. For example, there is a high incidence of both acute and chronic medical problems among patients with chronic mental illness. Studies of ambulatory psychiatric patients, who are most likely to be seen in primary care settings, reveal that up to 93% have medical problems, many of which were undiagnosed or inadequately treated (Bartsch, Shern, Feinberg, & Fuller, 1990; Felker, Yazel, & Short, 1996). Despite this evidence, the use of general care services is limited (Worley, Drago, & Hadley, 1990). The underdiagnosis of medical problems may be influenced by a lack of ability and resources of people with major psychiatric illness to access care and follow through with treatment (Crews et al., 1998). In addition, the behavior of psychiatric patients is sometimes seen as disruptive to medical personnel (Hall, Beresford, Gardner, & Popkin, 1982). Psychiatric patients also are less likely to engage in behaviors that enhance health and well-being. For example, Holmberg and Kane (1999) used the Health Promoting Lifestyle Profile (S. N. Walker, Sechrist, & Pender, 1987) and found that psychiatric patients engaged in more behaviors linked to premature death, such as overeating and smoking, than did comparison participants.

In addition, most medications and some behavioral treatments affect other areas of health and well-being. For example, an exercise-based intervention may lower depression and may also improve sleep, cause weight loss, or increase joint pain. An antidepressant may not only reduce depression but also increase a patient's attendance and productivity at work. Once again, these examples suggest that interventions have multiple, sometimes unknown, impacts that are not captured with measures specific to the main presenting complaint. Therefore, finding comprehensive, generic measures to assess all areas of health in each patient appears optimal.

Health-Related Quality of Life

It is clear that an individual's health affects his or her quality of life, and it is the goal of health care to maintain optimal functioning and decrease disabilities associated with chronic illnesses (Field & Gold, 1998). This emphasis has led to a focus on health-related quality of life (HRQOL). Broadly defined, HRQOL is a state of complete physical, mental, and social well-being and not merely the absence of disease or infirmity (World Health Organization, 1948). A number of domains of HRQOL have been identified, including physical health, emotional health, cognitive functioning, sexual functioning, social role performance, and work productivity (Ware & Sherbourne, 1992). As decisions are made regarding which treatments produce improvements in HRQOL, it is imperative that careful consideration be given to the measure(s) chosen to quantify changes in HRQOL.

Identifying the target behavior is an important first step in choosing a measure. Although program planners may not have the resources to collect the depth and breadth of information they would like, doing assessments regarding the impact of specific conditions, and having the ability to compare those conditions and translate findings in common units, are important considerations.

A number of approaches have been used in the measurement of HRQOL, both in psychiatric and medical conditions. Approaches to measurement of outcome include generic profile measures that yield dimension-specific scores (e.g., the Sickness Impact Profile; Bergner, Bobbitt, Kressel, et al., 1976; Bergner, Bobbitt, Pollard, Martin, & Gilson, 1976); the Medical Outcomes Study health survey, which is sometimes referred to as the *SF-36*; Ware & Gandek, 1998) or the use of single indexes (e.g., Karnofsky Performance Status and the Functional Living Index; Ganz, Haskell, Figlin, La Soto, & Siau, 1988). An alternative approach to the measurement of outcomes focuses on specific populations or diseases. One such instrument, developed specifically for use with psychiatric patients, is a broad-based assessment of recent and current life experiences in a variety of life areas that was developed by Lehman, Slaughter, and Myers (1991). Alternatively, investigators may use customized batteries of individual measures that attempt to capture specific dimensions of quality of life thought to be important in particular disorders (e.g., the Social Adjustment Scale, Patterson et al., 1997; Paykel, Weissman, & Prusoff, 1978); the Scales for Assessment of Positive and Negative Symptoms; Andreasen & Olsen, 1982).

Each of these approaches has limitations, including difficulties comparing across dimensions (i.e., weighting or nonweighting of specific dimensions) and across populations, diseases, or both. For the last 10 years, Kaplan and his colleagues have argued that mental and physical health should be assessed using a common measurement unit (Kaplan, 1990, 1994, 1996; Kaplan et al., 1995; Kaplan & California Policy Seminar, 1993; Kaplan, Feeny, & Revicki, 1999; Kaplan, Ganiats, Sieber, & Anderson, 1998). In fact, comparisons between any competing interventions or treatments in health care require that outcomes be expressed using some common denominator. Not all health care interventions are equally efficient in returning benefits for the expended dollar. In the next section, we review several generic approaches to outcomes evaluation and economic analysis in health care.

REVIEW OF SPECIFIC MEASURES

There are numerous methods for the assessment of HRQOL. There is now an entire journal devoted to HRQOL measurement and several professional societies that focus on the topic. Methods for assessing HRQOL represent at least two different conceptual traditions. One grows out of the tradition of psychometric theory, and the other has its roots in decision theory. Several efforts to develop measures of health status were launched in the late 1960s and early 1970s. All the projects were guided by the World Health Organization's definition of *health status* as a "complete state of physical, mental, and social well-being and not merely absence of disease" (World Health Organization, 1948). The projects resulted in a variety of assessment tools, including the Sickness Impact Profile (SIP; Bergner, Bobbitt, Kressel, et al., 1976), the Quality of Well-Being Scale (Kaplan, 1996; Kaplan et al., 1998), the SF-36 (Ware & Gandek, 1998), and the Nottingham Health Profile (Lowe, O'Grady, McEwen, & Williams, 1990). Many of the measures examine the effect of disease or disability on performance of social roles, ability to interact in the community, and physical functioning. Some of the systems have separate components for the measurement of physical, social, and mental health. The measures also differ in the extent to which they consider subjective aspects of life quality (Brown, Gordon, & Haddad, 2000).

The psychometric approach attempts to provide separate measures for the many different dimensions of quality of life. Perhaps the best known example of the psychometric tradition is the SIP, a 136-item measure that yields 12 different scores displayed in a format similar to a Minnesota Multiphasic Personality Inventory profile (Bergner, Bobbitt, Pollard, et al., 1976).

The decision theory approach attempts to weight the different dimensions of health in order to provide a single expression of health status. Supporters of this approach argue that psychometric methods fail to consider that different health problems are not of equal concern. A runny nose is not the same as severe chest pain. Experimental trials using the psychometric approach often find that some aspects of quality of life improve while others get worse. For example, a medication might reduce high blood pressure but also produce headaches and impotence. Many argue that the quality-of-life notion is the subjective evaluation of observable or objective health states. The decision theory approach attempts to provide an overall measure of quality of life that integrates subjective function states, preferences for these states, morbidity, and mortality.

Common Methods for the Measurement of Quality of Life

A variety of methods have been proposed to measure quality of life, but we cannot review and critique them all here. Instead, we present some of the most widely used psychometric and decision theory based methods. Readers interested in more detailed reviews should consult McDowell and Newell (1996) and S. R. Walker and Rosser (1993).

Psychometric Methods

SF-36. Perhaps the most commonly used outcome measure in the world today is the Medical Outcome Study Short Form–36 (SF-36). The SF-36 grew out of work by the RAND Corporation and the Medical Outcomes Study (Ware & Gandek, 1998). It was originally based on the measurement strategy from the RAND Health Insurance Study (Manning et al., 1987;

Newhouse et al., 1987). The SF-36 includes eight health concepts: (a) physical functioning, (b) role—physical, (c) bodily pain, (d) general health perceptions, (e) vitality, (f) social functioning, (g) role—emotional, and (h) mental health (Kosinski, Keller, Hatoum, Kong, & Ware, 1999). The SF-36 can be either administered by a trained interviewer or self-administered. It has many advantages. For example, it is brief, and there is substantial evidence for its reliability and validity. The SF-36 can be machine scored and has been evaluated in large population studies. The reliability and validity of the SF-36 are well documented (Keller, Ware, Hatoum, & Kong, 1999; Scott-Lennox, Wu, Boyer, & Ware, 1999; Stewart & Ware, 1992).

Despite its many advantages, the SF-36 also presents some disadvantages. For example, it does not have age-specific questions, and one cannot clearly determine whether it is equally appropriate at each level of the age continuum. The items for older retired individuals are the same as those for children (Stewart & Ware, 1992). Nevertheless, the SF-36 has become the most commonly used behavioral measure in contemporary medicine.

Dartmouth Primary Care Cooperative Information Project charts. Several methods have been developed for the assessment of health outcomes in primary care settings. The best developed among these is the Dartmouth Primary Care Cooperative Information Project (COOP; Wasson, Kairys, Nelson, Kalishman, & Baribeau, 1994). The purpose of this effort was to develop a practical system for measuring health status in primary care medicine (Nelson, Landgraf, Hays, Wasson, & Kirk, 1990). The system uses simple, self-rating charts in which physical, mental, and role functioning are self-rated. The COOP charts include the descriptive title and a question asking about functioning during the last 4 weeks. The 5-point response scale is presented in the form of a simple picture. The group developing the measure has performed extensive evaluative research and has documented the reliability and validity of the COOP measures (Larson, Hays, & Nelson, 1992).

Decision Theory Approaches

Quality-adjusted life years (QALYs) are generic measures of life expectancy with adjustments for quality of life (Gold, 1996). QALYs consider both benefits and side effects of programs in terms of the common outcome units. Although QALYs are typically assessed for patients, they can also be measured for others, including caregivers who are placed at risk because they experience stressful life events. The Institute of Medicine recommended that population health metrics be used to evaluate public programs and to assist the decision-making process (Field & Gold, 1998).

The need to integrate mortality and quality-of-life information is clearly apparent in studies of heart disease. Consider hypertension. People with high blood pressure may live shorter lives if untreated, longer if treated. Thus, one benefit of treatment is to add years to life. However, for most patients, high blood pressure does not produce symptoms for many years. Conversely, the treatment for high blood pressure may cause negative side effects. If one evaluates a treatment only in terms of changes in life expectancy, then the benefits of the program will be overestimated, because one has not taken side effects into consideration. On the other hand, considering only current quality of life will underestimate the treatment benefits, because information on mortality (death) is excluded. In fact, considering only current function might make the treatment look harmful, because the side effects of the treatment might be worse than the symptoms of hypertension. A comprehensive measurement system takes into consideration side effects and benefits and provides an overall estimate of the benefit of treatment (Russell, 1986).

How does one integrate side effects and benefits to estimate the overall impact of a disease and its treatment? If a man dies of heart disease at age 50, and one expected him to live to age 75, then one might conclude that the disease precipitated 25 lost life years. If 100 men died at age 50 (and also had a life expectancy of 75 years), one might conclude that 2500 (100 men × 25 years) life years had been lost. Yet death is not the only relevant outcome to consider. Many adults suffer myocardial infarctions that leave them somewhat disabled for long periods of time. Although they are still alive, they suffer diminished quality of life. QALYs take into consideration such consequences. For example, a disease that reduces quality of life by one half will take away 0.5 QALY over the course of each year. If the disease affects two people, it will take away 1 year (2 × 0.5) over each year. A medical treatment that improves quality of life by 0.2 for each of five individuals will result in the equivalent of 1 QALY if the benefit persists for 1 year. This system has the advantage of considering both benefits and side effects of programs in terms of the common QALY units.

Of the several different approaches for obtaining QALYs, most are similar. The three most commonly used methods are the EQ-5D (Feeny, Furlong, Mulhurn, Barr, & Hudson, 1999), the Health Utilities Index (HUI; Feeny et al., 1999), and the Quality of Well-Being Scale (QWB; Feeny et al., 1999).

EQ-5D. The approach most commonly used in the European community is the EQ-5D. This method, developed by Paul Kind and his associates (1997), has been developed by a collaborative group from Western Europe known as the *EuroQol group.* The intention of this effort was to develop a generic currency for health that could be used commonly across Europe. The concept of a common EuroQol was stimulated by the desire for a common European currency: the Euro dollar. The original version of the EuroQol included 14 health states in six different domains. In addition, respondents placed their health on a continuum ranging from death (0.0) to perfect health (1.0). The method was validated in postal surveys in England, Sweden, and the Netherlands. More recent versions of the EuroQol, known as the EQ-5D, are now in use in a substantial number of clinical and population studies (Gudex, Dolan, Kind, & Williams, 1996; Hurst, Kind, Ruta, Hunter, &

Stubbings, 1997). Although the EQ-5D is easy to use and comprehensive, there have been some problems with ceiling effects. Substantial numbers of people obtain the highest possible score.

HUI. Torrance, Feeny, Furlong, and their Canadian associates developed the HUI, which is derived from micro-economic theory (Feeny et al., 1999). There have been several versions of the measure, typically identified by "Mark." The HUI Mark I was developed for studies in the neonatal intensive care unit and had 960 unique health states. In 1992, the HUI Mark II was developed and included 24,000 unique health states. The HUI Mark III, released in 1995, had 972,000 health states. The eight components of the HUI Mark III include (a) vision (six levels), (b) hearing (six levels), (c) speech (five levels), (d) ambulation (six levels), (e) dexterity (six levels), (f) emotion (five levels), (g) cognition (six levels), and (h) pain (five levels). Multiplying the number of levels across the eight dimensions yields the 972,000 states. Using multi-attribute utility scaling methods, judges evaluate levels of wellness associated with each level of each domain. A multi-attribute model is used to map preference for the 972,000 possible states onto the 0.0–1.0 continuum. The HUI has been used in many population and clinical studies. Figure 16.1 shows estimates of the HUI for men and women in the American population. For overall health status, men obtain higher scores early in the life cycle; however, after about age 45, women obtain higher scores, and this difference grows systematically through the remainder of the life span (Kaplan & Erickson, 2000).

QWB. A third method, the QWB, integrates several components into a single score. First, patients are classified according to objective levels of functioning that are represented by scales of mobility, physical activity, and social activity. Once observable behavioral levels of functioning have been classified, each individual is placed on the 0–1.0 scale of wellness, which describes where a person lies on the continuum between optimum functioning and death (Kaplan, 1990, 1994, 1996; Kaplan et al., 1995, 1998, 1999; Kaplan & Bush, 1982; Kaplan & California Policy Seminar, 1993).

Most traditional measures used in medicine and public health consider only whether a person is dead or alive. In other words, all living people are assigned the same score. Yet there are different levels of wellness, and there is a need to quantify these levels. To accomplish this, the observable health states are weighted by quality ratings for the desirability of these conditions. Human value studies have been conducted to place the observable states onto a preference continuum, with an anchor of 0 for death and 1.0 for completely well. Studies have shown that the weights are highly stable over a 1-year period and that they are consistent across diverse groups of raters. Finally, one must consider the duration of stay in various health states. Having a cough or a headache for 1 day is not the same as having the problem for 1 year. A health measure must take these durations into consideration. Using this information, one can describe HRQOL in terms similar to years of

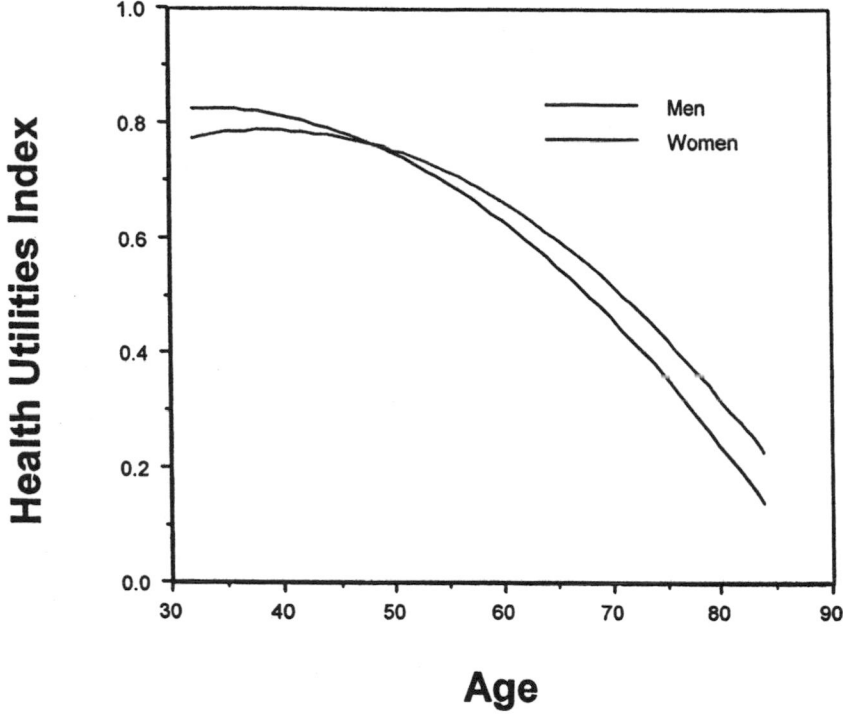

Figure 16.1. Health Utilities Index data for men and women in the American population. From "Gender Differences in Quality-Adjusted Survival Using a Health-Utilities Index" by R. M. Kaplan and P. Erickson, 2000, *American Journal of Preventive Medicine, 18*, p. 80. Copyright 2000 by Elsevier Science. Reprinted by permission.

life. For example, 1 year in a state assigned the weight of .5 is equivalent to 0.5 of a QALY.

Rating Methods

Cost–utility analysis requires an assessment of utilities for health states. A variety of different techniques have been used to assess these utilities. Some analysts do not measure utilities directly; instead, they evaluate health outcomes by simply assigning a reasonable utility. However, most current approaches have respondents assign weights to different health states on a scale ranging from 0 (for dead) to 1.0 (for wellness). The most common techniques include rating scales, the standard gamble, and the time trade-off. Rating scales provide simple techniques for assigning a numerical value to an object. There are several methods for obtaining rating scale information. One is the category scale. This is a simple partition method in which respondents are requested to assign each case a number selected from a set of numbered categories representing equal intervals. This method, exemplified by the familiar 10-point rating scale, is efficient, easy to use, and applicable in a large number of settings. In a typical administration, the respondent reads the description of a case and rates it on a 10-point scale ranging from 0 for dead to 10 for asymptomatic, optimum function. The endpoints of the scale are typically well defined.

Another common rating scale method is the visual analog scale. In the visual analog method, the respondent is presented with a line, typically 100 cm long, with well-defined endpoints. The respondent's task is to mark the line to indicate where his or her preference rests in relation to the two poles. The standard gamble offers a choice between two alternatives: Choice A—living in healthy state with certainty, or Choice B—taking a gamble on a new treatment for which the outcome is uncertain. The respondent is told that a hypothetical treatment will lead to perfect health with a probability of p or immediate death with a probability of $1 - p$. He or she can choose between remaining in a state that is intermediate between wellness and death or taking the gamble and trying the new treatment. The probability (p) is varied until the respondent is indifferent between Choices A and B. The concept of probability is difficult for most respondents and requires the use of visual aids or props to assist in the interview. Thus, an alternative to the standard gamble uses a trade-off in time, in which the respondent is offered a choice of living for a defined amount of time in perfect health or a variable amount of time in an alternative state that is less desirable. It is presumed that all respondents would choose a year of wellness versus a year with some health problem. However, by reducing the time of wellness and leaving fixed (e.g., 1 year) the time in the suboptimal health state, an indifference point can be determined. For example, a respondent may rate being severely depressed for 2 years as equivalent to perfect wellness for 1 year.

Internet Data Collection

A variety of new techniques are available to assess patient health status over the Internet. One good example is provided by Impact 3, an Online Survey Generation Instrument. Impact 3 was developed by Leslie Lenert at the University of California, San Diego. The site allows the user to build custom-based questionnaires that can collect a wide variety of data. It has standard data collection forms for background information, medical and health history, and demographic characteristics. The site also allows the user to select from a variety of standardized questionnaires. Furthermore, it allows data collection via common instruments such as the visual analog scale, the time tradeoff, willingness to pay, and the standard gamble (Lenert & Kaplan, 2000). The site is available to the public and has the attractive feature of allowing a researcher or clinician to quickly build his or her own Web site (see www.preferences.ucsd.edu).

Cost–Effectiveness Evaluations

In addition to health benefits, programs also have costs. Resources are limited, and good policy decisions require allocations that maximize life ex-

Cost/QALY for Selected Interventions

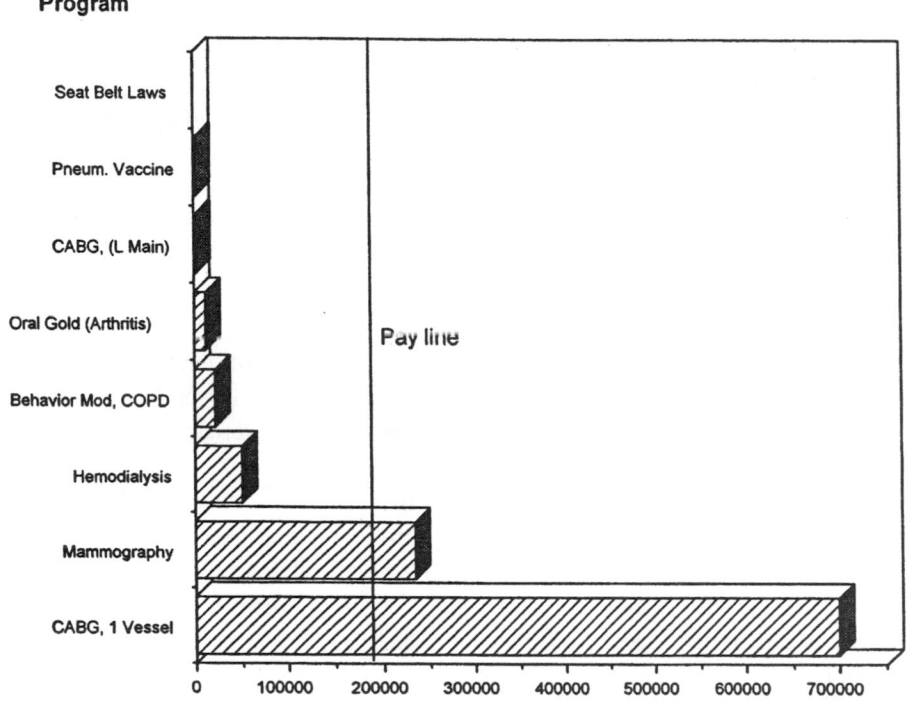

Cost/QALY

Figure 16.2. Comparison of several programs using cost–quality-adjusted life years (QALY) ratios. (From Kaplan 2001). Pneum. = pneumonia; CABG = coronary artery bypass graft; Mod = modification; COPD = chronic abstructive pulmonary disease.

pectancy and HRQOL. Methodologies for estimating costs have now become standardized (Gold, 1996). From an administrative perspective, cost estimates include all costs of treatment as well as costs associated with caring for any side effects of treatment. From a social perspective, costs are broader and may include costs of family members who are not working in order to provide care. When one is comparing programs for a given population with a given medical condition, cost-effectiveness is measured as the change in costs of care for the program compared with the existing therapy or program, relative to the change in health measured in a standardized unit such as the QALY. The difference in costs over the difference in effectiveness is the *incremental cost-effectiveness* and is usually expressed as the cost–QALY ratio. Because the objective of all programs is to produce QALYs, the cost–QALY ratio can be used to show the relative efficiency of different programs (Gold, 1996).

Figure 16.2 shows a comparison of different programs that have been analyzed using the cost–QALY ratio. Some traditional interventions, such as bypass surgery for one-vessel coronary heart disease, may cost as much as $700,000 to produce a QALY. Screening programs, such as mammography, may also require many resources to produce a QALY. On the other hand, public health programs, such as pneumonia vaccines for the elderly or laws requiring children to be in infant seats and adults to use seatbelts, may produce a QALY at a very low cost. The figure shows a hypothetical "pay line." It might be argued that programs to the left of the pay line should be funded, but those with cost–QALY ratios to the right of the line be examined more carefully.

Standards For Cost–Effectiveness Analysis

Contrary to the portrayal of cost–effectiveness analysis in the popular media, the purpose of the analysis is not to cut costs; rather, cost–effectiveness analysis attempts to identify which interventions produce the greatest amount of health using the resources that are available. Because of the confusion about cost–effectiveness analysis, the Office of Disease Prevention and Health Promotion in the Public Health Service appointed a panel to develop standards for cost–effectiveness analysis (Gold, 1996; Russell, Gold, Siegel, Daniels, & Weinstein, 1996; Siegel, Weinstein, Russell, & Gold, 1996; Weinstein, Siegel, Gold, Kamlet, & Russell, 1996). In the following sections, we review some of the major elements of cost–effectiveness analysis as defined by this panel.

Perspective. The results of cost–effectiveness analysis may depend on perspective. From the *societal* perspective, all health care benefits and costs are considered, regardless of who experiences them or pays for them. The *administrative* perspective evaluates the problem through the eyes of a specific agency. *Individual* perspectives consider costs and benefits from the viewpoint of an individual citizen or patient. There may be occasions on which results differ dramatically as a function of perspective. A health maintenance organization, for example, may save money by denying a particular mental health service. So, from an administrative perspective, costs may be reduced; however, from a societal perspective, costs may increase, because other agencies may be required to pay for this service or for the consequences of conditions being left untreated. The panel concluded that most analyses should incorporate the societal perspective.

Comparators. Virtually all decisions involve evaluation in comparison to some alternative. Evaluations of innovative new therapies should compare the new approach with care that was standard before the new intervention was available.

Accounting for costs. From the societal perspective, the cost component considers all resources required for the intervention and for the comparator. These include all costs for all people exposed to the program regardless of whether they eventually developed a health problem. In cost–benefit analysis, the cost savings in reduced health care are subtracted from the cost of an intervention. For example, a psychological intervention may reduce the number of visits to health care providers. If the resources saved by reduced visits exceed the costs of the programs, a *cost offset* has been achieved. Behavioral programs may offer cost offsets, but careful analysis rarely shows that intervention programs actually save money (Russell, 1986). Some cost–effectiveness analyses examine how changes in utilization as a result of a treatment or intervention affect health care costs.

Sensitivity analysis. Many analyses estimate values for variables, and there is uncertainty about whether these estimates are correct. A sensitivity analysis examines how the results of the cost-effectiveness analysis would change if these estimated values were allowed to vary between a realistic upper and lower bound. In other words, researchers examine and report how sensitive their results are to the estimates contained in their analyses.

Computer simulation and decision modeling. Although not a guideline in itself, the use of computers in simulating future outcomes of intervention in cost–effectiveness analysis has become popular. It involves developing a decision tree of all known outcomes of a treatment and using estimates of their likelihood to predict what the result would be if all patients were followed until they reach a certain age or their life expectancy is reached. The likelihood of each outcome is based on results from previous studies or the best estimates available. Sensitivity analyses become very important for evaluating the stability of findings based on these estimates, because the outcomes are estimated and are not observed. Published cost–effectiveness simulations using decision models are continuing to increase and are predicted to play an increasing role in health decision making.

The panel standards for cost–effectiveness are now widely recognized; however, they rarely have been applied in behavioral outcome studies. Kaplan and Groessl (2002) reviewed current cost–effectiveness studies in behavioral medicine and found only two studies consistent with the panel's criteria for high-quality analyses. However, several studies in mental health care in primary care settings have used current methodologies We describe one example in the following section.

SCREENING FOR DEPRESSION IN PRIMARY CARE

A recent example of a cost–utility analysis is provided by an evaluation of screening for depression in primary care. Depression provides a good example because of its high prevalence. Between 5% and 12% of men and between 10% and 25% of women experience at least one major depressive episode during their lifetimes (Kessler et al., 1994). Most of these individuals, if treated at all, are cared for in the primary care system rather than the mental health system. It has been suggested that patients would benefit if primary care physicians screened for depression and initiated early treatment.

However, resources available to primary care physicians are limited, and it is not known whether screening for depression is a good use of the resources in relation to other alternatives. We can no longer assume something should be implemented just because it intuitively makes sense.

Valenstein, Vijan, Zeber, Boehm, and Buttar (2001) performed a cost–utility analysis of the benefits of screening for depression in primary care. The purpose of this analysis was to estimate the cost to produce a QALY (utility). This outcome typically is estimated using one of the decision-based outcome measures such as the QWB, the HUI, or the EuroQol. The comparator was no depression screening. The investigators created a hypothetical cohort of 40-year-old primary care patients and assumed that these patients would either be screened for depression every year or that no screening would take place. The computer simulation followed the patients until they reached either age 90 or were assumed to have died of other causes. Screening consisted of the administration of a self-administered depression questionnaire with follow-up of positive cases by a nurse and primary care provider.

For each time period in the model, it was assumed that the patient was in one of eight states: (a) never depressed; (b) history of depression, in remission; (c) history of depression, still in treatment; (d) significant depressive symptoms; (e) significant depressive symptoms, in treatment; (f) major depression; (g) major depression, in treatment; (h) deceased. To meet the definition of an undetected depressive episode, a patient would need (a) two or more depressive symptoms for at least 2 weeks, (b) to be experiencing functional impairment, and (c) to not meet the *Diagnostic and Statistical Manual for Mental Disorders* (American Psychiatric Association, 1994) criteria for major depression. All patients who had a diagnosis of minor depression, dysthymia, or major depression were also considered to be depressed and were included. Estimates of the effectiveness of depression treatment and screening were obtained from a review of 350 articles published in the peer-reviewed literature. The prevalence of depression was estimated from published studies that examined patients in primary care settings.

The analysis suggested that, on average, depression screening measures had a sensitivity of 84% and an average specificity of 72% for major depression. For minor depression, sensitivities were significantly lower. Valenstein et al. (2001) used a sensitivity of 35% for depressive symptoms. It was assumed that primary care physicians would initiate treatment in 45% of the patients with major depression and 20% of the patients with depressive symptoms. Furthermore, it was assumed that 3%–5% of the patients would be referred to a mental health specialist and that 26% of those with major depression and 13% of those with symptoms would self-refer during a 12-month interval. Using the QWB, Valenstein et al. used utilities for depression of between .55 and .68. It was assumed that utilities for the general population who do not have depression were between .81 and .90.

The results suggest that, compared with no screening, the annual costs of screening in primary care are \$192,444/QALY. If screening is reduced from once a year to once every 5 years, costs are reduced to \$50,988/QALY. A one-time screening program (not repeated on a regular time interval) reduced that cost–QALY ratio to \$32,053. Valenstein et al. (2001) concluded that regular screening may not be competitive with other health care programs. However, one-time screening competes favorably with other options in health care (Valenstein et al., 2001). A variety of variables affect the analysis. One is the assumption that screening measures are not very good, particularly for minor depression. For example, given that there is a 5% prevalence of major depression in primary care, a sensitivity of .84 and a specificity of .72 lead to many false diagnoses. For every 100 patients screened, there would be 4 true positive cases and 27 false positive results (Kroenke, 2001). Each of these false positives adds significantly to the costs of the program, because each one must be followed up. The analysis also assumes that treatments are not very effective and that adherence to treatment is only about 50%. The study did not evaluate the benefits of cognitive–behavioral therapy in relation to pharmacological management of the condition.

The sensitivity analysis showed that cost of treatment was not an important factor. Varying the cost of professional visits and antidepressant medication by ±50% had only a small impact on the cost–effectiveness ratio. Similarly, cost offset did not have a large effect. For example, assuming that treatment of depression would reduce general medical expenses by 20% had only a minor effect on the cost–QALY estimates.

Although the Valenstein et al. (2001) study is important, it also suggests important directions for future research. In particular, the study makes clear that much work remains to be done. For example, studies have not prospectively evaluated the outcomes for patients who have been assigned to screening or to usual care. Valenstein et al. did the best they could with computer simulation, given the data published in the literature. However, considerably more needs to be known about health outcomes for patients treated for depression. At present, this information is usually estimated rather than measured.

SUMMARY AND CONCLUSIONS

The primary care setting has become an important venue for mental health care. This change in the delivery of health care has created many new problems. Health care has become expensive, and there is clearly a need to use resources in a way that provides the most benefit for the most people. Policy shifts have redistributed the way care is delivered. Psychiatrists and, to a lesser extent, psychologists, have lost market share to lower cost providers. Many providers have argued that the change in the way care is delivered will harm patients.

Unfortunately, we have little evidence that the changes in the delivery of care are better or worse for patients. To establish this, we need significantly more information on patient outcomes. A variety of measures are available to assess patient outcomes, each from a different perspective, with advantages and disadvantages. These measures include mental health specific measures and generic measures such as the SF-36, the COOP charts, the HUI, and the QWB.

Methodologies for evaluating costs should also be considered in health care decisions. The panel on cost–effectiveness in medicine and health care has offered standards for cost–effectiveness evaluations. Although a growing number of studies apply these methodologies, there are still relatively few systematic cost–effectiveness evaluations of mental health care. Given the lack of data, analyses must depend on the available information. Studies published in the literature offer some surprising findings. For example, regular screening for depression is relatively expensive to produce a QALY. On the other hand, one-time screening competes well with other health care services.

How the information gathered through the various assessment methods discussed in this chapter will shape the future of primary health care remains to be seen. Although it is clear that a large portion of mental health care is currently, and will undoubtedly continue to be, delivered in primary care settings, there is no agreed-on model for how this will be accomplished. A number of ways to manage patients have been discussed, including the referral model and a collaborative care model. Patients with serious mental illness are certainly best cared for in a referral model. The severity of the illness (e.g., schizophrenia vs. mild depression) will in part undoubtedly determine which model to follow. Lower spectrum anxiety and depression might be best cared for in a collaborative care model in which primary care physicians and mental health providers share management (Maser & Patterson, 2002). However, the costs and benefits of these various models of care depend, in part, on the perspective one takes. For example, it may be more cost-effective from the health care system's perspective for the primary care physician to provide the care. In contrast, from the patient's perspective, where improved quality of life is paramount, it is unclear which model is most useful. The data to conduct such cost–effectiveness analyses from each perspective do not currently exist. We encourage investigators to gather the data necessary to address these critical issues.

Many aspects of cost–effectiveness analysis are not covered in this chapter. For more details, readers are referred to Gold (1996), a much more comprehensive source. It is worth mentioning that our presentation of methods for making important health policy decisions may seem detached or insensitive to some readers. Placing dollar and QALY values on human lives raises important ethical issues (Dranove, 2003). Although we argue that these methods should be considered, we do not believe that cost–effectiveness should be the only information that is used to make these major health decisions. Cost–effectiveness analysis is an objective tool for the evaluation of health interventions that may maximize the overall health of a population. It should be one component of health policy decisions.

Mental health outcomes research offers unusual opportunities for basic methodological and applied research. We believe the most important opportunities are in demonstrations that mental health services in primary care result in benefits to patients. This can be demonstrated through studies that measure patient reported quality-of-life outcomes. The best examples of benefit will result from systematic randomized clinical trials. In addition to demonstration of patient benefit, more studies are needed that demonstrate that mental health services offer good value. More studies are necessary, too, to show that investments in mental health care produce an increment in benefit over more traditional care. It will be necessary to demonstrate that adding another service, which adds cost, can still be justified, because patients experience better outcomes and overall health care costs are reduced. To date, there have been very few systematic studies in this field. Although the work will be difficult, there are plenty of important opportunities in mental health services research.

REFERENCES

American Psychiatric Association. (1994). *Diagnostic and statistical manual of mental disorders* (4th ed.). Washington, DC: Author.

Andreasen, N. C., & Olsen, S. (1982). Negative vs. positive schizophrenia: Definition and validation. *Archives of General Psychiatry, 39*, 789–794.

Bartsch, D. A., Shern, D. L., Feinberg, L. E., & Fuller, B. B. (1990). Screening CMHC outpatients for physical illness. *Hospital & Community Psychiatry, 41*, 786–790.

Bergner, M., Bobbitt, R. A., Kressel, S., Pollard, W. E., Gilson, B. S., & Morris, J. R. (1976). The Sickness Impact Profile: Conceptual formulation and methodology for the development of a health status measure. *International Journal of Health Services, 6*, 393–415.

Bergner, M., Bobbitt, R. A., Pollard, W. E., Martin, D. P., & Gilson, B. S. (1976). The Sickness Impact Profile: Validation of a health status measure. *Medical Care, 14*, 57–67.

Blumenthal, D. (2001). Controlling health care expenditures. *New England Journal of Medicine, 344*, 766–769.

Brown, M., Gordon, W. A., & Haddad, L. (2000). Models for predicting subjective quality of life in individuals with traumatic brain injury. *Brain Injury, 14*, 5–19.

Burke, W., Baron, R. B., Lemon, M., Losh, D., & Novack, A. (1994). Training generalist physicians: Structural elements of the curriculum. *Journal of General Internal Medicine, 9*(4, Suppl. 1), S23–S30.

Coyne, J. C., Klinkman, M. S., & Nease, D. E. (2002). Emotional disorders in primary care. *Journal of Consulting and Clinical Psychology, 70*, 798–809.

Crews, C., Batal, H., Elasy, T., Casper, E., & Mehler, P. S. (1998). Primary care for those with severe and persistent mental illness. *Western Journal of Medicine, 169*, 245–250.

Dranove, D. (2003). *What's your life worth?* Upper Saddle River, NJ: Prentice Hall.

Feeny, D., Furlong, W., Mulhern, R. K., Barr, R. D., & Hudson, M. (1999). A framework for assessing health-related quality of life among children with cancer. *International Journal of Cancer Supplement, 12*, 2–9.

Felker, B., Yazel, J. J., & Short, D. (1996). Mortality and medical comorbidity among psychiatric patients: A review. *Psychiatric Services, 47*, 1356–1363.

Field, M. J., & Gold, M. R. (1998). *Summarizing population health.* Washington, DC: Institute of Medicine, National Academy Press.

Ganz, P. A., Haskell, C. M., Figlin, R. A., La Soto, N., & Siau, J. (1988). Estimating the quality of life in a clinical trial of patients with metastatic lung cancer using the Karnofsky performance status and the Functional Living Index—Cancer. *Cancer, 61*, 849–856.

Gold, M. R. (1996). *Cost-effectiveness in health and medicine.* New York: Oxford University Press.

Golini, A. (2001). Demographic trends and population policies. *Futures, 33*, 27–41.

Gudex, C., Dolan, P., Kind, P., & Williams, A. (1996). Health state valuations from the general public using the visual analogue scale. *Quality of Life Research, 5*, 521–531.

Hall, R. C., Beresford, T. P., Gardner, E. R., & Popkin, M. K. (1982). The medical care of psychiatric patients. *Hospital and Community Psychiatry, 33*, 25–34.

Heffler, S., Levit, K., Smith, S., Smith, C., Cowan, C., Lazenby, H., et al. (2001). Health spending growth up in 1999; faster growth expected in the future. *Health Affairs, 20*, 193–203.

Hirschfeld, R. M. A. (1998). American health care systems and depression: The past, present, and the future. *Journal of Clinical Psychiatry, 59*(Suppl. 20), 5–10.

Holmberg, S. K., & Kane, C. (1999). Health and self-care practices of persons with schizophrenia. *Psychiatric Services, 50*, 827–829.

Hurst, N. P., Kind, P., Ruta, D., Hunter, M., & Stubbings, A. (1997). Measuring health-related quality of life in rheumatoid arthritis: Validity, responsiveness and reliability of EuroQol (EQ-5D). *British Journal of Rheumatology, 36*, 551–559.

Iglehart, J. K. (1996). Managed care and mental health. *New England Journal of Medicine, 334*, 131–135.

Institute for the Future. (2000). *Health and health care 2010: The forecast, the challenge.* San Francisco: Jossey-Bass.

Kaplan, R. M. (1990). Behavior as the central outcome in health care. *American Psychologist, 45*, 1211–1220.

Kaplan, R. M. (1994). The Ziggy theorem: Toward an outcomes-focused health psychology. *Health Psychology, 13*, 451–460.

Kaplan, R. M. (1996). Measuring health outcomes for resource allocation. In R. L. Glueckauf, R. G. Frank, G. R. Bond, & J. H. McGrew (Eds.), *Psychological practice in a changing health care system* (pp. 101–133): New York: Springer.

Kaplan, R. M., Anderson, J. P., Patterson, T. L., McCutchan, J. A., Weinrich, J. D., Heaton, R. K., et al. (1995). Validity of the Quality of Well-Being Scale for persons with human immunodeficiency virus infection. *Psychosomatic Medicine, 57*, 138–147.

Kaplan, R. M., & Bush, J. W. (1982). Health-related quality of life measurement for evaluation research and policy analysis. *Health Psychology, 1*, 60–80.

Kaplan, R. M., & California Policy Seminar. (1993). *Allocating health resources in California: Learning from the Oregon experiment.* Berkeley: California Policy Seminar.

Kaplan, R. M., & Erickson, P. (2000). Gender differences in quality-adjusted survival using a Health-Utilities Index. *American Journal of Preventive Medicine, 18*, 77–82.

Kaplan, R. M., Feeny, D., & Revicki, D. A. (1999). Methods for assessing relative importance in preference based outcome measures. In E. C. R. B. Joyce, E. Hannah, & M. McGee (Eds.), *Individual quality of life: Approaches to conceptualisation and assessment* (pp. 135–149). Amsterdam: Harwood Academic Publishers.

Kaplan, R. M., Ganiats, T. G., Sieber, W. J., & Anderson, J. P. (1998). The Quality of Well-Being Scale: Critical similarities and differences with SF-36. *International Journal for Quality in Health Care, 10*, 509–520.

Kaplan, R. M., & Groessl, E. J. (2002). Applications of cost-effectiveness methodologies in behavioral medicine. *Journal of Consulting and Clinical Psychology, 70*, 482–493.

Keller, S. D., Ware, J. E., Jr., Hatoum, H. T., & Kong, S. X. (1999). The SF-36 Arthritis-Specific Health Index (ASHI): II. Tests of validity in four clinical trials. *Medical Care, 37*(5, Suppl.), MS51–MS60.

Kessler, R. C., McGonagle, K. A., Nelson, C. B., Hughes, M., Swartz, M., & Blazer, D. G. (1994). Sex and depression in the National Comorbidity Survey: Cohort effects. *Journal of Affective Disorders, 30*, 15–26.

Kind, P. (1997). The performance characteristics of EQ-5D, a measure of health related quality of life for use in technology assessment [Abstract]. *Annual Meeting of International Society of Technology Assessment in Health Care, 13*(5), 81.

Kosinski, M., Keller, S. D., Hatoum, H. T., Kong, S. X., & Ware, J. E., Jr. (1999). The SF-36 Health Survey as a generic outcome measure in clinical trials of patients with osteoarthritis and rheumatoid arthritis: Tests of data quality, scaling assumptions and score reliability. *Medical Care, 37*(5, Suppl.), MS10–MS22.

Kroenke, K. (2001). Depression screening is not enough. *Annals of Internal Medicine, 134*, 418–420.

Larson, C. O., Hays, R. D., & Nelson, E. C. (1992). Do the pictures influence scores on the Dartmouth COOP Charts? *Quality of Life Research, 1*, 247–249.

Lehman, A. F., Slaughter, J. G., & Myers, C. P. (1991). Quality of life in alternative residential settings. *Psychiatric Quarterly, 62*, 35–49.

Lenert, L., & Kaplan, R. M. (2000). Validity and interpretation of preference-based measures of health-related quality of life . *Medical Care, 38*(9, Suppl.), II138–II150.

Lowe, D., O'Grady, J. G., McEwen, J., & Williams, R. (1990). Quality of life following liver transplantation: A preliminary report. *Journal of the Royal College of Physicians of London, 24,* 43–46.

Manning, W. G., Newhouse, J. P., Duan, N., Keeler, E. B., Leibowitz, A., & Marquis, M. S. (1987). Health insurance and the demand for medical care: Evidence from a randomized experiment. *The American Economic Review, 77,* 251–277.

Maser, J., & Patterson, T. L. (2002). Spectrum and vosology: Implications for DSM–V. *Psychiatric Clinics of North America, 25,* 855–885.

McDowell, I., & Newell, C. (1996). *Measuring health: A guide to rating scales and questionnaires* (2nd ed.). New York: Oxford University Press.

Meyer, R. E. (1993). The economics of survival for academic psychiatry. *Academic Psychiatry, 17,* 149–160.

Nelson, E. C., Landgraf, J. M., Hays, R. D., Wasson, J. H., & Kirk, J. W. (1990). The functional status of patients: How can it be measured in physicians' offices? *Medical Care, 28,* 1111–1126.

Newhouse, J. P., Manning, W. G., Duan, N., Keeler, E. B., Leibowitz, A., & Marquis, M. S. (1987). The findings of the Rand Health Insurance experiment—A response to Welch et al. *Medical Care, 25,* 157–179.

Patterson, T. L., Semple, S. J., Shaw, W. S., Halpain, M., Moscona, S., Grant, I., et al. (1997). Self-reported social functioning among older patients with schizophrenia. *Schizophrenia Research, 27,* 199–210.

Paykel, E. S., Weissman, M. M., & Prusoff, B. A. (1978). Social maladjustment and severity of depression. *Comprehensive Psychiatry, 19,* 121–128.

Russell, L. B. (1986). *Is prevention better than cure?* Washington, DC: Brookings Institution.

Russell, L. B., Gold, M. R., Siegel, J. E., Daniels, N., & Weinstein, M. C. (1996). The role of cost-effectiveness analysis in health and medicine. *Journal of the American Medical Association, 276,* 1172–1177.

St. Peter, R. F., Reed, M. C., Kemper, P., & Blumenthal, D. (1999). The scope of care expected of primary care physicians: Is it greater than it should be? *Issue Brief: Center for the Study of Health System Change, 16*(24), 1–4.

Scott-Lennox, J. A., Wu, A. W., Boyer, J. G., & Ware, J. E., Jr. (1999). Reliability and validity of French, German, Italian, Dutch, and UK English translations of the Medical Outcomes Study HIV Health Survey. *Medical Care, 37,* 908–925.

Siegel, J. E., Weinstein, M. C., Russell, L. B., & Gold, M. R. (1996). Recommendations for reporting cost-effectiveness analyses. *Journal of the American Medical Association, 276,* 1339–1341.

Stafford, R. S., Saglam, D., Causino, N., Starfield, B., Culpepper, L., Marder, W. D., et al. (1999). Trends in adult visits to primary care physicians in the United States. *Archives of Family Medicine, 8,* 26–32.

Starfield, B. (2000). Is US health really the best in the world? *Journal of the American Medical Association, 284*, 483–485.

Stewart, A. L., & Ware, J. E. (1992). *Measuring functioning and well-being: The medical outcomes study approach*. Durham, NC: Duke University Press.

United States Department of Health and Human Services & Healthy People 2010. (2000). *Healthy People 2010*. Washington, DC: Author.

Valenstein, M., Vijan, S., Zeber, J. E., Boehm, K., & Buttar, A. (2001). The cost–utility of screening for depression in primary care. *Annals of Internal Medicine, 134*, 345–360.

Walker, S. N., Sechrist, K. R., & Pender, N. J. (1987). The Health-Promoting Lifestyle Profile: Development and psychometric characteristics. *Nursing Research, 36*, 76–81.

Walker, S. R., & Rosser, R. (1993). *Quality of life assessment: Key issues in the 1990s*. Boston: Kluwer Academic.

Ware, J. E., Jr., & Gandek, B. (1998). Overview of the SF-36 Health Survey and the International Quality of Life Assessment (IQOLA) Project. *Journal of Clinical Epidemiology, 51*, 903–912.

Ware, J. E., Jr., & Sherbourne, C. D. (1992). The MOS 36-item short-form health survey (SF-36): Conceptual framework and item selection. *Medical Care, 30*, 473–483.

Wasson, J. H., Kairys, S. W., Nelson, E. C., Kalishman, N., & Baribeau, P. (1994). A short survey for assessing health and social problems of adolescents: Dartmouth Primary Care Cooperative Information Project (The COOP). *Journal of Family Practice, 38*, 489–494.

Weinstein, M. C., Siegel, J. E., Gold, M. R., Kamlet, M. S., & Russell, L. B. (1996). Recommendations of the Panel on Cost-Effectiveness in Health and Medicine. *Journal of the American Medical Association, 276*, 1253–1258.

World Health Organization. (1948). *Constitution of the World Health Organization*. Geneva, Switzerland: Author.

Worley, N. K., Drago, L., & Hadley, T. (1990). Improving the physical health–mental health interface for the chronically mentally ill: Could nurse case managers make a difference? *Archives of Psychiatric Nursing, 4*, 108–113.

OUTCOME ASSESSMENT FOR RESOURCE ALLOCATION   *315*

17

THE FUTURE IS PRIMARY CARE

PATRICK H. DeLEON, NINA P. ROSSOMANDO,
AND BRIAN D. SMEDLEY

Primary care psychology is a natural result of the evolution of the discipline of professional psychology over the last 30 years. As the 21st century begins, psychology is becoming one of the nation's primary health care professions (DeLeon, VandenBos, Pollard et al., 1991). This evolving transformation in identity can be viewed as reflecting a movement from the profession's traditionally narrow focus on mental health diagnoses and treatment to a more generic psychosocial and behavioral orientation to health care. Psychologists collectively are finally coming to appreciate that mental health per se is an integral component of health care; that the psychosocial aspects of health and disease are critical, particularly to the all-important efforts to define *quality*; and that the underlying changes they are experiencing today reflect a gradual evolution toward comprehensive, integrative care, both within psychology and within the overall U.S. health care system.

Within the generic health care arena there has been a steady movement in resource allocation from a traditional—again, almost exclusive—focus on individual patient concerns, toward an increasing quest for accountability, cost-effectiveness evaluations, public health models, and the utilization of advanced technology both to provide clinical services and to objectively ascertain "golden standards" of care. Psychologists and other nonphysicians are being increasingly appointed to positions of high administrative and public policy formulation responsibility. These changes have resulted in significant modifications in the profession's practice, training, and scientific endeavors (Mauksch & Heldring, 1995).

It is important to appreciate that psychology is a relatively young profession. Although the discipline dates back to the founding of Wundt's laboratory in 1879, it was only in 1977 that Missouri became the last state in the nation to license psychology's practitioners. The following year, President Carter's Commission on Mental Health issued its landmark report (President's Commission on Mental Health, 1978). At that time, there were approximately 46,800 members of the American Psychological Association (APA) and 25,000 licensed psychologists. In the public's mind, psychology was synonymous with mental health care. At the turn of the 21st century, only slightly more than 20 years later, the first-ever Surgeon General's report on mental health (U.S. Department of Health and Human Services, 1999) was released. APA's membership exceeded 155,000, and there were an estimated 81,000 licensed psychologists. At the 1998 APA Annual Convention, in San Francisco, the ceremony heralding the 10th anniversary of the Committee for the American Psychological Association of Graduate Students, with its 40,000-plus members, clearly demonstrated that the field was undergoing a phenomenal expansion. Psychology remains one of the most popular, if not the most popular, undergraduate majors, and applications to graduate programs continue to far exceed available positions. At the public policy level, serious questions are being raised as to why mental health treatment should continue to be considered any differently than that of any other kind of health care services. Equally important has been the growing public awareness of the importance of the psychosocial aspects of health care and wellness. Nowhere is this more evident than in primary care.

From a legislative and public policy perspective, times have indeed changed. Psychology's legislative agenda has gradually expanded from an initial focus on individual state and federal efforts that were primarily intended to ensure private practice insurance reimbursement (e.g., "freedom of choice" bills) to encompass broader systems concerns that address scope-of-practice issues, facility (e.g., hospital) staff eligibility, and interdisciplinary collaboration. In addition, psychology has expanded its public interest advocacy, particularly to promote federal health promotion and disease prevention initiatives in areas such as HIV/AIDS, women's health, and minority health—which all are very important for the practice of primary care psychology. By the turn of the 21st century, professional psychology had been successful in obtaining recognition under a wide range of federal health care programs, including many of the health professions training initiatives of Title VII of the U.S. Public Health Service Act and the Graduate Medical Educational account of Medicare. This accomplishment represented a major change in orientation for the educational field. Psychology educators had previously relied on the generic, although steadily decreasing, support received from the National Institute of Mental Health and the Veterans Administration. Now, significant additional funding is being made available for targeted programmatic activities, reflecting federal health care priorities such as providing access to care within rural America and increasing the numbers of ethnic minority psychologists.

During the ultimately ill-fated Clinton Administration health care reform deliberations, individual psychologists and APA were active participants, with then-APA President Frank Farley meeting directly with Hillary Rodham Clinton. During this period of significant national debate, APA, as the national psychological organization, was committing significant resources and providing policy guidance for the development of credible and lasting state psychological association infrastructure and state-based political action efforts.

By the late 1990s, there were very few relevant federal health statutes enacted that did not expressly include psychology. Within the APA governance there was a gradually increasing awareness of the fundamentally interrelated nature of psychology's status within the public interest arena, the public sector, the private practice environment, and the field's educational mission. In our judgment, this heightened awareness will ultimately represent the next major evolution within professional psychology, as greater appreciation for the critical interface of the underlying missions of our educational institutions, society's public health needs, and clinical practice opportunities begins to directly affect APA's legislative goals. Simply stated, as psychology effectively addresses society's pressing priorities, U.S. elected officials will affirmatively respond to psychologists' educational, scientific, and clinical needs—whatever they may be. The corollary to this statement is that with educators and practitioners working collaboratively, both will acquire access to evolving national trends, including the importance of primary care and the opportunity to shape the nature of technology's exploding impact on health care.

It is interesting, in retrospect, that it now appears that while members of organized psychology were working to make psychology a greater political force on the national scene, the Clinton Administration's second term seems to have heralded a significant *devolution* within U.S. health policy thinking. At the time, there is no question that a number of highly regarded health policy experts were recommending monumental changes in the status quo at the federal level, for example, instituting national licensure requirements, ensuring consumer engagement in relevant policy boards, and the establishment of national commissions to determine professional scope-of-practice issues (Finocchio, Dower, Blick, Gragnola, & The Taskforce on Health Care Workforce Regulation, 1998; O'Neil & The Pew Health Professions Commission, 1998). The United States was undergoing unprecedented advances within the communications and technology industries, which were just beginning to directly affect health care. These were projected to be truly revolutionary in nature and thereby required a national response. Yet, again in retrospect, there did not appear to be the political will necessary to implement such far-reaching recommendations and thereby override traditional state public health responsibilities. Instead, it is now clear that a wide range of health care issues have increasingly been returned to the state and local levels for their determination.

The *Healthy People* report (U.S. Department of Health, Education, and Welfare, 1979) may have been the health policy hallmark of President Carter's administration, with substantial implications for primary care. "Let us make no mistake about the purpose of this, the first Surgeon General's Report on Health Promotion and Disease Prevention. Its purpose is to encourage a second public health revolution in the history of the United States. And let us make no mistake about the significance of this document. It represents an emerging consensus among scientists and the health community that the Nation's health strategy must be dramatically recast to emphasize the prevention of disease" (p. vii). The report further noted that

> In fact, of the 10 leading causes of death in the United States, at least seven could be substantially reduced if persons at risk improved just five habits: diet, smoking, lack of exercise, alcohol abuse, and use of antihypertensive medication. (U.S. Department of Health, Education, and Welfare, 1979, p. 14)

Primary care is the first, and often only, context in which most people are diagnosed and treated for these lifestyle-related problems.

This was an impressive step in potentially reconceptualizing the fundamental nature of the U.S. health delivery system as biopsychosocial, including the priorities of the health professions' educational training systems. Also, as seemingly is so often the case, the far-reaching policy recommendations contained in the *Healthy People* report were actually built upon the foundation laid by scholars at yet an earlier time. Approximately 5 years earlier, in April 1974, Marc Lalonde, then the Canadian Minister of National Health and Welfare, released *A New Perspective on the Health of Canadians: A Working Document*. Throughout this policy document, Canadian health policy experts were making a clear and unequivocal call for a broader view of health care: a vision rooted in primary care beyond that of focusing exclusively on individual patient clinical concerns.

> The Governments of the Provinces and of Canada have long recognized that good physical and mental health are necessary for the quality of life to which everyone aspires. Accordingly they have developed a health care system, which, though short of perfection, is the equal of any in the world. Included in the system has been a program of pre-paid health services, which substantially removes financial barriers to medical and hospital care. At the same time. . . . ominous counter-forces have been at

work to undo progress in raising the health status of Canadians. It is therefore necessary for Canadians themselves to be concerned with the gravity of environmental and behavioral risks before any real progress can be made. . . . When the full impact of environment and lifestyle has been assessed, and the foregoing is necessarily but a partial statement of their effect, there can be no doubt that the traditional view of equating the level of health in Canada with the availability of physicians and hospitals is inadequate. Marvelous though health care services are in Canada in comparison with many other countries, there is little doubt that future improvements in the level of health of Canadians lie mainly in improving the environment, moderating self-imposed risks and adding to our knowledge of human biology. (Lalonde, 1974, p. 18)

THE DEVELOPMENT OF HEALTH PSYCHOLOGY

Within organized psychology, perhaps the most significant indication of the collective recognition of the advances occurring within the U.S. health care system and professional psychology's potential leadership role was the establishment in 1978 of Division 38, the Division of Health Psychology. The division's first president was Joseph Matarazzo, professor of medical psychology at Oregon Health Sciences University, who in 1989 became APA's 97th president. Under his leadership, the APA board of directors established a special Presidential Task Force to explore the interrelationship between psychology and U.S. federal health policies. Once again, psychology's fledgling efforts at the national level built upon a foundation established earlier, this time at the divisional level.

In May 1983, Division 38 convened its National Working Conference on Education and Training in Health Psychology (Stone, 1983). The *Arden House Conference*, as it came to be known, reflected nearly 2 years of planning by scores of psychologists and 4 days of intense deliberations by 57 conference participants. In her opening remarks, Judith Rodin, now president of the University of Pennsylvania, raised a critical policy issue for psychology:

It certainly has reached the attention of the public, and it has been our knowledge for a long time, that the heaviest burdens of illness in the United States today are related to behavior—they originate in or are aggravated by unhealthy lifestyles. It is our discipline that has shown that behavior can be studied reliably, reproducibly, and systematically, and that it can be intervened upon. So, in that sense, we really have created this new field in a way to reflect our own knowledge base and to develop it through our efforts to address the behavioral aspects of health and illness. But. . ., as the behavioral contribution to our burden of illness has become clear, all of the health sciences have turned their attention to participation in behavioral approaches to illness. (Stone, 1983, p. 49)

From our public policy frame of reference, we wish to reiterate that a critical component of psychology's evolving response must be the active involvement of psychology's training programs in the actual delivery of health care.

In *Healthy People 2010: Understanding and Improving Health* (U.S. Department of Health and Human Services, 2000), the Clinton Administration called for a 21st-century health care system that focused on the community and the environment, cornerstones of primary care. "We have witnessed a great deal of progress in public health and medicine since our Nation first embarked on the national planning process for the Healthy People initiative. The process began in 1979 with *Healthy People*" (U.S. Department of Health and Human Services, 2000, p. ii).

> Over the years, it has become clear that individual health is closely linked to community health—the health of the community and environment in which individuals live, work, and play. Likewise, community health is profoundly affected by collective behaviors, attitudes, and beliefs of everyone who lives in the community. Indeed the underlying premise of *Healthy People 2010* is that the health of the individual is almost inseparable from the health of the larger community and that the health of every community in every State and territory determines the overall health status of the Nation. (U.S. Department of Health and Human Services, 2000, p. 3)

And, once again,

> The leading causes of death in the United States generally result from a mix of behaviors; injury, violence, and other factors in the environment; and the unavailability or inaccessibility of quality health services. Understanding and monitoring behaviors, environmental factors, and community health systems may prove more useful to monitoring the Nation's *true* health, and in driving health improvement activities, than the death rates that reflect the cumulative impact of these factors. (U.S. Department of Health and Human Services, 2000, p. 21)

The Institute of Medicine (IOM) was established in 1970 by the National Academy of Sciences and possesses a Congressional charter to serve as a formal advisor to the federal government. Over the years, the IOM has become as a highly credible health policy think tank, developing state-of-the-art policy documents on a wide range of issues. From their deliberations often evolve future health care agendas. The 1982 report *Health and Behavior* (Hamburg, Elliott, & Parron, 1982) restated that

> The heaviest burdens of illness in the United States today are related to aspects of individual behavior, especially long-term patterns of behavior often referred to as "lifestyle." As much as 50 percent of mortality from the 10 leading causes of death in the United States can be traced to lifestyle. (p. 3)

Also, "Diseases for which lifestyle factors are especially significant have a dominant position in causes of mortality and morbidity" (p. 7). The IOM report *Promoting Health* (Smedley & Syme, 2000) reiterated a very similar clinical and health policy message:

> The vast majority of the nation's health research resources have been directed towards biomedical research endeavors. By itself, however, biomedical research cannot address the most significant challenges to improving the public's health in the new century. Approximately half of all causes of mortality in the United States are linked to social and behavioral factors. . . . Yet, less than 5% of the approximately $1 trillion spent annually on health care in the United States is devoted to reducing risks posed by these preventable conditions. Behavioral and social interventions therefore offer great promise to reduce disease morbidity and mortality, but as yet their potential to improve the public's health has been relatively poorly tapped. (p. 1)

The authors of the latter report also discussed in considerable depth how evolving research protocols are identifying the locus and mechanisms for biobehavioral interventions. Particularly intriguing was the policy recommendation that "Children should be a major focus of intervention efforts. . . . The evidence is that interventions in early life can change the trajectory of these risk factors" (p. 5).

As the United States recognized the importance of psychology in the understanding and treatment of common illness, many areas of professional psychology began to recognize the importance of primary care. Pediatric psychology has a long history of training and practice in pediatric settings. Family psychology began an active alliance with family medicine in the late 1970s and early 1980s. Family medicine residency programs were required to have behavioral scientists, most of whom were psychologists, on the faculty. Today, family medicine is a training site for many psychology interns and Fellows. Family psychologists are also working in the primary care fields of internal medicine, pediatrics, and obstetrics–gynecology. APA has brought together psychologists trained in family, health, and pediatric psychology to encourage research and to fashion the most effective practice and education in primary care psychology.

Since 1998, APA has participated as a primary care professional organization in the Bureau of Health Professions Primary Care Policy Fellowship. With leaders from medicine, nursing, midwifery, dentistry, and other primary care disciplines, psychology has a representative to participate in a think tank about important primary care policy issues of the day. After advanced leadership and federal policy training, these Fellows present the results of their brainstorming in the form of recommendations about primary care policy to the Secretary of Health and Human Services. In this fellowship one also quickly learns the long-term importance of proselytizing to colleagues. All too often, practicing psychologists and the science and educational faculty of training institutions simply are not aware of the public policy implications of their work; neither do they feel it is their responsibility to teach public policy to students or to try to influence it. They remain unaware of the fundamental relevance of the public policy process to their personal and professional lives. Primary Care Policy Fellows help to shape federal policy, educate other primary care professionals, and promote primary care psychology within the discipline of psychology.

As the chapters in this volume demonstrate, psychology's increasing involvement in the primary care arena holds great promise. Psychology professionals' clinical skills and underlying scientific orientation will likely improve the quality of care. The field of psychology is poised to contribute to the further development of primary care through the marriage of scientist and practitioner. This model creates the skills needed for the next epoch of health care priorities. As the experience of the Department of Defense psychopharmacology fellows has clearly demonstrated, the psychological approach to medication utilization is qualitatively different than the traditional medical approach. Also within the Department of Defense, as Paul G. Wilson describes in his chapter of this volume, an innovative delivery system that truly integrates primary care and psychological services holds great promise. As the diverse models of psychological practice described in this volume are further tested and integrated, it is clear that a new psychology of primary care clearly beckons the profession.

REFERENCES

DeLeon, P. H., VandenBos, G. R., Pollard, M. R., Solarz, A. L., & Weinberg, R. B. (1991). Clinical psychology and the political scene. In M. Hersen, A. E. Kazdin, & A. S. Bellack (Eds.), *The clinical psychology handbook* (2nd ed., pp. 128–143). New York: Pergamon Press.

Finocchio, L. J., Dower, C. M., Blick, N. T., Gragnola, C. M., & The Taskforce on Health Care Workforce Regulation. (1998, October). *Strengthening consumer protection: Priorities for health care workforce regulation.* San Francisco: Pew Health Professions Commission.

Hamburg, D. A., Elliott, G. R., & Parron, D. L. (1982). *Health and behavior: Frontiers of research in the biobehavioral sciences.* Washington, DC: National Academy Press.

Lalonde, M. (1974). *A new perspective on the health care of Canadians: A working document.* Ottawa, Ontario, Canada: Government of Canada.

Mauksch, L., & Heldring, M. (1995). Behavioral scientists' views on work environment, roles, and teaching. *Family Medicine, 27,* 103–108.

O'Neil, E. H., & The Pew Health Professions Commission. (1998, December). *Recreating health professional practice for a new century: The fourth report of the*

Pew Health Professions Commission. San Francisco: Pew Health Professions Commission.

President's Commission on Mental Health. (1978). *Report to the President* (Vol. I). Washington, DC: U.S. Government Printing Office.

Smedley, B. D., & Syme, S. L. (Eds.). (2000). *Promoting health: Intervention strategies from social and behavioral research.* Washington, DC: National Academy Press.

Stone, G. C. (Ed.). (1983). Proceedings of the National Working Conference on Education and Training in Health Psychology: Arden House. *Health Psychology, 2*(5, Suppl.).

U.S. Department of Health, Education, and Welfare. (1979). *Healthy people: The Surgeon General's report on health promotion and disease prevention* (DHEW Publication No. PHS 79-55071). Washington, DC: U.S. Government Printing Office.

U.S. Department of Health and Human Services. (1999). *Mental health: A report of the Surgeon General.* Washington, DC: U.S. Government Printing Office.

U.S. Department of Health and Human Services. (2000). *Healthy people 2010: Understanding and improving health.* Washington, DC: U.S. Government Printing Office.

INDEX

Boulder model programs, 65
Boundary definition, 126
Bradley, Bill, 285
Branding, 267
Bray, J. H., 156
Bray, James H., 251
Briefness, 183
Bureau of Health Professions Primary Care Fellowship, 323
Bureau of Primary Care, 289
Burnout, 152
Burns, B. J., 152
Business efficiency, 27
Business relationship, 154
Buttar, A., 308

California, 248
Campbell, T. L., 158
Canada, 320–321
Capitated payment arrangements, 33, 101
Capitation, 27–28
Capitation models, 28
Cardinal Symptom model, 261–262, 270–273
Caregivers, 212, 220, 233, 235–236
Caring, 117–118
Carter administration, 318, 320
Carve-ins, 20, 38, 263
Carve-outs, 20, 38, 170, 196, 263
Category scale, 303–304
Chaney, J. M., 159
Chapel Hill Pediatrics, 161–164
Child care, 212
Child Health Insurance Program (CHIP), 197, 265, 283, 288
Child Manifestations section of DSM–PC, 195
Children, 189–202
    barriers to psychosocial services for, 190–191
    with chronic health conditions, 265, 271
    collaboration strategies for, 198–202
    and family needs, 197–198
    models of collaboration for, 161–164, 192–196
    needs of low-income, 196–197
    psychology–pediatric collaboration for, 191–192
    uninsured, 282
CHIP. *See* Child Health Insurance Program
Chronic gynecologic conditions, 222

Chronic health conditions, 11, 259–265, 268–273
    Cardinal Symptom model of care for, 270–273
    care for patients with, 119
    care programs for, 262–264
    definition of, 259
    funding of care management for, 264–265
    and information economy, 268–270
    management of, 10
    and primary care, 260–262
    primary care vs. specialists for, 269
    psychosocial management of, 12
    women with, 216–218
Chronic pain, 35, 218
Chwa, H., 228
"Clean" referrals, 139
Clinical assessment, 74–76
Clinical education, 126
Clinical interventions, 76–78
Clinical services, 102
Clinton, Bill, 24, 284
Clinton, Hillary Rodham, 319
Clinton administration, 319, 322
Clinton health care reform proposal, 32, 268
Coding systems
    CPT, 19
    diagnostic, 39, 194–196
Cognitive components of health/illness, 68–69
Cognitive impairment, 231–232
Collaboration, 12, 98–101
    advantages of, 127–128
    approaching prospects for, 155
    beginning the, 157–159
    education/training of, 78–80
    examples of, 161–165
    finding a practice partner for, 155
    independent practice case study of, 136–138
    maintaining, 159–161
    models of, 128, 149–152
    negotiating relationship for, 155–156
    overcoming barriers to, 125–127
    preparation for medical setting, 156–157
    pros and cons of, 152–154
    in rural health care, 250–251
    self-assessment stage in, 154–155
    success factors for, 154–161
    time-related problems in, 105–106

toleration vs., 125
Collaborative-but-traditional model, 128
Collaborative care model, 310
Collaborative family healthcare approach, 114–129
    guidelines for, 125–129
    medical family therapy in, 121–124
    patients/families in, 118–121
    and power, 115–118
Collaborative model, 128
Collaborative relationships, 154
Collaborative team model, 150
Collaborative treatment models, 19
Columbia/HCA, 26
Columbia Healthcare, 26
Commission on Mental Health, 318
Committee for the Advancement of Professional Practice (APA), 12, 35
Committee on the Future of Primary Care (IOM), 14
Commonwealth Fund 1993 Survey on Women's Health, 217
Commonwealth Fund 1998 Survey of Women's Health, 212
Communication
    of bad news, 56–58
    in collaboration, 126
    importance of effective, 119
    and independent practice, 139
    in independent practices, 135
    of knowledge, 107
    need for clear, 154
    with payors, 144–146
    physician and psychologist, 97
    in physician–patient relationship, 48
    with physicians, 104–105
    with support staff, 142–143
Communion, 122
Community–collaborator model, 192, 194
Community integration, 102
Comorbidity, 231, 296–297
Comorbidity syndromes, 20
Comparators, 306, 308
Complexity issues, 231
Comprehensive health care, 9, 12–13
Computerized materials, 199–200
Computer simulation, 307
Conciseness, 183
Confidentiality, 105, 126, 157
Congressional Budget Office, 265
Congressional Fellows Program, 289
Conjoint patient visits, 106

Consolidation, health care industry, 25–26
Consultants, 101, 251, 270
Consultation model, 150, 192–193
Consultation reports, 106
Consultations, 159
Consultation services, 102
Continuing responsibility, 8, 10
Continuous care, 8–9
COOP (Dartmouth Primary Care Cooperative Information Project), 300
Cooper-Patrick, L., 282
Coordinative function, 9–10
Cordes, John, 127
Corporatization of health care, 25–27
Cost containment, 27–28, 34
Cost effectiveness
    incremental, 305
    standards for analysis of, 305–306
Cost–effectiveness analysis, 305–306, 310–311
Cost–effectiveness ratio, 309
Cost offset effect, 13–14, 307, 309
Cost–QALY ratio, 305, 309
Costs
    accounting for, 306–307
    of chronic health conditions, 259–260
    depression-related, 15
    of depression screening, 309
    of health care in U.S., 295
    opportunity, 295–296
    overhead, 135
    pharmacy, 175–176
    of prescription drugs, 262
    and quality of life, 304–306
    rising health care, 32
    Tinker Project impact of, 174–177
Cost savings, 153
Council of Representatives (APA), 36, 37
Council on Graduate Medical Education, 10
Couples communication training, 119
CPT codes, 19
Crabtree, B. F., 20
Crisis points, 217
"Critical Challenges" (Pew Commission), 254
Cross-subsidization, 266–268
Cultural sensitivity, 102, 287
Culture, 288
    fitting into, 179–181
    learning about differences in, 126, 157, 158
    and medications, 220

time-related clashes of, 105–106
Cummings, N. A., 234
Cunningham, C., 161

Dartmouth Primary Care Cooperative Information Project (COOP), 300
Databases, 146, 200
Data collection, 304
Decision-based outcome measures, 308
Decision modeling, 307
Decision theory approach, 299, 300–303
DeGruy, 11, 14
DeGruy, F., 251
DeGruy, Frank, 254
Dementia, 231–232, 235
Department of Social Services, 162
Depression, 11
    costs associated with, 15
    in older adults, 229, 232, 235
    in rural patients, 246, 248, 249
    screening for, 307–309
    and subthreshold syndromes, 19–20
    in women, 213–216
Developmental aspects of health/illness, 70–71
Developmental disorders, 195
Developmental guidelines, 195
Developmental problems, 195
Developmental variations, 195
Diabetes, 262
Diabetes case study, 46–58
Diabetes Treatment Centers of America, 263
Diagnoses
    differences in use of, 179
    need for appropriate, 16
Diagnostic and Statistical Manual for Primary Care (DSM–PC), 194–196, 201
Diagnostic and Statistical Manual of Mental Disorders (DSM), 15, 108, 191, 194, 308
Diagnostic codes, 194–196
Disease management programs, 262–263
Disease prevention, 10
Disorders, developmental, 195
Distressing procedures, 219
Division 38, 321
Documentation, 139–140
    briefness of, 183–184
    for patient, 142
    for third-party payors, 146
Doherty, W. J., 158
Domestic violence, 212

Drotar, D., 154, 192, 193, 199, 201
Drugs
    abuse of, 13, 216, 251–252
    female use of, 212
DSM. *See Diagnostic and Statistical Manual of Mental Disorders*
DSM–PC. *See Diagnostic and Statistical Manual for Primary Care*
Durlak, J. A., 200

Early intervention, 199, 200
Eating disorders, 246
Eberhardt, T. L., 56
Economic indicators, 200
Economies of scale, 267
Education, 38–39, 103
    and primary care, 17–18
    for referring provider, 159
Education and training, 63–82
    affective components of health/illness in, 69–70
    assumptions for curriculum of, 66
    behavioral/developmental aspects of health/illness in, 70–71
    biological components of health/illness in, 67–68
    of clinical assessment, 74–76
    of clinical interventions, 76–78
    cognitive components of health/illness in, 68–69
    for common primary care problems, 73–74
    of core knowledge/skills, 65–82
    for ethical issues, 80
    health policy and health care systems in, 72–73
    of interprofessional collaboration, 78–80
    for legal issues, 80–81
    levels of, 65
    need for, 64
    for professional issues, 81–82
    resources for development of, 66–67
    sociocultural components of health/illness in, 71–72
Education levels, 249
Education services, 102
Eggebeen, D. J., 245
Eisenberg, L., 33
Eisenstat, S. A., 212
Elliott, G. R., 322
Emergent needs, 182, 183

Emotions
    and medical family therapy, 123
    patients' expressions of, 51–52, 58
Empathy, 51, 58
Employee pension funds, 31
Employee Retirement Income Security Act
    (ERISA), 31
Employee status, 152
Employer-focused health care, 23
Employer-paid health plans, 24–25
Employment, 212
Employment-based insurance, 283–284
Empowerment, 118
Encarta, 266
Encounters, relationships vs., 33
Encyclopedia Britannica, 266
End-of-life issues, 233–234
Enright, Michael F., 251
Epidemiological Catchment Area, 245
Epstein, R. M., 50
EQ-5D, 301–302
ERISA (Employee Retirement Income Se-
    curity Act), 31
Ethical issues, 80
"Ethic of accommodation," 120
Ethnic disparities, 281, 282
EuroQol group, 301
Evaluation (of reason for referral), 159
Evidence-based medicine, 33–34
Ewart, C. K., 119
Expectations, 141, 180–181
Expertise, complementary areas of, 107–108

Fallowfield, L., 119
Families
    as care providers, 118–119
    definitions of, 12, 114
    as health care team members, 120–121
    and independent practice, 141
    older adults and issues with, 233
    and primary providers, 197–198
Family medicine, 164, 323
Family Medicine Clinic, 171–177, 180, 181,
    183
Family nurse practitioners, 11
Family-of-origin experiences, 155
Family Oriented Primary Care (S.H. Daniel,
    T. L. Campbell, D. B. Seaburn), 159
Family physicians, 10
Family psychologists, 114
Family Psychology Associates (FPA), 133–
    147

Family relationships, 118
Family support specialists, 271
Family therapy, master's of, 294
Family therapy, medical, 121–124
Family violence, 116
Farley, Frank, 319
Farmer, Janet, 271
Feedback
    brief, 183
    in collaboration, 129
    on communications skills, 56–58
    to physicians, 141
    in rural health care, 249–250
    to/from patients, 142, 177–178
Fee-for-service basis, 146
Feeny, D., 302
Fellowship model, 65
First-contact care, 8
Flashbacks, 213
Flexibility, 157, 179
Flowers, K., 50
Follow-up
    information from, 105, 140, 143
    opportunities for long-term, 152
Forrest, 9
FPA. *See* Family Psychology Associates
Frank, Arthur, 122
Frank, R. G., 261
Frank, Robert, 289
Frankel, R. M., 49, 50
Free market economy approach, 27
Freud, Sigmund, 115–116
Funding, 162, 200, 264–265
Funk and Wagnall's encyclopedia, 266
Furlong, W., 302

Gatekeepers, 11, 33, 96, 201
Gender, 281–282
Generalists, 13, 32, 181
Geographically adjacent practices, 151
Geographic colocation, 150, 181
Gerber, P. D., 246
Geropsychology. *See* Older adults
Girgis, A., 56
Glenn, Michael, 128
Global case rates, 28
Goals
    in collaboration, 125
    of primary care, 46–48
    for Tinker Project, 171
Gold, M. R., 310
Goldberg, I D., 189

Good, M. J. D., 15, 248
"Good enough treatment," 199
"Good health," 286
Government health care coverage, 25, 264–265
Government intervention, 24
Government policing of health care, 26–27
Groessl, E. J., 307
Group Health Cooperative, 263
Group models, 30
Group practices, 100
Group support
    and older adults, 234
    for women, 222–223
Guggenbuhl-Craig, Adolf, 117
Guidelines and Principles for Accreditation
        of Programs in Professional Psychol-
        ogy (APA), 64
Gutek, Barbara, 33
Gynecologic conditions, chronic, 222

Haggerty, R., 202
Hagglund, Kris, 289
Haley, W. E., 228
"Hallway consultations," 173, 181–183
Hamburg, D. A, 322
Handouts, 198
HCA (Hospital Corporation of America), 26
Health
    defining good, 286
    focus on, 119–120
Health and Behavior (D. A. Hamburg, G. R.
        Elliott, D. L. Parron), 322
Health care, comprehensive, 9, 12–13
Health care industry, 25–26
Health care information systems, 29
Health care systems, 72–73
Health care transformation, 23–40
    corporatization effects on, 25–27
    cost containment/risk allocation effects
        on, 27–28
    ERISA effects on, 31
    and growth of managed care, 29–30
    organized systems of care effects on, 28–
        29
    primary care emphasis in, 31–34
    and psychology in primary care, 34–40
    public policy effects on, 24
    third-party payment effects on, 24–25
Health maintenance organizations (HMOs)
    legislation enabling, 24
    and older adults, 229
    primary care in, 32

and rural patients, 247
Health promotion, 10, 216
Health psychology services
    development of, 321–324
    and women, 210
Health-related quality of life (HRQOL),
        297–307
    assessment of, 298–307
    and cost–effectiveness evaluations, 304–
        306
    decision theory approaches to measure-
        ment of, 300–303
    Internet data collection for measure-
        ment of, 304
    psychometric methods for measurement
        of, 299–300
    rating methods for, 303–304
Health service providers, psychologists as, 36
Health status (definition), 298–299
Health Utilities Index (HUI), 302, 303
Healthy People 2010 project, 287, 296–298,
        322
Healthy People report, 320, 322
Helgeson, V. S., 121
Help, collaboration vs., 125
High utilizers, 176–177, 183
Himmelstein, D. U., 231
HIV, 281
HMO Act of 1973, 24, 29
HMO plans, 29–30
HMOs. *See* Health maintenance organiza-
        tions
Holmberg, S. K., 297
Home health care, 98
Home-visiting programs, 200
Honesty, 145
Horizontal integration, 28
Horwitz, 16
Hospital Corporation of America (HCA), 26
Hospitalizations, 153
HRQOL. *See* Health-related quality of life
HUI. *See* Health Utilities Index
HUI Mark I, 302
HUI Mark II, 302
HUI Mark III, 302
Hybrid reimbursement systems, 28
Hyperarchy, 266, 271

ICD–10 (International Classification of Dis-
        eases), 15
Identification of behavioral health problems,
        173–174

Illness stories, 122, 123
Impact 3, 304
Incremental cost–effectiveness, 305
Incrementalism, 285
Independent practice, 133–147
    core assumptions for, 133–134
    and patients/families, 141
    and payors, 144–146
    and physicians/nurse practitioners, 135–141
    problems with, 150–151
    structural overview of, 134–135
    and support staff, 142–143
Independent practice associations (IPAs), 30, 144, 146
Individual perspective, 306
Individuals with Disabilities Education Act, 265
Infertility, 218
Information
    follow-up, 105
    payor, 145, 146
Information economy, 265–270
"Information intensity," 54
Information systems, 29, 98
Infrastructure, 134–135
Inpatient care, 32
Institute for the Future, 295
Institute of Medicine (IOM), 8, 9, 14, 260, 261, 300, 322
Insurance companies, 144–146, 162, 191, 294
Insurance coverage, 197, 281–285
Integrated psychosocial care, 153
Interdisciplinary model, 192–194
Internal clinic referrals, 182
Internal medicine physicians, 10
International Classification of Diseases (ICD–10), 15
International Classification of Functioning, Disability and Health, 39
Internet
    consumer use of, 270
    data collection using, 304
    standards for, 266
Internship experiences, 126
Interprofessional collaboration, 78–80
Interruptions, interview, 49–50
Interventions, clinical
    adaptations for older adult, 235–236
    education/training for, 76–78
Interviewing skills, 15

Interviews
    medical, 48–52
    psychological, 98
    and rates of adherence, 54–55
Introduction (to patient), 97
IOM. *See* Institute of Medicine
IPAs. *See* Independent practice associations

Jargon, 107, 108
Johnson, Gary, 37
Journals, 142

Kaiser, 30
Kaiser Permanente Health Care System, 263
Kane, C., 297
Kaplan, R. M., 298, 307
Kerker, 16
Kiesler, C. A., 196, 199
Kind, Paul, 301
Kosinski, M., 237
Kraemer, H. C., 119
Kroenke, 16
Kwang, C. Y., 287

Lalonde, Marc, 320
Landlord–tenant relationships, 151
Language, 157
Lavigne, J. V., 201
Leaf, 16
Legal issues, 80–81
Lehman, A. F., 298
Lenert, Leslie, 304
Letter writing, 142
Leventhal, 16
Levine, C., 120
Lichter, D. T., 245
Life cycle stage, 122–123
Lifestyle modifications, 296
Life-threatening conditions, 216–218
Linkage Project, 251–254
Linkages with primary care physicians, 100
Linking of products, 266–267
Lipkin, M., 15
Lobbying efforts, 237, 289
Lobo, R. A., 287

Madsen, W. C, 141
Magellan Health Services, 26
Maguire, P., 56
Managed care
    and children, 189, 196, 199
    and chronic health conditions, 265

and diagnostic codes for children, 195
gatekeepers in, 96
growth of, 29–30
and interdisciplinary teams, 193–194
and older adults, 237
and patient satisfaction, 20
pediatrician impacted by, 162
and rising health care costs, 284
Management
of acute medical conditions, 10, 12
of chronic medical conditions, 10, 12
of medication, 139
psychosocial, 12
Mangelsdorff, 16
Market-driven health care, 23
Marvel, M. K., 50
Matarazzo, Joseph, 321
Maternal and Child Health Bureau (Title V),
265
McDaniel, S. H., 106, 158
McDaniel, Susan, 289
McDowell, I., 299
McElreath, L., 235
Measures of outcome, 296–298
Medicaid
and children's health coverage, 197, 200
and chronic health conditions, 260, 265
creation of, 283
enactment of, 24
and interdisciplinary teams, 193
and managed care, 30
state support of, 281
and third-party payments, 25
Medical family therapy, 121–124
"Medical–industrial complex," 25
Medical Outcomes Study, 299
Medical Outcome Study Short Form–36 (SF-
36), 299–300
Medicare
and chronic health conditions, 259–
260, 264–265, 269
creation of, 283
and dementia, 232
doctor shortage in, 281
enactment of, 24
for-profit hospital billing of, 26
and managed care, 30
and older adult psychological services,
236–237
and prescription drug coverage, 288
projected budget of, 230
psychologists reimbursed by, 39

and rising health care costs, 284
and third-party payments, 25
Medicare + Choice program, 264
Medication
management of, 139
and older adults, 231
paying for, 220
MedLine database, 49
Meetings, 159, 182
Menopausal issues, 221–222
Menstrual issues, 220–221
Mental health care
changes in, 294
and cost offset effect, 13–14
and primary care, 14–15
Mental Health Clinic, 172, 173, 181
Microsoft, 266
Minnesota Multiphasic Personality Inven-
tory profile, 299
Minority populations, 281
Miranda, J., 235
Miscommunication, 101
Mission, common, 126
Missouri, 318
Missouri Partnership for Enhanced Delivery
of Services (MO-PEDS), 271–272
Mixed model plans, 30
Model primary care curriculum, 18
Models of collaboration, 149–152
Models of service delivery, 20
Mohl, P. C., 199
Monetarization of medicine, 33
Mood disorders, 246
MO-PEDS. See Missouri Partnership for En-
hanced Delivery of Services
Morisky, D. E., 119
Mossey, J. A., 235
Motivation, 160
Mullins, L. L., 159
Multiple physical problems, 216–217
Myers, C. P., 298

Nahill, Arthur, 56
Narrative therapists, 142
National Academy of Sciences, 322
National Household Survey on Drug Abuse,
216
National Institute of Mental Health, 20, 114,
162, 245, 251
National Institute on Alcoholism and Alco-
hol Abuse, 20
National Institutes of Health, 35, 281

National Survey of Families and Households, 245
Network models, 30
Network of mutual commitment, 114
Neurocognitive evaluations, 200
Newell, C., 299
New England Journal of Medicine, 25
New Mexico, 37
A New Perspective On The Health of Canadians (Marc Lalonde), 320
Newspapers, 266
Nonpsychiatric physicians, 14
Nonpsychotropic medications, 175
Nonverbal behavior, 51
"Normalizing effect," 143
Normative model, 150
Nottingham Health Profile, 299
Nurse practitioners, 11, 135–141, 271

Obesity, 15
Obstetricians–gynecologists, 11
Occupational stress, 212
Office of Disease Prevention and Health Promotion in the Public Service, 306
Office of the Surgeon General, 15
Office staff, 160
Older adults, 227–238
    assessment adaptations for, 234–235
    cognitive impairment in, 231–232
    comorbidity/complexity issues for, 231
    depression/anxiety/substance abuse/suicide in, 232–233
    and end-of-life issues, 233–234
    and family issues, 233
    intervention adaptations for, 235–236
    need for psychological services for, 227–230
    and reimbursement systems, 236–237
    and role issues for psychologists, 237–238
    special issues in serving, 230–236
    and special settings/systems of care, 234
    and training issues, 236
Olfson, 14
Olson, R. A., 159
Online Survey Generation Instrument, 304
Open mindedness, 158
Opportunity cost problem, 295–296
Organized systems of care, 28–29
Outcome measurement, 296–298
Out-of-pocket spending, 264
Outpatient care, 32

Overhead costs, 135
Oxman, T. E., 246

Pace, T. M., 159
Pace (of appointments), 157
Packaged mental health services, 294
Pain, chronic, 35, 218
Palermo, T. M., 199
Pamphlets, 198
Paradigm sharing, 154
Parallel primary care mental health system, 11
Parron, D. L., 322
Partner, finding a, 155
Partner violence, 212–213
Patient materials, 198
Patient rights, 268
Patient satisfaction, 20, 46, 177–178
Payment systems, 32
Payors, 144–146
PCPs. *See* Primary care practitioners
PDP (Psychopharmacology Demonstration Project), 37
Pediatricians, 10, 161–164, 190–191
Pension funds, 31
Perrin, E. C., 200
Perrin, Ellen, 125
Personalized type of care, 10
Personal relationships, 125–126
Personnel, 140, 160
Perspective, 306, 310
Pew Health Professions Commission, 32, 254
Pharmaceutical industry, 262, 263
Pharmacy costs, 175–176
Philbrick, J. T., 246
Phone numbers, 140
Physical proximity, 97
Physician–patient relationship, 45–59
    agenda setting in, 49–51
    building the, 51–52
    communication in, 48
    and delivering bad news, 55–58
    delivering diagnostic recommendations/negotiating treatment decisions in, 52–58
    diabetes case study of, 46–58
    and goals of primary care, 46–48
    medical interviews in, 48–52
    power in, 117
Physicians. *See* Primary care practitioners
Piedmont Health Survey, 245
Pless, I. B., 202

Plichta, 16

Point-of-service plans (POSs), 30

Policy development, 35–39

Polivka, L. A., 228

POSs (point-of-service plans), 30

Postreferral feedback, 249

Posttraumatic stress disorder (PTSD), 213

Poverty, 282

Power, 115–118

PPOs (preferred provider organizations), 30

Practical tips for clinicians, 95–110, 178–184
    collaboration, 98–101
    complementary areas of expertise, 107–108
    explaining referral to patient, 104–105
    fitting into culture, 179–181
    generalists vs. specialists, 108–109
    making yourself available, 181–182
    physical health assessment, 98–99
    psychological assessment, 106–107
    range of services, 101–104
    referral alternatives, 97–98
    referring out, 109–110
    scheduling appointments, 182–183
    time-related problems, 105–106

Practitioner's Toolbox Series (APA), 96

Precepting, 18

Preconsultation discussion, 159

Preferred provider organizations (PPOs), 30

Pregnancy-related issues, 220–221

Prepaid heath plans, 24

Prereferral collaboration, 152

Prescription drugs, 262, 288

Prescriptive authority movement, 37–38

"Presenting the concern," 50

Prevention services, 8–9, 200, 287

Price, Reynolds, 118

Primary care, 7–21
    aspects of, 8–10
    changes in, 293–294
    clinical assessment of common conditions in, 74–76
    clinical interventions in, 76–78
    common problems in, 73–74
    critical content areas within, 10
    definitions of, 8, 261
    educational needs/opportunities in, 17–18
    ethical issues in, 80
    goals of, 46–48
    interprofessional collaboration in, 78–80

    legal issues in, 80–81
    mental/behavioral/health problems in, 14–16
    opportunities for psychologists in, 35
    practice needs/opportunities in, 18–19
    professional issues in, 81–82
    psychologists in, 11–14, 16–17
    psychology in, 34–40
    research needs/opportunities in, 19–20
    rising emphasis on, 31–34

Primary care model, 263

Primary care practitioners (PCPs), 8
    benefits of collaboration for, 128–129, 152–154
    efficacy of, 8
    and independent practice psychologists, 135–141
    patient relationship with. *See* Physician–patient relationship
    specialties in, 10–11

Primary care psychology
    definition of, 12
    education/training in. *See* Education and training
    expertise areas of, 12
    future of, 317–324

Primary Care Task Force (APA), 12–13, 35–36, 154, 198, 199

Prioritization, agenda-setting, 50

Private sector, 284

Privatization, 30

Problems, developmental, 195

Product loyalty, 267

"Product" options, 30

Professional development, 102

Professional issues, 81–82

Professional relationships, 138

Promoting Health (B. D. Smedley & S. L. Syme), 323

Protocol form, 159

Proximity of providers, 154, 163

Psychiatric illnesses, 13–14

Psychiatrists, 294

Psychoeducation, 123

Psychoeducational support groups, 123, 160

Psychological assessment, 106–107

Psychologists, 34–40
    advocacy/policy development by, 35–38
    benefits of collaboration for, 128–129, 152–154
    Cardinal Symptom team role of, 272–273

and changes in mental health care, 294
as community collaborators, 194
as consultants, 192–193
external advocacy/education by, 38–39
future of primary care, 39–40
as interdisciplinary team members, 193–194
number of licensed, 318
and older adults, 237–238
performance reviews of, 146
and primary care, 11–14
primary care opportunities for, 35
and public health, 288–289
as tertiary providers, 192
training of, 38
Psychology
gero-. *See* Older adults
and health care transformation, 34–40
primary care. *See* Primary care psychology
and public health, 288–289
Psychometric assessments, 183, 299–300
Psychopharmacology Demonstration Project (PDP), 37
Psychosocial management, 12
Psychotropic medications
and collaboration, 153, 162, 165
costs of, 175
nonpsychiatric physicians prescribing, 14, 247
and women, 214
Ptacer, J. T., 56
PTSD (posttraumatic stress disorder), 213
Public health policy, 24, 72–73, 102, 279–289
current issues in, 281–282
historical perspectives on, 283–285
issues and questions in, 285–288
and psychology, 288–289
upcoming issues in, 288
Public Health Service Primary Care Policy Fellowship, 39
Public service, 289
Pure staff model, 30
Purpose, common, 154

Quality-adjusted life years (QALYs), 300–303
Quality of life, 297–298. *See also* Health-related quality of life
Quality of Well-Being (QWB) Scale, 299, 302, 308

Qualls, S. H., 236
QWB. *See* Quality of Well-Being Scale

Racial disparities, 281, 282
Rakel, 11
RAND Corporation, 299
RAND Health Insurance Study, 299
Referral model, 310
Referral(s), 10, 12, 17
alternatives to, 97–98
clean, 139
evaluation of reason for, 159
explaining reasons for, 104–105
focusing/clarifying the reason for, 105–106
and independent-practice model, 150–151
from other clinics, 182
pediatric, 201
and proximity, 163
self-, 26–27
sources of, 152
Referring out, 109–110, 160
Regier, D., 161
Regier, D. A., 189
Rehabilitation teams, 270
Reimbursement systems
and children with mental health problems, 191
and collaboration, 101
hybrid, 28
and independent practices, 144–146
and interdisciplinary teams, 193–194
for Medicare, 281
for older adult psychological services, 236–237
procedure-based, 32
for psychologists, 39
for rural health care, 249
Relationally-based health problems, 116
Relationships
collaborative, 154
encounters vs., 33
negotiating collaborative, 155–156
physician–patient. *See* Physician–patient relationship
professional, 138
with support staff, 143
Release-of-information forms, 140
Reports
consultation, 106
to physicians, 139–140

U.S. Bureau of Census, 244
U.S. Bureau of Community Health Services, 251
U.S. Congress, 30, 37
U.S. Department of Defense, 37, 324
U.S. Department of Education, 289
U.S. Department of Health and Human Services, 289
U.S. Public Health Service, 39
Utilization management, 28

Valenstein, M., 308, 309
Variations, developmental, 195
Vaughn, L. M., 198
Verbal behavior, 51
Vertical integration, 28–29
Victimization of women, 212–213
Video feedback coaching, 56–58
Videotapes, 198, 199
Vijan, S., 308
Violence
    family, 116
    in relationships, 16
    against women, 212–213
Visual analog scale, 304

Walker, S. R., 299
Ware, J. E., 237
Webb, C. E., 27
Wedding, Danny, 289
"Well-person" checkups, 9
Wells, A. M., 200
Wherry, J., 248, 249
Wilcox, S. M., 231
Williams, C., 248, 249
Willingness to be trained, 107
Wilson, Paul G., 324
"Window of opportunity," 52
Wirth, D. P., 287

Wofford, Harris, 284
Women, 16, 209–223
    adherence by, 219–220
    with chronic gynecologic conditions, 222
    chronic/life-threatening conditions in, 216–218
    consultation/treatment issues for, 211–222
    elderly, 228
    and group support, 222–223
    health promotion in, 216
    interdisciplinary care collaboration for, 223
    and menopausal issues, 221–222
    and menstrual issues, 220–221
    mood/anxiety/mental health disorders among, 213–216
    multiple roles of, 212–213
    and pregnancy-related issues, 220–221
    procedure preparations for, 218–219
    psychology–primary care integration for, 211–222
    psychosocial stressors for, 212–214
    with sexual concerns, 222
    victimization of, 212–213
Woolhandler, S., 231
Work Group on Expanding the Rose of Psychology in the Health Care Delivery System, 36
World Health Organization, 39, 281, 298
Wright, L., 152
Wundt, Wilhelm, 318
Wyoming, 252

Yuen, E. J., 247

Zeber, J. E., 308
Zuckerman, C., 120

ABOUT THE EDITORS

Robert G. Frank, PhD, is dean of the College of Health Professions at the University of Florida, where he is also professor in the Department of Clinical and Health Psychology. His first appointment was at the University of Missouri—Columbia School of Medicine, Department of Physical Medicine and Rehabilitation, where he established the Division of Clinical Health Psychology and Neuropsychology. He was a Robert Wood Johnson Health Policy Fellow (1991–1992) and has worked with Sen. Jeff Bingaman (D–NM). After completing the fellowship, Dr. Frank returned to the University of Missouri where, as assistant to the dean for health policy, he continued to work on federal and state health policy. He continued to work with Sen. Bingaman and managed Missouri's state health reform effort, the ShowMe Health Reform Initiative. Dr. Frank has a doctorate in clinical psychology from the University of New Mexico. He is a diplomate in clinical psychology of the American Board of Professional Psychology. He is past president and a fellow of Division 22 (Rehabilitation Psychology) of the American Psychological Association (APA) and a fellow of Division 38 (Health Psychology). He currently chairs the Health Care Task Force for the Florida Developmental Disabilities Council and has chaired the APA Committee on Professional Continuing Education (1997) and its Board of Educational Affairs (2000).

Susan H. McDaniel, PhD, is professor of psychiatry and family medicine, director of the Family and Marriage Programs and the Wynne Center for Family Research in Psychiatry, and associate chair of Family Medicine at the University of Rochester School of Medicine and Dentistry in Rochester, New York. She is known for her publications in the areas of medical family psychology, family systems medicine, and family therapy supervision and consultation. Her special areas of interest are assisted-reproductive technologies, somatization, genetic testing, and gender and health. She is a frequent speaker at meetings of both health and mental health professionals.

Dr. McDaniel is coeditor, with Thomas Campbell, MD, of the multidisciplinary journal *Families, Systems, & Health*, and serves on several other journal boards. She coauthored or coedited the following books: *Systems Consultation* (1986), *Family-Oriented Primary Care* (1990, 2003), *Medical Family Therapy* (1992), *Integrating Family Therapy* (American Psychological Association, 1995), *Counseling Families With Chronic Illness* (1995), *The Shared Experience of Illness* (1997), *Casebook for Integrating Family Therapy* (2001), *The Biopsychosocial Model: Past, Present, and Future* (2003), two of which have been translated into several languages, one exclusively in German.

Dr. McDaniel was chair of the Commission on Accreditation for Marriage and Family Therapy Education in 1998 and president of Division 43 (Family Psychology) of the American Psychological Association (APA) in 1999. She was recognized by the APA as the 1995 Family Psychologist of the Year. In 1998, she was the first psychologist to be a fellow in the Public Health Service Primary Care Policy Fellowship, and in 2000 she received the award for Innovative Contributions to Family Therapy from the American Family Therapy Academy. She also served as chair of the APA Publications and Communcations Board in 2003.

James H. Bray, PhD, is director of the Family Psychology Programs and associate professor in the Department of Family and Community Medicine, Baylor College of Medicine, in Houston, Texas. Dr. Bray has published and presented numerous works in the areas of divorce, remarriage, adolescent substance use, intergenerational family relationships, and collaboration between physicians and psychologists. He was the principal investigator of the federally funded longitudinal study "Developmental Issues in Step-Families Research Project" and has appeared on the *Today Show, 20/20, Good Morning America*, and various radio and television programs in regard to his work. He is currently working on a federally funded project on alcohol and other drug abuse in families with adolescents.

Dr. Bray has received numerous awards, including recent election into the National Academies of Practice for Psychology and the Karl F. Heiser Presidential Award for Advocacy on Behalf of Professional Psychology from the American Psychological Association. As a clinical psychologist, he conducts research and teaches resident physicians, medical students, and psychology students. In addition to his research, he also maintains an active clinical practice focusing on children and families.

Margaret Heldring, PhD, is the president and executive director of America's HealthTogether, a nonprofit, bipartisan organization. The mission of America's HealthTogether is to advance a broad view of health and health care, provide effective public education about universal health care, and promote health and social justice.

Dr. Heldring is a clinical psychologist with more than 30 years experience in health care. From 1984 until 2001, she was a clinical assistant professor in the Department of Family Medicine at the University of Washington. She practiced psychology independently and has published and lectured widely in both mental health and primary care. She is a past president of the Washington State Psychological Association and past chair of the American Psychological Association's Committee of State Leaders. She has been honored on the state and national levels for her leadership.

Dr. Heldring served as the director of Health Policy for Bill Bradley's (D–NJ) 2000 Presidential campaign and, previously, as chief health advisor to Sens. Bradley and Paul Wellstone (D–MN). She provided congressional staff leadership for the 1996 maternity stay legislation and the 1997 provision for mental health services for children in the Child Health Insurance Program.

Dr. Heldring is the editor of the Department of Family Health Policy journal *Families, Systems, & Health* and is on the editorial advisory board for the journal *American Family Physician*.

Dr. Heldring was the first psychologist to run for public office in Washington state.

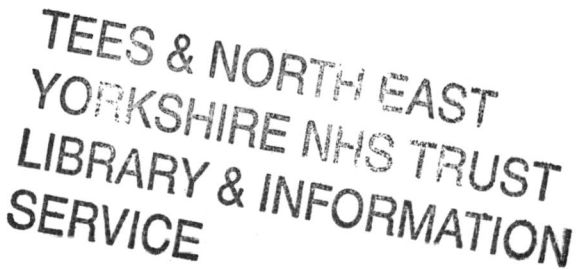